The Peregrine Reader

The Peregrine Reader

Edited by
Mikel Vause and
Carl Porter

SALT LAKE CITY

GIBBS·SMITH
P
PUBLISHER

First Edition

99 98 97 96 4 3 2 1

Some works in this anthology appeared originally in the following publications: "A Few Words About Minimalism," the *New York Times Book Review*; "Letter to the Lady of the House," the *New Yorker*; "Skeletons," the *New Yorker*; "Watermelon Rind Jelly," "In the Garden Again," "In the Garden," "No Sorry," "Tent Song," "El Paso," all from *Rock Farm*; "Any Friend of Nicholas Nickleby's Is a Friend of Mine," *I Sing the Body Electric*; "A Good Scent from a Strange Mountain," *New England Review*; "The Writer in the Family," *The Lives of the Poets*; "Errand," the *New Yorker*; "John Gardner: The Writer as Teacher," *Fires*; "On Where I'm Calling From," *No Heroics Please*; "Writing It Down For James: Some Thoughts on Reading Toward the New Millennium," *Antioch Review*; "Edie: A Life," *Epoch*; "Book Codes II," "Book Codes III," both from *No Roses Review*; "The Testimony of Light," "The Garden Shukkei-en," "Elegy," all from *Angels of History*; "Optimists," *Esquire*; "First Things First: One More Writer's Beginnings," *Harpers*; "Corpse Cradle," "While I Sit in a Sunny Place," both from *Moon Crossing Bridge*; "Now That I Am Never Alone," *New Poets of the Nineties*; "Black Valentine," *Ploughshares*; "Moon Crossing Bridge," "Northwest by Northwest," both from *Haydens Ferry Review*; "Picking Bones," *Seattle Review*; "My Father's Love Letters," *American Poetry Review*; "The Right Thing to Do at the Time," *The Sound of Writing, Volume I*; "Faith," *Ploughshares*; "O Furo," *The Sound of Writing, Volume I*; all of Maxine Kumin's poems are from *The Long Approach*; "Attending the Forest," *Perfecting an Unspeakable Act*; "Waiting for the Elf," *Wisdom of Silenius*; "In the Land of Men," *Triquarterly* and *Redbook*; "The Lives of the Dead," *Esquire*; "newborn thrown in trash and dies," *The Stories of John Edgar Wideman*; "The Liar," *Back in the World*; "Lumumba Lives," *River Styx and other Stories*.

The works listed above are used here by permission.

This is a Peregrine Smith Book,
published by Gibbs Smith, Publisher
P.O. Box 667, Layton, UT 84041

Design by Scott Van Kampen
Edited by Gail Yngve

All cover art by and copyright of © Royden Card

Printed and bound in the United States of America

Library of Congress Cataloging-in-Publication Data

The Peregrine reader / edited by Mikel Vause and Carl Porter.–1st ed.

p. cm.
"A Peregrine Smith book"–T.p. verso.
ISBN 0-87905-794-7
1. College readers. 2. American literature–20th century.
3. United States–Literary collections. I. Vause, Mikel, 1952-
II. Porter, Carl.
PE1122.P44 1997
810.8'0054–dc20   96-38193

Contents

Introduction

*I*n 1980, as a nontraditional student on my way to graduate school, I was invited to read before students and faculty at the annual English Department awards program. Some months before I had written "Frankenstein: The Creation of Innocence and Evil" for Dr. Gerald Grove's British Romantic Literature class. I was thrilled by the invitation to read that paper and still regard it as a capstone to my schooling at Weber State College. Now, some fifteen years later, I am on the faculty at Weber, and I've had the opportunity to read both critical and creative papers in New York; Tromso, Norway; Vancouver, B.C.; Reno; Las Vegas; Pittsburgh; Sheffield, England; as well as many other places. Each of these has been exciting, but none compares with reading that spring afternoon of 1980 in the Social Science building at Weber State.

At the time, I wished more of my classmates could have had the same opportunity to read, but obviously that would have been impossible. The National Undergraduate Literature Conference is a direct result of that personal recognition given me by the English Department. I went off to graduate school on that very positive note. There were several more similar opportunities to read my papers in graduate school, but none of those experiences were equal to the first at Weber State.

Upon completion of my degree, I found myself back at Weber, not as a student, but as an instructor. During my second year of teaching, I approached Dr. Candadai Seshachari, the Department Chairman, with the idea of starting a conference that would enable the students of Weber State to show their wares to students from the other in-state institutions. This forum was to provide the same wonderful experience of my final year to a far greater number of students. I felt that to provide our students the opportunity to see how they compared with students from other schools in Utah was very important. Sesh's support was immediate.

My colleague Michael Myer and I headed off to the Rocky Mountain Modern Language Conference with fists full of flyers inviting students from the other Utah schools to participate in what we had dubbed as the Utah State Undergraduate Literature Conference. We intended this conference to include readings and workshops by the best writers in the world. For the first year we were able to land both John Barth and Tobias Wolff as our keynote speakers. No sooner had we started to distribute the flyers than Professor Scott Samuelson from Ricks College in Idaho asked if his students could submit papers. In fifteen minutes the conference had evolved into the Western States Undergraduate Literature Conference. However, within that same hour a professor from Florida asked if her students might also come to our conference. We considered our day at the RMMLA quite a success as our idea had started as a quiet little in-state get together but in a few hours had exploded into the **National Undergraduate Literature Conference**.

This brings me to the real purpose of this little reminiscence. Along with providing undergraduate students an audience for their works, we wanted to provide them an opportunity to meet and listen to writers who had "made it." So we set our sights high by approaching the best writers in the world. We figured the worst that could happen was we would be told no or to go to hell. But what more could happen? Our first call was to John Barth.

A colleague in the Weber State University History Department upon hearing what some were calling our "crass and arrogant project," said, "If you land John Barth, it will be a miracle." He continued, "Weber State University has never had on campus an author of Barth's stature."

We made the call. Professor Barth gladly accepted and was thrilled to be speaking to undergraduates. He read from his then unfinished *Tidewater Tales*.

Along with Professor Barth, we asked Tobias Wolff to come. A professor at Syracuse University's Creative Writing Program, Wolff is recognized as one of America's finest short-story writers. He, too, jumped at the chance to be involved with our enterprise. Professor Wolff arrived in Utah with an excellent essay on minimalism and his short stories "The Liar" and "In the Garden of the North American Martyrs."

The conference was not only off the ground, it was soaring. Barth and Wolff gladly provided us with suggestions on how to make the conference better and Wolff suggested we ask Richard Ford for the next year. Ford brought his friend Raymond Carver, and after Carver, came Ray Bradbury and Alan Cheuse. Cheuse has become a mainstay to our one-of-a-kind conference by helping bring folks like Larry McMurtry, Tess Gallagher, Anne Beattie, Richard Bausch, George Garrett, and all the other contributors to this anthology to Ogden, Utah.

The conference, as well as Weber State University, has been very fortunate to have had the support of so many sterling writers. Their willingness to be involved with this anthology is just another example of the support they have shown us.

Included is a MacArthur Award winner, John Edgar Wideman; Pulitzer Prize winners, Maxine Kumin, Robert Olen Butler, and Richard Ford; Strauss Award winners, Raymond Carver and Robert Stone; National Book Award winners, Tim O'Brien and Larry McMurtry; and numerous PEN/Hemingway and PEN/Faulkner award winners, Guggenheim fellows, and National Endowment for the Arts recipients.

Some of the world's greatest poets are also represented here: Maxine Kumin, George Garrett, Carolyn Forche, Tess Gallagher, Catherine Bowman, and Howard McCord. They are all careful examiners of the human condition, as well as of the natural world.

The common thread that runs through all of the stories, poems, and essays in this collection is the concern for careful reading and good writing as a means of finding and sharing truth. Ray Bradbury, in numerous interviews, has expressed the concern that the future of civilization rests upon the next generation's literacy. Currently, he is concerned, as should we all be, that children from elementary school through college ages are not learning to love knowledge and are not being taught to read for the purpose of gaining insight and inspiration. The by-product of these practices translates into their inability to write. Our culture is fast becoming one that relies on television and other forms of electronic media for all its information. Thus with machines, we are killing the intimacy that comes from contact with the printed page, and, for that matter, with the feel of a pencil. We are selling our "birthrights" for a keypad and a mouse.

This collection reflects a reverence for reading and writing by those who practice the ancient and noble craft of storytelling, which has for them become the most powerful means of presenting the reward that comes to them from, as Thoreau said, "living life deliberately, on its own terms." They are compelled to share their world views in, as Blake said, in his introduction to *Songs of Innocence:* "In a book that all may read."

The purpose of literature is to tell the truth as George Garrett points out in "The Right Thing to do at the Time":

> This a true story about my father, a true story with the shape of a piece of fiction. Well, why not? Where do you suppose all the shapes and forms of fiction came from in the first place? And what's the purpose of fiction anyway, whether it's carved out of the knotty hardwood of personal experience or spun out of the slick thin air like soap bubbles? "What's the purpose of the bayonet?" they used to yell when I was a soldier years ago. The correct answer was: "To kill, to Kill, to KILL!"

Whether it's in the poetry, or the fiction, or the essays herein, if read carefully the reader will find truth conveyed in humanity's highest form of communication—through the written word.

There are a number of individuals who deserve to be recognized for their support of the conference that has led to this outstanding collection, who have perennially supported our efforts: Scott Samualson, from Ricks College; Glen Selander and Helen Lojek, Boise State University; Earl Kirk, Baker University; Brad Roghaar, Candadai and Neila Seshachari, Merlin and Donna Cheney, Richard Alston, Levi Peterson, Carl Porter, Glen Wiese, Russel Burrows, President Paul Thompson, Provost Robert Smith, Dean Sherwin Howard, Dean June Phillips, Scott Loughton, John Sillito, University Librarian Joan Hubbard and Weber State University Friends of the Library, Weber State University; Gibbs Smith, Gail Yngve, of Gibbs Smith, Publisher; The Rich Foundation; and Bob Sawatski of the Weber County Libraries. To all those listed above, and to the many others not listed but who have helped with both the conference and the production of this book, please know how much your support is appreciated.

Mikel Vause
Weber State University

Reading and Writing*

E. L. Doctorow

I thought of myself as a writer for many years, before I ever wrote a thing. It's a very effective way to begin. I suppose I started to think of myself as a writer when I was in the third grade, and with such conviction that for many years I didn't feel any obligation to actually write anything in order to be a writer.

Of course, I was reading constantly. I read enormous amounts. I read everything. I read all the time. I don't remember everything—every author I read, of course, but I had the advantage of growing up in a time before there was television.

Oh, I remember Rafael Sabtini was one of the writers—he wrote a wonderful book called *Captain Blood*. And then there was Will James—not the brother of Henry, but the cowboy writer, who wrote a wonderful novel about a horse called *Smokey*. I think that's still in print.

I read Howard Pees, an adventure writer; John R. Tunis, who wrote terrific sports novels; and a writer named Joseph Altsheler, who wrote a marvelous novel about the Alamo.

I grew up in a kind of a poor neighborhood, and paperbacks were not really accessible in the local bookstore or drugstore, so the major source of our reading was the public library. The very word *library* still calls up in my mind the neighborhood branch of the New York Public Library that I marched to each and every week on Washington Avenue in the East Bronx.

It was one of those old libraries with oak shelves and oak tables that were marked and scored, and huge globe lights hung from the ceiling on long chains. It was a bit of a walk from my house, a long walk actually, through new and strange neighborhoods. And, fittingly enough, to get there I had to pass a bread-baking factory, a bakery from which emanated each evening's delicious smells of fresh baking rye and pumpernickel bread. So I always associated reading with nourishment.

I remember wandering through the stacks—all these marvelous shelves filled with books covered with library bindings. With the gilt-lettered titles and authors' names worn almost entirely away from use and handling. Libraries in those days hadn't figured out to leave books in their original wrappers and they disdained paperbacks so that the bindings were uniform, thick and utilitarian. I loved those worn-out books. Big thick novels that had been read so many times that the pages had a soft, pliant touch—almost like cloth, the felt.

I'd pick out things that looked interesting, things I had no business reading, authors I had discovered for myself without knowing who they were: Voltaire, and Cervantes, and Dostoevsky. I read whatever I could find by Jack London. I read a racy French novel called *Mademoiselle du' Maupin* that made my heart beat and my ears turn red. And Dumas's, *The Count of Monte Cristo, The Three Musketeers*—I was crazy about all those swashbuckling novels; and *Les Miserables,* a book I read over one whole summer on the subway in New York going to the allergist every week for my shots. It put those painful shots in perspective to know that Hugo's hero, Jean Valjean, had a tougher life than I did.

I think I always managed to identify as a kind of older brother or sister, the author of the story in my hands. That is to say I could suffer with the experiences of the characters of any given book while at the same time appreciating the act of composition that was unfolding before me. This appreciation could exist at the lowest level of my awareness, but it is indisputably an additional thing that happens to a young, self-declared writer when he reads, which may not happen in the minds of other people. That is, a feeling of bonding with the author, or more confusingly, an assumption that he, or she, and you, were writing the book together, as you read it.

*Used with the permission of the author.

The Tidewater Tales

John Barth

KATHERINE SHERRITT SAGAMORE, THIRTY-NINE YEARS
OLD AND EIGHT AND A HALF MONTHS PREGNANT,
BECALMED IN OUR ENGINELESS SMALL SAILBOAT
AT THE END OF A STICKY JUNE CHESAPEAKE AFTERNOON
AMID EVERY SIGN OF THUNDERSTORMS APPROACHING
FROM ACROSS THE BAY,
AND SPEAKING AS SHE SOMETIMES DOES IN VERSE,
SETS HER HUSBAND A TASK.

Tell me a story of women and men
Like us: like us in love for ten
Years, lovers for seven, spouses
Two, or two point five. *Their House's
Increase* is the tale I wish you'd tell.

Why did that perfectly happy pair,
Like us, decide this late to bear
A child? Why toil so to conceive
One (or more), when they both believe
The world's aboard a handbasket bound for Hell?
Well?

Sentimentality, was it? A yen
Like ours to be one person, blend
Their flesh forever, so to speak—
Although the world could end next week
And that dear incarnation be H-bomb-fried?

Maybe they thought that by joining their
(Like our) so different genes—her
Blue-blooded, his blue-collared—they'd make
A blue-eyed Wunderkind who'd take
The end of civilization in his/her stride?
What pride!

Or maybe they weren't thinking at all,

13

But (unlike us) obeyed the call
Of blind instinct and half-blind custom:
"Reproduce your kind, and trust them
To fortune's winds and tides, life's warmth and frost!"

Perhaps they considered all the above
(Like us, exactly)—instinct, love,
The world's decline from bad to worse
In more respects than the reverse—
And decided to pay, but not to count, the cost.
Fingers crossed.

Well:
Tell me their story as if it weren't ours,
But *like* ours enough so that the Powers
That drive and steer good stories might
Fetch them beyond *our* present plight

and navigate the tale itself to an ending more rich and strange than everyday realism ordinarily permits; a bottom line that will make art if not sense out of the predicament your sperm and my egg, with a lot of help from their producers, have got us into; in short, yet another rhyme as it were for *cost* to end this poem with, even if we have to abandon verse for prose or prose for verse to reach it: a rhyme less discouraging, more pregnant so to speak with hope, than *lost*.

Okay?

PETER SAGAMORE, THIRTY-NINE YEARS AND
EIGHT AND A HALF MONTHS OLD,
AN AUTHOR WITH CERTAIN DIFFICULTIES
THOUGH CERTAINLY NOT A DIFFICULT AUTHOR,
AT THE TILLER OF OUR LITTLE SLOOP STORY,
RESPONDS IN PROSE.

Blam. Blooey.
Katherine Sherritt begs his pardon?
BLAM! BLOOEY!
Twin thunderstorms struck Chesapeake Bay at about the same hour two weeks apart in the last spring and summer of the eighth decade of the twentieth century of the Christian era and bracketed our story like artillery zeroing in.
The first storm—*Blam!*—was born to a sultry low-pressure cell that squatted over Maryland all Sunday, June 15, 1980, last weekend before the solstice. At afternoon's end she let go a squall below Baltimore that spun across the Bay like an uncorked genie and blammed the middle Eastern Shore of Maryland, in particular the lower Miles and upper Tred Avon rivers. Wondrous, thunderous, frightening lightning! Hail and minitwisters: trees downed, roofs unroofed, doors unhinged, windows blown . . . and our story begun.

14

The second storm—*Blooey!*—offsprang from a Canadian high that swept pregnant across the upper Mississippi and the Great Lakes on Sunday, June 29, 1980, first weekend after the solstice. Astraddle the Appalachian ridge she delivered a passel of young roughnecks, the roughest of whom tore into Druid Hill Park and the Baltimore Zoo at happy hour EDST, knocked down with a ninety-knot punch a big traveling crane at the Dundalk Marine Terminal, lost steam drowning two hubristic sportfishermen in small boats out on the Bay, and blooeyed the upper Shore at seventy knots plus before cooling off in the cornfields of Kent County. Near the old fishing village of Rock Hall, a big cruising sailboat in dry storage named *Buy, Baby,* owned by a Philadelphia investment counselor, was blown right out of its cradle. Farther up the peninsula, behind Ordinary Point on the Sassafras, some yachts dragged anchor, some others didn't . . . and our story came 'round on itself.

Here's how.

SET ME A TASK!

As Kathy Sherritt will tell it next fall, when we're home in Baltimore and she's back at work as Director of Folklore and Oral History at the Enoch Pratt Free Library, *The Tidewater Tales: A Novel* saw daylight at about six P.M. during Blooey! along with the other things she gave birth to that remarkable evening aboard *Story,* at anchor with the weekend fleet aswarm behind Ordinary Point, up near the cervix of Chesapeake Bay. But it was conceived just prior to Blam! two weeks before at Nopoint Point, the Sherritt spread on Goldsborough Creek, off the Tred Avon, off the Choptank, off that same Chesapeake, farther down that Eastern Shore, when pent-up Peter Sagamore, that Kathy's best friend, best lover, best husband, moderately celebrated author of short and shorter stories, and father of the whole kaboodle in her womb, cried For pity's sake, Kathy, set me a task!—thereby setting *her* one.

NOPOINT POINT

A lover's task is what Peter meant: something he could do to demonstrate to Katherine Sherritt that he loves her like life and language themselves despite mosquitoes, heat, humidity, her parents' trying unsuccessfully not to be a bother, precious little sex since Kath's on the cusp, no tennis but brutal with macho male Sherritts all save Andy the youngest of whom blow him off the family court in straight sets, every day less swimming in Sherritt Cove, less windsurfing and waterskiing out in Goldsborough Creek, because on each new tide the sea nettles move a bit farther in like a billion old condoms with their miserable sting and beautiful name, *Chrysaora quinquecirrha,* which means five-filamented gold-edge but ought to mean God's five-month curse upon the Talbot County Gold Coast, no respite from Kathy's old prep-school and college chums, family friends, and fellow ASPS (American Society for the Preservation of Storytelling), swarming like sheepflies on Nopoint Point, including her onetime (one time) lesbian lover, a black-belt balladeer and sometime pain in our marital tush, though Kathy won't hear May Jump spoken ill of except by Peter in extremis. And more.

Now, P welcomes these diversions for good K's sake, but so much company gets to a chap who, while no solitary, is a duetary unabashedly and for sure: Give him him and

Kathy Sherritt; the rest of the world is just . . . material. And on the bottom line—by reason of these manifold irritations and distractions and the low-grade, high-level suspense of when for pity's sake will she unload, and what and how many . . . Well.

To be sure, it's been no picnic for Katherine Shorter Sherritt, these two weeks on Nopoint Point; P.S. knows that. She loves the man as does he her and is as grateful for his uncomplaint as is he hers, but *she's* the one with the fabulous bellyful, Estimated Date of Confinement two weeks hence by our best reckoning: 29 June '80, 266 nights since a certain blessed one last fall—though inasmuch as all such EDCs are + two weeks, she might just unload here in mid-sentence and set him a task indeed. She's the one hors de combat, on maternity leave from the great Pratt's Word of Mouth Department; from supervising oral history projects through the neighborhood branches, collecting urban folklore and recording immigrant folktales out of Baltimore's ethnic smorgasbord; from telling apprentice-level tales under May Jump's ongoing tutelage to the very young and very old and the blind and the unlettered, working toward her brown belt in recitation; from conducting seminars in otolaryngeal narrative and taking them in narration; from assuming the wheel herself sometimes of the Inner City Talemobile in winter or one of the Storycycles in summer to carry forth the word from Cathedral Street as well as bring it back; and in general from looking after the library's Office of Oral Input as May (once upon a time) looked after its Out-. She misses that. A writer may be his own best company: Desert Island or Manhattan Island, for Peter Sagamore it's scratch and scribble, scribble and scratch. But a mouth needs an ear, an ear a mouth; Kath's as gregarious as Pete's egregious; it's mainly the human flow through Nopoint Point, with its freight of anecdote and inquiry, that has eased the tedium of this fortnight in the First Guest Cottage. Bored out of her skull is Katie, by enforced inactivity and unresponsibility; as gratefully surfeited as Peter with her parents' benevolent overkill; weary as he of making more shift than love, and on top of all straining her lumbars to haul who knew how many of who could say what, given that equivocal ultrasound scan, from poolside to courtside to dockside to dinnertableside to husbandside at last in bed.

The month of May normally gets our man into high gear and happy fits of abbreviation: His teaching's done, but Kathy's still at work; our Baltimore apartment he has all to himself from half past eight to half past five. Four hours of making long notes for short paragraphs; an hour of lunch and mail; two of sweet mindless physicality in some nearby school's gymnasium or on its tennis court; another two of chores, odd jobs, and errands about beflowered Baltimore; two or three more of building and eating dinner with Katherine Shorter Sherritt, comparing days, conferring upon the wider world—our favorite time, which we do not rush: wine and candles every blessed weekday, Telemann on tape, good food and quiet talk till cleanup's done at eight or nine; the balance of the evening reading, walking, letter-writing, very occasional movie- or theatergoing, perhaps with friends. Some okay restaurant weekly, some better one monthly, a semesterly party of some sort. To this routine add typically those two weeks in June of sailing on the Bay; now and then a quick winter ski trip or Caribbean beach-out when the cash flow flows. The occasional off-campus lecture junket for Peter or, for Katherine, library scientists' convention. Twice in our decade together short visits to Europe, whither in our earlier decades apart Kathy Sherritt had gone often, briefly, and Peter Sagamore once for a corner-turning year.

Thus our life, reader, which we love. Thus, normally, our May. Come June, we'd normally close our Stony Run flat, spend a long weekend with the Sherritts at Nopoint Point commissioning and provisioning old *Story* and baffling Henry Sherritt once again with our preference for an engineless, unamenitied little sloop over *Katydid IV,* his fifty-foot ketch with three staterooms, two hot showers, full electronics, and a mighty diesel, which we're welcome to use with or without the paid hand. After a happy fortnight's sailing and drifting, back to steamy Baltimore and to work, returning most weekends to Nopoint Point, where there's never not room aplenty.

A regular life and a tranquil; a privileged life and an easy. Yet a busy life, a productive—and a too too swiftly running. Normally.

This May, no; this June, no. Jack Bass, the family obstetrician-gynecologist, who delivered Katherine early in his practice, has half retired to a spread of his own across Goldsborough Creek, but is still sought after by Gold Coasties in the family way and supervises the pregnancies of those he once delivered. Kath's is a case Doctor Jack has followed with more than routine interest: He delivered her first husband, Porter "Poonie" Baldwin, Jr., and shrugged his shoulders at that marriage, which all four parents cheered; he tisked his tongue at its early breakup and aborted young Mrs. Baldwin's pregnancy back when abortion was not much done in Talbot County; he consoled Henry Sherritt on the golf course and prescribed Valium for Irma; he approved K's subsequent pairing with Captain Fritz Sagamore's son from across the broad Choptank, despite that family's much lower social rank; he applauded our decision eight years later to get married and pregnant if P's old vasectomy could be surgically reversed, and steered him to a Boston urologist whose specialty is iffy reanastomosis; he rejoiced with us at evidence of motile sperm, danced at our wedding, and coached our late-procreative efforts when success did not at once crown them; he toasted our eventual pregnancy and monitored its regrettable miscarriage; he counseled Kathy—who by then was thirty-eight and getting no younger—on our final long-shot strategy and cheered its clear payoff in early winter; he informed us in March that he heard two heartbeats in there, in April two at least, and ordered an ultrasound scan to clarify matters wombwise; then he put an arm about Peter Sagamore's shoulders, took Kathy Sherritt's hand in his, regarded with us in equal awe the wondrous video display of what looked like a sibling-incestuous, polymorphousperverse prenatal orgy of Siamese septuplets, such was the tangle of shadowy arms and legs and umbilici flickering before us, and could or would not say further than that the delivery was definitely going to be multiple and that a week or two might be subtracted from our EDC. He recommended that Kath begin her maternity leave on the first of June instead of its ides and move to Nopoint Point for the entire summer, where he'd be five minutes away from the First Guest Cottage by Boston Whaler and no more than fifteen by Jaguar from either Chez Sherritt or Easton Memorial Hospital. Inasmuch as he knows us Sherritt-Sagamores to be great lookers-up and checkers-out of information, he felt constrained to forewarn us that morbidity and mortality rates increase for second-born twins, second- and third-born triplets, second-, third-, and fourth-born quadruplets, to say no further. Delivery by cesarean section was more than a possibility, despite our hopes to go the natural route.

Well!

We remind ourselves now that we reminded ourselves then that going on and then off the Pill plus hitting the fertilizer improves the odds not only for conception (that was our half-year long shot), but for multiple conception. Given Kathy's age, we told ourselves, and the seventy-percent lowered fertility rate of men with vasovasectomies, it is unlikely we'll give pregnancy another go. Something to be said, in short, for putting all one's eggs in this one basket, if one wants more than one.

But who wants? Though we both affirm that a child sans siblings is the poorer for that lack, we ourselves have each in fact one close to her/his heart, one not; it seems a toss-up. And even with Help, each privately sees—at the prospect of *two* (-plus) infants, *two* (-plus) preschoolers—our duetary peace and quiet, already but a dear memory since 1 June, receding that much further into the future. Not till 1998, by Peter's gloomy private reckoning, two years before the millennium, when he'll be pushing sixty, will the kids be off to college and the apartment tranquil enough again for him to write—should world and colleges, himself and writing, survive so long. Broods Kathy to her glummest self Hah: quintuplets in a high-crime city low-rise? We're in the *housing* market, Peter *mio*: the *big* housing market. With eleven-percent mortgages a bargain already and thirteenpercenters soon to be nostalgia, but real estate prices booming in the Baltimore-Washington corridor, you and I are going to have to buy a multibedroomed, play-basemented, fancy-kitchened, laundry-roomed, central-AC'd, automatic garage-doored, quiet low-crime side-streeted playyarded azaleaed dogwooded magnoliaed suburban for Christ's sake *house!*

As Hank and Irma Sherritt's only daughter, Princess Kate growing up on Nopoint Point had two of everything including brothers, trikes, bikes, cars, mailing addresses, coming-out parties, rs and ts in her family name, and, in time, colleges, degrees, husbands, and uncompleted pregnancies. One day she'll have the best of that again, compounded: her share of the old, abundant Sherritt pile. She's glad of that, because she honors her parents and because there are at least three causes she looks forward to philanthropizing massively: her husband, who has paid his workaday dues and should be freed to give his remaining prime time, all of it, to his everterser art; her ASPS, of which she and May Jump are founding members; and her HOSCA (Hands Off South and Central America), an organization devoted to the frustration of U.S. meddling in the governments of its southern neighbors. But in the middle while between rich and rich—if only, she grants, like a person stepping coatless into the cold from a warm room to which she'll presently return—she's pleased to do with little in the ownership way, K, a good deal less than our twin salaries could afford: our light and airy but spare apartment; a modest wardrobe from Loehmann's discountery and L. L. Bean's mail-order outdoorsery, her chief indulgence. No car of her own; no television; art mostly from the Baltimore Museum's rental gallery; tapes, records, and books on loan from the Pratt. It is marshy Hoopers Island Peter, public-high-school state-university Peter, who bought and treasures our secondhand BMW and thirdhand sailboat of his late father's manufacture, the threadbare Herizes, Tabrizes, and Bokharas on our floors, the Japanese brush drawings and stereo, Scandinavian furniture and French food processor and German coffeemaker and cabinetful of okay Bordeaux. But until we can afford to commission some architect friend to design us a simple, high-tech, energy-efficient, unostentatious, unobtrusive little gem tucked into the trees on some high point of land on the Chester or the Sassafras, say, where we can swim naked in the natural element instead of suited up in the Sherritts' filtered and chlorinated tank, he wants a house no more than she.

A house! And then, no doubt, pet animals; he sure loved his in boyhood days: the world of Kitty Litter, Hartz flea collars, fish tanks, gerbil cages. Are there Boy and Girl Scouts still? Merit badges? Peter Sagamore was born into a moderately poor family made poorer by the Great Depression in historically poor lower Dorchester County, Maryland; he grew up without benefit of baby-sitters, nursery schools, summer camps, special-education fast tracks, and pressure from his parents to excel, both of whom had gone to work at sixteen and were delighted to see their children finish South Dorchester High. Katherine Sherritt was born into a moderately rich family made richer by every declared war in U.S. history in historically rich Talbot County, Maryland; she too grew up without baby-sitters (the Sherritts had live-in nannies and governesses), without summer camps (the Sherritts spent their Augusts in Maine or Spain), without special-ed fast tracks (a Sherritt's ed is special from prekindergarten on), without pressure from her parents to excel (the Sherritts have taken excellence in one form or another for granted since the eighteenth century). Having so much inexperience in common, we understandably share some apprehension about dealing with Pampers and PTAs, especially in triplicate or quadruplicate.

But we made up our minds two years ago, not impulsively, to join genes, and we're not displeased with our success, only dismayed by its extent; Peter Sagamore especially. One child, small, was what *he* had in mind, by whose lights a windy sentence is one with more than two clauses or three commas; whose longest short story in recent years runs maybe six pages, his recenter ones three or two, his recentest— you'll see. The world has things enough in it already; more than enough; too many. One ought ever to add to their number with reluctance. Pete's Cartesian, Kath Rabelaisian. Sentences, paragraphs like these must be hers, under whose good breasts are lungs like a marathoner's, a Met soprano's. This green-belt raconteuse can recite Homer's Catalogue of Ships or Gargantua's of bumswipes at the clip of a Gilbert and Sullivan patter song and make you call not only Bravo but Encore. She can enjoy the Ocean City public beach and boardwalk on a July Fourth afternoon with a third of a million fellow humans schooled like smelts, or the common fitting room at Loehmann's just before High Holidays, for which no simile will serve. If Less Is More is Pete, More Is More is Kath. Pete's pet poet is Emily Dickinson: *zero at the bone.* Katherine Sherritt's is Walt Whitman: *I contain multitudes.*

In sum, a well-coupled couple, and not only Jack Sprat-wise. At abundant Kathy's core, her friend discovered years ago, like hurricane's eye or black hole in a plenum, is a small but central bubble not of nothing but of Nothingness: an empty point where some Big Bang must have banged, since from it her universe busies out in all directions, particularly his. Peter Sagamore's life has been by contrast all but void of scenes, events, things, relations, distractions; son of monotonous marshes stretching sky to sky, he thrives upon silence, sparseness. But as in fact those wetlands teem and nurse the elsewise lifeless oceans, so at Peter's center, his friend discovered years ago, is not only a wistful, detached affection for the variety and busyness of the world, but a certain hard tireless dedicated energy, like a quasar blazing X rays in the universe's crawlspace. From that core his lean art radiates, as do by the way his attraction to and patience with the busy life of Nopoint Point, in measured doses, and his measureless delight in Katherine Sherritt.

DO THE WOMAN.

That won't be easy from our coupled point of view—P's promptings, K's cadenzas—but she'll draw a great breath; we'll try. Here's the woman of us, in her man's opinion: Katherine Shorter Sherritt at thirty-nine is a rangy, long-limbed looker looking thirty-three tops and topped with beach-colored hair (both the dry beach and the wet), streaked straight past fine strong shoulders when she lets it down. She has Hank Sherritt's Episcopalian bright gray eyes, Irma Shorter's twenty-four-carat skin and cultured-pearl dentition. She'll dress to the nines when occasion calls and sophisticate in three languages, Kate, but she's easy in the preppie drag she wears to work: tweed skirts, cable-knit crewnecks over oxford-cloth buttondowns; easier yet in soft jeans and hiking boots and flannels, swapping stories with her ASPS across an Ozark campfire; easiest of all in the all-but-altogether with Peter Sagamore, spanking along in *Story* through a summer afternoon or splashing naked by moonlight with the noctilucae. When Katherine takes her clothes off later in this prologue and stands in the First Guest Cottage wearing only earrings, wedding band, and fine gold chain necklace, you'll see those aforesung breasts engorged by pregnancy beyond their normal trim, their russet aureoles stretched cookie-size: athletic buttocks fairly firm even this far gone; smoothmuscled, fineskinned calves and thighs, flawless; and what was till the turn of the year a hard flat belly with God's thumbprint for a navel. All this, mind, in her husband's opinion (and May Jump's). She's an Outward Bound type, Kath: backpacker, white-water canoeist, distance swimmer. She's a green-belt karateist as well as raconteuse, don't mess with K.S.S., though that belly's thrown her balance off. Under all that skin she is intuitive but clearheaded, even hardheaded when necessary. She is memorious, practical, capable, Kathy, but more dependent than she wishes upon Peter's stability and good humor to level out her swings from up to down to up. Life having been generous to her, she is in his opinion generous with hers: Much of that Pratt work is hardcore inner-city, and she is forever volunteering for good-citizenly chores over and above: Operation Head Start, the League of Women Voters, the Museum board, the Better Baltimore Committee, her prep school's board of trustees, her college's alumnae association, the local chapter of Amnesty International, and of course her ASPS and HOSCA. She has enjoyed vigorously, Katherine, every stage of her privileged life—her childhood, girlhood, adolescence, young womanhood, mature adulthood—except the period of her marriage to Poonie Baldwin. Strong-charactered and principled, she learned from that experience to prize good character above all else in others. She dislikes pettiness, foolishness, weakness, coquetry, moral laziness, snobbishness, cowardice, dissembling, bad faith; also drunkenness, narcosis, philandering, and sexual sadism. She is not, is Katherine Sherritt, modish, intellectual, high-style, cute, very worldly, "sexy," very political, submissive, very dependent, carping, devious, vain, contentious, affected, very fastidious, "passionate," fearful, reckless, jealous. She is neither genius nor virtuoso, though she's a whiz at collecting stories and getting better all the time at telling them. What she is, in her husband's view, is knowledgeable, sensible, well-organized, ardent, reasonable, energetic, sexual, loyal, dependable, moodier than she approves of being, quick-minded and intelligent, well-educated, physically and morally courageous, articulate, resourceful, prevailingly cheerful, self-reliant but not entirely, damned good-looking, we said that already, and, she adds, much drawn to genuine talent and virtuosity.

Kathy Sherritt knows who she is. She does? She does. With the strength of a certain WASP cultural tradition behind her, of which she largely but not uncritically approves, she relates easily to others who know who they are, however foreign: an asset in her ethnic-oral-history work. She would hit it off with a Masai chieftain or the Baal Shem Tov. Homosexual men are not uncomfortable in Kathy's company; straight women like her; lesbians are powerfully drawn herward, Q.E.D., as are heterosexual men of various classes, races, ages.

Katherine, Kathy, Katie-Kath-Kate! *He's* drawn to you, too, who just now helped draw you! Lucky the man whose woman is Katherine Sherritt.

NOW DO THE MAN.

With pleasure: Lucky Katherine, in her and this narrative's opinion, to have for the man of us good Peter Sagamore. That surname is Algonquian for "minor chieftain"—we remember Teddy Roosevelt's Sagamore Hill, up in Oyster Bay—but "Captain" Fritz Sagamore was a German immigrant carpenter's son. The word is not given in our German-English dictionary: *Sage mehr* ("Say more"), we wonder, metamorphosed by some immigration clerk like many another new American's name? *Zage mir?* Nobody knows. Capn Fritz felt more or less German, but was never taught the tongue; the Sagamores presume themselves a line of sturdy Kraut carpenters going back forever and take no interest in family history. Transplanted to Hoopers Island, on the Chesapeake side of lower Dorchester, Fritz's father enlarged his trade to include boat carpentry, in which the son specialized; Fritz established himself in time as a regionally famous builder of Chesapeake Bay workboats—especially those long, narrow oyster-tong boats with inverted, "duck's-ass" transoms—and, toward the end of his career, small wooden cruising sailboats built "by rack of eye," without full-scale laid-out plans. Our Peter and Jacob, his older brother, even their mother and Sue-Ann, their younger sister, all worked about the yard and became adept with the boatwright's tools—joinery and brightwork were adolescent Peter's special skills—but only Jake took up the trade. Some voice spoke to Peter Sagamore early on, who knows whose in those trackless wetlands, saying Honor thy father and thy mother and thy place of birth, but put kilometrage as soon as possible 'twixt thee and them.

Pete's parenting was benign but inattentive. Lapsed Lutherans, Fritz and Nora always smiled, never quarreled, but were too busy and indifferent to do more than work, eat, sleep. P felt affection for but not much kinship with his mother: A good-natured, rawboned farm woman used to self-sacrifice and hard work without complaint, she's in a down-county nursing home now, senile early, cheerful, deaf, incontinent. All day long she drinks coffee and smokes cigarettes (it is not a strict nursing home), turns the television up too loud but doesn't look at it, and makes pencil drawings that her attendants can't decipher but her children recognize at a glance to be of the wooden parts of her late husband's boats: knees, stemheads, keelsons, bitts. P respected and felt kinship with but not much closeness to his father: a sound craftsman; an honest businessman with little head for business; an energetic and incorruptible citizen who served term after term as county commissioner in addition to running the Sagamore boatyard; a shrug-shouldered father like his father, who never disciplined and almost never rebuked his children because there was almost never need to, but who did not talk or do much with them, either. Peter sees Fritz Sagamore now as having been a principled, benevolent, hardworking, unadventurous, good-humored, civic-minded, rather shy and selfish fellow who made the best of his limitations without complaint and mildly left his children to their own devices. Pete misses him, honors his memory, wishes they two had been able to converse and do more of the usual father-son things, wonders whether Capn Fritz felt the same about his father, and finally shrugs. He worries that for want of better models, experience, and genes he'll be no closer to our children, despite his resolve to be, than his father was to him. Don't worry, says his wife, but sometimes she does too.

So how does a lower-middle-class, unaffluent, semirural, semiredneck, semicivilized, semieducated boy make his way out of the salt marsh into the corridors of literature? He bloody doesn't, as a rule: not into literature's or any other profession's corridors. If he does, it will likely be by accident and indirection. What your Sherritts take for granted, he'll pay for with his youth. Though he may outstrip, he'll never catch up. Though he scale in his lifework the high, dry summit of Parnassus, he'll go to his grave almost as wet behind the ears as if he'd never crawled out of the marsh. He will? He will. He had better therefore make a virtue of this limitation, become a hedgehog as he'll never be a fox. He will stumble into some university on scholarship, nearly drown there but not quite, and learn to float if never swim in the academic enterprise. Coming from no very defined cultural tradition, he will have not only all civilizations to discover, but Civilization. Having unlike Kathy no very defined self, he will grope his way into art with the one advantage of being unable, ipso facto, to practice it as self-expression; he will be free therefore either to invent himself in and for his stories or—what in his opinion comes to the same thing—to efface himself in his invention. Because he has everything to learn, he'll approach the medium without preconceptions, and this innocence may not be altogether a liability. Because he does not quite know who he is, he may never quite learn what he cannot do, and this ignorance, if it does not ruin him, may be his strength. This sounds more like the man of us talking than the woman; let her have her say.

Okay: On the cusp of forty, Peter Sagamore is a handsome U.S. sixfooter, lean and healthy, even athletic, with curly hair the color of his woman's and skin to match its darker locks; some south European input into that lost line of carpenters gave all the Sagamores mahogany eyes and permanent suntans. He wears no mustache, beard, or eyeglasses. When he takes his clothes off later in Day Zero and stands in *Story's* cockpit wearing only wedding band, wristwatch, and brown bead necklace, you'll see long flat swimmer's muscles under more of that permanent tan, body hair barley-gold and fine but for the tobacco-brown bush of underarms and pubes, the latter fleecier than Kathy's tight-curled nap but identical in color. Exercise and a lucky metabolism have kept P. Sagamore almost as trim as a healthy thirty-year-old. The skin that girdles his butt and gut is less tan than the rest; Katherine Shorter Sherritt's pleasure is to kiss right 'round those borders when on warm weekends we're sailing stripped and out of ready view: more particularly if, as happens, her friend is steering momentarily with the tiller-tip squeezed between his buns while trimming *Story's* mainsheet or making entries in the log. His genital equipment—there it hangs, mildly curious reader—is circumcised, normal in magnitude, reliable in function. Inasmuch as husband and wife, neither either green or jaded, are satisfied quite with each other as sexual partners, an aspect of our life together that we enjoy as much as any other, there'll be little more to say in our story upon this head, though there may be some.

When our chap wears clothes, they'll generally be in the khaki-slacks/navy-blazer/madras-shirt category on teaching days, the jeans-and-rugbyshirt on others, cutoff denims and deck moccasins in summer. Except in town and on special occasions, he wears neither shirt nor socks from Flag Day to Labor Day. We dislike air-conditioning and are fond of skin; we are neither exhibitionists nor voyeurs, but nudity comes as easily to us in humid tidewaterland as to north Europeans on a south European beach.

All right. Some things Peter Sagamore is not, in his wife's opinion, are colorful, eccentric, high-energetic, very outgoing, Romantic, religious, politically enthusiastic, vain, gregarious, affected, promiscuous, devious, personally subtle, and ideological, though he sure does have opinions. Some things he is are personable, introspective, vigorous, unassuming, mild-mannered, stoical, prevailingly serene and good-humored, moderate in his habits, well organized, firmly principled, rational, virile (though forty is not twenty), patient with himself and others, a touch absentminded and forgetful, a touch passive in his dealings with the world and therefore dependent in many ways upon Kathy—and immune to doubts about his vocation, though not about his accomplishment. His personal culture is less broad than Kath's, though she finds it deeper. He reads not widely, massively, or systematically, but what he reads becomes a working part of him; he has a gift for language, none for languages; neither a scholar on the one hand nor a primitive on the other, he is an okay instructor in the art of literature from its manufacturers' point of view and a first-rate coach and critic of apprentice writers. Fairly said. As a writer himself . . .

That is another story, even shorter. Enough here to establish that while our woman, who is without invention, can recount spellbindingly anything except her husband's stories, which must come silently from the page through the eye and mind into the soul, our man can recount nothing to good effect; can't even tell a joke. He merely and strictly invents, sets down. And that for this inventing and setting down, the fellow trains, like a spiritual and physical athlete. Mens sana in corpore sano: All that swimming, running, stretching exercise and the rest are not just for his physical well-being, any more than his memory-, breathing-, concentration-, and relaxation-exercises are merely for his psychological well-being. They are to bring him to the mark—the last mark he put upon yesterday's white page—in both Olympic and Olympian condition.

Henry and Irma Sherritt, it goes without saying, had early trouble with this connection of Princess Kate's and even now are less than perfectly easy with it. But they are chastened by their former advocacy of Poonie Baldwin, Jr., and they cannot but like Pete personally and approve his character. They respect the chap's integrity, and so far from perceiving him as a threat to their conservative values, with Kathy's help they see him as a moderating influence upon their daughter: His politics, for example, are more skeptical and middle-of-the-road than hers. If he were more famous, they'd be less uneasy; if he were less so, they'd be more. Not only the *New York Times,* after all, but even the *Wall Street Journal* has assured them that their laconic son-in-law is something different: a writer's writer's writer?

The writer Peter Sagamore: That sums him up. As another, asked what he is, might say, "I'm a black militant poet," "I'm a fifty-year-old divorced chamber musician with grown-up Hasidic twin daughters," or "I'm a Chilean Marxist on the staff of Orlando Letelier, Salvador Allende's ambassador to the U.S."; as Henry Sherritt would say, "I'm a Republican businessman Episcopalian Sherritt," and Irma, "I'm Mrs. Henry Sherritt," and Katherine, "I'm Kath"; so Peter Sagamore would answer I'm a writer. And it is because this writer, honed to this edge, had been these several seasons ever more distracted by seven several circumstances from writing, and especially this fortnight pent on Nopoint Point like a Preakness thoroughbred stuck in the gates at Pimlico, that in the sultry mid-afternoon of 15 June '80 Peter Sagamore cried out to Katherine Sherritt in the First Guest Cottage For pity's sake, Kathy, set me a task!

Thereby setting her one.

A Few Words About Minimalism

*L*ess is more," said Walter Gropius, or Alberto Giacometti, or Laszlo Molholy-Nagy, or Henri Guadier-Brzeska, or Constantin Brancusi, or Le Corbusier, or Ludwig Mies van der Rohe; the remark (first made in fact by Robert Browning) has been severally attributed to all of those more or less celebrated more or less minimalists. Like the Bauhaus motto, "Form follows function," it is itself a memorable specimen of the minimalist esthetic, of which a cardinal principle is that artistic effect may be enhanced by a radical economy of artistic means, even where such parsimony compromises other values: completeness, for example, or richness or precision of statement.

The power of that esthetic principle is easy to demonstrate: contrast my eminently forgettable formulation of it above—"artistic effect may be enhanced," etc.—with the unforgettable assertion "less is more." Or consider the following proposition, first with, and then without, its parenthetical elements:

Minimalism (of one sort or another) is the principle (one of the principles, anyhow) underlying (what I and many another interested observer consider to be perhaps) the most impressive phenomenon on the current (North American, especially the United States) literary scene (the gringo equivalent to *el boom* in the Latin American novel): I mean the new flowering of the (North) American short story (in particular the kind of terse, oblique, realistic or hyperrealistic, slightly plotted, extrospective, cool-surfaced fiction associated in the last five or ten years with such excellent writers as Frederick Barthelme, Ann Beattie, Raymond Carver, Bobbie Ann Mason, James Robison, Mary Robison, and Tobias Wolff, and both praised and damned under such labels as "K-Mart realism," "hick chic," "Diet-Pepsi minimalism" and "post-Vietnam, post-literary, postmodernist blue-collar neo-early-Hemingwayism").

Like any clutch of artists collectively labeled, the writers just mentioned are at least as different from one another as they are similar. Minimalism, moreover, is not the only and may not be the most important attribute that their fiction more or less shares; those labels themselves suggest some other aspects and concerns of the New American Short Story and its proportionate counterpart, the three-eighth-inch novel. But it is their minimalism I shall speak of (briefly) here, and its antecedence: the idea that, in art at least, less is more.

It is an idea surely as old, as enduringly attractive and as ubiquitous as its opposite. In the beginning was the Word: only later came the Bible, not to mention the three-decker Victorian novel. The oracle at Delphi did not say, "Exhaustive analysis and comprehension of one's own psyche may be prerequisite to an understanding of one's behavior and of the world at large"; it said, "Know thyself." Such inherently minimalist genres as oracles (from the Delphic shrine of Apollo to the modern fortune cookie), proverbs, maxims, aphorisms, epigrams, pensées, mottoes, slogans and quips are popular in every human century and culture—especially in oral cultures and subcultures, where mnemonic staying power has high priority—and many specimens of them are self-reflexive or self-demonstrative: minimalism about minimalism. "Brevity is the soul of wit." "Silence is golden." *"Vita brevis est, ars longa"* Seneca warns aspiring poets in his third Epistle; "Eschew surplusage," recommends Mark Twain.

Against the large-scale classical prose pleasures of Herodotus, Thucydides, and Petronius, there are the miniature delights of Aesop's fables and Theophrastus' *Characters*. Against such verse epics as *The Iliad, The Odyssey*, and the *Aeneid*—and the much longer Sanskrit *Ramayana, Mahabharata* and *Ocean of Story*—are such venerable supercompressive poetic forms as the palindrome (there are long examples, but the ones we remember are "Madam, I'm Adam" and "Sex at noon taxes"), or the single couplet (a modern instance is Ogden Nash's "Candy is dandy / But liquor is quicker"), or the feudal Japanese haiku and its Western echoes in the early-20th-century imagists up to the contemporary "skinny poems" of, say, Robert Creeley. There are even single-word poems, or single words that ought to be poems; the best one I know of I found in the *Guinness Book of World Records,* listed as the "most succinct word": The Tierra del Fuegian word "mamihlapinatapei." In the language of the Land of Fire, "mamihlapinatapei" is said to mean: looking into each other's eyes, each hoping that the other will initiate what both want to do but neither chooses to commence.

The genre of the short story, as Poe distinguished it from the traditional tale in his 1842 review of Hawthorne's first collection of stories, is an early manifesto of modern narrative minimalism: "In the whole composition there should be no word written, of which the tendency . . . is not to the pre-established design. . . . Undue length is . . . to be avoided." Poe's codification informs such later 19th-century masters of terseness, selectivity, and implicitness (as opposed to leisurely once-upon-a-timelessness, luxuriant abundance, explicit and extended analysis) as Guy de Maupassant and Anton Chekhov. Show, don't tell, said Henry James in effect and at length in his prefaces to the 1908 New York edition of his novels. And don't tell a word more than you absolutely need to, added young Ernest Hemingway, who thus described his "new theory" in the early 1920s: "You could omit anything if you knew that you omitted, and the omitted part would strengthen the story and make people feel something more than they understood."

The Bauhaus Functionalists were by then already busy unornamenting and abstracting modern architecture, painting and design; and while functionalism and minimalism are not the same thing, to say nothing of abstractionism and minimalism (there is nothing abstract about those early Hemingway stories), they spring from the same impulse: to strip away the superfluous in order to reveal the necessary, the essential. Never mind that Voltaire had pointed out, a century and a half before, how indispensable the superfluous can be (*"Le superflu, chose si nécessaire"*); just as, in modern painting, the process of stripping away leads from Post-Impressionism through Cubism to the radical minimalism of Dasimir Malevich's "White on White" of 1918, and Ad Reinhardt's all but imageless "black paintings" of the 1950s, so in 20th-century literature the minimalist succession leads through Hemingway's "new theory" to the shorter *ficciones* of Jorge Luis Borges and the ever-terser texts of Samuel Beckett, perhaps culminating in his play *Breath* (1969): The curtain opens on a dimly lit stage, empty but for scattered rubbish: there is heard a single recorded human cry, then a single amplified inspiration and expiration of breath accompanied by a brightening and redimming of the lights, then again the cry. Thirty-five seconds after it opened, the curtain closes.

But it closes only on the play, not on the modern tradition of literary minimalism, which honorably continues in such next-generation writers as, in America, Donald Barthelme ("The fragment is the only form I trust," says a character in his slender novel *Snow White*) and, in the literary generation overlapping and following his, the plentiful authors of the New American Short Story.

Old or new, fiction can be minimalist in any or all of several ways. There are minimalisms of unit, form and scale: short words, short sentences and paragraphs, super-short stories, those three-eighth-inch thin novels aforementioned, and even minimal bibliographies (Borges's fiction adds up to a few modest, though powerfully influential, short-story collections). There are minimalisms of style: stripped-down vocabulary; a stripped-down syntax that avoids periodic sentences, serial predications and complex subordinating constructions; a stripped-down rhetoric that may eschew figurative language altogether; a stripped-down, non-emotive tone. And there are minimalisms of material: minimal characters, minimal exposition ("all that David Copperfield kind of crap," says J. D. Salinger's catcher in the rye), *minimal mises en scène,* minimal action, minimal plot.

Found together in their purest forms, these several minimalisms add up to an art that—in the words of its arch-priest, Samuel Beckett, speaking of the painter Bram Van Velde—expresses "that there is nothing to express, nothing with which to express, nothing from which to express, no power to express, no desire to express—together with the obligation to express." But they are not always found together. There are very short works of great rhetorical, emotional and thematic richness, such as Borges's essential page, "Borges and I"; and there are instances of what may fairly be called long-winded minimalism, such as Samuel Beckett's stark-monumental trilogy from the early '50s: *Molloy, Malone Dies* and *The Unnameable.* Parallels abound in the other arts: the miniature, in painting, is characteristically brimful (miniaturism is not minimalism); Joseph Cornell's little boxes contain universes. The large paintings of Mark Rothko, Franz Kline and Barnett Newman, on the other hand, are as undetailed as the Washington Monument.

The medieval Roman Catholic Church recognized two opposite roads to grace; the *via negativa* of the monk's cell and the hermit's cave, and the *via affirmativa* of immersion in human affairs, of being in the world whether or not one is of it. Critics have aptly borrowed those terms to characterize the difference between Mr. Beckett, for example, and his erstwhile master James Joyce, himself a maximalist except in his early works. Other than bone-deep disposition, which is no doubt the great determinant, what inclines a writer—sometimes almost a cultural generation of writers—to the Negational Path?

For individuals, it may be by their own acknowledgment largely a matter of past or present personal circumstances. Raymond Carver writes of a literary apprenticeship in which his short poems and stories were carved in precious quarter-hours stolen from a harrowing domestic and economic situation; though he now has professional time aplenty, the notion besets him that should he presume to attempt even a short novel, he'll wake to find himself back in those wretched circumstances. An opposite case was Borges's: his near-total blindness in his later decades obliged him to the short forms that he had elected for other, nonphysical reasons when he was sighted.

. . .

To account for a trend, literary sociologists and culture watchers point to more general historical and philosophical factors—not excluding the factor, of powerful models like Borges and Beckett. The influence of early Hemingway on Raymond Carver, say, is as apparent as the influence of Mr. Carver in turn on a host of other New American Short-Story writers, and on a much more numerous host of apprentices in American college fiction-writing programs. But why this model rather than that, other than its mere and sheer artistic prowess, on which after all it has no monopoly? Doubtless because this one is felt, by the writers thus more or less influenced, to speak more strongly to their condition and that of their readers.

And what is that condition, in the case of the cool-surface realist-minimalist story-tellers of the American 1970s and '80s? In my conversation with them, my reading of their critics both positive and negative and my dealings with recent and current apprentice writers, I have heard cited, among other factors, these half-dozen, ranked here in no particular order:

■ Our national hangover from the Vietnam War, felt by many to be a trauma literally and figuratively unspeakable. "I don't want to talk about it" is the characteristic attitude of "Nam" veterans in the fiction of Ann Beattie, Jayne Anne Phillips and Bobbie Ann Mason—as it is among many of their real-life counterparts (and as it was among their numberless 20th-century forerunners, especially after the First World War). This is, of course, one of the two classic attitudes to trauma, the other being its opposite, and it can certainly conduce to hedged, nonintrospective, even minimalist discourse: one remembers Hemingway's early story "Soldier's Home."

■ The more or less coincident energy crisis of 1973–76, and the associated reaction against American excess and wastefulness in general. The popularity of the sub-compact car parallels that (in literary circles, at least) of the subcompact novel and the minifiction—though not, one observes, of the miniskirt, which had nothing to do with conserving material.

■ The national decline in reading and writing skills, not only among the young (including even young apprentice writers, as a group), but among their teachers, many of whom are themselves the product of an ever-less-demanding educational system and a society whose narrative-dramatic entertainment and tastes come far more from movies and television than from literature. This is not to disparage the literacy and general education of those writers mentioned above, or to suggest that the great writers of the past were uniformly flawless spellers and grammarians, of wide personal literary culture. Some were, some weren't; some of today's are, some aren't. But at least among those of our aspiring writers promising enough to be admitted into good graduate writing programs—and surely they are not the *inferior* specimens of their breed—the general decline in basic language skills over the last two decades is inarguable enough to make me worry in some instances about their teaching undergraduates. Rarely in their own writing, whatever its considerable other merits, will one find a sentence of any syntactical complexity, for example, and inasmuch as a language's repertoire of other-than-basic syntactical devices permits its users to articulate other-than-basic thoughts and feelings, Dick-and-Jane prose tends to be emotionally and intellectually poorer than Henry James prose. Among the great minimalist writers, this impoverishment is elected and strategic: simplification in the interest of strength, or of some other value. Among the less great it may be *faute de mieux*. Among today's "common readers" it is pandemic.

■ Along with this decline, an ever-dwindling readerly attention span. The long popular novel still has its devotees, especially aboard large airplanes and on beaches; but it can scarcely be doubted that many of the hours we bourgeois now spend with our televisions and video cassette recorders, and in our cars and at the movies, we used to spend reading novels and novellas and not-so-short stories, partly because those glitzy other distractions weren't there and partly because we were more generally conditioned for sustained concentration, in our pleasures as well as in our work. The Austrian novelist Robert Musil was complaining by 1930 (in his maxi-novel *The Man Without Qualities*) that we live in "the age of the magazine," too impatient already in the twitchy '20s to read books. Half a century later, in America at least, even the large-circulation magazine market for fiction had dwindled to a handful of outlets; the readers weren't there. It is a touching paradox of the New American Short Story—so admirably straightforward and democratic access, so steeped in brand names and the popular culture—that it perforce appears mainly in very small-circulation literary quarterlies instead of the likes of *Collier's, Liberty,* and the *Saturday Evening Post.* But the *New Yorker* and *Esquire* can't publish everybody.

■ Together with all the above, a reaction on these authors' part against the ironic, black-humoristic "fabulism" and/or the (sometimes academic) intellectuality and/or the density, here byzantine, there baroque, of some of their immediate American literary antecedents: the likes of Donald Barthelme, Robert Coover, Stanley Elkin, William Gaddis and William Gass, John Hawkes, Joseph Heller, Thomas Pynchon, Kurt Vonnegut, (and, I shall presume, myself as well). This reaction, where it exists, would seem to pertain as much to our successors' relentless realism as to their minimalism: among the distinguished brothers Barthelme, Donald's productions are no less lean that Frederick's or the up-and-coming Steven's; but their characteristic material, angle of attack and resultant flavor are different indeed. The formal intricacy of Elder Brother's story "Sentence," for example (a single nine-page nonsentence), or the direct though satirical intellectuality of his "Kierkegaard Unfair to Schlegel," are as foreign to the K-Mart Realists as are the manic flights of *Gravity's Rainbow.* So it goes: The dialogue between fantast and realist, fabulator and quotidianist, like the dialogue between maximalist and minimalist, is as old as storytelling, and by no means always adversary. There are innumerable combinations, coalitions, line-crossings, and workings of both sides of the street.

■ The reaction against the all but inescapable hyperbole of American advertising, both commercial and political, with its high-tech manipulativeness and glamourous lies, as ubiquitous as and more polluted than the air we breathe. How understandable that such an ambiance, together with whatever other items in this catalogue, might inspire a fiction dedicated to homely, understated, programmatically unglamorous, even minimalistic Telling It Like It Is.

That has ever been the ground inspiration, moral-philosophical in character, of minimalism and its kissing cousin realism in their many avatars over the centuries, in the fine arts and elsewhere: the feeling that the language (or whatever) has for whatever reasons become excessive, cluttered, corrupted, fancy, false. It is the Puritans' reaction against baroque Catholicism; it is Thoreau's putting behind him even the meager comforts of the village of Concord.

To the Lost Generation of World War I survivors, says one of their famous spokesmen (Frederic Henry in Hemingway's *A Farewell to Arms*), "Abstract words such as glory, honor, courage, or hallow were obscene." Wassily Kandinsky said he sought "not the shell, but the nut." The functionalism of the Bauhaus was inspired in part by admiration for machine technology, in part by revulsion against the fancy clutter of the Gilded Age, in language as well as elsewhere. The sinking of the elegant *Titanic* has come to symbolize the end of that age, as the sight of some workmen crushed by a falling Victorian cornice symbolized for young Frank Lloyd Wright the dead weight of functionless architectural decoration. Flaubert raged against the *blague* of bourgeois speech, bureaucratic speech in particular; his passion for the *mot juste* involved far more subtraction than addition. The baroque inspires its opposite: after the excesses of scholasticism comes Descartes's radical reductionism—let us doubt and discard everything not self-evident and see whether anything indubitable remains upon which to rebuild. And among the scholastics themselves, three centuries before Descartes, William of Ockham honed his celebrated razor: *Entia non sunt multiplicanda* ("Entities are not to be multiplied").

In short, less is more.

Beyond their individual and historically local impulses, then, the more or less minimalist authors of the New American Short Story are reenacting a cyclical correction in the history (and the microhistories) of literature and of art in general; a cycle to be found as well, with linger rhythms, in the history of philosophy, the history of the culture. Renaissances beget Reformations, which then beget Counter-Reformations; the seven fat years are succeeded by seven lean, after which we, no less than the people of Genesis, may look forward to the recorrection.

For if there is much to admire in artistic austerity, its opposite is not without merits and joys as well. There are the minimalist pleasures of Emily Dickinson—"Zero at the Bone"—and the maximalist ones of Walt Whitman; the low-fat rewards of Samuel Beckett's *Texts for Nothing* and the high-calorie delights of Gabriel García Márquez's *One Hundred Years of Solitude*. There truly are more ways than one to heaven. As between minimalism and its opposite, I pity the reader—or the writer, or the age— too addicted to either to savor the other.

Letter to the Lady of the House

Richard Bausch

*I*t's exactly twenty minutes to midnight, on this the eve of my seventieth birthday, and I've decided to address you, for a change, in writing—odd as that might seem. I'm perfectly aware of how many years we've been together, even if I haven't been very good about remembering to commemorate certain dates, certain days of the year. I'm also perfectly aware of how you're going to take the fact that I'm doing this at all, so late at night, with everybody due to arrive tomorrow, and the house still unready. I haven't spent almost five decades with you without learning a few things about you that I can predict and describe with some accuracy, though I admit that, as you put it, lately we've been more like strangers than husband and wife. Well, so if we are like strangers, perhaps there are some things I can tell you that you won't have already figured out about the way I feel.

Tonight, we had another one of those long, silent evenings after an argument (remember?) over pepper. We had been bickering all day, really, but at dinner I put pepper on my potatoes and you said that about how I shouldn't have pepper because it always upsets my stomach. I bothered to remark that I used to eat chili peppers for breakfast and if I wanted to put plain old ordinary black pepper on my potatoes, as I had been doing for more than sixty years, that was my privilege. Writing this now, it sounds far more testy than I meant it, but that isn't really the point.

In any case, you chose to overlook my tone. You simply said, "John, you were up all night the last time you had pepper with your dinner."

I said, "I was up all night because I ate green peppers. Not black pepper, but green peppers."

"A pepper is a pepper, isn't it?" you said. And then I started in on you. I got, as you call it, legal with you—pointing out that green peppers are not black pepper—and from there we moved on to an evening of mutual disregard for each other that ended with your decision to go to bed early. The grandchildren will make you tired, and there's still the house to do; you had every reason to want to get some rest, and yet I felt that you were also making a point of getting yourself out of proximity with me, leaving me to my displeasure, with another ridiculous argument settling between us like a fog.

So, after you went to bed, I got out the whiskey and started pouring drinks, and I had every intention of putting myself into a stupor. It was almost my birthday, after all, and—forgive this, it's the way I felt at the time—you had nagged me into an argument and then gone off to bed; the day had ended as so many of our days end now, and I felt, well, entitled. I had a few drinks, without any appreciable effect (though you might well see this letter as firm evidence to the contrary), and then I decided to do something to shake you up. I would leave. I'd make a lot of noise going out the door; I'd take a walk around the neighborhood and make you wonder where I could be. Perhaps I'd go check into a motel for the night. The thought even crossed my mind that I might leave you altogether. I admit that I entertained the thought, Marie. I saw our life together now as the day-to-day round of petty quarreling and tension that it's mostly been over the past couple of years or so, and I wanted out as sincerely as I ever wanted anything.

My God, I wanted an end to it, and I got up from my seat in front of the television and walked back down the hall to the entrance of our room to look at you. I suppose I hoped you'd still be awake so I could tell you of this momentous decision I felt I'd reached. And maybe you were awake: one of our oldest areas of contention being the noise I make—the feather-thin membrane of your sleep that I am always disturbing with my restlessness in the nights. All right. Assuming you were asleep and don't know that I stood in the doorway of our room, I will say that I stood there for perhaps five minutes, looking at you in the half-dark, the shape of your body under the blanket—you really did look like one of the girls when they were little and I used to stand in the doorway of their rooms; your illness last year made you so small again—and, as I said, I thought I had decided to leave you, for your peace as well as mine. I know you have gone to sleep crying, Marie. I know you've felt sorry about things and wished we could find some way to stop irritating each other so much.

Well, of course I didn't go anywhere. I came back to this room and drank more of the whiskey and watched television. It was like all the other nights. The shows came on and ended, and the whiskey began to wear off. There was a little rain shower. I had a moment of the shock of knowing I was seventy. After the rain ended, I did go outside for a few minutes. I stood on the sidewalk and looked at the house. The kids, with their kids, were on the road somewhere between their homes and here. I walked up to the end of the block and back, and a pleasant breeze blew and shook the drops out of the trees. My stomach was bothering me some, and maybe it was the pepper I'd put on my potatoes. It could just as well have been the whiskey. Anyway, as I came back to the house, I began to have the eerie feeling that I had reached the last night of my life. There was this small discomfort in my stomach, and no other physical pang or pain, and I am used to the small ills and side effects of my way of eating and drinking; yet I felt the sense of the end of things more strongly than I can describe. When I stood in the entrance of our room and looked at you again, wondering if I would make it through to the morning, I suddenly found myself trying to think what I would say to you if indeed this *were* the last time I would ever be able to speak to you. And I began to know I would write you this letter.

At least words in a letter aren't blurred by tone of voice, by the old aggravating sound of me talking to you. I began with this and with the idea that, after months of thinking about it, I would at last try to say something to you that wasn't colored by our disaffections. What I have to tell you must be explained in a rather roundabout way.

32

I've been thinking about my cousin Louise and her husband. When he died and she stayed with us last summer, something brought back to me what is really only the memory of a moment; yet it reached me, that moment, across more than fifty years. As you know, Louise is nine years older than I, and more like an older sister than a cousin. I must have told you at one time or another that I spent some weeks with her, back in 1933, when she was first married. The memory I'm talking about comes from that time, and what I have decided I have to tell you comes from that memory.

Father had been dead four years. We were all used to the fact that times were hard and that there was no man in the house, though I suppose I filled that role in some titular way. In any case, when Mother became ill there was the problem of us, her children. Though I was the oldest, I wasn't old enough to stay in the house alone, or to nurse her, either. My grandfather came up with the solution—and everybody went along with it—that I would go to Louise's for a time, and the two girls would go to stay with Grandfather. You'll remember that people did pretty much what that old man wanted them to do.

So we closed up the house, and I got on a train to Virginia. I was a few weeks shy of fourteen years old. I remember that I was not able to believe that anything truly bad would come of Mother's pleurisy, and was consequently glad of the opportunity it afforded me to travel the hundred miles south to Charlottesville, where cousin Louise had moved with her new husband only a month earlier, after her wedding. Because we traveled so much at the beginning, you never got to really know Charles when he was young—in 1933 he was a very tall, imposing fellow, with bright red hair and a graceful way of moving that always made me think of athletics, contests of skill. He had worked at the Navy Yard in Washington, and had been laid off in the first months of Roosevelt's New Deal. Louise was teaching in a day school in Charlottesville so they could make ends meet, and Charles was spending most of his time looking for work and fixing up the house. I had only met Charles once or twice before the wedding, but already I admired him and wanted to emulate him. The prospect of spending time in his house, of perhaps going fishing with him in the small streams of central Virginia, was all I thought about on the way down. And I remember that we did go fishing one weekend, that I wound up spending a lot of time with Charles, helping to paint the house and to run water lines under it for indoor plumbing. Oh, I had time with Louise, too—listening to her read from the books she wanted me to be interested in, walking with her around Charlottesville in the evenings and looking at the city as it was then. Or sitting on her small porch and talking about the family, Mother's stubborn illness, the children Louise saw every day at school. But what I want to tell you has to do with the very first day I was there.

I know you think I use far too much energy thinking about and pining away for the past, and I therefore know that I'm taking a risk by talking about this ancient history, and by trying to make you see it. But this all has to do with you and me, my dear, and our late inability to find ourselves in the same room together without bitterness and pain.

That summer, 1933, was unusually warm in Virginia, and the heat, along with my impatience to arrive, made the train almost unbearable. I think it was just past noon when it pulled into the station at Charlottesville, with me hanging out one of the windows, looking for Louise or Charles. It was Charles who had come to meet me. He stood in a crisp-looking seersucker suit, with a straw boater cocked at just the angle you'd expect a young, newly married man to wear a straw boater, even in the middle of economic disaster. I waved at him and he waved back, and I might've jumped out the window if the train had slowed even a little more than it had before it stopped in the shade of the platform. I made my way out, carrying the cloth bag my grandfather had given me for the trip—Mother had said through her rheum that I looked like a carpetbagger—and when I stepped down to shake hands with Charles I noticed that what I thought was a new suit was tattered at the ends of the sleeves.

"Well," he said. "Young John."

I smiled at him. I was perceptive enough to see that his cheerfulness was not entirely effortless. He was a man out of work, after all, and so in spite of himself there was worry in his face, the slightest shadow in an otherwise glad and proud countenance. We walked through the station to the street, and on up the steep hill to the house, which was a small clapboard structure, a cottage, really, with a porch at the end of a short sidewalk lined with flowers—they were marigolds, I think—and here was Louise, coming out of the house, her arms already stretched wide to embrace me. "Lord," she said. "I swear you've grown since the wedding, John." Charles took my bag and went inside.

"Let me look at you, young man," Louise said.

I stood for inspection. And as she looked me over I saw that her hair was pulled back, that a few strands of it had come loose, that it was brilliantly auburn in the sun. I suppose I was a little in love with her. She was grown, and married now. She was a part of what seemed a great mystery to me, even as I was about to enter it, and of course you remember how that feels, Marie, when one is on the verge of things—nearly adult, nearly old enough to fall in love. I looked at Louise's happy, flushed face, and felt a deep ache as she ushered me into her house. I wanted so to be older.

Inside, Charles had poured lemonade for us and was sitting in the easy chair by the fireplace, already sipping his. Louise wanted to show me the house and the backyard—which she had tilled and turned into a small vegetable garden—but she must've sensed how thirsty I was, and so she asked me to sit down and have a cool drink before she showed me the upstairs. Now, of course, looking back on it, I remember that those rooms she was so anxious to show me were meager indeed. They were not much bigger than closets, really, and the paint was faded and dull; the furniture she'd arranged so artfully was coming apart; the pictures she'd put on the walls were prints she'd cut out—magazine covers, mostly—and the curtains over the windows were the same ones that had hung in her childhood bedroom for twenty years. ("Recognize these?" she said with a deprecating smile.) Of course, the quality of her pride had nothing to do with the fineness—or lack of it—in these things, but in the fact that they belonged to her, and that she was a married lady in her own house.

On this day in July, in 1933, she and Charles were waiting for the delivery of a fan they had scrounged enough money to buy from Sears, through the catalog. There were things they would rather have been doing, especially in this heat, and especially with me there. Monticello wasn't far away, the university was within walking distance, and without too much expense one could ride a taxi to one of the lakes nearby. They had hoped that the fan would arrive before I did, but since it hadn't, and since neither Louise nor Charles was willing to leave the other alone while traipsing off with me that day, there wasn't anything to do but wait around for it. Louise had opened the windows and shut the shades, and we sat in her small living room and drank the lemonade, fanning ourselves with folded parts of Charles's morning newspaper. From time to time an anemic breath of air would move the shades slightly, but then everything grew still again. Louise sat on the arm of Charles's chair, and I sat on the sofa. We talked about pleurisy and, I think, about the fact that Thomas Jefferson had invented the dumbwaiter, how the plumbing at Monticello was at least a century ahead of its time. Charles remarked that it was the spirit of invention that would make a man's career in these days. "That's what I'm aiming for, to be inventive in a job. No matter what it winds up being."

When the lemonade ran out, Louise got up and went into the kitchen to make some more. Charles and I talked about taking a weekend to go fishing. He leaned back in his chair and put his hands behind his head, looking satisfied. In the kitchen, Louise was chipping ice for our glasses, and she began singing something low, for her own pleasure, a barely audible lilting, and Charles and I sat listening. It occurred to me that I was very happy. I had the sense that soon I would be embarked on my own life, as Charles was, and that an attractive woman like Louise would be there with me. Charles yawned and said, "God, listen to that. Doesn't Louise have the loveliest voice?"

And that's all I have from that day. I don't even know if the fan arrived later, and I have no clear memory of how we spent the rest of the afternoon and evening. I remember Louise singing a song, her husband leaning back in his chair, folding his hands behind his head, expressing his pleasure in his young wife's voice. I remember that I felt quite extraordinarily content just then. And that's all I remember.

But there are, of course, the things we both know: we know they moved to Colorado to be near Charles's parents; we know they never had any children; we know that Charles fell down a shaft at a construction site in the fall of 1957 and was hurt so badly that he never walked again. And I know that when she came to stay with us last summer she told me she'd learned to hate him, and not for what she'd had to help him do all those years. No, it started earlier and was deeper than that. She hadn't minded the care of him—the washing and feeding and all the numberless small tasks she had to perform each and every day, all day—she hadn't minded this. In fact, she thought there was something in her makeup that liked being needed so completely. The trouble was simply that whatever she had once loved in him she had stopped loving, and for many, many years before he died, she'd felt only suffocation when he was near enough to touch her, only irritation and anxiety when he spoke. She said all this, and then looked at me, her cousin, who had been fortunate enough to have children, and to be in love over time, and said, "John, how have you and Marie managed it?"

And what I wanted to tell you has to do with this fact—that while you and I had had one of our whispering arguments only moments before, I felt quite certain of the simple truth of the matter, which is that whatever our complications, we *have* managed to be in love over time.

"Louise," I said.

"People start out with such high hopes," she said, as if I wasn't there. She looked at me. "Don't they?"

"Yes," I said.

She seemed to consider this a moment. Then she said, "I wonder how it happens."

I said, "You ought to get some rest." Or something equally pointless and admonitory.

As she moved away from me, I had an image of Charles standing on the station platform in Charlottesville that summer, the straw boater set at its cocky angle. It was an image I would see most of the rest of that night, and on many another night since.

I can almost hear your voice as you point out that once again I've managed to dwell too long on the memory of something that's past and gone. The difference is that I'm not grieving over the past now. I'm merely reporting a memory, so that you might understand what I'm about to say to you.

The fact is, we aren't the people we were even then, just a year ago. I know that. As I know things have been slowly eroding between us for a very long time; we are a little tired of each other, and there are annoyances and old scars that won't be obliterated with a letter—even a long one written in the middle of the night in desperate sincerity, under the influence, admittedly, of a considerable portion of bourbon whiskey, but nevertheless with the best intention and hope: that you may know how, over the course of this night, I came to the end of needing an explanation for our difficulty. We have reached this—place. Everything we say seems rather aggravatingly mindless and automatic, like something one stranger might say to another in any of the thousand circumstances where strangers are thrown together for a time, and the silence begins to grow heavy on their minds, and someone has to say something. Darling, we go so long these days without having anything at all to do with each other, and the children are arriving tomorrow, and once more we'll be in the position of making all the gestures that give them back their parents as they think their parents are, and what I wanted to say to you, what came to me as I thought about Louise and Charles on that day so long ago, when they were young and so obviously glad of each other, and I looked at them and knew it and was happy—what came to me was that even the harsh things that happened to them, even the years of anger and silence, even the disappointment and the bitterness and the wanting not to be in the same room anymore, even all that must have been worth it for such loveliness. At least I am here, at seventy years old, hoping so. Tonight, I went back to our room again and stood gazing at you asleep, dreaming whatever you were dreaming, and I had a moment of thinking how we were always friends, too. Because what I wanted finally to say was that I remember well our own sweet times, our own old loveliness, and I would like to think that even if at the very beginning of our lives together I had somehow been shown that we would end up here, with this longing to be away from each other, this feeling of being trapped together, of being tied to each other in a way that makes us wish for other times, some other place—I would have known enough to accept it all freely for the chance at that love. And if I could, I would do it all again, Marie. All of it, even the sorrow. My sweet, my dear adversary. For everything that I remember.

36

Skeletons

Ann Beattie

Usually she was the artist.

Today she was the model. She had on sweatpants—both she and Garrett wore medium, although his sweatpants fit her better than they did him, because she did not have his long legs—and a Chinese jacket, plum-colored, patterned with blue octagons, edged in silver thread, that seemed to float among the lavender flowers that were as big as the palm of a hand raised for the high-five. A frog, Nancy thought; that was what the piece was called—the near-knot she fingered, the little fastener she never closed.

It was late Saturday afternoon, and, as usual, Nancy Niles was spending the day with Garrett. She had met him in a drawing class she took at night. During the week, he worked in an artists' supply store, but he had the weekends off. Until recently, when the weather turned cold, they had often taken long walks on Saturday or Sunday, and sometimes Kyle Brown—an undergraduate at the University of Pennsylvania, who was the other tenant in the rooming house Garrett lived in, in a run-down neighborhood twenty minutes from the campus—had walked with them. It was Kyle who had told Garrett about the empty room in the house. His first week in Philadelphia, Garrett had been in line to pay his check at a coffee shop when the cashier asked Kyle for a penny, which he didn't have. Then she looked behind Kyle to Garrett and said, "Well, would you have a penny?" Leaving, Kyle and Garrett struck up the conversation that had led to Garrett's moving into the house. And now the cashier's question had become a running joke. Just that morning, Garrett was outside the bathroom, and when Kyle came out, wrapped in his towel, he asked, "Well, got a penny *now?*"

It was easy to amuse Kyle, and he had a lovely smile, Nancy thought. He once told her that he was the first member of his family to leave Utah to go to college. It had strained relations with his parents, but they couldn't argue with Kyle's insistence that the English department at Penn was excellent. The landlady's married daughter had gone to Penn, and Kyle felt sure that had been the deciding factor in his getting the room. That and the fact that when the landlady told him where the nearest Episcopal church was, he told her that he was a Mormon. "At least you have *some* religion," she said. When she interviewed Garrett and described the neighborhood and told him where the Episcopal church was, Kyle had already tipped him; Garrett flipped open a notebook and wrote down the address.

Now, as Garrett and Nancy sat talking as he sketched (Garrett cared so much about drawing that Nancy was sure that he was happy that the weather had turned, so he had an excuse to stay indoors), Kyle was frying chicken downstairs. A few minutes earlier, he had looked in on them and stayed to talk. He complained that he was tired of being known as "the Mormon" to the landlady. Not condescendingly, that he could see—she just said it the way a person might use the Latin name for a plant instead of its common one. He showed them a telephone message from his father she had written down, with "MORMON" printed at the top.

Kyle Brown lived on hydroponic tomatoes, Shake 'n Bake chicken, and Pepperidge Farm rolls. On Saturdays, Garrett and Nancy ate with him. They contributed apple cider—smoky, with a smell you could taste; the last pressing of the season—and sometimes turnovers from the corner bakery.

Above the sputtering chicken Nancy could hear Kyle singing now, in his strong baritone: "The truth is, I *never* left you . . ."

"Sit still," Garrett said, looking up from his sketchbook. "Don't you know your role in life?"

Nancy cupped her hands below her breasts, turned her head to the side, and pursed her lips.

"Don't do that," he said, throwing the crayon stub. "Don't put yourself down, even as a joke."

"Oh, don't analyze everything so seriously," she said, hopping off the window seat and picking up the conte crayon. She threw it back to him. He caught it one-handed. He was the second person she had ever slept with. The other one, much to her embarrassment now, had been a deliberate experiment.

"Tell your shrink that your actions don't mean anything," he said.

"You hate it that I go to a shrink," she said, watching him bend over the sketchbook again. "Half the world sees a shrink. What are you worried about—that somebody might know something about me you don't know?"

He raised his eyebrows, as he often did when he was concentrating on something in a drawing. "I know a few things he doesn't know," he said.

"It's not a competition," she said.

"*Everything* is a competition. At some very serious, very deep level, every single thing—"

"You already made that joke," she said, sighing.

He stopped drawing and looked over at her in a different way. "I know," he said. "I shouldn't have taken it back. I really do believe that's what exists. One person jockeying for position, another person dodging."

"I can't tell when you're kidding. Now you're kidding, right?"

"No. I'm serious. I just took it back this morning because I could tell I was scaring you."

"Oh. Now are you going to tell me that you're in competition with me?"

"Why do you think I'm kidding?" he said. "It would *kill* me if you got a better grade in any course than I got. And you're so good. When you draw, you make strokes that look as if they were put on the paper with a feather. I'd take your technique away from you if I could. It's just that I know I can't, so I bite my tongue. Really. I envy you so much my heart races. I could never share a studio with you. I wouldn't be able to be in the same room with somebody who can be so patient and so exact at the same time. Compared to you, I might as well be wearing a catcher's mitt when I draw."

Nancy pulled her knees up to her chest and rested her cheek against one of them. She started to laugh.

"Really," he said.

"O.K.—*really,*" she said, going poker-faced. "I know, darling Garrett. You really do mean it."

"I do," he said.

She stood up. "Then we don't have to share a studio," she said. "But you can't take it back that you said you wanted to marry me." She rubbed her hands through her hair and let one hand linger to massage her neck. Her body was cold from sitting on the window seat. Clasping her legs, she had realized that the thigh muscles ached.

"Maybe all that envy and anxiety has to be burnt away with constant passion," she said. "I mean—I really, *really* mean that." She smiled. "Really," she said. "Maybe you just want to give in to it—like scratching a mosquito bite until it's so sore you cry."

They were within seconds of touching each other, but just at the moment when she was about to step toward him they heard the old oak stairs creaking beneath Kyle's feet.

"This will come as no surprise to you," Kyle said, standing in the doorway, "but I'm checking to make sure that you know you're invited to dinner. I provide the chicken, sliced tomatoes, and bread—right? You bring dessert and something to drink."

Even in her disappointment, Nancy could smile at him. Of course he knew that he had stumbled into something. Probably he wanted to turn and run back down the stairs. It wasn't easy to be the younger extra person in a threesome. When she raised her head, Garrett caught her eye, and in that moment they both knew how embarrassed Kyle must be. His need for them was never masked as well as he thought. The two of them, clearly lovers, were forgoing candlelight and deliberately bumped knees and the intimacy of holding glasses to each other's lips in order to have dinner with him. Kyle had once told Nancy, on one of their late-fall walks, that one of his worst fears had always been that someone might be able to read his mind. It was clear to her that he had fantasies about them. At the time, Nancy had tried to pass it off lightly; she told him that when she was drawing she always sensed the model's bones and muscles, and what she did was stroke a soft surface over them until a body took form.

Kyle wanted to stay close to them—meant to stay close—but time passed, and after they all had moved several times he lost track of them. He knew nothing of Nancy Niles's life, had no idea that in October, 1985, she was out trick-or-treating with Garrett and their two-year-old child, Fraser, who was dressed up as a goblin for his first real Halloween. A plastic orange pumpkin, lit by batteries, bobbed in front of her as she walked a few steps ahead of them. She was dressed in a skeleton costume, but she might have been an angel, beaming salvation into the depths of the mines. Where she lived—their part of Providence, Rhode Island—was as grim and dark as an underground labyrinth.

It was ironic that men thought she could lead the way for them, because Nancy had realized all along that she had little sense of direction. She felt isolated, angry at herself for not pursuing her career as an artist, for no longer being in love. It would have surprised her to know that in a moment of crisis, late that night, in Warrenton, Virginia, when leaves, like shadows on an X ray, suddenly flew up and obscured his vision and his car went into a skid, Kyle Brown would see her again, in a vision. Nancy Niles! he thought, in that instant of fear and shock. There she was, for a split second—her face, ghostly pale under the gas-station lights, metamorphosed into brightness. In a flash, she was again the embodiment of beauty to him. As his car spun in a widening circle and then came to rest with its back wheels on an embankment, Nancy Niles the skeleton was walking slowly down the sidewalk. Leaves flew past her like footsteps, quickly descending the stairs.

Watermelon Rind Jelly

Catherine Bowman

This poem begins with a cauldron,
then a coffin, then a bed, then a boat,
then a prayer.

Cauldron: Latin for warm bath.
So sit back and relax.
Don't worry,

I don't mean some witchy blast-furnace,
or scientific crucible at some trinity site
those nuclear types figure themselves into.

No, I just mean that old pickling pot
my grandmother bought
at the PX on sale.

There she is, sweat over her top
lip, rousing watermelon rinds
with a seismoscopic spoon

to a double-time-sized shellac, thick,
thickest, now thicker than mud-gum,
moan-brine, hush-clove, and fool-July.

Nasty, grandfather says. Our faces and hands
sticky from feasting on triple-sugar-mountain
helpings and more. Seeds stuck

to our arms and toes and hair. Flies
everywhere. This goes on and on
and on for twelve summers straight.

Grandmother calls her recipe My Famous
Virgin of Guadalupe Pickled Watermelon Rind Jelly.
I don't know why. She's not

a religious woman. All she worships is
money, work, bourbon, and earth,
in that order.

She saves every vinegary dime. She says
if you're going to eat the gift of the fruit,
you had better eat that bitter rind.

Please lower the lights and direct your attention to:

Grandfather laid out in his open casket in full
dress uniform, a pecan branch in his left hand.

—A Lime Green coffin, imagine that, says one aunt.
—More Creme de Menthe, says another.
—Watermelon Jelly Green, says the third.
—She did it just to spite him for leaving her all alone
in their big old bed.
—Imagine that.
—Excuse me, ladies, the funeral director, a personal friend,
says. I'll have you know the Colonel's coffin is not Lime, or Mint, or Melon, but
rather what we call a pale Sea Foam. The deceased before he passed left a one-
word note: *Economical*.
—That's right, says grandmother in her matching pale Sea Foam dress. Besides,
she says, they've got him so cooked in sour juices he doesn't need some oak or
mahogany boat to float to the place I'm sure that bastard's going.

Excuse me, ladies, the prayer:
    O cauldron O coffin O bed O boat
O clove of syrup O mystical rose
Lay me down tonight on the star-filled sky
That is her cloak in the folds of her dress
In that place where her hands pray
Under a spinning world of work
And earth and bourbon and vinegary dimes
For the water is deep the night so wide
Listen as the whippoorwill begins her sad cry
Under a new moon that is our bed and our boat
My honey my darling the sweet sun
On our face and our legs and our neck
The sweat and the salt that we lick off
The skin of this hot July day the words
That come from your mouth and your tongue
The bitterness of the rind
The burning gift of the fruit.

In the Garden

She is watching the creatures of paradise.
How the cheetah, in paradise, rises at dawn
hunting the swift gazelle, in paradise,
smothering it with just a paw, then in the cool
morning air, wanting for nothing, eating at leisure
in the shade of paradise. How the hyena's jaw
is so strong that in paradise it can crush
a large bone with one bite to get to the marrow.

The locust, the vulture, the shark, the piranha,
all the innocent creatures of paradise.
How she listens with pleasure to the music
of the lion's satisfied grunts,
its tongue so rough it can mangle
as it licks, in paradise.

In the Garden Again

1.
The translations are all wrong.
It wasn't just an apple.
Something more French, all sugar and butter,
the licking of fingers, something with heat.
We don't have a word in our language.
The closest we can get is an idea
that would mean all at once
goose-stuffed-with-ocean-cypress-fat-apples-
wind-in-winter-coffee-starlight-afternoon-rain.

As for the serpent or snake,
another mistranslation,
a common mistake.
On closer inspection,
a fancy green garter
of handmade lace.

And the angel's fiery sword,
turning in every direction,
in truth, the rays of the sun,
i.e., the hands of the clock.
They had so little time together.

Later texts consistently omit the *me'thode* champagne,
the cinnamon oils, the ocean smell.
Not one apple, but fields of musky apples,
how she spreads her legs,
between his legs,
the really great kissing,
how good it tasted.

Misread and misinterpreted—
there was no storm or thunder,
only a little shame.
What sent them out into the world
was simply the music of crickets
or perhaps a four-part fugue.

What has been lost in modern renderings
is that the word apple at the time
was not so much in the curve
of her hip, or even in the idea
of the curve, but in the heart.
As in: *She gave her heart to him.*
As in, when their eyes opened,
they put two and two together,
two pair of eyes,
and saw each other for a moment
no longer bound, but free,
not knowing, but giving.

2.
Forget the apple.
Since this is paradise
why not something French?
Say, an apple tatin,
with a glass of crisp champagne.
Let's kill a goose, darling,
here in the garden and stuff it
with apples. All I need
is a knife and an apron, and—voila!—
a buttery goose cassoulet.
Let's get up at dawn, dear,
and work for hours, then
a long nap where we'll dream
about apples or something like that,
it's so strange, so wonderful,
how good it tastes—
like the ocean, here between your legs,
the taste of musky apples,
the tangled roots of cypress,
the wind on water, the stars,
your eyes all over me
like mystics hungry for a vision,
like jeweled flies on horseshit,
like dogs on a deer scent,
your hands on my thighs, Thank You God
for these thighs, the fields, the sky,
the down across your belly,
the apple world veined with ores and metals,
all honeyed and sweet, licking each layer,
10,000 crickets rub legs together
in this world, this paradise
where we are always falling.

No Sorry

Do you have any scissors I could borrow? *No, I'm sorry I don't.* What about a knife? You got any knives? A good paring knife would do or a simple butcher knife or maybe a cleaver? *No, sorry, all I have is this old bread knife my grandfather used to butter his bread with every morning.* Well then, how about a hand drill or hammer, a bike chain, or some barbed wire? You got any rusty, razor-edged barbed wire? You got a chain saw? *No, sorry I don't.* Well then maybe you might have some sticks? *I'm sorry, I don't have any sticks.* How about some stones? *No, I don't have any sticks or stones.* Well how about a stone tied to a stick? *You mean a club?* Yeah, a club. You got a club? *No, sorry, I don't have any clubs.* What about some fighting picks, war axes, military forks, or tomahawks? *No, sorry, I don't have any kind of war fork, ax, or tomahawk.* What about a morning star? *A morning star?* Yeah, you know, those spiked ball and chains they sell for riot control. *No, nothing like that. Sorry.* Now I know you said you don't have a knife except for that dull old thing your grandfather used to butter his bread with every morning, and that he passed down to you, but I thought maybe you just might have an Australian dagger with a quartz blade and a wood handle, or a bone dagger, or a Bowie, you know it doesn't hurt to ask? Or perhaps one of those lethal multipurpose stilettos? *No, sorry.* Or maybe you have a simple blow pipe? Or a complex airgun? *No, I don't have a simple blow pipe or a complex airgun.* Well then maybe you have a jungle carbine, a Colt, a revolver, a Ruger, an axis bolt-action repeating rifle with telescopic sight for sniping, a sawed-off shotgun? Or better yet a gas-operated self-loading fully automatic assault weapon? *No, sorry I don't.* How about a hand grenade? *No.* How about a tank? *No.* Shrapnel? *No.* Napalm? *No.* Napalm 2. *No, sorry, I don't.* Then let me ask you this. Do you have any intercontinental ballistic missiles? Or submarine-launched cruise missiles? Or multiple independently targeted reentry missiles? Or terminally guided anti-tank shells or projectiles? Do you have any fission bombs or hydrogen bombs? Let me ask you this. Do you have any thermonuclear warheads? Got any electronic measures or electronic counter-measures or electronic counter-counter-measures? Got any biological weapons or germ warfare, preferably in aerosol form? Got any enhanced tactical neutron lasers emitting massive doses of wholebody gamma radiation? Wait a minute. Got any plutonium? Got any chemical agents, nerve agents, blister agents, you know, like mustard gas, any choking agents or incapacitating agents or toxin agents? *Well, I'm not sure. What do they look like?* Liquid vapor powder colorless gas. Invisible. *I'm not sure. What do they smell like?* They smell like fruit, garlic, fish or soap, new-mown hay, apple blossoms, or like those little green peppers that your grandfather probably would tend to in his garden every morning after he buttered his bread with that old bread knife that he passed down to you.

Tent Song

We do not remember what brought us to the woods.
But we were there. You with your funny eyes.

We had thrown away the map and the legends.
We were beyond the open coast. Beyond the cold

place with the warm name. We had left our local
tales at the finish line. It was before the war.

We were married here. The horse we rode was our horse.
The old growth echoed across the ridge. The black clouds

sectioned and resectioned themselves far to the south.
The moon cracked and burst on the pond's surface.

Poplar leaves spooned and spun like silver dollars.
Your fingers smelled like grass and dirt and mineral.

You wrote your name on my stomach. The storm held us.
It was that kind of day. It was that kind of night.

El Paso

She came to me that night like a lover
    but it wasn't a lover, just my old Granny
        dead now some twenty-five years.

I could tell it was Natalia S.
    by her rhinestone slippers
        and her scent of Evening in Paris.

As I turned my head up to the heavens,
    Granny's tears poured over my vision,
        through her saline lens the world

refracted, split into a thousand
    pieces, I was traveling fast,
        back to my bordertown of superstition

and illusion, where all points,
    all surfaces, all angles of every
        broken mirror appear farther

or nearer or equal in distance,
    where on the White Sands Range
        praying families around picnic tables

in an instant become Hercules
    Missiles, for the compass was spinning,
        I was traveling fast, wrapped

in rush-light and tumbleweed static,
    back through the spirit and smoke
        of Black Cat firecrackers, down

and down through hymnologies of fire ants,
    the multitudes in daily lustrations,
        chain-praying under this tent cloth that is

desert that is light that is desert that is El Paso,
    the passage through whiskey burn and memory burn,
        where cars zodiac the windsheets of highway and storm,

fireships scorpioid and chromed,
    dissolving into a carboniferous horizon
        like prison fare for the sun.

Open the gates and let the greyhounds run,
    light the safety matches in the drainage
        ditches where children disappear,

smell the sage and electric tension
    as pages from a lost book spiral
        in a whirlwind blur, the dervish of lost

songs, lost love letters, whirlpooled on
    the river's mirror, reflected in reverse
        alphabet on clouds above.

The stars fall, Christmas yards fill with luminarios,
    beeswax amulets against 77 fevers, God's eyes
        are everywhere, Granny says, in the ashes,

metabolites, rising up from the burnt grasses,
    in the heatwaves ciphering upward
        from the burning cement, the cypress trees,

corpse candles, coronaed, enhaloed,
    the smokestacks, the gem-strewn towers,
        salt pillars rising from the refinery and smelter,

illumined in Orphic code against
    the mountain's oiled parchment, orphreyed
        skein of orphan night where across the dark

I saw the dead spinning and arcing
    through veins of lightning, heat lightning veins,
        all those passed and passing through

to the other side of life. I saw
    Natalia, Donald, Pete, Nanny,
        Carmen, Ruth, Doris, George,

Pauline, Samuel, Frank T., Valerie,
    David, Ben, Sylvia, Yancy,
        Daniel, Martha, J. J., little Rose,

some I recognised, some I did not
  speaking to me all at once,
    tongues in pentecost, spirit-driven

voices, solid light, fireballs, speeding
  over the high voltage wires,
    gutturals to the cottonwood roots,

sibilants over jack rabbit hair,
  cactus splinter aspirations, hammers
    on this hammerstone that is El Paso

where I made my first passage with my
  eyes and ears and hands and mouth
    stuffed and crammed with big light and sky,

where I'll always see the mountain at the edges
  of my left eye, the big A for Anne, my beautiful
    laughing skinny mother's middle name,

who taught me to pray in El Paso,
  where I'm always traveling every minute
    of every night and day,

open wide the gates
  and let the greyhounds run,
    light the safety matches,

the corona of cypress branches,
  for God's eyes are everywhere,
    my Granny's mineral tears.

Any Friend of Nicholas Nickleby's Is a Friend of Mine

Ray Bradbury

Imagine a summer that would never end.

Nineteen twenty-nine. Imagine a boy who would never grow up.

Me.

Imagine a barber who was never young.

Mr. Wyneski.

Imagine a dog that would live forever.

Mine.

Imagine a small town, the kind that isn't lived in anymore.

Ready? Begin . . .

Green Town, Illinois . . . Late June.

Dog barking outside a one-chair barbershop.

Inside, Mr. Wyneski, circling his victim, a customer snoozing in the steambath drowse of noon.

Inside, me, Ralph Spaulding, a boy of some twelve years, standing still as an iron Civil War statue, listening to the hot wind, feeling all that hot summer dust out there, a bakery world where nobody could be bad or good, boys just lay gummed to dogs, dogs used boys for pillows under trees that lazed with leaves which whispered in despair: Nothing Will Ever Happen Again.

The only motion anywhere was the cool water dripping from the huge coffin-sized ice block in the hardware store window.

The only cool person in miles was Miss Frostbite, the traveling magician's assistant, tucked into that lady-shaped long cavity hollowed in the ice block displayed for three days now without, they said, her breathing, eating, or talking. That last, I thought, must have been terrible hard on a woman.

Nothing moved in the street but the barbershop striped pole which turned slowly to show its red, white, and then red again, slid up out of nowhere to vanish nowhere, a motion between two mysteries.

"... hey ..."

I pricked my ears.

"... something's coming ..."

"Only the noon train, Ralph." Mr. Wyneski snicked his jackdaw scissors, peering in his customer's ear. "Only the train that comes at noon."

"No ..." I gasped, eyes shut, leaning. "Something's *really* coming ..."

I heard the far whistle wail, lonesome, sad, enough to pull your soul out of your body.

"*You* feel it, don't you, Dog?"

Dog barked.

Mr. Wyneski sniffed. "What can a dog feel?"

"Big things. Important things. Circumstantial coincidences. Collisions you can't escape. Dog says. I say. *We* say."

"That makes *four* of you. Some team." Mr. Wyneski turned from the summer-dead man in the white porcelain chair. "Now, Ralph, my problem is hair. Sweep."

I swept a ton of hair. "Gosh, you'd think this stuff just grew up out of the floor."

Mr. Wyneski watched my broom. "Right! I didn't cut all that. Darn stuff just grows, I swear, lying there. Leave it a week, come back, and you need hip boots to trod a path." He pointed with his scissors. "Look. You ever *see* so many shades, hues, and tints of forelocks and chin fuzz? There's Mr. Tompkins's receding hairline. There's Charlie Smith's topknot. And here, here's all that's left of Mr. Harry Joe Flynn."

I stared at Mr. Wyneski as if he had just read from Revelations. "Gosh, Mr. Wyneski, I guess you know everything in the world!"

"Just about."

"I—I'm going to grow up and be—a barber."

Mr. Wyneski, to hide his pleasure, got busy.

"Then watch this hedgehog, Ralph, peel an eye. Elbows thus, wrists so! Make the scissors *talk*. Customers appreciate. Sound *twice* as busy as you are. Snickety-snick, boy, snickety-snick. Learned this from the French! Oh, yes, the French! They *do* prowl about the chair light on their toes, and the sharp scissors whispering and nib-bling, Ralph, nibbling and whispering, you *hear!*"

"Boy!" I said, at his elbow, right in with the whispers and nibbles, then stopped: for the wind blew a wail way off in summer country, so sad, so strange.

"There it is again. The train. And something *on* the train ..."

"Noon train don't stop here."

"But I got this feeling—"

"The hair's going to grab me, Ralph ..."

I swept hair.

After a long while I said, "I'm thinking of changing my name."

Mr. Wyneski sighed. The summer-dead customer stayed dead.

"What's *wrong* with you today, boy?"

"It's not me. It's the name is out of hand. Just listen. Ralph." I grred it. "Rrrralph."

53

"Ain't exactly harp music . . ."

"Sounds like a mad dog." I caught myself.

"No offense, Dog."

Mr. Wyneski glanced down. "He seems pretty calm about the whole subject."

"Ralph's dumb. Gonna change my name by tonight."

Mr. Wyneski mused. "Julius for Caesar? Alexander for the Great?"

"Don't care what. Help me, huh, Mr. Wyneski? Find me a *name* . . ."

Dog sat up. I dropped the broom.

For way down in the hot cinder railroad yards a train furnaced itself in, all pomp, all fire-blast shout and tidal churn, summer in its iron belly bigger than the summer outside.

"Here it comes!"

"There it goes," said Mr. Wyneski.

"No, there it *doesn't* go!"

It was Mr. Wyneski's turn to almost drop his scissors.

"Goshen. Darn noon train's putting on the brakes!"

We heard the train stop.

"How many people getting off the train, Dog?"

Dog barked once.

Mr. Wyneski shifted uneasily. "U.S. mailbags—"

"No . . . a *man!* Walking light. Not much luggage. Heading for our house. A new boarder at Grandma's, I bet. And he'll take the empty room right next to you, Mr. Wyneski! Right, Dog?"

Dog barked.

"That dog talks too much," said Mr. Wyneski.

"I just *gotta* go see, Mr. Wyneski. Please?"

The far footsteps faded in the hot and silent streets.

Mr. Wyneski shivered.

"A goose just stepped on my grave."

Then he added, almost sadly:

"Get along, Ralph."

"Name ain't Ralph."

"Whatchamacallit . . . run see . . . come tell the worst."

"Oh, thanks, Mr. Wyneski, thanks!"

I ran. Dog ran. Up a street, along an alley, around back, we ducked in the ferns by my grandma's house. "Down, boy," I whispered. "Here the Big Event comes, *whatever* it is!"

And down the street and up the walk and up the steps at a brisk jaunt came this man who swung a cane and carried a carpetbag and had long browngray hair and silken mustaches and a goatee, politeness all about him like a flock of birds.

On the porch near the old rusty chain swing, among the potted geraniums, he surveyed Green Town.

Far away, maybe, he heard the insect hum from the barbershop, where Mr. Wyneski, who would soon be his enemy, told fortunes by the lumpy heads under his hands as he buzzed the electric clippers. Far away, maybe, he could hear the empty library where the golden dust slid down the raw sunlight and way in back someone scratched and tapped and scratched forever with pen and ink, a quiet woman like a great lonely mouse burrowed away. And she was to be part of this new man's life, too, but right now . . .

The stranger removed his tall moss-green hat, mopped his brow, and not looking at anything but the hot blind sky said:

"Hello, boy. Hello, dog."

Dog and I rose up among the ferns.

"Heck. How'd you know where we were hiding?"

The stranger peered into his hat for the answer. "In another incarnation, I was a boy. Time before that, if memory serves, I was a more than usually happy dog. But . . . !" His cane rapped the cardboard sign BOARD AND ROOM thumbtacked on the porch rail. "Does the sign say true, boy?"

"Best rooms on the block."

"Beds?"

"Mattresses so deep you sink down and drown the third time, happy."

"Boarders at table?"

"Talk just enough, not too much."

"Food?"

"Hot biscuits every morning, peach pie noon, shortcake every supper!"

The stranger inhaled, exhaled those savors.

"I'll sign my soul away!"

"I beg your pardon?!" Grandma was suddenly at the screen door, scowling out.

"A manner of speaking, ma'am." The stranger turned. "Not meant to sound un-Christian."

And he was inside, him talking, Grandma talking, him writing and flourishing the pen on the registry book, and me and Dog inside, breathless watching, spelling:

"C.H."

"Read upside down, do you, boy?" said the stranger, merrily, giving pause with the inky pen.

"Yes, sir!"

On he wrote. On I spelled:

"A.R.L.E.S. Charles!"

"Right."

Grandma peered at the calligraphy. "Oh, what a fine hand."

"Thank you, ma'am." On the pen scurried. And on I chanted. "D.I.C.K.E.N S."

I faltered and stopped. The pen stopped. The stranger tilted his head and closed one eye, watchful of me.

"Yes?" He dared me, "What, *what?*"

"Dickens!" I cried.

"Good!"

"Charles Dickens, Grandma!"

"I can read, Ralph. A *nice* name . . ."

"Nice?" I said, agape. "It's *great!* But . . . I thought you were—"

55

"Dead?" The stranger laughed. "No. Alive, in fine fettle, and glad to meet a recognizer, fan, and fellow reader here!"

And we were up the stairs, Grandma bringing fresh towels and pillowcases and me carrying the carpetbag, gasping, and us meeting Grandpa, a great ship of a man, sailing down the other way.

"Grandpa," I said, watching his face for shock. "I want you to meet . . . Mr. Charles Dickens!"

Grandpa stopped for a long breath, looked at the new boarder from top to bottom, then reached out, took hold of the man's hand, shook it firmly, and said:

"Any friend of Nicholas Nickleby's is a friend of mine!"

Mr. Dickens fell back from the effusion, recovered, bowed, said, "Thank you, sir," and went on up the stairs, while Grandpa winked, pinched my cheek, and left me standing there, stunned.

In the tower cupola room, with windows bright, open, and running with cool creeks of wind in all directions, Mr. Dickens drew off his horse-carriage coat and nodded at the carpetbag.

"Anywhere will do, Pip. Oh, you don't mind I call you Pip, eh?"

"Pip?!" My cheeks burned, my face glowed with astonishing happiness. "Oh, boy. Oh, no, sir. Pip's *fine!*"

Grandma cut between us. "Here are your clean linens, Mr. . . . ?"

"Dickens, ma'am." Our boarder patted his pockets, each in turn. "Dear me, Pip, I seem to be fresh out of pads and pencils. Might it be possible—"

He saw one of my hands steal up to find something behind my ear. "I'll be darned," I said, "a yellow Ticonderoga Number 2!" My other hand slipped to my back pants pocket. "And hey, an Iron-Face Indian Ring-Back Notepad Number 12!"

"Extraordinary!"

"Extraordinary!"

Mr. Dickens wheeled about, surveying the world from each and every window, speaking now north, now north by east, now east, now south:

"I've traveled two long weeks with an idea. Bastille Day. Do you know it?"

"The French Fourth of July?"

"Remarkable boy! By Bastille Day this book must be in full flood. Will you help me breach the tide gates of the Revolution, Pip?"

"With *these?*" I looked at the pad and pencil in my hands.

"Lick the pencil tip, boy!"

I licked.

"Top of the page: the title. Title." Mr. Dickens mused, head down, rubbing his chin whiskers. "Pip, what's a rare fine title for a novel that happens half in London, half in Paris?"

"A—" I ventured.

"Yes?"

"A *Tale,*" I went on.

"Yes?!"

"A *Tale of . . . Two Cities?!*"

56

"Madame!" Grandma looked up as he spoke. "This boy is a genius!"

"I read about this day in the Bible," said Grandma. "Everything ends by noon."

"Put it down, Pip." Mr. Dickens tapped my pad. "Quick. *A Tale of Two Cities*. Then, mid-page. Book the First. 'Recalled to Life.' Chapter 1. 'The Period.'"

I scribbled. Grandma worked. Mr. Dickens squinted at the sky and at last intoned:

"It was the best of times, it was the worst of times, it was the age of wisdom, it was the age of foolishness, it was the epoch of belief, it was the epoch of incredulity, it was the season of Light, it was the season of Darkness, it was the spring of hope, it was the winter—"

"My," said Grandma, "you speak *fine*."

"Madame." The author nodded, then, eyes shut, snapped his fingers to remember, on the air. "Where was I, Pip?"

"It was the winter," I said, "of *despair*."

Very late in the afternoon I heard Grandma calling someone named Ralph, Ralph, down below. I didn't know who that was. I was writing hard.

A minute later, Grandpa called, "Pip!"

I jumped. "Yes, sir!"

"Dinnertime, Pip," said Grandpa, up the stairwell.

I sat down at the table, hair wet, hands damp. I looked over at Grandpa. "How did you know . . . Pip?"

"Heard the name fall out the window an hour ago."

"Pip?" said Mr. Wyneski, just come in, sitting down.

"Boy," I said. "I been everywhere this afternoon. The Dover Coach on the Dover Road. Paris! Traveled so much I got writer's cramp! I—"

"Pip?" said Mr. Wyneski, again.

Grandpa came warm and easy to my rescue.

"When I was twelve, changed my name—on several occasions." He counted the tines on his fork. "Dick. That was Dead-Eye Dick. And . . . John. That was for Long John Silver. Then: Hyde. That was for the other half of Jekyll."

"I never had any other name except Bernard Samuel Wyneski," said Mr. Wyneski, his eyes still fixed to me.

"None?" cried Grandpa, startled.

"None."

"Have you proof of childhood, then, sir?" asked Grandpa. "Or are you a natural phenomenon, like a ship becalmed at sea?"

"Eh?" said Mr. Wyneski.

Grandpa gave up and handed him his full plate.

"Fall to, Bernard Samuel, fall to."

Mr. Wyneski let his plate lie. "Dover Coach . . . ?"

"With Mr. Dickens, of course," supplied Grandpa. "Bernard Samuel, we have a new boarder, a novelist, who is starting a new book and has chosen Pip there, Ralph, to work as his secretary—"

"Worked all afternoon," I said. "Made a quarter!"

I slapped my hand to my mouth. A swift dark cloud had come over Mr.

Wyneski's face.

"A novelist? Named Dickens? Surely you don't believe—"

"I believe what a man tells me until he tells me otherwise, then I believe that. Pass the butter," said Grandpa.

The butter was passed in silence.

". . . hell's fires . . ." Mr. Wyneski muttered.

I slunk low in my chair.

Grandpa, slicing the chicken, heaping the plates, said, "A man with a good demeanor has entered our house. He says his name is Dickens. For all I know that is his name. He implies he is writing a book. I pass his door, look in, and, yes, he is indeed writing. Should I run tell him not to? It is obvious he needs to set the book down—"

"*A Tale of Two Cities!*" I said.

"*A Tale!*" cried Mr. Wyneski, outraged, "*of Two*—"

"Hush," said Grandma.

For down the stairs and now at the door of the dining room there was the man with the long hair and the fine goatee and mustaches, nodding, smiling, peering in at us doubtful and saying, "Friends . . . ?"

"Mr. Dickens," I said, trying to save the day. "I want you to meet Mr. Wyneski, the greatest barber in the world—"

The two men looked at each other for a long moment.

"Mr. Dickens," said Grandpa. "Will you lend us your talent, sir, for grace?"

"An honor, sir."

We bowed our heads. Mr. Wyneski did not.

Mr. Dickens looked at him gently.

Muttering, the barber glanced at the floor.

Mr. Dickens prayed:

"O Lord of the bounteous table, O Lord who furnishes forth an infinite harvest for your most respectful servants gathered here in loving humiliation, O Lord who garnishes our feast with the bright radish and the resplendent chicken, who sets before us the wine of the summer season, lemonade, and maketh us humble before simple potato pleasures, the lowborn onion and, in the finale, so my nostrils tell me, the bread of vast experiments and fine success, the highborn strawberry shortcake, most beautifully smothered and amiably drowned in fruit from your own warm garden patch, for these, and this good company, much thanks. Amen."

"Amen," said everyone but Mr. Wyneski.

We waited.

"Amen, I guess," he said.

O what a summer that was!

None like it before in Green Town history.

I never got up so early so happy ever in my life! Out of bed at five minutes to, in Paris by one minute after . . . six in the morning the English Channel boat from Calais, the White Cliffs, sky a blizzard of seagulls, Dover, then the London Coach and London Bridge by noon! Lunch and lemonade out under the trees with Mr. Dickens,

Dog licking our cheeks to cool us, then back to Paris and tea at four and . . .

"Bring up the cannon, Pip!"

"Yes, *sir!*"

"Mob the Bastille!"

"Yes, sir!"

And the guns were fired and the mobs ran and there I was, Mr. C. Dickens A-1 First Class Green Town, Illinois, secretary, my eyes bugging, my ears popping, my chest busting with joy, for I dreamt of being a writer someday, too, and here I was unravelling a tale with the very finest best.

"Madame Defarge, oh how she sat and knitted, knitted, sat—"

I looked up to find Grandma knitting in the window.

"Sidney Carton, what and who was he? A man of sensibility a reading man of gentle thought and capable action . . ."

Grandpa strolled by mowing the grass.

Drums sounded beyond the hills with guns; a summer storm cracked and dropped unseen walls . . .

Mr. Wyneski?

Somehow I neglected his shop, somehow I forgot the mysterious barber pole that came up from nothing and spiraled away to nothing, and the fabulous hair that grew on his white tile floor . . .

So Mr. Wyneski then had to come home every night to find that writer with all the long hair in need of cutting, standing there at the same table thanking the Lord for this, that, and t'other, and Mr. Wyneski not thankful. For there I sat staring at Mr. Dickens like *he* was God until one night:

"Shall we say grace?" said Grandma.

"Mr. Wyneski is out brooding in the yard," said Grandpa.

"Brooding?" I glanced guiltily from the window.

Grandpa tilted his chair back so he could see.

"Brooding's the word. Saw him kick the rose bush, kick the green ferns by the porch, decide against kicking the apple tree. God made it too firm. There, he just jumped on a dandelion. Oh, oh. Here he comes, Moses crossing a Black Sea of bile."

The door slammed. Mr. Wyneski stood at the head of the table.

"I'll say grace tonight!"

He glared at Mr. Dickens.

"Why, I mean," said Grandma. "Yes. Please."

Mr. Wyneski shut his eyes tight and began his prayer of destruction:

"O Lord, who delivered me a fine June and a less fine July, help me to get through August somehow.

"O Lord, deliver me from mobs and riots in the streets of London and Paris which drum through my room night and morn, chief members of said riot being one boy who walks in his sleep, a man with a strange name and a Dog who barks after the ragtag and bobtail.

"Give me strength to resist the cries of Fraud, Thief, Fool, and Bunk Artists which rise in my mouth.

"Help me not to run shouting all the way to the Police Chief to yell that in all probability the man who shares our simple bread has a true name of Red Joe Pyke from Wilkesboro, wanted for counterfeiting life, or Bull Hammer from Hornbill, Arkansas, much desired for mean spitefulness and pennypilfering in Oskaloosa.

"Lord, deliver the innocent boys of this world from the fell clutch of those who would tomfool their credibility.

"And Lord, help me to say, quietly, and with all deference to the lady present, that if one Charles Dickens is not on the noon train tomorrow bound for Potters Grave, Lands End, or Kankakee, I shall like Delilah, with malice, shear the black lamb and fry his mutton-chop whiskers for twilight dinners and late midnight snacks.

"I ask, Lord, not mercy for the mean, but simple justice for the malignant.

"All those agreed, say 'Amen.'"

He sat down and stabbed a potato.

There was a long moment with everyone frozen.

And then Mr. Dickens, eyes shut said, moaning:

"Ohhhhhhhhhh . . . !"

It was a moan, a cry, a despair so long and deep it sounded like the train way off in the country the day this man had arrived.

"Mr. Dickens," I said.

But I was too late.

He was on his feet, blind, wheeling, touching the furniture, holding to the wall, clutching at the doorframe, blundering into the hall, groping up the stairs.

"Ohhhhh . . ."

It was the long cry of a man gone over a cliff into Eternity.

It seemed we sat waiting to hear him hit bottom.

Far off in the hills in the upper part of the house, his door banged shut.

My soul turned over and died.

"Charlie," I said. "Oh, Charlie."

Late that night, Dog howled.

And the reason he howled was that sound, that similar, muffled cry from up in the tower cupola room.

"Holy Cow," I said. "Call the plumber. Everything's down the drain."

Mr. Wyneski strode by on the sidewalk, walking nowhere, off and gone.

"That's his fourth time around the block." Grandpa struck a match and lit his pipe.

"Mr. Wyneski!" I called.

No answer. The footsteps went away.

"Boy oh boy, I feel like I lost a war," I said.

"No, Ralph, beg pardon, Pip," said Grandpa, sitting down on the step with me. "You just changed generals in midstream is all. And now one of the generals is so unhappy he's turned mean."

"Mr. Wyneski? I—I almost hate him!"

Grandpa puffed gently on his pipe. "I don't think he even knows why he is so unhappy and mean. He has had a tooth pulled during the night by a mysterious dentist and now his tongue is aching around the empty place where the tooth was."

"We're not in church, Grandpa."

"Cut the Parables, huh? In simple words, Ralph, you used to sweep the hair off that man's shop floor. And he's a man with no wife, no family, just a job. A man with no family needs someone somewhere in the world, whether he knows it or not."

"I," I said. "I'll wash the barbershop windows tomorrow. I—I'll oil the red-and-white striped pole so it spins like crazy."

"I know you will, son."

A train went by in the night.

Dog howled.

Mr. Dickens answered in a strange cry from his room.

I went to bed and heard the town clock strike one and then two and at last three.

Then it was I heard the soft crying. I went out in the hall to listen by our boarder's door.

"Mr. Dickens?"

The soft sound stopped.

The door was unlocked. I dared open it.

"Mr. Dickens?"

And there he lay in the moonlight, tears streaming from his eyes, eyes wide open staring at the ceiling, motionless.

"Mr. Dickens?"

"Nobody by that name here," said he. His head moved side to side. "Nobody by that name in this room in this bed in this world."

"You," I said. "You're Charlie Dickens."

"You ought to know better," was the mourned reply. "Long after midnight, moving on toward morning."

"All I know is," I said, "I seen you writing every day. I heard you talking every night."

"Right, right."

"And you finish one book and start another, and write a fine calligraphy sort of hand."

"I do that." A nod. "Oh yes, by the demon possessions, I do."

"So!" I circled the bed. "What call you got to feel sorry for yourself, a world-famous author?"

"You know and I know, I'm Mr. Nobody from Nowhere, on my way to Eternity with a dead flashlight and no candles."

"Hells bells," I said. I started for the door. I was mad because he wasn't holding up his end. He was ruining a grand summer. "Good night!" I rattled the doorknob.

"Wait!"

It was such a terrible soft cry of need and almost pain, I dropped my hand, but I didn't turn.

"Pip," said the old man in the bed.

"Yeah?" I said, grouching.

"Let's both be quiet. Sit down."

I slowly sat on the spindly wooden chair by the night table.

"Talk to me, Pip."

"Holy Cow, at three—"

"—in the morning, yes. Oh, it's a fierce awful time of night. A long way back to sunset, and ten thousand miles on to dawn. We have need of friends then. *Friend,* Pip? Ask me things."

"Like what?"

"I think you know."

I brooded a moment and sighed. "Okay, okay. Who are you?"

He was very quiet for a moment lying there in his bed and then traced the words on the ceiling with a long invisible tip of his nose and said, "I'm a man who could never fit his dream."

"What?"

"I mean, Pip, I never became what I wanted to be."

I was quiet now, too, "What'd you *want* to be?"

"A writer."

"Did you try?"

"Try!" he cried, and almost gagged on a strange wild laugh. "Try," he said, controlling himself. "Why Lord of Mercy, son, you never saw so much spit, ink, and sweat fly. I wrote my way through an ink factory, broke and busted a paper company, ruined and dilapidated six dozen typewriters, devoured and scribbled to the bone ten thousand Ticonderoga Soft Lead pencils."

"Wow!"

"You may well say Wow."

"What did you write?"

"What *didn't* I write. The poem. The essay. The play *tragique.* The farce. The short story. The novel. A thousand words a day, boy, every day for thirty years, no day passed I did not scriven and assault the page. Millions of words passed from my fingers onto paper and it was all bad."

"It couldn't have been!"

"It *was.* Not mediocre, not passing fair. Just plain outright mudbath bad. Friends knew it, editors knew it, teachers knew it, publishers knew it, and one strange fine day about four in the afternoon, when I was fifty, I knew it."

"But you can't write thirty years without—"

"Stumbling upon excellence? Striking a chord? Gaze long, gaze hard, Pip, look upon a man of peculiar talent, outstanding ability, the only man in history who put down five million words without slapping to life one small base of a story that might rear up on its frail legs and cry Eureka! we've done it!"

"You never sold *one* story?!"

"Not a two-line joke. Not a throwaway newspaper sonnet. Not a want ad or obit. Not a home-bottled autumn pickle recipe. Isn't that rare? To be so outstandingly dull, so ridiculously inept, that nothing ever brought a chuckle, caused a tear, raised a temper, or discharged a blow. And do you know what I did on the day I discovered I would never be a writer? I killed myself."

"Killed?!"

"Did away with, destroyed. How? I packed me up and took me away on a long train ride and sat on the back smoking-car platform a long time in the night and then one by one let the confetti of my manuscripts fly like panicked birds away down the tracks. I scattered a novel across Nebraska, my Homeric legends over North, my love sonnets through South Dakota. I abandoned my familiar essays in the men's room at the Harvey House in Clear Springs, Idaho. The late summer wheatfields knew my prose. Grand fertilizer, it probably jumped up bumper crops of corn long after I passed. I rode two trunks of my soul on that long summer's journey, celebrating my badly served self. And one by one, slow at first, and then faster, faster, over I chucked them, story after story, out, out of my arms out of my head, out of my life, and down they went, sunk drowning night rivers of prairie dust, in lost continents of sand and lonely rock. And the train wallowed around a curve in a great wail of darkness and release, and I opened my fingers and let the last stillborn darlings fall. . . .

"When I reached the far terminus of the line, the trunks were empty. I had drunk much, eaten little, wept on occasion in my private room, but had heaved away my anchors, dead-weights, and dreams, and came to the sliding soft-chuffing end of my journey, praise God, in a kind of noble peace and certainty. I felt reborn. I said to myself, why, what's this, what's this? I'm—I'm a new man."

He saw it all on the ceiling, and I saw it, too, like a movie run up the wall in the moonlit night.

"I—I'm a new man I said, and when I got off the train at the end of that long summer of disposal and sudden rebirth, I looked in a fly-specked, rainfreckled gummachine mirror at a lost depot in Peachgum, Missouri, and my beard grown long in two months of travel and my hair gone wild with wind that combed it this way sane, that way mad, and I peered and stood back and exclaimed softly, 'Why, Charlie Dickens, is that you?!'"

The man in the bed laughed softly.

"'Why, Charlie,' said I, 'Mr. Dickens, there you are!' And the reflection in the mirror cried out, 'Dammit, sir, who else *would* it be!? Stand back. I'm off to a great lecture!'"

"Did you really say that, Mr. Dickens?"

"God's pillars and temples of truth, Pip. And I got out of his way! And I strode through a strange town and I knew who I was at last and grew fevers thinking on what I might do in my lifetime now reborn and all that grand fine work ahead! For, Pip, this thing *must* have been growing. All those years of writing and snuffing up defeat, my old subconscious must have been whispering, 'Just you wait. Things will be black midnight bad but then in the nick of time, *I'll* save you!'

"And maybe the thing that saved me was the thing that ruined me in the first place: respect for my elders; the grand moguls and tall muckymucks in the lush literary highlands and me in the dry river bottom with my canoe.

"For, oh God, Pip, how I devoured Tolstoy, drank Dostoevsky, feasted on De Maupassant, had wine and chicken picnics with Flaubert and Molière. I gazed at gods too high. I read too *much!* So, when my work vanished, theirs stayed. Suddenly I found I could *not* forget their books, Pip!"

"Couldn't?"

"I mean I could not forget any letter of any word of any sentence or any paragraph of any book ever passed under these hungry omnivorous eyes!"

"Photographic memory!"

"Bull's-eye! All of Dickens, Hardy, Austen, Poe, Hawthorne, trapped in this old box Brownie waiting to be printed off my tongue, all those years, never knew, Pip, never guessed, I had hid it all away. Ask me to speak in tongues. Kipling is one. Thackeray another. Weigh flesh, I'm Shylock. Snuff out the light, I'm Othello. All, all, Pip, all!"

"And then? And so?"

"Why then and so, Pip, I looked another time in that fly-specked mirror and said, 'Mr. Dickens, all this being true, *when* do you write your first book?'

"'Now!' I cried. And bought fresh paper and ink and have been delirious and joyful, lunatic and happy frantic ever since, writing all the books of my own dear self, me, I, Charles Dickens, one by one.

"I have traveled the continental vastness of the United States of North America and settled me in to write and act, act and write, lecturing here, pondering there, half in and then half out of my mania, known and unknown, lingering here to finish *Copperfield,* loitering there for *Dombey and Son,* turning up for tea with Marley's Ghost on some pale Christmas noon. Sometimes I lie whole snowbound winters in little whistle stops and no one there guessing that Charlie Dickens bides hibernation there, then pop forth like the ottermole of spring and so move on. Sometimes I stay whole summers in one town before I'm driven off. Oh, yes, driven. For such as your Mr. Wyneski cannot forgive the fantastic, Pip, no matter how particularly practical that fantastic be.

"For he has no humor, boy.

"He does not see that we all do what we must to survive, survive.

"Some laugh, some cry, some bang the world with fists, some run, but it all sums up the same: they *make do.*

"The world swarms with people, each one drowning, but each swimming a different stroke to the far shore.

"And Mr. Wyneski? He makes do with scissors and understands not my inky pen and littered papers on which I would flypaper-catch my borrowed English soul."

Mr. Dickens put his feet out of bed and reached for his carpetbag.

"So I must pick up and go."

I grabbed the bag first.

"No! You can't leave! You haven't finished the book!"

"Pip, dear boy, you haven't been listening—"

"The world's waiting! You can't just quit in the middle of *Two Cities!*"

He took the bag quietly from me.

"Pip, Pip . . ."

"You can't, Charlie!"

He looked into my face and it must have been so white hot he flinched away.

"I'm waiting," I cried. "They're waiting!"

"They . . . ?"

"The mob at the Bastille. Paris! London. The Dover sea. The guillotine!"

I ran to throw all the windows even wider as if the night wind and the moonlight might bring in sounds and shadows to crawl on the rug and sneak in his eyes, and the curtains blew out in phantom gestures and I swore I heard, Charlie heard, the crowds, the coach wheels, the great slicing downfall of the cutting blades and the cabbage heads falling and battle songs and all that on the wind . . .

"Oh, Pip, Pip . . ."

Tears welled from his eyes.

I had my pencil out and my pad.

"Well?" I said.

"Where were we, this afternoon, Pip?"

"Madame Defarge, knitting."

He let the carpetbag fall. He sat on the edge of the bed and his hands began to tumble, weave, knit, motion, tie and untie, and he looked and saw his hands and spoke and I wrote and he spoke again, stronger, and stronger, all through the rest of the night . . .

"Madame Defarge . . . yes . . . well. Take this, Pip. She—"

"Morning, Mr. Dickens!"

I flung myself into the dining-room chair. Mr. Dickens was already half through his stack of pancakes.

I took one bite and then saw the even greater stack of pages lying on the table between us.

"Mr. Dickens?" I said. "The *Tale of Two Cities*. It's . . . finished?"

"Done." Mr. Dickens ate, eyes down. "Got up at six. Been working steady. Done. Finished. Through."

"Wow!" I said.

A train whistle blew. Charlie sat up, then rose suddenly, to leave the rest of his breakfast and hurry out in the hall. I heard the front door slam and tore out on the porch to see Mr. Dickens half down the walk, carrying his carpetbag.

He was walking so fast I had to run to circle round and round him as he headed for the rail depot.

"Mr. Dickens, the book's finished, yeah, but not *published* yet!"

"You be my executor, Pip."

He fled. I pursued, gasping.

"What about David Copperfield?! Little Dorrit?!"

"Friends of yours, Pip?"

"Yours, Mr. Dickens, Charlie, oh, gosh, if you don't write them, they'll never *live*."

"They'll get on somehow." He vanished around a corner. I jumped after.

"Charlie, wait. I'll give you—a new title! *Pickwick Papers*, sure, *Pickwick Papers!*"

The train was pulling into the station.

Charlie ran fast.

"And after that, *Bleak House*, Charlie, and *Hard Times* and *Great*—Mr. Dickens, listen—*Expectations!* Oh, my gosh!"

For he was far ahead now and I could only yell after him:

"Oh, blast, go on! get off! get away! You know what I'm going to do!? You don't deserve reading! You don't! So right now, and from here on, see if I even bother to finish reading *Tale of Two Cities!* Not me! Not this one! No!"

The bell was tolling in the station. The steam was rising. But, Mr. Dickens had slowed. He stood in the middle of the sidewalk. I came up to stare at his back.

"Pip," he said softly. "You mean what you just said?"

"You!" I cried. "You're nothing but—" I searched in my mind and seized a thought: "—a blot of mustard, some undigested bit of raw potato—!"

"'Bah, Humbug, Pip?'"

"Humbug! I don't give a blast *what* happens to Sidney Carton!"

"Why, it's a far, far better thing I do than I have ever done, Pip. You must read it."

"Why!?"

He turned to look at me with great sad eyes.

"Because I wrote it for you."

It took all my strength to half-yell back: "So—?"

"So," said Mr. Dickens, "I have just missed my train. Forty minutes till the next one—"

"Then you got time," I said.

"Time for what?"

"To meet someone. Meet them, Charlie, and I promise I'll finish reading your book. In there. In *there,* Charlie."

He pulled back.

"That place? The library?!"

"Ten minutes, Mr. Dickens, give me ten minutes, just ten, Charlie. Please."

"Ten?"

And at last, like a blind man, he let me lead him up the library steps and half-fearful, sidle in.

The library was like a stone quarry where no rain had fallen in ten thousand years.

Way off in that direction: silence.

Way off in that direction: hush.

It was the time between things finished and things begun. Nobody died here. Nobody was born. The library, and all its books, just *were.*

We waited, Mr. Dickens and I, on the edge of the silence.

Mr. Dickens trembled. And I suddenly remembered I had never seen him here all summer. He was afraid I might take him near the fiction shelves and see all his books, written, done, finished, printed, stamped, bound, borrowed, read, repaired, and shelved.

But I wouldn't be that dumb. Even so, he took my elbow and whispered:

"Pip, what are we doing here? Let's go. There's . . ."

"Listen!" I hissed.

And a long way off in the stacks somewhere, there was a sound like a moth turning over in its sleep.

"Bless me," Mr. Dickens's eyes widened. "I know that sound."

"Sure!"

"It's the sound," he said, holding his breath, then nodding, "of someone writing."

"Yes, sir."

"Writing with a pen. And . . . and writing . . ."

"What?"

"Poetry," gasped Mr. Dickens. "That's it. Someone off there in a room, how many fathoms deep, Pip, I swear, writing a poem. There! Eh? Flourish, flourish, scratch, flourish on, on, on, that's not figures, Pip, not numerals, not dusty-dry facts, you feel it *sweep,* feel it *scurry?* A poem, by God, yes, sir, no doubt, a poem!"

"Ma'am," I called.

The moth-sound ceased.

"Don't stop her!" hissed Mr. Dickens. "Middle of inspiration. Let her go!"

The moth-scratch started again.

Flourish, flourish, scratch, on, on, stop. Flourish, flourish. I bobbed my head. I moved my lips, as did Mr. Dickens, both of us suspended, held, leant forward on the cool marble air listening to the vaults and stacks and echoes in the subterrane.

Flourish, flourish, scratch, on, on.

Silence.

"There." Mr. Dickens nudged me.

"Ma'am!" I called ever so urgently soft.

And something rustled in the corridors.

And there stood the librarian, a lady between years, not young, not old; between colors, not dark, not pale; between heights, not short, not tall, but rather frail, a woman you often heard talking to herself off in the dark dust-stacks with a whisper like turned pages, a woman who glided as if on hidden wheels.

She came carrying her soft lamp of face, lighting her way with her glance.

Her lips were moving, she was busy with words in the vast room behind her clouded gaze.

Charlie read her lips eagerly. He nodded. He waited for her to halt and bring us to focus, which she did, suddenly. She gasped and laughed at herself.

"Oh, Ralph, it's you and—" A look of recognition warmed her face. "Why, you're Ralph's friend. Mr. Dickens, isn't it?"

Charlie stared at her with a quiet and almost alarming devotion.

"Mr. Dickens," I said. "I want you to meet—"

"'Because I could not stop for Death—'" Charlie, eyes shut, quoted from memory.

The librarian blinked swiftly and her brow like a lamp turned high, took white color.

"Miss Emily," he said.

"Her name is—" I said.

"Miss Emily." He put out his hand to touch hers.

"Pleased," she said. "But how did you—?"

"Know your name? Why, bless me, ma'am, I heard you scratching way off in there, runalong rush, only poets do *that!*"

"It's nothing."

"Head high, chin up," he said, gently. "It's something. 'Because I could not stop for death' is a fine A-1 first-class poem."

"My own poems are so poor," she said, nervously. "I copy hers out to learn."

"Copy *who?*" I blurted.

"Excellent way to learn."

"Is it, *really?*" She looked close at Charlie. "You're not . . . ?"

"Joking? No, not with Emily Dickinson, ma'am!"

"Emily Dickinson?" I said.

"That means much coming from you, Mr. Dickens," she flushed. "I have read all your books."

"All?" He backed off.

"All," she added hastily, "that you have published so far, sir."

"Just finished a new one." I put in, "Sockdolager! *A Tale of Two Cities.*"

"And you, ma'am?" he asked, kindly.

She opened her small hands as if to let a bird go.

"Me? Why, I haven't even sent a poem to our town newspaper."

"You must!" he cried, with true passion and meaning. "Tomorrow. No, today!"

"But," her voice faded. "I have no one to read them to, first."

"Why," said Charlie quietly. "You have Pip here, and, accept my card, C. Dickens, Esquire. Who will, if allowed, stop by on occasion, to see if all's well in this Arcadian silo of books."

She took his card. "I couldn't—"

"Tut! You must. For I shall offer only warm sliced white bread. Your words must be the marmalade and summer honey jam. I shall read long and plain. You: short and rapturous of life and tempted by that odd delicious Death you often lean upon. Enough." He pointed. "There. At the far end of the corridor, her lamp lit ready to guide your hand . . . the Muse awaits. Keep and feed her well. Good-bye."

"Good-bye?" she asked. "Doesn't that mean 'God be with you'?"

"So I have heard, dear lady, so I have heard."

And suddenly we were back out in the sunlight, Mr. Dickens almost stumbling over his carpetbag waiting there.

In the middle of the lawn, Mr. Dickens stood very still and said, "The sky is blue, boy."

"Yes, sir."

"The grass is green."

"Sure." Then I stopped and really looked around. "I mean, heck, yeah!"

"And the wind . . . smell that sweet wind?"

We both smelled it. He said:

"And in this world are remarkable boys with vast imaginations who know the secrets of salvation . . ."

He patted my shoulder. Head down, I didn't know what to do. And then I was saved by a whistle:

"Hey, the next train! Here it comes!"

We waited.

After a long while, Mr. Dickens said:

"There it goes . . . and let's go home, boy."

"Home!" I cried, joyfully, and then stopped. "But what about . . . Mr. Wyneski?"

"Oh, after all this, I have such confidence in you, Pip. Every afternoon while I'm having tea and resting my wits, you must trot down to the barbershop and—"

"Sweep hair!"

"Brave lad. It's little enough. A loan of friendship from the Bank of England to the First National Bank of Green Town, Illinois. And now, Pip . . . pencil!"

I tried behind one ear, found gum; tried the other ear and found: "Pencil!"

"Paper?"

"Paper!"

We strode along under the soft green summer trees.

"Title, Pip—"

He reached up with his cane to write a mystery on the sky. I squinted at the invisible penmanship.

"The—"

He blocked out a second word on the air.

"Old," I translated.

A third.

"C.U." I spelled. "R.I. . . . Curiosity!"

"How's that for a title, Pip?"

I hesitated. "It . . . doesn't seem, well, quite finished, sir."

"What a Christian you are. There!"

He flourished a final word on the sun.

"S.H.O. . . . Shop! *The Old Curiosity Shop*."

"Take a novel, Pip!"

"Yes, sir," I cried. "Chapter One!"

A blizzard of snow blew through the trees.

"What's that?" I asked, and answered:

Why, summer gone. The calendar pages, all the hours and days, like in the movies, the way they just blow off over the hills. Charlie and I working together, finished, through. Many days at the library, over! Many nights reading aloud with Miss Emily done! Trains come and gone. Moons waxed and waned. New trains arriving and new lives teetering on the brink, and Miss Emily suddenly standing right there, and Charlie here with all their suitcases and handing me a paper sack.

"What's this?"

"Rice, Pip, plain ordinary white rice, for the fertility ritual. Throw it at us, boy. Drive us happily away. Hear those bells, Pip? Here goes Mr. and Mrs. Charlie Dickens! Throw, boy, throw! Throw!"

I threw and ran, ran and threw, and them on the back train platform waving out of sight and me yelling good-bye, Happy marriage, Charlie! Happy times! Come back! Happy . . . Happy . . .

And by then I guess I was crying, and Dog chewing my shoes, jealous, glad to have me alone again, and Mr. Wyneski waiting at the barbershop to hand me my broom and make me his son once more.

And autumn came and lingered and at last a letter arrived from the married and traveling couple.

I kept the letter sealed all day and at dusk, while Grandpa was raking leaves by the front porch I went out to sit and watch and hold the letter and wait for him to look up and at last he did and I opened the letter and read it out loud in the October twilight:

"Dear Pip," I read, and had to stop for a moment seeing my old special name again, my eyes were so full.

"Dear Pip. We are in Aurora tonight and Felicity tomorrow and Elgin the night after that. Charlie has six months of lectures lined up and looking forward. Charlie and I are both working steadily and are most happy . . . very happy . . . need I say?

"He calls me Emily.

"Pip, I don't think you know who she was, but there was a lady poet once, and I hope you'll get her books out of the library someday.

"Well, Charlie looks at me and says: 'This is my Emily' and I almost believe. No, I do believe."

I stopped and swallowed hard and read on:

"We are crazy, Pip.

"People have said it. We know it. Yet we go on. But being crazy together is fine.

"It was being crazy alone I couldn't stand any longer.

"Charlie sends his regards and wants you to know he has indeed started a fine new book, perhaps his best yet . . . one you suggested the title for, *Bleak House*.

"So we write and move, move and write, Pip. And some year soon we may come back on the train which stops for water at your town. And if you're there and call our names as we know ourselves now, we shall step off the train. But perhaps meanwhile you will get too old. And if when the train stops, Pip, you're not there, we shall understand, and let the train move us on to another and another town.

"Signed, Emily Dickinson.

"P.S. Charlie says your grandfather is a dead ringer for Plato, but not to tell him.

"P.P.S. Charlie is my darling."

"Charlie is my darling," repeated Grandpa, sitting down and taking the letter to read it again. "Well, well . . ." he sighed. "Well, well . . ."

We sat there a long while, looking at the burning soft October sky and the new stars. A mile off, a dog barked. Miles off, on the horizon line, a train moved along, whistled, and tolled its bell, once, twice, three times, gone.

"You know," I said. "I don't think they're crazy."

"Neither do I, Pip," said Grandpa, lighting his pipe and blowing out the match. "Neither do I."

A Good Scent from a Strange Mountain

Robert Olen Butler

H̱ô Chí Minh came to me again last night, his hands covered with confectioners' sugar. This was something of a surprise to me, the first time I saw him beside my bed, in the dim light from the open shade. My oldest daughter leaves my shades open, I think so that I will not forget that the sun has risen again in the morning. I am a very old man. She seems to expect that one morning I will simply forget to keep living. This is very foolish. I will one night rise up from my bed and slip into her room and open the shade there. Let *her* see the sun in the morning. She is sixty-four years old and she should worry for herself. I could never die from forgetting.

But the light from the street was enough to let me recognize Hồ when I woke, and he said to me, "Đao, my old friend, I have heard it is time to visit you." Already on that first night there was a sweet smell about him, very strong in the dark, even before I could see his hands. I said nothing, but I stretched to the nightstand beside me and I turned on the light to see if he would go away. And he did not. He stood there beside the bed—I could even see him reflected in the window—and I knew it was real because he did not appear as he was when I'd known him but as he was when he'd died. This was Uncle Hồ before me, the thin old man with the dewlap beard wearing the dark clothes of a peasant and the rubber sandals, just like in the news pictures I studied with such a strange feeling for all those years. Strange because when I knew him, he was not yet Hồ Chí Minh. It was 1917 and he was Nguyễn Aí Quốc and we were both young men with clean-shaven faces, the best of friends, and we worked at the Carlton Hotel in London, where I was a dishwasher and he was a pastry cook under the great Escoffier. We were the best of friends and we saw snow for the first time together. This was before we began to work at the hotel. We shoveled snow and Hồ would stop for a moment and blow his breath out before him and it would make him smile, to see what was inside him, as if it were the casting of bones to tell the future.

On that first night when he came to me in my house in New Orleans, I finally saw what it was that smelled so sweet and I said to him, "Your hands are covered with sugar."

He looked at them with a kind of sadness.

71

I have received that look myself in the past week. It is time now for me to see my family, and the friends I have made who are still alive. This is our custom from Vietnam. When you are very old, you put aside a week or two to receive the people of your life so that you can tell one another your feelings, or try at last to understand one another, or simply say good-bye. It is a formal leave-taking, and with good luck you can do this before you have your final illness. I have lived almost a century and perhaps I should have called them all to me sooner, but at last I felt a deep weariness and I said to my oldest daughter that it was time.

They look at me with sadness, some of them. Usually the dull-witted ones, or the insincere ones. But Hồ's look was, of course, not dull-witted or insincere. He considered his hands and said, "The glaze. Maestro's glaze."

There was the soft edge of yearning in his voice and I had the thought that perhaps he had come to me for some sort of help. I said to him, "I don't remember. I only washed dishes." As soon as the words were out of my mouth, I decided it was foolish for me to think he had come to ask me about the glaze.

But Hồ did not treat me as foolish. He looked at me and shook his head. "It's all right," he said. "I remember the temperature now. Two hundred and thirty degrees, when the sugar is between the large thread stage and the small orb stage. The Maestro was very clear about that and I remember." I knew from his eyes, however, that there was much more that still eluded him. His eyes did not seem to move at all from my face, but there was some little shifting of them, a restlessness that perhaps only I could see, since I was his close friend from the days when the world did not know him.

I am nearly one hundred years old, but I can still read a man's face. Perhaps better than I ever have. I sit in the overstuffed chair in my living room and I receive my visitors and I want these people, even the dull-witted and insincere ones—please excuse an old man's ill temper for calling them that—I want them all to be good with one another. A Vietnamese family is extended as far as the bloodline strings us together, like so many paper lanterns around a village square. And we all give off light together. That's the way it has always been in our culture. But these people who come to visit me have been in America for a long time and there are very strange things going on that I can see in their faces.

None stranger than this morning. I was in my overstuffed chair and with me there were four of the many members of my family: my son-in-law Thắng, a former colonel in the Army of the Republic of Vietnam and one of the insincere ones, sitting on my Castro convertible couch; his youngest son, Lợi, who had come in late, just a few minutes earlier, and had thrown himself down on the couch as well, youngest but a man old enough to have served as a lieutenant under his father as our country fell to the communists more than a decade ago; my daughter Lâm, who is Thắng's wife, hovering behind the both of them and refusing all invitations to sit down; and my oldest daughter, leaning against the door frame, having no doubt just returned from my room, where she had opened the shade that I had closed when I awoke.

It was Thắng who gave me the sad look I have grown accustomed to, and I perhaps seemed to him at that moment a little weak, a little distant. I had stopped listening to the small talk of these people and I had let my eyes half close, though I could still see them clearly and I was very alert. Thắng has a steady face and the quick eyes of a man who is ready to come under fire, but I have always read much more there, in spite of his efforts to show nothing. So after he thought I'd faded from the room, it was with slow eyes, not quick, that he moved to his son and began to speak of the killing.

You should understand that Mr. Nguyễn Bích Lê had been shot dead in our community here in New Orleans just last week. There are many of us Vietnamese living in New Orleans and one man, Mr. Lê, published a little newspaper for all of us. He had recently made the fatal error—though it should not be that in America—of writing that it was time to accept the reality of the communist government in Vietnam and begin to talk with them. We had to work now with those who controlled our country. He said that he remained a patriot to the Republic of Vietnam, and I believed him. If anyone had asked an old man's opinion on this whole matter, I would not have been afraid to say that Mr. Lê was right.

But he was shot dead last week. He was forty-five years old and he had a wife and three children and he was shot as he sat behind the wheel of his Chevrolet pickup truck. I find a detail like that especially moving, that this man was killed in his Chevrolet, which I understand is a strongly American thing. We knew this in Saigon.

In Saigon it was very American to own a Chevrolet, just as it was French to own a Citroën.

And Mr. Lê had taken one more step in his trusting embrace of this new culture. He had bought not only a Chevrolet but a Chevrolet pickup truck, which made him not only American but also a man of Louisiana, where there are many pickup trucks. He did not, however, also purchase a gun rack for the back window, another sign of this place. Perhaps it would have been well if he had, for it was through the back window that the bullet was fired. Someone had hidden in the bed of his truck and had killed him from behind in his Chevrolet and the reason for this act was made very clear in a phone call to the newspaper office by a nameless representative of the Vietnamese Party for the Annihilation of Communism and for the National Restoration.

And Thắng, my son-in-law, said to his youngest son, Lợi, "There is no murder weapon." What I saw was a faint lift of his eyebrows as he said this, like he was inviting his son to listen beneath his words. Then he said it again, more slowly, like it was code. "There is no *weapon*." My grandson nodded his head once, a crisp little snap. Then my daughter Lâm said in a very loud voice, with her eyes on me, "That was a terrible thing, the death of Mr. Lê." She nudged her husband and son, and both men turned their faces sharply to me and they looked at me squarely and said, also in very loud voices, "Yes, it was terrible."

I am not deaf, and I closed my eyes further, having seen enough and wanting them to think that their loud talk had not only failed to awake me but had put me more completely to sleep. I did not like to deceive them, however, even though I have already spoken critically of these members of my family. I am a Hòa Hao Buddhist and I believe in harmony among all living things, especially the members of a Vietnamese family.

After Hồ had reassured me, on that first visit, about the temperature needed to heat Maestro Escoffier's glaze, he said, "Đạo, my old friend, do you still follow the path you chose in Paris?"

He meant by this my religion. It was in Paris that I embraced the Buddha and disappointed Hồ. We went to France in early 1918, with the war still on, and we lived in
the poorest street of the poorest part of the Seventeenth Arrondissement. Number
nine, Impasse Compoint, a blind alley with a few crumbling houses, all but ours
rented out for storage. The cobblestones were littered with fallen roof tiles and Quốc
and I each had a tiny single room with only an iron bedstead and a crate to sit on. I
could see my friend Quốc in the light of the tallow candle and he was dressed in a
dark suit and a bowler hat and he looked very foolish. I did not say so, but he knew it
himself and he kept seating and reseating the hat and shaking his head very slowly,
with a loudly silent anger. This was near the end of our time together, for I was visiting daily with a Buddhist monk and he was drawing me back to the religion of my
father. I had run from my father, gone to sea, and that was where I had met Nguyễn Aí
Quốc and we had gone to London and to Paris and now my father was calling me
back, through a Vietnamese monk I met in the Tuileries.

Quốc, on the other hand, was being called not from his past but from his future.
He had rented the dark suit and bowler and he would spend the following weeks in
Versailles, walking up and down the mirrored corridors of the Palace trying to gain
an audience with Woodrow Wilson. Quốc had eight requests for the Western world
concerning Indochina. Simple things. Equal rights, freedom of assembly, freedom of
the press. The essential things that he knew Wilson would understand, based as they
were on Wilson's own Fourteen Points. And Quốc did not even intend to ask for
independence. He wanted Vietnamese representatives in the French Parliament.
That was all he would ask. But his bowler made him angry. He wrenched out of the
puddle of candlelight, both his hands clutching the bowler, and I heard him muttering in the darkness and I felt that this was a bad sign already, even before he had set
foot in Versailles. And as it turned out, he never saw Wilson, or Lloyd George either,
or even Clemenceau. But somehow his frustration with his hat was what made me
sad, even now, and I reached out from my bedside and said, "Uncle Hồ, it's all right."

He was still beside me. This was not an awakening, as you might expect, this was
not a dream ending with the bowler in Paris and I awaking to find that Hồ was never
there. He was still beside my bed, though he was just beyond my outstretched hand
and he did not move to me. He smiled on one side of his mouth, a smile full of
irony, as if he, too, was thinking about the night he'd tried on his rented clothes. He
said, "Do you remember how I worked in Paris?"

I thought about this and I did remember, with the words of his advertisement in
the newspaper *La Vie Ouvrière*: "If you would like a lifelong memento of your family, have your photos retouched at Nguyễn Aí Quốc's." This was his work in Paris; he
retouched photos with a very delicate hand, the same fine hand that Monsieur
Escoffier had admired in London. I said, "Yes, I remember."

Hồ nodded gravely. "I painted the blush into the cheeks of Frenchmen."

I said, "A lovely portrait in a lovely frame for forty francs," another phrase from his
advertisement.

"Forty-five," Hồ said.

I thought now of his question that I had not answered. I motioned to the far corner of the room where the prayer table stood. "I still follow the path."

He looked and said, "At least you became a Hòa Hao."

He could tell this from the simplicity of the table. There was only a red cloth upon it and four Chinese characters: Bao Sơn Kỳ Hương. This is the saying of the Hòa Haos. We follow the teachings of a monk who broke away from the fancy rituals of the other Buddhists. We do not need elaborate pagodas or rituals. The Hòa Hao believes that the maintenance of our spirits is very simple, and the mystery of joy is simple, too. The four characters mean "A good scent from a strange mountain."

I had always admired the sense of humor of my friend Quốc, so I said, "You never did stop painting the blush into the faces of Westerners."

Hồ looked back to me but he did not smile. I was surprised at this but more surprised at my little joke seeming to remind him of his hands. He raised them and studied them and said, "After the heating, what was the surface for the glaze?"

"My old friend," I said, "you worry me now."

But Hồ did not seem to hear. He turned away and crossed the room and I knew he was real because he did not vanish from my sight but opened the door and went out and closed the door behind him with a loud click.

I rang for my daughter. She had given me a porcelain bell, and after allowing Hồ enough time to go down the stairs and out the front door, if that was where he was headed, I rang the bell, and my daughter, who is a very light sleeper, soon appeared.

"What is it, Father?" she asked with great patience in her voice. She is a good girl. She understands about Vietnamese families and she is a smart girl.

"Please feel the doorknob," I said.

She did so without the slightest hesitation and this was a lovely gesture on her part, a thing that made me wish to rise up and embrace her, though I was very tired and did not move.

"Yes?" she asked after touching the knob.

"Is it sticky?"

She touched it again. "Ever so slightly," she said. "Would you like to me to clean it?"

"In the morning," I said.

She smiled and crossed the room and kissed me on the forehead. She smelled of lavender and fresh bedclothes and there are so many who have gone on before me into the world of spirits and I yearn for them all, yearn to find them all together in a village square, my wife there smelling of lavender and our own sweat, like on a night in Saigon soon after the terrible fighting in 1968 when we finally opened the windows onto the night and there were sounds of bombs falling on the horizon and there was no breeze at all, just the heavy stillness of the time between the dry season and the wet, and Saigon smelled of tar and motorcycle exhaust and cordite but when I opened the window and turned to my wife, the room was full of a wonderful scent, a sweet smell that made her sit up, for she sensed it, too. This was a smell that had nothing to do with flowers but instead reminded us that flowers were always ready to fall into dust, while this smell was as if a gemstone had begun to give off a scent, as if a mountain of emerald had found its own scent. I crossed the room to my wife and we were already old, we had already buried children and grandchildren that we prayed waited for us in that village square at the foot of the strange mountain, but when I came near the bed, she lifted her silk gown and threw it aside and I pressed close to her and our own sweat smelled sweet on that night. I want to be with her in that square and with the rest of those we'd buried, the tiny limbs and the sullen eyes and the gray faces of the puzzled children and the surprised adults and the weary old people who have gone before us, who know the secrets now. And the sweet smell of the glaze on Hồ's hands reminds me of others that I would want in the square, the people from the ship, too, the Vietnamese boy from a village near my own who died of a fever in the Indian Ocean and the natives in Dakar who were forced by colonial officials to swim out to our ship in shark-infested waters to secure the moorings and two were killed before our eyes without a French regret. Hồ was very moved by this and I want those men in our square and I want the Frenchman, too, who called Hồ "monsieur" for the first time. A man on the dock in Marseilles. Hồ spoke of him twice more during our years together and I want that Frenchman there. And, of course, Hồ. Was he in the village square even now, waiting? Heating his glaze fondant? My daughter was smoothing my covers around me and the smell of lavender on her was still strong.

"He was in this room," I said to her to explain the sticky doorknob.

"Who was?"

But I was very sleepy and I could say no more, though perhaps she would not have understood anyway, in spite of being the smart girl that she is.

The next night I left my light on to watch for Hồ's arrival, but I dozed off and he had to wake me. He was sitting in a chair that he'd brought from across the room. He said to me, "Đao. Wake up, my old friend."

I must have awakened when he pulled the chair near to me, for I heard each of these words. "I am awake," I said. "I was thinking of the poor men who had to swim out to our ship."

"They are already among those I have served," Hồ said. "Before I forgot." And he raised his hands and they were still covered with sugar.

I said, "Wasn't it a marble slab?" I had a memory, strangely clear after these many years, as strange as my memory of Hồ's Paris business card.

"A marble slab," Hồ repeated, puzzled.

"That you poured the heated sugar on."

"Yes." Hồ's sweet-smelling hands came forward but they did not quite touch me. I thought to reach out from beneath the covers and take them in my own hands, but Hồ leaped up and paced about the room. "The marble slab, moderately oiled. Of course. I am to let the sugar half cool and then use the spatula to move it about in all directions, every bit of it, so that it doesn't harden and form lumps."

I asked, "Have you seen my wife?"

Hồ had wandered to the far side of the room, but he turned and crossed back to me at this. "I'm sorry, my friend. I never knew her."

I must have shown some disappointment in my face, for Hồ sat down and brought his own face near mine. "I'm sorry," he said. "There are many other people that I must find here."

76

"Are you very disappointed in me?" I asked. "For not having traveled the road with you?"

"It's very complicated," Hồ said softly. "You felt that you'd taken action. I am no longer in a position to question another soul's choice."

"Are you at peace, where you are?" I asked this knowing of his worry over the recipe for the glaze, but I hoped that this was only a minor difficulty in the afterlife, like the natural anticipation of the good cook expecting guests when everything always turns out fine in the end.

But Hồ said, "I am not at peace."

"Is Monsieur Escoffier over there?"

"I have not seen him. This has nothing to do with him, directly."

"What is it about?"

"I don't know."

"You won the country. You know that, don't you?"

Hồ shrugged. "There are no countries here."

I should have remembered Hồ's shrug when I began to see things in the faces of my son-in-law and grandson this morning. But something quickened in me, a suspicion. I kept my eyes shut and laid my head to the side, as if I was fast asleep, encouraging them to talk more.

My daughter said, "This is not the place to speak."

But the men did not regard her. "How?" Lợi asked his father, referring to the missing murder weapon.

"It's best not to know too much," Thắng said.

Then there was a silence. For all the quickness I'd felt at the first suspicion, I was very slow now. In fact, I did think of Hồ from that second night. Not his shrug. He had fallen silent for a long time and I had closed my eyes, for the light seemed very bright. I listened to his silence just as I listened to the silence of these two conspirators before me.

And then Hồ said, "They were fools, but I can't bring myself to grow angry anymore."

I opened my eyes in the bedroom and the light was off. Hồ had turned it off, knowing that it was bothering me. "Who were fools?" I asked.

"We had fought together to throw out the Japanese. I had very good friends among them. I smoked their lovely Salem cigarettes. They had been repressed by colonialists themselves. Did they not know their own history?"

"Do you mean the Americans?"

"There are a million souls here with me, the young men of our country, and they are all dressed in black suits and bowler hats. In the mirrors they are made ten million, a hundred million."

"I chose my path, my dear friend Quốc, so that there might be harmony."

And even with that yearning for harmony I could not overlook what my mind made of what my ears had heard this morning. Thắng was telling Lợi that the murder weapon had been disposed of. Thắng and Lợi both knew the killers, were in sympathy with them, perhaps were part of the killing. The father and son had been airborne rangers and I had several times heard them talk bitterly of the exile of our people. We were fools for trusting the Americans all along, they said.

We should have taken matters forward and disposed of the infinitely corrupt Thiệu and done what needed to be done. Whenever they spoke like this in front of me, there was soon a quick exchange of sideways glances at me and then a turn and an apology. "We're sorry, Grandfather. Old times often bring old anger. We are happy our family is living a new life."

I would wave my hand at this, glad to have the peace of the family restored. Glad to turn my face and smell the dogwood tree or even smell the coffee plant across the highway. These things had come to be the new smells of our family. But then a weakness often came upon me. The others would drift away, the men, and perhaps one of my daughters would come to me and stroke my head and not say a word and none of them ever would ask why I was weeping. I would smell the rich blood smells of the afterbirth and I would hold our first son, still slippery in my arms, and there was the smell of dust from the square and the smell of the South China Sea just over the rise of the hill and there was the smell of the blood and of the inner flesh from my wife as my son's own private sea flowed from this woman that I loved, flowed and carried him into the life that would disappear from him so soon. In the afterlife would he stand before me on unsteady child's legs? Would I have to bend low to greet him or would he be a man now?

My grandson said, after the silence had nearly carried me into real sleep, troubled sleep, my grandson Lợi said to his father, "I would be a coward not to know."

Thắng laughed and said, "You have proved yourself no coward."

And I wished then to sleep, I wished to fall asleep and let go of life somewhere in my dreams and seek my village square. I have lived too long, I thought. My daughter was saying, "Are you both mad?" And then she changed her voice, making the words very precise. "Let Grandfather sleep."

So when Hồ came tonight for the third time, I wanted to ask advice. His hands were still covered with sugar and his mind was, had been for the past two nights, very much distracted. "There's something still wrong with the glaze," he said to me in the dark, and I pulled back the covers and swung my legs around to get up. He did not try to stop me, but he did draw back quietly into the shadows. "I want to pace the room with you," I said. "As we did in Paris, the tiny rooms of ours. We would talk about Marx and about Buddha and I must pace with you now."

"Very well," he said. "Perhaps it will help me remember."

I slipped on my sandals and I stood up and Hồ's shadow moved me, through the spill of streetlight and into the dark near the river. I followed him, smelling the sugar on his hands, first before and then moving past me as I went on into the darkness he'd left. I stopped as I turned and I could see Hồ outlined before the window and I said, "I believe my son-in-law and grandson are involved in the killing of a man. A political killing."

Hồ stayed where he was, a dark shape against the light, and he said nothing and I could not smell his hands from across the room. I smelled only the sourness of Lợi as he laid his head on my shoulder. He was a baby and my daughter Lâm retreated to

78

our balcony window after handing him to me and the boy turned his head and I turned mine to him and I could smell his mother's milk, sour on his breath, he had a sour smell and there was incense burning the room, jasmine, the smoke of souls, and the boy sighed on my shoulder, and I turned my face away from the smell of him. Thắng was across the room and his eyes were quick to find his wife and he was waiting for her to take the child from me.

"You have never done the political thing," Hồ said. "Is this true?"

"Of course."

I asked, "Are there politics where you are now, my friend?"

I did not see him moving toward me, but the smell of the sugar on his hands grew stronger, very strong, and I felt Hồ Chí Minh very close to me, though I could not see him. He was very close and the smell was strong and sweet and it was filling my lungs as if from the inside, as if Hồ was passing through my very body, and I heard the door open behind me and then close softly shut.

I moved across the room to the bed. I turned to sit down but I was facing the window, the scattering of a streetlamp on the window like a nova in some far part of the universe. I stepped to the window and touched the reflected light there, wondering if there was a great smell when a star explodes, a great burning smell of gas and dust. Then I closed the shade and slipped into bed, quite gracefully, I felt, I was quite wonderfully graceful, and I lie here now waiting for sleep. Hồ is right, of course. I will never say a word about my grandson. And perhaps I will be as restless as Hồ when I join him. But that will be all right. He and I will be together again and perhaps we can help each other. I know now what it is that he has forgotten. He has used confectioners' sugar for his glaze fondant and he should be using granulated sugar. I was only a washer of dishes but I did listen carefully when Monsieur Escoffier spoke. I wanted to understand everything. His kitchen was full of such smells that you knew you had to understand everything or you would be incomplete forever.

Keith

Ron Carlson

*B*arbara Peterson didn't need some weird guy sending her notes. In fact, she didn't need anything at all. They were lab partners. It was that simple, how they met. She was the Barbara Peterson, President of half the school offices and Queen of the rest. He was Keith Zetterstrom, a character, an oddball, a Z. His name was called last. The spring of their senior year at their equipment drawer she spoke to him for the first time in all their grades together:

"Are you my lab partner?"

He spread the gear on the counter for the inventory and looked at her. "Yes, I am," he said. "I haven't lied to you this far, and I'm not going to start now."

After school Barbara Peterson met her boyfriend, Brian Woodworth, in the parking lot. They had twin red scooters because Brian had given her one at Christmas. "That guy," Barbara said, pointing to where Keith stood in the bus line, "is my lab partner."

"Who is he?" Brian said.

Keith was the window, wallpaper, woodwork. He'd been there for years, and they'd never seen him. This was complicated, because for years he was short and then he grew tall. And then he grew a long black slash of hair and now he had a crew cut. He was hard to see, to fix in one's vision.

The experiments in chemistry that spring concerned states of matter, and Barbara and Keith worked well together, quietly and methodically testing the elements.

"You're Barbara Peterson," he said finally as they waited for a beaker to boil. "We were on the same kickball team in fourth grade, and I stood behind you in the sixth-grade Christmas play. I was a Russian soldier."

Barbara Peterson did not know what to say to these things. She couldn't remember the sixth-grade play . . . and fourth grade? So she said, "What are you doing after graduation?"

"The sky's the limit," he said. "And you are going off to Brown University."

"I got in. I'm not sure if Barbara Peterson goes away to Brown. She might stay here and go to school with Brian."

"Her boyfriend."

"Right," she said. Their mixture boiled, and Keith poured some off into a cooling tray. "So what do you do?" he asked her. Barbara eyed him. She was used to classmates having curiosity about her, and she had developed a pleasant condescension, but Keith had her off-guard.

"What do you mean?"

"On a date with Brian, your boyfriend. What do you do?"

"Lots of things. We play miniature golf."

"You go on your scooters and play miniature golf."

"Yes."

"Who wins? The golf."

"Brian," Barbara said. "He does."

Barbara showed the note to Dana, her best friend.

REASONS YOU SHOULD GO WITH ME

A. You are my lab partner.

B. Just to see. (You, too, contain the restless germ of curiosity that has led humanity out of the complacency of our dark caves into the bright world, where we invented bowling—among other things.)

C. It's not a "date."

"Great," Dana said. "We certainly believe this! But who wants to graduate without a night out with a bald guy? Go. Tell Brian that you're staying at my house."

Keith drove a Chevy pickup, forest green, and when Barbara climbed in, she asked, "Why don't you drive this to school?"

"There's a bus. I love the bus. Have you ever been on one?"

"Not a school bus."

"Oh, try it," he said. "It's so big, and it doesn't drop you off right at your house."

"You're weird."

The evening went like this: Keith turned onto Bloomfield, the broad business avenue that stretched from near the airport all the way back to the university. He told her, "I want you to point out your least-favorite building on this street."

"So we're not going bowling?"

"No, we're saving that. I thought we'd just get a little something to eat. So keep your eyes open; any places you can't stand?" By the time they reached the airport, Barbara had pointed out four she thought were ugly. When they turned around, Keith added: "Now, your final choice please. And not someplace you just don't like. We're looking for genuine aversion."

Barbara selected a five-story metal building near downtown with a marquee above the main doors that read INSURANCE.

"Excellent," Keith said as he swung the pickup to the curb. He got out and began unloading his truck. "This is truly garish. The architect here is now serving time."

"This is where my father used to work."

Keith paused, his arms full of equipment. "When . . ."

"When he divorced my mom. His office was right up there."

She pointed. "I hate driving by this place."

"Good," Keith said with renewed conviction. "Come over here and sit down. Have a Coke."

Barbara sat in a chaise lounge that Keith had set on the floodlit front lawn next to a folding table. He handed her a Coke. "We're eating here?"

"Yes, Miss," he said, toting over a cooler and a little propane stove. "It's rustic but traditional: cheese omelets and hash browns. Sliced tomatoes for a salad and—for dessert—ice cream. On the way home, of course." Keith poured some oil into the frying pan. "There is nothing like a meal to alter the chemistry of a place."

On the way home they did stop for ice cream and Barbara asked him, "Wasn't your hair long last year, like in your face and down like this?" She swept her hand past his eye.

"It was."

"Why is it so short now?"

Keith ran his hand back over his head. "Seasonal cut. Summer's a-coming in. I want to lead the way."

It was a weird week for Barbara. She actually did feel differently about the insurance building as she drove her scooter by it on the way to school. When she told Dana about dinner, she said, "I saw you! You were like camped out, right?"

Wonder spread on Barbara's face as she thought it over.

"Yeah, it was cool. He cooked."

"Right. But please, I've known a lot of guys who cook and they're some of the slickest. High School Confidential says, 'There are three million seductions and only one goal.'"

In chemistry, it was sulfur; liquid, solid, and gas. The hallways of the chemistry annex smelled like rotten eggs. Barbara winced through the white wispy smoke as Keith stirred the melting sulfur nuggets.

"This is awful," Barbara said."

"This is wonderful," Keith said. "This is the exact smell that greets sinners at the gates of hell. They think it's awful; here we get to enjoy it for free."

Barbara looked at him. "My lab partner is a certifiable . . ."

"Your lab partner will meet you tonight at seven o'clock."

"Keith," she said, taking the stir stick from him and prodding the undissolved sulfur. "I have a boyfriend. Remember?"

"Good for you," he said. "Now tell me something I don't know. Listen, I'll pick you up at seven. This isn't a date. This is errands. Necessary errands for your friends. You'll be home by nine. Young Mr. Brian can scoot by then." Keith leaned toward her, the streams of acrid sulfur rising past his face. "I'm not lying to you."

When she got into the truck that night, Keith asked her, "What did you tell Brian?"

"I told him I'd be at my aunt's and to come by at ten."

"That's awfully late on a school night. I mean, why didn't you tell him you'd be with me for two hours?" He looked at her. "I have trouble lending credibility to a relationship that is almost one year old in which one of the members has given the other an actual full-size, road-worthy motor vehicle, and yet one of the members lies to the other when she plans to spend two hours with her lab partner, a person with whom she has inhaled the very vapors of hell."

"Stop the truck, Keith. I'm getting out."

"And miss bowling? And the search for bowling balls?" Half an hour later, they were in Veteran's Thrift, reading the bowling balls. They'd already bought five at

Desert Thrift Shops and the Salvation Army. Keith's rule was that they had to be less than two dollars. They'd bought PATTY for Dana, BETSY and KIM for two more of Barbara's friends, an initialed B.R. ball for Brian, even though his last name was Woodworth ("Puzzle him," Keith said), and WALT for their chemistry teacher, Mr. Walter Miles. They found three more in the bins in Veteran's Thrift, one marked SKIP, one marked COSMO ("A must," Keith said), and a brilliant green ball, run deeply with hypnotic swirls, that had no name at all.

Barbara was touring the wide shelves of used appliances and kitchen utensils. "Where do they get this stuff? This is a dime?" She held up a large plastic tray with a picture of the Beatles on it.

"That," Keith said, taking it from her and placing it in the cart with their bowling balls, "came from the home of a fan of the first magnitude. Oh, it's a sad story. It's enough to say that this is here tonight because of Yoko Ono." Keith's attention was taken by a large trophy, standing among the dozen other trophies on the top shelf. "Whoa," he said, pulling it down. It was huge, over three feet tall: six golden columns, ascending from a white marble base to a silver obelisk, framed by two embossed silver wreaths, and topped by a silver woman on a rearing motorcycle. The inscription on the base read WIDOWMAKER HILL CLIMB—FIRST PLACE 1987. Keith held it out to show her, like a man holding a huge bottle of aspirin in a television commercial. "But this is another story altogether." He placed it reverently in the basket.

"And that would be?"

"No time. You've got to get back and meet Brian, a person who doesn't know where you are." Keith led her to the checkout. He was quiet all the way to the truck. He placed the balls carefully in the truck bed and then set the huge trophy between them on the seat.

"You don't know where this trophy's from," said Barbara.

Keith put a finger to his lips: "Shhhh." He started the truck and headed to Barbara's house. After several blocks of silence, Barbara folded her arms. "It's a tragic, tragic story," he said in a low voice. "I mean, this girl was a golden girl, an angel, the light in everybody's life."

"Do I want to hear this tragic story?"

"She was a wonder. Straight A's, with an A-plus in chemistry. The girl could do no wrong. And then," Keith looked at Barbara, "she got involved with motorcycles."

"Is this her on top of the trophy?"

"The very girl." Keith nodded grimly. "Oh, it started innocently enough with a little red scooter, a toy really. She ran errands for the Ladies' Society every Sunday when she wasn't home studying." Keith turned to Barbara, moving the trophy forward so he could see her. "I should add here that her fine academic standing got her where she was going that fateful fall." Keith laid the trophy back. "When her thirst for speed grew and grew, breaking over her good common sense like a tidal wave, sending her into the arms of an eight-eight-three Harley, one of the most powerful two-wheel vehicles in the history of mankind." They turned onto Barbara's street, and suddenly Barbara ducked, her head against Keith's knee.

"Drive by," she whispered. "Just keep going."

"What?" Keith said. "If I do that, Brian won't see you." Keith could see Brian leaning against his scooter in the driveway.

"Is that guy always early?"

Keith turned the next corner and Barbara sat up and opened her door. "I'll go down the alley."

"Cool," Keith said. "So you sneak down the alley to meet your boyfriend? Pretty sexy. But there's one last thing, partner. I'll pick you up at four to deliver these bowling balls."

"Four?"

"Four A.M. Brian will be gone, won't he?"

"Keith!"

"It's not a date. We've got to finish this program, right?"

Barbara looked at Keith as she opened the truck door.

"Okay, but meet me there," she pointed, "by the mailbox."

She was there. The streets of the suburbs were dark and eerily quiet, everything in its place, sleeping, but Barbara stood in the humming lamplight, hugging her elbows. She could hear Keith coming for two or three blocks before he turned onto her street. He had the heater on, and when she climbed in he handed her a blue cardigan, which she quickly put on. She rubbed her hands over the air vent. "Now this is weird out here."

"Yeah," Keith said. "Four o'clock makes it a different planet. I recommend it. But bring a sweater." He looked at her. "You look good. This is the face you ought to bring to school."

Barbara looked at Keith and smiled. "No makeup, okay? It's four A.M." His face looked tired, and in the pale dash lights, with his short, short hair, he looked more like a child, a lithe boy. "What do we do?"

"We give each of these babies"—Keith nodded back at the bowling balls in the truck bed—"a new home."

They delivered the balls, placing them carefully on her friends' porches, including Dana and Brian, and then they spent half an hour finding Mr. Miles's house, which was across town, a tan spilt-level. Keith handed Barbara the ball marked WALT and made her walk it up to the front porch. When she returned to the truck, Keith said, "Years from now you'll be able to say, 'When I was seventeen I put a bowling ball on my chemistry's teacher's front porch.'"

"His name was Walt," Barbara added.

At 5:30, as the first gray light rose, Barbara and Keith walked into Jewel's Cafe carrying the last two balls: the green beauty and COSMO. Jewel's was the oldest cafe in the city, an all night diner full of mailmen. "So," Barbara said, as they slid into one of the huge maroon booths, "who gets these last two?" She was radiant now, fully awake, and energized by the new day. The waitress appeared and they ordered Round-the-World omelets, hash browns, juice, milk, coffee, and muffins, and Barbara ate with gusto, looking up halfway through. "So, where next?" She saw his plate. "Hey, you're not eating."

Keith looked odd, his face milky, his eyes gray. "This food is full of the exact amino acids to have a certifiably chemical day," he said. "I'll get to it." He pushed his

84

plate aside and turned the place mat over and began to write on it.

"Are you feeling all right?" Barbara said.

"I'm okay." She tilted her head at him skeptically. "Hey. I'm okay. I haven't lied to you this far. Why would I start now?" He showed her the note he had written:

Dear Waitress: My girlfriend and I are from different sides of the tracks, races, creeds, colors, and zip codes, and if they found out we had been out bowling all night, they would banish us to prison schools on separate planets. Please, please find a good home for our only bowling balls. Our enormous sadness is only mitigated by the fact that we know you'll take care of them. With sweet sorrow. COSMO

In the truck, Barbara said, "Mitigated?"

"Always leave them something to look up."

"You're sick, aren't you?" she said.

"You look good in that sweater," he said. When she started to remove it, he said, "Don't. I'll get it after class, in just"—he looked at his watch—"two hours and twenty minutes." But he wasn't there. He wasn't there all week. The class did experiments with oxidation and Mr. Miles spent two days explaining and diagramming rust.

On Friday, Mr. Miles worked with Barbara and she asked him what was wrong with Keith. "I'm not sure," he said. "But I think he's on medication." Barbara had a tennis match at school on Tuesday afternoon, and Brian picked her up and drove her home. Usually he came in and they'd watch TV, but for the first time she begged off, claiming homework, kissing him quickly and running inside. On Friday, during her away match at Viewpoint, she felt odd again. She knew Brian was in the stands. When she walked off the court after the match, it was nearly dark and he was waiting. She gave Dana her rackets and climbed on Brian's scooter without a word. "You weren't that bad," he said. "Viewpoint always has a good team."

"Brian, let's just go home."

Barbara could tell by the way he was driving that he was mad, and she felt strangely glad about it. She didn't want to invite him in, let him grope her on the couch. She held on as he took the corners too fast and slipped through the stop signs, but all the way home she didn't put her chin on his shoulder. At her house, she got the scene she'd been expecting "What is the matter with you?" Brian said.

For some reason, when he'd gone to kiss her, she averted her face. Her heart burned with pleasure and shame. She was going to make up a lie about tennis, but then she just said, "Oh, Brian. Just leave me alone for a while, will you. Just go home." Inside, she couldn't settle down. She didn't shower or change clothes. She sat in the dark of her room for a while and then, using only the tiny spot of her desk lamp, she copied her chemistry notes for the week and called Dana.

It was midnight when Dana picked her up. Dana was smoking a Marlboro and blowing smoke into the windshield. She said, "High School Confidential Part Five: Young Barbara Peterson, still in her foxy tennis clothes, and her old friend Dana meet at midnight, cruise the Strip, pick up two guys with tattoos, and are never seen alive again. Is that it? Count me in."

"Not quite. It goes like this: Two sultry babes, one who has just been a royal bitch to her boyfriend for no reason, drive to eleven forty Fairmont to drop off the week's chemistry notes."

"That would be Keith Zetterstrom's address, I'd guess."

"He's my lab partner."

"Of course he is," Dana said.

"He missed all last week. Mr. Miles told me that he's sick."

"Oh my God!" Dana clamped the steering wheel. "He's got cancer. That's that scary hairdo."

"No he doesn't. He's going to Dickinson."

"Not for long, honey. I should've known this." Dana inhaled and blew smoke thoughtfully out of the side of her mouth. "Bald kids in high school without earrings have got cancer."

Keith was in class the following Monday for the chemistry exam: sulfur and rust. After class, Barbara Peterson took him by the arm and led him to her locker. "Thanks for the notes, partner," he said, "They were absolutely chemical."

"You were sick last week."

"Last week," he pondered. "Oh, you mean because I wasn't here. What do you do, come every day? I just couldn't; it would take away the something special I feel for this place."

"I know what's the matter with you."

"Good for you, Barbara Peterson. And I know what's the matter with you too; sounds like a promising relationship."

Barbara pulled his folded sweater from the locker and handed it to him. As she did, Brian came up. "Oh I see," he said. He started to walk away.

"Brian," Keith said. "I'm not a threat to you." Brian stood, his eyes narrowed. Keith went on: "She's not stupid. What am I going to do, trick her? I'm her lab partner. Relax." Keith took Brian's hand and shook it. "I'm serious, Woodworth." Brian stood for a moment longer until Barbara said, "I'll see you at lunch," and then he disappeared down the hall.

When he was gone, Barbara said, "Are you tricking me?"

"I don't know. Something's going on. I'm a little confused."

"You're confused. Where have you been, Keith Zetterstrom? Who are you? I've been going to school with you all these years and I've never even seen you and then we're delivering bowling balls together and now you're sick. Where were you last year? What are you doing? What are you doing next year?"

"Last year I got a C in Spanish with Mrs. Whitehead. It was gruesome. This year is somewhat worse, with a few exceptions, but all in all, I'd say the sky is the limit." Keith took her wrist. "Quote me on that."

Barbara took a sharp breath and quietly began to cry.

"Oh, let's not," Keith said, pushing a handkerchief into her hand. "Here. Think of this." He moved her back against the wall, out of the way of students passing by. "If I was having a good year, I might never have spoken to you. Extreme times require extreme solutions. I went all those years sitting in the back, and then I had to get to this edge to start talking. Now that's something, isn't it? Besides, I've got a plan. I'll pick you up at nine. Bring pajamas and a robe."

Barbara looked at him over the handkerchief.

"Hey. Trust me. You're the one who's crying. I'll see you at nine o'clock. This will cheer you up."

The hospital was on the hill and Keith parked in the farthest corner of the vast parking lot. Beneath them in the dark night the city teemed and shimmered, a million lights.

"It looks like a city on another planet," Barbara Peterson said, as she stepped out of the truck.

"It does, indeed," Keith said, grabbing his bag. "Now if we only knew if the residents were friendly." He took her arm.

"And now I'm going to cheer you up. I'm going to take you in that building"—Keith pointed at the huge hospital, lit like an ocean liner in the night—"and buy you a package of gum."

They changed clothes in the fifth-floor rest rooms and met in the hallway, in pajamas and robes, and stuffed their street clothes into Barbara's bag. "I feel better already," Barbara said.

"Now take my arm like this," Keith moved next to her and placed her hand above his elbow, "And look down like this." He put his chin on his chest. Barbara tried it. "No, not such a sad face, more serious, be strong. Now walk just like this, little sub steps, real slow."

They started down the hallway, creeping along one side.

"How far is it?" Barbara said. People passed them quietly in groups of two or three. It was the end of visiting hours. "A hundred yards to the elevators and down three floors, then out a hundred more. Keep your face down."

"Are people looking at us?"

"Well, yes. They've never seen a braver couple. And they've never seen such chemical pajamas."

They continued along the windows, through the lobby and down the elevator, in which they stood side by side, their four hands clasped together, while they looked at their tennis shoes. The other people in the car gave them room out of respect. The main hall was worse, thick with people, everyone going five miles an hour faster than Barbara and Keith, who shuffled along whispering.

In the gift shop, finally, they parted the waters. The small room was crowded, but the people stepped aside and Keith and Barbara stood right at the counter. "A package of chewing gum, please," Keith said.

"Which kind?" asked the candy striper.

"Sugarless. My sister and I want our teeth to last forever."

They ran to the truck, leaping and swinging their arms. Keith threw the bag containing their clothes into the truck bed and climbed in the cab. Barbara climbed in, laughing, and Keith said, "You feel better! You're cured!" She slid across the seat meaning to hug him, but it changed for both of them into a kiss. She pulled him to her side, one of her arms around his neck and one of her hands on his face. They fell into a spin there in the truck, eyes closed, holding onto each other in their pajamas, her robe open, their heads against the backseat, kissing. Barbara shifted and Keith sat up; the look they exchanged held. Below them, the city's lights flickered in a simmering network. Barbara cupped her hand carefully on the top of Keith's bald scalp. She pulled him forward. When she looked in his eyes again she knew what was going to happen, and it was a powerful feeling that gave her strange new certainty as she went for his mouth again.

There were other moments that surfaced in the truck in the night above the ancient city. Something Keith did, his hand, reminded her of Brian, but that thought vanished as they were beyond Brian in a moment. Later, well beyond even her notions of what to do and what not to do, breathing as if in toil, she heard herself say "okay." She said that several times.

She looked for Keith everywhere, catching glimpses of his head, his shoulder, in the hallways. In chemistry they didn't talk; there were final reports, no need to work together. Finally, three days before graduation, they stood together cleaning out their chemistry locker, waiting for Mr. Miles to check them off. Keith's manner was what? Easy, too confident, too neutral. He seemed to take up too much space in the room. She hated the way he kept his face blank and open as if fishing for the first remark. She held off, feeling the restraint as a physical pang. Mr. Miles inventoried their cupboard and asked for their keys. Keith handed his to Mr. Miles, and then Barbara Peterson found her key in the side of her purse and handed it to the teacher. She hated relinquishing the key; it was the only thing she had that meant she would see Keith, and now with it gone, something opened in her and it hurt in a way she'd never hurt before. Keith turned to her and seeing something in her face, shrugged and said, "The end of chemistry as we know it. Which isn't really very well."

"Who are you?" Barbara said, her voice a kind of surprise to her. "You're so glib. Such a little actor." Mr. Miles looked up from his check sheet and several students turned toward them. Barbara was speaking loudly; she couldn't help it.

"What are you doing to me? If this is good-bye, it's pretty chicken." Everyone was looking at her. Then her face would not work at all, the tears coming from some hot place, and she walked from the room.

Mr. Miles looked at Keith, alarmed. Keith dropped his head and worked his eyes with his forefingers. He whispered: "Don't worry, Mr. Miles. She was addressing her remarks to me."

The night before graduation, while her classmates met in the bright, noisy gym for the yearbook-signing party, Barbara drove out to the airport and met Keith where he said he'd be: at the last gate, H17. There on an empty stretch of maroon carpet in front of three large banks of seats full of travelers, he was waiting. He handed her a pretty green canvas valise and an empty ticket sleeve.

"You can't even talk as yourself," she said. "You always need a setting. Now we're pretending I'm going away?"

He looked serious tonight, weary. There were gray shadows under his eyes. "You wanted a good-bye scene," he said.

"It's all a joke," she said. "You joke all the time."

"You know what the counselor said?" He smiled thinly as if glad to give her this point. "He said this is a phase, that I'll stop joking soon." Their eyes met and the look held again. She stepped close to him. He put his hand on her elbow.

"You want a farewell speech. Okay, here you go. You better call Brian and get your scooter back. Tell him I tricked you. I just wanted to see if I could give Barbara Peterson a whirl. And I did. It was selfish, okay? I just cranked you around a little. You said it yourself: It was a joke. That's my speech."

"You didn't crank me around, Keith." Barbara moved his hand and put her arms around his neck so she could speak in his ear. She could see some of the people watching them. "You screwed me." She held him tighter. "And good for you. Extreme times require extreme solutions." She was whispering as they stood alone on that carpet in their embrace. "You were a surprise. Way to go. That pajama bit was great; I'll remember it." Now people were deplaning, entering the gate area and streaming around them. Barbara felt Keith begin to tremble and she closed her eyes. "It wasn't a joke. I screwed you too. Remember? You were there," she said. "I'm glad for it. I've been wondering all year how I was going to give that scooter back." He laughed and hugged her. For a moment she was keenly aware of the public scene they were making, but that disappeared and they twisted tighter, kissing. The mock ticket slipped from her fingers behind his neck; a young woman in a business suit knelt and retrieved it and tapped Barbara on the hand. Barbara clutched the ticket and dropped her head to Keith's chest.

"Keith," she said. "What are these people thinking? Make something up."

"No need. They've got it right. That's why we came out here. They think we're saying good-bye."

Simply put, that was the last time Barbara Peterson saw Keith Zetterstrom. She received two postcards from a clinic in Minnesota and then that fall, when she arrived in Providence for her freshman year at Brown, there was a package waiting for her, a large trophy topped by a girl on a motorcycle. She kept it in her dorm window where it was visible four stories from the ground and she told her roommates that it meant a lot to her, that it represented a lot of fun and hard work but her goal had been to win the Widowmaker Hill Climb, and once she'd done that, she sold her bikes and gave up her motorcycles forever.

Notes
on Keith

The first signal from the real world for the story "Keith": I saw a woman in the hospital. I was in the University of Utah Hospital visiting a friend, and walking along the fifth floor corridor, the glassed part which offers a view of the whole valley below, I passed a young woman who was coming the other way dressed in pajamas and a robe. She was walking very slowly, little stab steps, and she had one hand at the throat of the robe, holding it together. She was very beautiful there moving like that on a floor where only dire things transpired. We were alone for a moment in that strange daylight and then gone and I never saw her again.

But I thought about her, trying to make sense of her youth and her beauty and the implications of her being in that serious place in her bedclothes.

I was teaching in a high school at the time, as a visiting writer, and the hundred people I dealt with every day were young and healthy and full of energy and foolish wisdom, and of course being around such people and reading their stories proves soon enough that their worries are real and that they are young and old at once. My wife and I taught in a boarding school for ten years, long enough to see that high school is a little world with all the allegiances and betrayals any small planet needs. There's a good deal of drama every day in a high school. And it was there I made this odd connection: the young woman I saw wasn't gravely ill, she was simply on a lark. She'd come up to the hospital, changed into her pajamas and was walking around. It was a kind of theater; I saw ten examples of it every day at school. And then—logically—I had the other thought: that would be a great date. You go to the hospital with your girlfriend, change into your pajamas and walk around. It might seem oddly out of context, but to a fiction writer working in a high school who was bothered by a woman he'd seen, it made real good sense. So many times as a writer, you ask "what if?" and then follow the premise as it connects to others.

Many years before I saw the woman in the hospital, while I was teaching high school English in Connecticut, I had taught a story which stayed with me for some reason. The story was "How Beautiful with Shoes," (and I can't find the story or the author's name now) and it was set in the thirties, I think, and it was about the night that an escaped inmate from an insane asylum changes the life of a rural farm girl. Two worlds collide, you could say: he's crazy, incandescent, poetic, doomed. She's stolid, prosaic, asleep. The idea took hold of me. There's a moment in that story when after her rescue from a long night with the lunatic, her fiancé—a sturdy farmhand—comes up and embraces her and she tells him something like: Oh, just go away. Leave me alone. It's the first time she's stood up to him. I loved that and pay tribute to it in "Keith."

When I started writing "Keith," I named the girl Barbara Peterson because I wanted it to be a "standard" name and I wanted her to be a standard success in high school, a type. (Also, Barbara Peterson is the name of one of my friends—one, coincidentally, who definitely breaks type.) I find that many times in my stories I start with a person who could be a stereotype, a generic character unit, and then work to earn them credibility, personhood. I did it with homeless people in a story called, "The Governor's Ball," and I did it with DeRay who starts as a biker in "DeRay" and proves himself a kind of rocket scientist. All I wanted my Barbara Peterson in the story to be was a person from the "right" world who meets someone who shows her other possibilities.

I pinched the name Zetterstrom from a fine friend of mine in Connecticut, a wonderful photographer, because the name is not typical and it starts with a Z.

The first hint that Keith might be sick emerged with the writing of the story. I was kind of playing with that option until Barbara's friend Dana said, "Bald kids in high school who don't have earrings have got cancer." Then it tipped for me, and that informed the rest of the story with that notion—that he had a life-threatening disease. The idea that he was doomed came from "How Beautiful with Shoes." The madman in that story was also fated for trouble, and I wanted Keith to be speaking from an edge, an extreme time. Being there has caused him to speak out, and it colors what he says and how he says it. There was some ambiguity in early drafts that he might be acting at being sick for the purpose of tricking, seducing Barbara, but that vanished when I found my final scene in the airport. Their frank exchange in this good-bye scene nailed both characters for me. It is an important moment for Barbara because she gets to climb into personhood, take charge, announce an agenda of her own. I knew all along that she wasn't in the story to be a backboard or counterpoint for Keith. If the story was going to be any good, she'd have to be a full person too. What she tells him there by the boarding gate lets me feel that she's arrived, that in fact she's always been in there, measuring things as well as Keith has.

The airport setting was a bit of a surprise and I found it by looking back through the story at the other sets he'd chosen for their "non-dates." The public picnic, the thrift stores, the restaurant, the hospital. The airport as theatre felt simply like a natural extension for Keith, something he would choose.

He was such a pleasure to write. In each moment I simply conjured what would be the thing that would most challenge the expected response and I let him do or say that. He makes that statement about sulfur. He writes her that note. In their discussion about his truck, he tells Barbara to try riding the school bus—as a kind of adventure. No ordinary high school kid would every associate himself with that kind of remark. And that's what I was after: the non-ordinary.

I have a long personal history with thrift shops, which I won't go into here, except to say I'm always arrested by the bowling balls (most weight for your dollar anywhere) and the trophies, and I've bought more than a few. And there actually used to be a motorcycle hill climbing contest called The Widowmaker Hill Climb in south Salt Lake near where I lived. Having my characters find that big trophy was fun because it felt like a real moment and that's all I'm ever after is a real moment. I didn't see the connection to scooters at the time and I certainly didn't see that the icon of the trophy would become so important in allowing me to close the story quickly in a single paragraph with just the implication I'd hoped for. I didn't see the trophy (big as it was) coming back into the story until I was typing that page.

"Keith" was a story I had in the drawer a long time before I made the final decisions about it and trimmed it up. I'm glad I did. I write from part to whole, staying as specific as I can as I go along in order to create an inventory that might tell me where to go next. "Keith" turned out to be a simple story of moments that speak of a world where wit and a sense of humor might have a chance against the forces of convention.

Errand

Raymond Carver

hekhov. On the evening of March 22, 1897, he went to dinner in Moscow with his friend and confidant Alexei Suvorin. This Suvorin was a very rich newspaper and book publisher, a reactionary, a self-made man whose father was a private at the battle of Borodino. Like Chekhov, he was the grandson of a serf. They had that in common: each had peasant's blood in his veins. Otherwise, politically and temperamentally, they were miles apart. Nevertheless, Suvorin was one of Chekhov's few intimates, and Chekhov enjoyed his company.

Naturally, they went to the best restaurant in the city, a former town house called the Hermitage—a place where it could take hours, half the night even, to get through a ten-course meal that would, of course, include several wines, liqueurs, and coffee. Chekhov was impeccably dressed, as always—a dark suit and waistcoat, his usual pince-nez. He looked that night very much as he looks in the photographs taken of him during this period. He was relaxed, jovial. He shook hands with the maitre d', and with a glance took in the large dining room. It was brilliantly illuminated by ornate chandeliers, the tables occupied by elegantly dressed men and women. Waiters came and went ceaselessly. He had just been seated across the table from Suvorin when suddenly, without warning, blood began gushing from his mouth. Suvorin and two waiters helped him to the gentlemen's room and tried to stanch the flow of blood with ice packs. Suvorin saw him back to his own hotel and had a bed prepared for Chekhov in one of the rooms of the suite. Later, after another hemorrhage, Chekhov allowed himself to be moved to a clinic that specialized in the treatment of tuberculosis and related respiratory infections. When Suvorin visited him there, Chekhov apologized for the "scandal" at the restaurant three nights earlier but continued to insist there was nothing seriously wrong. "He laughed and jested as usual," Suvorin noted in his diary, "while spitting blood into a large vessel."

Maria Chekhov, his younger sister, visited Chekhov in the clinic during the last days of March. The weather was miserable; a sleet storm was in progress, and frozen heaps of snow lay everywhere. It was hard for her to wave down a carriage to take her to the hospital. By the time she arrived she was filled with dread and anxiety.

"Anton Pavlovich lay on his back," Maria wrote in her *Memoirs*. "He was not allowed to speak. After greeting him, I went over to the table to hide my emotions." There, among bottles of champagne, jars of caviar, bouquets of flowers from well-wishers, she saw something that terrified her: a freehand drawing, obviously done by a specialist in these matters, of Chekhov's lungs. It was the kind of sketch a doctor often makes in order to show his patient what he thinks is taking place. The lungs were outlined in blue, but the upper parts were filled in with red. "I realized they were diseased," Maria wrote.

Leo Tolstoy was another visitor. The hospital staff were awed to find themselves in the presence of the country's greatest writer. The most famous man in Russia? Of course they had to let him in to see Chekhov, even though "nonessential" visitors were forbidden. With much obsequiousness on the part of the nurses and resident doctors, the bearded, fierce-looking old man was shown into Chekhov's room. Despite his low opinion of Chekhov's abilities as a playwright (Tolstoy felt the plays were static and lacking in any moral vision. "Where do your characters take you?" he once demanded of Chekhov. "From the sofa to the junk room and back.") Tolstoy liked Chekhov's short stories. Furthermore, and quite simply, he loved the man. He told Gorky, "What a beautiful, magnificent man: modest and quiet, like a girl. He even walks like a girl. He's simply wonderful." And Tolstoy wrote in his journal (everyone kept a journal or a diary in those days), "I am glad I love . . . Chekhov."

Tolstoy removed his woollen scarf and bearskin coat, then lowered himself into a chair next to Chekhov's bed. Never mind that Chekhov was taking medication and not permitted to talk, much less carry on a conversation. He had to listen, amazedly, as the Count began to discourse on his theories of the immortality of the soul. Concerning that visit, Chekhov later wrote, "Tolstoy assumes that all of us (humans and animals alike) will live on in a principle (such as reason or love) the essence and goals of which are a mystery to us. . . . I have no use for that kind of immortality. I don't understand it, and Lev Nikolayevich was astonished I didn't."

Nevertheless, Chekhov was impressed with the solicitude shown by Tolstoy's visit. But, unlike Tolstoy, Chekhov didn't believe in an afterlife and never had. He didn't believe in anything that couldn't be apprehended by one or more of his five senses. And as far as his outlook on life and writing went, he once told someone that he lacked "a political, religious, and philosophical world view. I change it every month, so I'll have to limit myself to the description of how my heroes love, marry, give birth, die, and how they speak."

Earlier, before his t.b. was diagnosed, Chekhov had remarked, "When a peasant has consumption, he says, 'There's nothing I can do. I'll go off in the spring with the melting of the snows.'" (Chekhov himself died in the summer, during a heat wave.) But once Chekhov's own tuberculosis was discovered he continually tried to minimize the seriousness of his condition. To all appearances, it was as if he felt, right up to the end, that he might be able to throw off the disease as he would a lingering catarrh. Well into his final days, he spoke with seeming conviction of the possibility of an improvement. In fact, in a letter written shortly before his end, he went so far as to tell his sister that he was "getting fat" and felt much better now that he was in Badenweiler.

Badenweiler is a spa and resort city in the western area of the Black Forest, not far from Basel. The Vosges are visible from nearly anywhere in the city, and in those days the air was pure and invigorating. Russians had been going there for years to soak in the hot mineral baths and promenade on the boulevards. In June, 1904, Chekhov went there to die.

Earlier that month, he'd made a difficult journey by train from Moscow to Berlin. He traveled with his wife, the actress Olga Knipper, a woman he'd met in 1898 during rehearsals for *The Seagull*. Her contemporaries describe her as an excellent actress. She was talented, pretty, and almost ten years younger than the playwright. Chekhov had been immediately attracted to her but was slow to act on his feelings. As always, he preferred a flirtation to marriage. Finally, after a three-year courtship involving many separations, letters, and the inevitable misunderstandings, they were at last married, in a private ceremony in Moscow, on May 25, 1901. Chekhov was enormously happy. He called Olga his "pony," and sometimes "dog" or "puppy." He was also fond of addressing her as "little turkey" or simply as "my joy."

In Berlin, Chekhov consulted with a renowned specialist in pulmonary disorders, a Dr. Karl Ewald. But, according to an eyewitness, after the doctor examined Chekhov he threw up his hands and left the room without a word. Chekhov was too far gone for help: this Dr. Ewald was furious with himself for not being able to work miracles and with Chekhov for being so ill.

A Russian journalist happened to visit the Chekhovs at their hotel and sent back this dispatch to his editor: "Chekhov's days are numbered. He seems mortally ill, is terribly thin, coughs all the time, gasps for breath at the slightest movement, and is running a high temperature." This same journalist saw the Chekhovs off at Potsdam Station when they boarded their train for Badenweiler. According to his account, "Chekhov had trouble making his way up the small staircase at the station. He had to sit down for several minutes to catch his breath." In fact, it was painful for Chekhov to move: his legs ached continually and his insides hurt. The disease had attacked his intestines and spinal cord. At this point he had less than a month to live. When Chekhov spoke of his condition now, it was, according to Olga, "with an almost reckless indifference."

Dr. Schwohrer was one of the many Badenweiler physicians who earned a good living by treating the well-to-do who came to the spa seeking relief from various maladies. Some of his patients were ill and infirm, others simply old and hypochondriacal. But Chekhov's was a special case: he was clearly beyond help and in his last days. He was also very famous. Even Dr. Schwohrer knew his name: he'd read some of Chekhov's stories in a German magazine. When he examined the writer early in June, he voiced his appreciation of Chekhov's art but kept his medical opinions to himself. Instead, he prescribed a diet of cocoa, oatmeal drenched in butter, and strawberry tea. This last was supposed to help Chekhov sleep at night.

On June 13, less than three weeks before he died, Chekhov wrote a letter to his mother in which he told her his health was on the mend. In it he said, "It's likely that I'll be completely cured in a week." Who knows why he said this? What could he have been thinking? He was a doctor himself, and he knew better. He was dying; it was as simple and as unavoidable as that. Nevertheless, he sat out on the balcony of his hotel room and read railway timetables. He asked for information on sailings of boats bound for Odessa from Marseilles. But he *knew*. At this stage he had to have known. Yet in one of the last letters he ever wrote he told his sister he was growing stronger by the day.

He no longer had any appetite for literary work, and hadn't for a long time. In fact, he had very nearly failed to complete *The Cherry Orchard* the year before. Writing that play was the hardest thing he'd ever done in his life. Toward the end, he was able to manage only six or seven lines a day. "I've started losing heart," he wrote Olga. "I feel I'm finished as a writer, and every sentence strikes me as worthless and of no use whatever." But he didn't stop. He finished his play in October, 1903. It was the last thing he ever wrote, except for letters and a few entries in his notebook.

A little after midnight on July 2, 1904, Olga sent someone to fetch Dr. Schwohrer. It was an emergency: Chekhov was delirious. Two young Russians on holiday happened to have the adjacent room, and Olga hurried next door to explain what was happening. One of the youths was in his bed asleep, but the other was still awake, smoking and reading. He left the hotel at a run to find Dr. Schwohrer. "I can still hear the sound of the gravel under his shoes in the silence of that stifling July night," Olga wrote later on in her memoirs. Chekhov was hallucinating, talking about sailors, and there were snatches of something about the Japanese. "You don't put ice on an empty stomach," he said when she tried to place an ice pack on his chest.

Dr. Schwohrer arrived and unpacked his bag, all the while keeping his gaze fastened on Chekhov, who lay gasping in the bed. The sick man's pupils were dilated and his temples glistened with sweat. Dr. Schwohrer's face didn't register anything. He was not an emotional man, but he knew Chekhov's end was near. Still, he was a doctor, sworn to do his utmost, and Chekhov held on to life, however tenuously. Dr. Schwohrer prepared a hypodermic and administered an injection of camphor, something that was supposed to speed up the heart. But the injection didn't help—nothing, of course, could have helped. Nevertheless, the doctor made known to Olga his intention of sending for oxygen. Suddenly, Chekhov roused himself, became lucid, and said quietly, "What's the use? Before it arrives I'll be a corpse."

Dr. Schwohrer pulled on his big mustache and stared at Chekhov. The writer's cheeks were sunken and gray, his complexion waxen; his breath was raspy. Dr. Schwohrer knew the time could be reckoned in minutes. Without a word, without conferring with Olga, he went over to an alcove where there was a telephone on the wall. He read the instructions for using the device. If he activated it by holding his finger on a button and turning a handle on the side of the phone, he could reach the lower regions of the hotel—the kitchen. He picked up the receiver, held it to his ear, and did as the instructions told him. When someone finally answered, Dr. Schwohrer ordered a bottle of the hotel's best champagne. "How many glasses?" he was asked. "Three glasses!" the doctor shouted into the mouthpiece. "And hurry, do you hear?" It was one of those rare moments of inspiration that can easily enough be overlooked later on, because the action is so entirely appropriate it seems inevitable.

The champagne was brought to the door by a tired-looking young man whose blond hair was standing up. The trousers of his uniform were wrinkled, the creases gone, and in his haste he'd missed a loop while buttoning his jacket. His appearance was that of someone who'd been resting (slumped in a chair, say, dozing a little), when off in the distance the phone had clamored in the early-morning hours—great

God in Heaven!—and the next thing he knew he was being shaken awake by a superior and told to deliver a bottle of Moet to Room 211. "And hurry, do you hear?"

The young man entered the room carrying a silver ice bucket with the champagne in it and a silver tray with three cut-crystal glasses. He found a place on the table for the bucket and glasses, all the while craning his neck, trying to see into the other room, where someone panted ferociously for breath. It was a dreadful, harrowing sound, and the young man lowered his chin into his collar and turned away as the ratchety breathing worsened. Forgetting himself, he stared out the open window toward the darkened city. Then this big imposing man with a thick mustache pressed some coins into his hand—a large tip, by the feel of it—and suddenly the young man saw the door open. He took some steps and found himself on the landing, where he opened his hand and looked at the coins in amazement.

Methodically, the way he did everything, the doctor went about the business of working the cork out of the bottle. He did it in such a way as to minimize, as much as possible, the festive explosion. He poured three glasses and, out of habit, pushed the cork back into the neck of the bottle. He then took the glasses of champagne over to the bed. Olga momentarily released her grip on Chekhov's hand—a hand, she said later, that burned her fingers. She arranged another pillow behind his head. Then she put the cool glass of champagne against Chekhov's palm and made sure his fingers closed around the stem. They exchanged looks—Chekhov, Olga, Dr. Schwohrer. They didn't touch glasses. There was no toast. What on earth was there to drink to? To death? Chekhov summoned his remaining strength and said, "It's been so long since I've had champagne." He brought the glass to his lips and drank. In a minute or two Olga took the empty glass from his hand and set it on the nightstand. Then Chekhov turned onto his side. He closed his eyes and sighed. A minute later, his breathing stopped.

Dr. Schwohrer picked up Chekhov's hand from the bedsheet. He held his fingers to Chekhov's wrist and drew a gold watch from his vest pocket, opening the lid of the watch as he did so. The second hand on the watch moved slowly, very slowly. He let it move around the face of the watch three times while he waited for signs of a pulse. It was three o'clock in the morning and still sultry in the room. Badenweiler was in the grip of its worst heat wave in years. All the windows in both rooms stood open, but there was no sign of a breeze. A large, black-winged moth flew through a window and banged wildly against the electric lamp. Dr. Schwohrer let go of Chekhov's wrist. "It's over," he said. He closed the lid of his watch and returned it to his vest pocket.

At once Olga dried her eyes and set about composing herself. She thanked the doctor for coming. He asked if she wanted some medication—laudanum, perhaps, or a few drops of valerian. She shook her head. She did have one request, though: before the authorities were notified and the newspapers found out, before the time came when Chekhov was no longer in her keeping, she wanted to be alone with him for a while. Could the doctor help with this? Could he withhold, for a while anyway, news of what had just occurred?

Dr. Schwohrer stroked his moustache with the back of a finger. Why not? After all, what difference would it make to anyone whether this matter became known now or a few hours from now? The only detail that remained was to fill out a death certificate, and this could be done at his office later on in the morning, after he'd slept a few hours. Dr. Schwohrer nodded his agreement and prepared to leave. He murmured a few words of condolence. Olga inclined her head. "An honor," Dr. Schwohrer said. He picked up his bag and left the room and, for that matter, history.

It was at this moment that the cork popped out of the champagne bottle; foam spilled down onto the table. Olga went back to Chekhov's bedside. She sat on a foot-stool, holding his hand, from time to time stroking his face. "There were no human voices, no everyday sounds," she wrote. "There was only beauty, peace, and the grandeur of death."

She stayed with Chekhov until daybreak, when thrushes began to call from the garden below. Then came the sound of tables and chairs being moved about down there. Before long, voices carried up to her. It was then a knock sounded at the door. Of course she thought it must be an official of some sort—the medical examiner, say, or someone from the police who had questions to ask and forms for her to fill out, or maybe, just maybe, it could be Dr. Schwohrer returning with a mortician to render assistance in embalming and transporting Chekhov's remains back to Russia.

But, instead, it was the same blond young man who'd brought the champagne a few hours earlier. This time, however, his uniform trousers were neatly pressed, with stiff creases in front, and every button on his snug green jacket was fastened. He seemed quite another person. Not only was he wide awake but his plump cheeks were smooth-shaven, his hair was in place, and he appeared anxious to please. He was hold-ing a porcelain vase with three long-stemmed yellow roses. He presented these to Olga with a smart click of his heels. She stepped back and let him into the room. He was there, he said, to collect the glasses, ice bucket, and tray, yes. But he also wanted to say that, because of the extreme heat, breakfast would be served in the garden this morning. He hoped this weather wasn't too bothersome; he apologized for it.

The woman seemed distracted. While he talked, she turned her eyes away and looked down at something in the carpet. She crossed her arms and held her elbows. Meanwhile, still holding his vase, waiting for a sign, the young man took in the details of the room. Bright sunlight flooded through the open windows. The room was tidy and seemed undisturbed, almost untouched. No garments were flung over chairs, no shoes, stockings, braces, or stays were in evidence, no open suitcases. In short, there was no clutter, nothing but the usual heavy pieces of hotel-room furniture. Then, because the woman was still looking down, he looked down, too, and at once spied a cork near the toe of his shoe. The woman did not see it—she was looking somewhere else. The young man wanted to bend over and pick up the cork, but he was still hold-ing the roses and was afraid of seeming to intrude even more by drawing any further attention to himself. Reluctantly, he left the cork where it was and raised his eyes. Everything was in order except for the uncorked, half-empty bottle of champagne that stood alongside two crystal glasses over on the little table. He cast his gaze about once more. Through an open door he saw that the third glass was in the bedroom, on the nightstand. But someone still occupied the bed! He couldn't see a face, but the figure under the covers lay perfectly motionless and quiet. He noted the figure and looked elsewhere. Then, for a reason he couldn't understand, a feeling of uneasiness took hold of him. He cleared his throat and moved his weight to the other leg. The woman still didn't look up or break her silence. The young man felt his cheeks grow warm. It occurred to him, quite without his having thought it through, that he should perhaps suggest an alternative to breakfast in the garden. He coughed, hoping to focus the woman's attention, but she didn't look at him. The distinguished foreign guests could, he said, take breakfast in their rooms this morning if they wished. The young man (his name hasn't survived, and it's likely he perished in the Great War) said he would be happy to bring up a tray. Two trays, he added, glancing uncertainly once again in the direction of the bedroom.

He fell silent and ran a finger around the inside of his collar. He didn't understand. He wasn't even sure the woman had been listening. He didn't know what else to do now; he was still holding the vase. The sweet odor of the roses filled his nostrils and inexplicably caused a pang of regret. The entire time he'd been waiting, the woman had apparently been lost in thought. It was as if all the while he'd been standing there, talking, shifting his weight, holding his flowers, she had been someplace else, somewhere far from Badenweiler. But now she came back to herself, and her face assumed another expression. She raised her eyes, looked at him, and then shook her head. She seemed to be struggling to understand what on earth this young man could be doing there in the room holding a vase with three yellow roses. Flowers? She hadn't ordered flowers.

The moment passed. She went over to her handbag and scooped up some coins. She drew out a number of banknotes as well. The young man touched his lips with his tongue; another large tip was forthcoming, but for what? What did she want him to do? He'd never before waited on such guests. He cleared his throat once more.

No breakfast, the woman said. Not yet, at any rate. Breakfast wasn't the important thing this morning. She required something else. She needed him to go out and bring back a mortician. Did he understand her? Herr Chekhov was dead, you see. Comprenez-vous? Young man? Anton Chekhov was dead. Now listen carefully to me, she said. She wanted him to go downstairs and ask someone at the front desk where he could go to find the most respected mortician in the city. Someone reliable, who took great pains in his work and whose manner was appropriately reserved. A mortician, in short, worthy of a great artist. Here, she said, and pressed the money on him. Tell them downstairs that I have specifically requested you to perform this duty for me. Are you listening? Do you understand what I'm saying to you?

The young man grappled to take in what she was saying. He chose not to look again in the direction of the other room. He had sensed that something was not right. He became aware of his heart beating rapidly under his jacket, and he felt perspiration break out on his forehead. He didn't know where he should turn his eyes. He wanted to put the vase down.

Please do this for me, the woman said. I'll remember you with gratitude. Tell them downstairs that I insist. Say that.

But don't call any unnecessary attention to yourself or to the situation. Just say that this is necessary, that I request it—and that's all. Do you hear me? Nod if you understand. Above all, don't raise an alarm. Everything else, all the rest, the commotion—that'll come soon enough. The worst is over. Do we understand each other?

The young man's face had grown pale. He stood rigid, clasping the vase. He managed to nod his head.

After securing permission to leave the hotel he was to proceed quietly and resolutely, though without any unbecoming haste, to the mortician's. He was to behave exactly as if he were engaged on a very important errand, nothing more. He was engaged on an important errand, she said. And if it would help keep his movements purposeful he should imagine himself as someone moving down the busy sidewalk carrying in his arms a porcelain vase of roses that he had to deliver to an important man. (She spoke quietly, almost confidentially, as if to a relative or a friend.) He could even tell himself that the man he was going to see was expecting him, was perhaps impatient for him to arrive with his flowers. Nevertheless, the young man was not to become excited and run, or otherwise break his stride. Remember the vase he was carrying! He was to walk briskly, comporting himself at all times in as dignified a manner as possible. He should keep walking until he came to the mortician's house and stood before the door. He would then raise the brass knocker and let it fall, once, twice, three times. In a minute the mortician himself would answer.

This mortician would be in his forties, no doubt, or maybe early fifties—bald, solidly built, wearing steel-frame spectacles set very low on his nose. He would be modest, unassuming, a man who would ask only the most direct and necessary questions. An apron. Probably he would be wearing an apron. He might even be wiping his hands on a dark towel while he listened to what was being said. There'd be a faint whiff of formaldehyde on his clothes. But it was all right, and the young man shouldn't worry. He was nearly a grown-up now and shouldn't be frightened or repelled by any of this. The mortician would hear him out. He was a man of restraint and bearing, this mortician, someone who could help allay people's fears in this situation, not increase them. Long ago he'd acquainted himself with death in all its various guises and forms; death held no surprises for him any longer, no hidden secrets. It was this man whose services were required this morning.

The mortician takes the vase of roses. Only once while the young man is speaking does the mortician betray the least flicker of interest, or indicate that he's heard anything out of the ordinary. But the one time the young man mentions the name of the deceased, the mortician's eyebrows rise just a little. Chekhov, you say? Just a minute, and I'll be with you.

Do you understand what I'm saying, Olga said to the young man. Leave the glasses. Don't worry about them. Forget about crystal wineglasses and such. Leave the room as it is. Everything is ready now. We're ready. Will you go?

But at that moment the young man was thinking of the cork still resting near the toe of his shoe. To retrieve it he would have to bend over, still gripping the vase. He would do this. He leaned over. Without looking down, he reached out and closed it into his hand.

On Where I'm Calling From

I wrote and published my first short story in 1963, twenty-five years ago, and have been drawn to short-story writing ever since. I think in part (but only in part) this inclination toward brevity and intensity has to do with the fact that I am a poet as well as a story writer. I began writing and publishing poetry and fiction at more or less the same time, back in the early 1960s when I was still an undergraduate. But this dual relationship as poet and short-story writer doesn't explain everything. I'm hooked on writing short stories and couldn't get off them even if I wanted to. Which I don't.

I love the swift leap of a good story, the excitement that often commences in the first sentence, the sense of beauty and mystery found in the best of them; and the fact—so crucially important to me back at the beginning and even now still a consideration—that the story can be written and read in one sitting. (Like poems!)

In the beginning—and perhaps still—the most important short-story writers to me were Isaac Babel, Anton Chekhov, Frank O'Connor, and V. S. Pritchett. I forget who first passed along a copy of Babel's *Collected Stories* to me, but I do remember coming across a line from one of his greatest stories. I copied it into the little notebook I carried around with me everywhere in those days. The narrator, speaking about Maupassant and the writing of fiction, says: "No iron can stab the heart with such force as a period put at the right place."

When I first read this, it came to me with the force of revelation. This is what I wanted to do with my own stories: line up the right words, the precise images, as well as the exact and correct punctuation so that the reader got pulled in and involved in the story and wouldn't be able to turn away his eyes from the text unless the house caught fire. Vain wishes perhaps, to ask words to assume the power of actions, but clearly a young writer's wishes. Still, the idea of writing clearly with authority enough to hold and engage the reader persisted. This remains one of my primary goals today.

My first book of stories, *Will You Please Be Quiet, Please?*, did not appear until 1976, thirteen years after my first story was written. This long delay between composition, magazine, and book publication was due in part to a young marriage, the exigencies of child rearing and blue-collar laboring jobs, a little education on the fly—and never enough money to go around at the end of each month. (It was during this long period, too, that I was trying to learn my craft as a writer, how to be as subtle as a river current when very little else in life was subtle.)

After the thirteen-year period it took to put the first book together and to find a publisher who, I might add, was most reluctant to engage in such a cockeyed enterprise—a first book of stories by an unknown writer!—I tried to write fast when I had the time, writing stories when the spirit was with me and letting them pile up in a drawer; and then going back to look at them carefully and coldly later on, from a remove, after things had calmed down, after things had, all too regrettably, gone back to "normal."

Inevitably, life being what it is, there were often great swatches of time that simply disappeared, long periods when I did not write any fiction. (How I wish I had those years back now!) Sometimes a year or two would pass when I couldn't even think about writing stories. Often, though, I was able to spend some of that time writing poems, and this proved important because in writing the poetry the flame didn't entirely putter out, as I sometimes feared it might. Mysteriously, or so it would seem to me, there would come a time to turn to fiction again. The circumstances in my life would be right or at least improved and the ferocious desire to write would take hold of me, and I would begin.

I wrote *Cathedral*—eight of those stories are reprinted here—in a period of fifteen months. But during that two-year period before I began to work on those stories, I found myself in a period of stock-taking, of trying to discover where I wanted to go with whatever new stories I was going to write and how I wanted to write them. My previous book, *What We Talk about When We talk about Love,* had been in many ways a watershed book for me, but it was a book I didn't want to duplicate or write again. So I simply waited. I taught at Syracuse University. I wrote some poems and book reviews, and an essay or two. And then one morning something happened. After a good night's sleep, I went to my desk and wrote the story "Cathedral." I knew it was a different kind of story for me, no question. Somehow I had found another direction I wanted to move toward. And I moved. And quickly.

The new stories that are included here, stories which were written after *Cathedral* and after I had intentionally, happily, taken "time out" for two years to write two books of poetry, are, I'm sure different in kind and degree from the earlier stories. (At the least I think they're different from the earlier stories, and I suspect readers may feel the same. But any writer will tell you he wants to believe his work will undergo a metamorphosis, a sea-change, a process of enrichment if he's been at it long enough.)

V. S. Pritchett's definition of a short story is "something glimpsed from the corner of the eye, in passing." First the glimpse. Then the glimpse given life, turned into something that will illuminate the moment and just maybe lock it indelibly into the reader's consciousness. Make it a part of the reader's own experience, as Hemingway so nicely put it. Forever the writer hopes. Forever.

If we're lucky, writer and reader alike, we'll finish the last line or two of a short story and then just sit for a minute, quietly. Ideally, we'll ponder what we've just written or read; maybe our hearts or our intellects will have been moved off the peg just a little from where they were before. Our body temperature will have gone up, or down, by a degree. Then, breathing evenly and steadily once more, we'll collect ourselves, writers and readers alike, get up, "created of warm blood and nerves," as a Chekhov character puts it, and go on to the next thing: Life. Always life.

John Gardner: The Writer as Teacher

(This essay formed the Foreword to John Gardner's
On Becoming a Novelist, *New York, 1983.)*

A long time ago—it was the summer of 1958—my wife and I and our two baby children moved from Yakima, Washington, to a little town outside of Chico, California. There we found an old house and paid twenty-five dollars a month rent. In order to finance this move, I'd had to borrow a hundred and twenty-five dollars from a druggist I'd delivered prescriptions for, a man named Bill Barton.

This is by way of saying that in those days my wife and I were stone broke. We had to eke out a living, but the plan was that I would take classes at what was then called Chico State College. But for as far back as I can remember, long before we moved to California in search of a different life and our slice of the American pie, I'd wanted to be a writer. I wanted to write, and I wanted to write anything—fiction, of course, but also poetry, plays, scripts, articles for *Sports Afield, True Argosy,* and *Rogue* (some of the magazines I was then reading), pieces for the local newspaper—anything that involved putting words together to make something coherent and of interest to someone besides myself. But at the time of our move, I felt in my bones I had to get some education in order to go along with being a writer. I put a very high premium on education then—much higher in those days than now, I'm sure, but that's because I'm older and have an education. Understand that nobody in my family had ever gone to college or for that matter had gotten beyond the mandatory eighth grade in high school. I didn't *know anything,* but I knew I didn't know anything.

So along with this desire to get an education, I had this very strong desire to write; it was a desire so strong that, with the encouragement I was given in college, and the insight acquired, I kept on writing long after "good sense" and the "cold facts"—the "realities" of my life told me, time and again, that I ought to quit, stop the dreaming, quietly go ahead and do something else.

That fall at Chico State I enrolled in classes that most freshman students have to take, but I enrolled as well for something called Creative Writing 101. This course was going to be taught by a new faculty member named John Gardner, who was already surrounded by a bit of mystery and romance. It was said that he'd taught previously at Oberlin College but had left there for some reason that wasn't made clear.

One student said Gardner had been fired—students, like everyone else, thrive on rumor and intrigue—and another student said Gardner had simply quit after some kind of flap. Someone else said his teaching load at Oberlin, four or five classes of freshman English each semester, had been too heavy and that he couldn't find time to write. For it was said that Gardner was a real, that is to say a practicing, writer—someone who had written novels and short stories. In any case, he was going to teach CW 101 at Chico State, and I signed up.

I was excited about taking a course from a real writer. I'd never laid eyes on a writer before, and I was in awe. But where were these novels and short stories, I wanted to know. Well, nothing had been published yet. It was said that he couldn't get his work published and that he carried it around with him in boxes. (After I became his student, I was to see those boxes of manuscript. Gardner had become aware of my difficulty in finding a place to work. He knew I had a young family and cramped quarters at home. He offered me the key to his office. I see that gift now as a turning point. It was a gift not made casually, and I took it, I think, as a kind of mandate—for that's what it was. I spent part of every Saturday and Sunday in his office, which is where he kept the boxes of manuscript. The boxes were stacked up on the floor beside the desk. *Nickel Mountain,* grease-penciled on one of the boxes, is the only title I recall. But it was in his office, within sight of his unpublished books, that I undertook my first serious attempts at writing.)

When I met Gardner, he was behind a table at registration in the women's gym. I signed the class roster and was given a course card. He didn't look anywhere near what I had imagined a writer should look like. The truth is, in those days he looked and dressed like a Presbyterian minister, or an FBI man. He always wore a black suit, a white shirt, and a tie. And he had a crewcut. (Most of the young men my age wore their hair in what was called a "DA" style—a "duck's ass"—the hair combed back along the sides of the head onto the nape and plastered down with hair oil or cream.) I'm saying that Gardner looked very square. And to complete the picture he drove a black four-door Chevrolet with black-wall tires, a car so lacking in any amenities it didn't even have a car radio. After I'd gotten to know him, had been given the key, and was regularly using his office as a place to work, I'd be at his desk in front of the window on a Sunday morning, pounding away on his typewriter. But I'd be watching for his car to pull up and park on the street out in front, as it always did every Sunday. Then Gardner and his first wife, Joan, would get out and, all dressed up in their dark, severe-looking clothes, walk down the sidewalk to the church where they would go inside and attend services. An hour and a half later I'd be watching for them as they came out, walked back down the sidewalk to their black car, got inside, and drove away.

Gardner had a crewcut, dressed like a minister or an FBI man, and went to church on Sundays. But he was unconventional in other ways. He started breaking the *rules* on the first day of class; he was a chain smoker and he smoked continuously in the classroom. When another faculty member who used the same room reported on him, Gardner merely remarked to us on the man's pettiness and narrowmindedness, opened windows, and went on smoking.

For short story writers in his class, the requirement was one story, ten to fifteen pages in length. For people who wanted to write a novel—I think there must have been one or two of these souls—a chapter of around twenty pages, along with an outline of the rest. The kicker was that this one short story, or the chapter of the novel, might have to be revised ten times in the course of the semester for Gardner to be satisfied with it. It was a basic tenet of his that a writer found what he wanted to say in the ongoing process of *seeing* what he'd said. And this seeing, or seeing more clearly, came about through revision. He believed in revision, endless revision; it was something very close to his heart and something he felt was vital for writers, at whatever the stage of their development. And he never seemed to lose patience rereading a student story, even though he might have seen it in five previous incarnations.

I think his idea of a short story in 1958 was still pretty much his idea of a short story in 1982; it was something that had a recognizable beginning, middle, and an end to it. Once in a while he'd go to the blackboard and draw a diagram to illustrate a point he wanted to make about rising or falling emotion in a story—peaks, valleys, plateaus, resolution, *denouement,* things like that. Try as I might, I couldn't muster a great deal of interest to really understand this side of things, the stuff he put on the blackboard. But what I did understand was the way he would comment on a story that was undergoing class discussion. Gardner might wonder aloud about the author's reasons for writing a story about a crippled person, say, and leaving out the fact of the character's crippledness until the very end of the story. "So you think it's a good idea not to let the reader of the story know this man is crippled until the last sentence?" His tone of voice conveyed his disapproval, and it didn't take more than an instant for everyone in the class to see that it wasn't a good strategy to use. Any strategy that kept important and necessary information away from the reader in the hope of overcoming him by surprise at the end of the story was cheating.

In class he was always referring to writers whose names I was not familiar with. Or if I knew their names, I'd never read the work. Conrad. Céline. Katherine Anne Porter. Isaac Babel. Walter van Tilburg. Chekhov. Hortense Calisher. Curt Harnack. Robert Penn Warren. (We read a story of Warren's called "Blackberry Winter." For one reason or another, I didn't care for it, and I said so to Gardner. "You'd better read it again," he said, and he was not joking.) William Gass was another writer he mentioned. Gardner was just starting his magazine, *MSS,* and was about to publish "The Pedersen Kid" in the first issue. I began reading the story in manuscript, but I didn't understand it and again I complained to Gardner. This time he didn't tell me I should read it again; he simply took the story away from me. He talked about James Joyce and Flaubert and Isak Dinesen as if they lived just down the road, in Yuba City. He said, "I'm here to tell you who to read as well as teach you how to write." I'd leave class in a daze and make straight for the library to find books by these writers he was talking about.

Hemingway and Faulkner were the reigning authors in those days. But altogether I'd probably read at the most two or three books by these fellows. Anyway, they were so well-known and so much talked about, they couldn't be all that good, could they? I remember Gardner telling me, "Read all the Faulkner you can get your hands on, and then read all of Hemingway to clean the Faulkner out of your system."

He introduced us to the "little" or literary periodicals by bringing a box of these magazines to class one day and passing them around so that we could acquaint ourselves with their names, see what they felt like to hold in the hand. He told us that this was where most of the best fiction in the country and just about all of the poetry was appearing. Fiction, poetry, literary essays, book reviews of recent books, criticism of *living* authors *by* living authors. I felt wild with discovery in those days.

For the seven or eight of us who were in his class, he ordered heavy black binders and told us we should keep our written work in these. He kept his own work in such binders, he said, and of course that settled it for us. We carried our stories in those binders and felt we were special, exclusive, singled out from others. And so we were.

I don't know how Gardner might have been with other students when it came time to have conferences with them about their work. I suspect he gave everybody a good amount of attention. But it was and still is my impression that during that period he took my stories more seriously, read them closer and more carefully, than I had any right to expect. I was completely unprepared for the kind of criticism I received from him. Before our conference he would have marked up my story, crossing out unacceptable sentences, phrases, individual words, even some of the punctuation; and he gave me to understand that these deletions were not negotiable. In other cases he would bracket sentences, phrases, or individual words, and these were items we'd talk about, these cases were negotiable. And he wouldn't hesitate to add something to what I'd written—a word here and there, or else a few words, maybe a sentence that would make clear what I was trying to say. We'd discuss commas in my story as if nothing else in the world mattered more at that moment—and, indeed, it did not. He was always looking to find something to praise. When there was a sentence, a line of dialogue, or a narrative passage that he liked, something that he thought "worked" and moved the story along in a pleasant or unexpected way, he'd write "Nice" in the margin, or else "Good!" And seeing these comments, my heart would lift.

It was close, line-by-line criticism he was giving me, and the reasons behind the criticism, why something ought to be this way instead of that; and it was invaluable to me in my development as a writer. After this kind of detailed talk about the text, we'd talk about the larger concerns of the story, the "problem" it was trying to throw light on, the conflict it was trying to grapple with, and how the story might or might not fit into the grand scheme of story writing. It was his conviction that if the words were blurred because of the author's insensitivity, carelessness, or sentimentality, then the story suffered from a tremendous handicap. But there was something even worse and something that must be avoided at all costs: if the words and the sentiments were dishonest, the author was faking it, writing about things he didn't care about or believe in, then nobody could ever care anything about it.

A writer's values and craft. This is what the man taught and what he stood for, and this is what I've kept by me in the years since that brief but all-important time.

This book of Gardner's seems to me to be a wise and honest assessment of what it is like and what is necessary to become a writer and stay a writer. It is informed by common sense, magnanimity, and a set of values that is not negotiable. Anyone reading it must be struck by the absolute and unyielding honesty of the author, as well as by his good humor and highmindedness. Throughout this book, if you notice, the author keeps saying: "it has been my experience. . . ." It was his experience—and it has been mine, in my role as a teacher of creative writing—that certain aspects of writing can be taught and handed over to other, usually younger, writers. This idea shouldn't come as a surprise to any person seriously interested in education and the creative act. Most good or even great conductors, composers, microbiologists, ballerinas, mathematicians, visual artists, astronomers, or fighter pilots, learned their business from older and more accomplished practitioners. Taking classes in creative writing, like taking classes in pottery or medicine, won't in itself make anyone a great writer, potter, or doctor—it may not even make the person *good* at any of these things. But Gardner was convinced that it wouldn't hurt your chances either.

One of the dangers in teaching or taking creative writing classes lies—and here I'm speaking from my experience again—in the overencouragement of young writers. But I learned from Gardner to take that risk rather than err on the other side. He gave and kept giving, even when the vital signs fluctuated wildly, as they do when someone is young and learning. A young writer certainly needs as much, I would even say more, encouragement than young people trying to enter other professions. And it ought to go without saying that the encouragement must always be honest encouragement and never hype. What makes this book particularly fine is the quality of its encouragement.

Failure and dashed hopes are common to us all. The suspicion that we're taking on water and that things are not working out in our life the way we'd planned hits most of us at some time or another. By the time you're nineteen you have a pretty good idea of some of the things you're *not* going to be; but more often, this sense of one's limitations, the really penetrating understanding, happens in late youth or early middle age. No teacher or any amount of education can make a better writer out of someone who is constitutionally incapable of becoming a writer in the first place. But anyone embarking on a career, or pursuing a calling, risks setbacks and failure. There are failed policemen, politicians, generals, interior decorators, engineers, bus drivers, editors, literary agents, businessmen, basket weavers. There are also failed and disillusioned creative writing teachers and failed and disillusioned writers. John Gardner was neither of these.

My own debt is great and can only be touched on in this brief context. I miss him more than I can say. But I consider myself the luckiest of men to have had his criticism and his generous encouragement.

The Tennessee Waltz

Alan Cheuse

1
Martin

I was dancing with my darling when the feeling hit, and I stopped dead on my feet, Sue Beth bumping up against me just as the laws of physics describe.

"Not again, honey," she said, her usually soft voice verging on annoyance. "Sugar, we got to do something for you."

We were clinging to each other, her arms about my neck, my hands on her hips, a rock formation in the middle of the great flow of dancers at Boots 'n Saddle, a favorite cowboy bar of hers. I liked it well enough, its Cotton-Eyed Joe and mournful country songs just about perfect for the kind of mood I found myself in on Saturday nights when Arlene went out to her "drama" club and the kids ran off with their friends.

"Would you like to go?" Sue Beth, arching up on tiptoe, spoke into my ear.

From the velocity of the dancers and the density of the smoke and musk and whiskey-fog, I could tell that the night was moving along and that, if I could overcome my problem leaving might not be such a bad idea. For the past four Saturdays, while Arlene was at her "rehearsals" and Sue Beth's Andy (Andrew Jackson Goins) worked the night shift at the Telephone Company, we turned and strolled around the dance floor and then repaired to a nearby motel. My house in Oak Ridge was off limits. Even with Arlene away the kids were always in and out. The trailer that Sue Beth shared with her lineman, a tobacco-chewing, salt-and-pepperbearded East Tennessean with a limp—and a smile, I guessed, that usually dared you to say I dare you to talk about something—that was forbidden territory. Not that Sue Beth hadn't suggested we go there the first time. I told her that it was a law of courtesy that kept me from doing that—I wouldn't befoul another man's turf—but of course it was just plain fear. I read the *News-Sentinel* every night after the *Tennessean* and the *Wall Street Journal*. I knew what deep-feeling creatures, prone as much to murder as suicide if pricked by self-doubt or a heart gone wrong, were the local caballeros.

What if Andy came home from work unexpectedly and found us together?

"You're cute," Sue Beth had told me when I finally broke down and explained why I'd rather take a motel way out in Kingston Pike.

"Oh, I am, I am," I joked with her, mind whirling about from place to place in the universe, the lab, my house, the desert where I spent my adolescence, the warm but as yet undiscovered planet where I hoped to spend my old age. Last year I had tried running away from home and that hadn't done any good—but way led on to way and the fuss made by security led to my session, once a week, with the division psychoanalyst, who had run into personnel problems one sunny morn and hired temporary help in the person of Sue Beth Reals.

If that's not fate, then I don't know Einstein.

"You look real nervous," she'd said when I showed up for that Saturday morning session.

"I am," I told her, "nervous like I never was at my senior prom."

And I talked about New Jersey, and she mentioned dancing, and the next thing you know I was asking her to show me one of those cowboy bars some evening if both of us could get free. One or two weekends later and, just like tonight, we were parking alongside one another in the big lot behind Boots 'n Saddle and lining up to get our hands stamped at the door. I hadn't figured out too well just what I was in for—not in the way of the spectacle, that is—and had arrived sporting a string tie that Arlene had bought me many years ago in Taos and a pair of boots I usually wore only when I was mowing the lawn. Sue Beth made my heart leap a little by the care she'd put into her own costume. She had combed out her medium-length, honey-colored hair into a moderate version of the thing we used to call a ducktail, buttoned herself into a shirt with frilly collar and cuffs so white it gave back every scintilla of light it passed beneath, and eased into jeans that boldly outlined her thighs high up.

I was more nervous about stepping out (single step or two-step, whatever the rhythm turned out to be) in my own town than I'd been about pulling a Gauguin and heading without so much as a word of notice for Hereheretue, belle isle of the tropics. Who could say why? It was much more of a scandal to take off the way I did than any rumors the sight of me and Sue Beth arm in arm prancing to "Waltz Across Texas" could inspire—and who that knew me frequented a place such as Boots 'n Saddle? The head of our company? The chief of security? The FBI, CIA, NBC, CBS? I'd never been good with other people. I'd backed into romance and a marriage and family with Arlene the way I used to find my way around the streets of a big city like New York, bumped and shoved and half-pushed by others. The desert years had been the happiest, blessed by air perfect for my adolescent's skin and a welcome absence of people. I lived and ate and slept the project and nobody could get through to me who didn't work with me, and they were for the most part odd ducks like myself, all of them older but all of them, like me, or at least the way I used to be, most cheerful when thinking about numbers, alone in a room or under the sky.

Sue Beth said she wanted to hear about what I used to do and I was willing to drink Irish coffee and talk as a way of calming myself down. So I told her about all that—I thought that I might as well have been describing the adolescence of a Martian as far as she was concerned, her own life was so different. But somehow she understood the problem it led up to, the sensation that I was an intern on call from another dimension. She'd learned about moments like that by growing up with her preacher "Daddy," as she called him in the familiar tone that we Yankees give up after our first hairs sprout on our chins and elsewhere. Reverend Reals was a man who had always claimed to have been in touch with the Ancient of Days. Though he had gone to his rest fairly early in her life, when Sue Beth was just budding in the chest and getting itchy around boys, hundreds of sinners had felt his touch as he brusquely shoved them beneath the sluggish waters of the Hiwassee. But for each one he'd baptised he'd apparently taken their sins on his shoulders, or in his liver, to be exact, tipping back a cup and then another and another of homemade corn liquor when they were first starting out. During the successful years, when boys in the Kinney community with bulging muscles and their hands in their coveralls sidled up to Sue Beth, the preacher's daughter, as though she might have been royalty, he switched to Jack Daniels.

At his funeral, a stringy-haired woman in a pale blue dress showed up and told the assembled family members that she was going to fight them for the possession of the estate.

"There weren't none," Sue Beth explained to me, "but he'd been keeping her all those years by telling her that he was investing money in stocks that was bound to build up and make him rich in his old age. Men! Oh, Lordy! I'm so glad I'm with you tonight, honey, instead of one of them go-rillas I growed up with."

"I'm still a man," I said, sweat pouring down my sides.

"I know, and I'm going to teach you the two-step."

And she did.

When it got to be that time on this one particular evening, multitudes sang along with the establishment's theme as it poured out of the loud speakers: "I got the boots 'n you got the saddle." The chill settled upon our sweating necks and arms and we shivered in the parking lot.

"There's another dance we're doing," I said as I opened the passenger door and watched her, slightly astonished, slide onto the seat.

"What's that, sugar?" Sue Beth, a smile on her narrow painted lips, walked spidery fingers along my shoulder.

"I used to hear it on the radio all the time when I was in New Mexico," I said. "I can't remember the name of the singer, but the song was called 'The Tennessee Waltz.'"

"Piggy Lee," she said.

"Who?" I said.

"Piggy Lee," she said.

"You mean *Peggy?*"

"That's what I said. Piggy. Piggy Lee."

"Here piggy piggy," I said, crooking my finger. "It was Patti Page."

"You making fun of me?" Her mouth opened into an almost perfect O.

"I'm *having* fun," I said. "And it's been so long I can hardly remember that it's not supposed to hurt."

The little death, the French call it, and it felt that way again this latest time. My heart was luffing like a hawk caught in a crosswind. This was supposed to soothe me, I told myself as I drove Sue Beth back to the dance hall parking lot, so why does it throw me into such quantum despond?

"You know what?" Sue Beth said with a sigh, as though she somehow understood even after disengaging from me the deep sadness I felt at the awareness of my own particles, waltzing, whirling, in time to some music whistled by a God or cosmic band with flute and Jew's harp, some country music combo of the cosmos ever mourning the impending divorce among all the matter in the universe.

"What's that?" I heard my voice as flat and uncaring as ever, the way I spoke to Arlene, the way that led me to catch myself when I spoke to the kids. "Sugar," I added. "Sugar, sugar."

"Sugar . . ." She snuggled close to me, the way my daughter did when she was very young. "Sugar, I'm craving one of them doughnuts."

Here was our famous local doughnut, its factory and coffee shop on the corner coming up. Here we stopped and dunked our Krispy Kremes into our coffees. Here we lingered, as was appropriate, animals dreamy if not sad in the wake of our coupling, seeking immediate replenishment of the sugar we had expended in our haste.

I drove the rest of the way to the parking lot without fear of coming apart. But as soon as we rolled over the lip of the entrance Sue Beth shrieked and grabbed the wheel.

"Don't stop!" she yelled—hollered might be more exact. "Keep goin', it's Andy; he's standing right there by that car over there, keep goin'!"

"Was he armed?" I inquired as I turned and rolled us right out of the lot again.

"The ugly go-rilla was standing there talking to a little girl!"

"He'll get in trouble with the police that way," I said, steering us back up the street toward the doughnut shop.

"He's in trouble all right! We're all in trouble. Oh, Lordy," and her voice cracked.

"I thought he was supposed to be working on Saturday nights," I said, feeling the wind without opening a window. My legs trembled and my arms shook even as I held the wheel on a newly paved road.

"That's what he told me," Sue Beth said, "but looks like he's been out sneaking around with some teenage girl. And he always told me, too, he don't like to come to the dance hall because of his leg."

"His leg?"

"His limp. Pull up here," she said, and I turned into the Krispy Kreme parking lot once more.

"Would you like another doughnut?"

"At a time like this? When I just discovered the go-rilla I'm living with is a cheater?"

"Why not?"

"Would it do me good?"

"Nothing can hurt you any more," I said.

"Who you think I am? Piggy Lee?"

I hugged her right then and there. "You made a pun, didn't you?"

"Did I? I guess I did."

A few minutes later I deposited Sue Beth back at the parking lot which was safe now, with her gorilla apparently gone off with the girl. On the drive back to Oak Ridge, rolling past mile after mile of kudzu vine still growing in the dark despite the onset of autumn, I heard Simon and Garfunkel sing "Scarborough Fair" on the radio. And I wept because I couldn't go with them. I had a project in the lab that I had to finish—or it must finish me—and hungers that kept me rummaging about the town, and nothing Arlene or the kids, who were spending the night with friends, as it turned out, nothing they could still. One day the entire earth might be covered with nothing but water and desert and kudzu. Remember me to one who lives there.

2

Andy

All the songs you hear as a boy out in the country, they tell you there's nothing so lonesome as a train whistle blowing in the night. But I think that's got to change. I left work early—unusual, but my stomach was kicking hell out of me. Something I ate, maybe, but probably something I was chewing. It was a Co-Cola I drank along with a little pinch of Red Man and a dash of the good white powder my friend Dewey brung back from a roofing job he done for a rich kid out in Sequoyah. Supposed to clear out your head, but what it did for me after the clearing, like somebody set a bomb under that roof, was everything caved in on top of me. My stomach started kicking like hell. So I come back. And like I was saying about lonesome, it used to be the train whistle in the night, but the new lonesome, *lonesome for our time,* like they might say on the television, is walking into the trailer expecting to find the best gal you ever had sitting up in front of the television waiting for you wearing nothing but one of her shortest nightgowns, a glass of whiskey in her hand, a smile on her face, that look in her eyes, and your own glass set right there on the table where she's got her pretty feet all propped up, waiting for you to pour yourself a taste—and, instead you find "Love Boat" showing on the screen with nobody watching, the sound way down, a half-filled cup of coffee on the kitchen table, a few ants enjoying themselves with a bit of crumbled Twinkies on the counter, smell of cigarettes and whiskey on the air.

I went right into the bedroom, and my heart sunk like a tire iron in Loudon Lake. There was a depression at the end of the bed big enough for Sue Beth's sweet behind, the odor of her perfume, honeysuckle, and along with her, gone is also her best cowgirl dancing clothes.

"Well, shee-it," a voice says in my ear. "Shee-it."

"And your Wichita lineman, is still on the line," was going through my head while I was driving to the dance hall, don't know why; well, I do, because I'm a lineman and she likes Glen Campbell, and I guess, well, I figure she's stringing me along and the way my heart feels, all swole up, I might as well be the fellow in the song. I pass motel after motel on the way down the Pike, and hamburger joints, and some movie theaters, and more motels, more motels, and Saturday night when I'm working overtime I never think about what the rest of the world is doing; but tonight here I am driving past these places, and I know that everybody is drinking and eating and making love while I'm just passing by, my stomach one hell of a party.

Who is she to be running off like that? Who is she? I give her what I do, help her make her car payments and fix up the trailer! She quit her job as ticket taker, I help her get through. She quit her job in the supermarket, I help her get through. She takes the job at the doctor's office and keeps on working, and you think I never did help her when she needed me. The doctor's office. The doctor?

I know her. She's a sweet thing, but she also got a big pull for money. And I can't go up against no doctor and hold my own. Not when it comes to money.

There's the sign, and the parking lot as full as I ever seen it. Her car ain't nowhere in sight, but then I can't go looking through the whole lot when I got to go inside and find her in the flesh.

And her daddy was a preacher.

Who knows what she wants? I'll bet she sure don't.

The way things has changed since I was a boy, and that wasn't all that long ago.

What's that there psychiatrist's name?

"Good evenin'."

"Howdy."

"That'll be two dollars. I need to stamp your hand."

I held out my paw to the gal with the ink stamp, trying to look past her into the dark insides of the hall.

"You seen a pretty blonde, hair all frizzed up, wearing probably a white cowgirl blouse or something and tight jeans? Oh, shee-it!" Bad enough I got this bum leg and I have to go put it in my mouth besides! There must have been a hundred and fifty-two thousand of blondes dressed like that, and the gal with the ink stamp gives me a look that tells me I sure ought to know something as simple as that. So I didn't say nothing else and hurried inside and went right up to the bar.

"Stranger?" There's this big guy with glasses under a Stetson serving up the drinks.

I ordered him to pour me a Jack Black. The music started up real loud just then. Willie Nelson, "Bloody Mary Morning." "Willie!" people was yelling, "Willie!" like he was playing live in the place instead of just on a record. I drank up and bought a few more, watching the crowd pouring round the dance floor, seeing nobody I knew, a lot of things out of the past flying through my mind like I was a drowning man, and wondering at the same time if these other sonsabitches at the bar looking so cool, if this bartender with his fancy eyeglasses and his Stetson trying to act city and cowboy at the same time, wondering if they could tell I was feeling low and lonesome? I had got Daddy in my mind, watching him waving good-bye or hello, picturing him in the door frame of the house on Crab Orchard Mountain. I never knew if he was coming in the door or leaving on his rig—and the train calling up from the valley, my stomach churning, remembering how many times he took me up on his knee and told me the story about how when he went west with his folks in the dust storms and got to California and ate the leavings from the fields and the garbage cans and how they must have fixed him up so bad that he had got bad blood and he passed it along to me by way of my one leg shorter than the other.

"Stranger?" the bartender said.

"I had enough of these by now I should be your friend."

Now where was I? Daddy, I was remembering. And he's gone now, and how he'd whoop and holler if he could see me a lineman, regular check, my own little pickup. Of course this Mister Jack Daniels is helping me to forget for a second that because of my leg I'm not up and dancing like the rest of those hairy, horny creatures out on the floor and that Sue Beth was fixing to leave me while I was heading out to work.

"*Friend,*" the bartender says to me, "have one of these," and he slides his knuckles up to my glass and shows me the little red pill he's hiding underneath like the pea in a shell game.

"You know, buddy," I said, after I picked it up and popped it, "you're a lucky fellow, because something got into my head to take your glasses off and feed 'em to you lens by lens."

"*Friend,*" he said, "why'd you want to go and do that?"

"'Cause you're mule shit," I said, feeling this whooping ball of hate drive up out of my aching stomach into my chest and throat.

"On the house," the bartender said, without a crinkle in his cool way of talking, and he knuckled another red one over to me.

Everybody was singing, "*I got the boots 'n you got the saddle.*"

Next thing I know this little bitty woman—perfect body, hear this, just little, kind of like a doll-size female—comes right up to where I'm sitting. I acted real surprised, like nobody had ever done that before.

"Come on, you big hunk," she said, looking me straight between the eyes.

I didn't know whether it was me or Jack D. or the reds talking, but I heard some- one using my voice say, "Sure do 'preciate it, but I'd just like to take you home."

Usual I'm not so bold. When I first got to meet Sue Beth it took me about two times before I even tried to do more than kiss her, though once we got past that everything went real fast. So I didn't know what would happen next. She kept on staring and staring, like she wanted to recognize somebody inside of me—and a friend instead of a stranger—before she'd talk again.

"Well . . . awright," she said, like I was the second prize she won when she really wanted a big stuffed panda bear.

"Does your momma know you're out this late?" I said to her when we got to the parking lot. I was trying not to limp and be real charming and make her laugh, because I was flying high inside.

She swung quick and hard, leaving me with a stinging jaw. I pulled back and slapped her in the head—she was so low I missed her face—and she bumped up against a car and dropped her keys. We got down on our knees to look for them and she started laughing, laughing.

"What's the joke, sugar?" I said.

And she looked up at me from where she was kneeling shoulder-high alongside me and said, "Looks like a dang prayer meeting, don't you think, Mr. Cool Hand Luke?"

3
Sue Beth

I was laying in the dark waiting for Andy to come on back, thinking about where I been, where I want to go, listening to the whistle of the L & N freight rumbling in from Nashville and then I must have dreamed because the next thing I knew I was sitting up in bed, feeling around in the empty place where Andy should have been and remembering that I had seen the woman in the blue dress rising up out of the waters of the Hiwassee, and she had a big grin on her face and I saw Daddy, his ugly big-nosed smile lighting up the world, and he annointed her a second time with the waters of the slow-flowing river, the same dream pretty much I had on and off for years now, and then Momma reaching out to me across the stream, and she's saying, "Little lamby, the Lord gave you feet to dance and Piggy Lee to sing with," and I blushed all over—this being a new part of the dream, I just didn't know it was coming—and the woman in blue was standing there at my side, and she handed me a kerchief and I dabbed at little spots of blood on my knees and my ankles, all this talk about sinning in a dream of old-timey washing away of sins. I was trying to ponder on it when the sun come bright smack through the window of the trailer and I got up real slow, wishing I'd a brought some of them Krispy Kremes home with me instead of eating two more while waiting for Andy to leave the parking lot. The handsomest preacher was on the TV, his hair all blowed dry like Farrah Fawcett's, and I was thinking what Daddy would have looked like if he'd a lived long enough; and the next thing I know Andy comes through the door, smelling like he spent the night in a barrel of fish and tobacco juice.

"Lordy," he said in a moan like a hurt dog.

"How you like 'em?" I heard myself asking him.

"Like what?" He held both hands to his head, like he was trying to keep it from falling into two pieces. His shirt was tore and he had a scratch like from a child or an animal along his right cheek.

"Your eggs," I said.

He looked at me like he was trying to decide whether to kill me or kiss me, and I gave him the same look back, figuring that if we both was to be true to what we said we believed in he would turn right around and walk out the door and I would pack and go my own way, and the only thing left in this God-forsook trailer would be the eggs frying in the skillet alongside the curling bacon, and the preacher with movie star's hair working his mouth without sound, alone, all alone on the screen that you could hardly see now because of the angle of the light coming in the window. Sometimes it seems like our lives was made of trying to be music, but nobody was singing now.

Writing It Down for James: Some Thoughts on Reading Towards the Millennium

On a rainy Washington December night, this traveler drove over to the Congressional Office Building on Capitol Hill to attend the Christmas party of a local literacy council. A group of young professionals, many of them lawyers and college teachers, who serve as tutors for the District's largest adult literacy project—not an official part of either the D.C. or federal government, but rather a nonprofit organization that belongs to a national umbrella group fostering the teaching of reading to adults—served plates of roast turkey and baked ham and many side dishes to a couple of dozen adults and a few teenagers, almost all of them black, who share the desire to learn how to read.

One of these late bloomers was a fifty-three-year-old truck driver from South Carolina named James. James picked up a newspaper only about a year and a half ago after a lifetime of work and raising a family. He had dropped out of school at the age of six to pick crops at nearby farms and never went back. Though unable to read a word, he'd performed such tasks as stevedore and foreman at a shipping company; for the last two decades he has been working as a teamster, in some instances hauling his load as far away as the Canadian border without knowing how to read the road signs.

When I expressed my astonishment at this feat, James laughed and said, "Hey, once you pass the driver's test, the rest ain't all that hard. It's usually just a matter of counting. Counting the stop signs, things like that. You recognize landmarks in town or out on the road and you sort of steer by them."

But after a lifetime of living in his own country as though it were a foreign land where he didn't know the language, James decided that since all his children had learned to read and had gone on to good jobs, he could take the time out to learn how to read himself. This he told me over a plate of food, his right leg moving up and down, up and down, his plate shaking on his lap.

"I wanted to learn to read a newspaper, see? I wanted to *read* about life, not just live it. So I can just about do that now. And now I want to read a whole book. I want to read a story. A good story." The desire for a good story—that had been on my own mind ever since I could remember. And for the last three decades reading and writing had become a large portion of my daily life. I write, usually, into the early afternoon, and the rest of the day, when I'm not leading a workshop or at the gym or the supermarket or the movies, I give over to reading. Read, read, read, a rage to read. It's an appetite as great as that for sex and food and even for the air we breathe. Death will be a great disappointment if no love or family or friends come with it, but I'd even forgo food in the next life (if there is one) if I could go on reading the good new novels as they come out. In the last ten years I've reviewed nearly five hundred books for National Public Radio's evening newsmagazine *All Things Considered* and, like most people who love narrative, whether fiction or history or politics or science (though fiction is the best narrative of them all), I've read a lot more than those I've reviewed during this past decade, rereading books as I teach them to my writing students (because as I explain to them, thinking that at the same time if I have to explain it to them then perhaps they are already lost, good writers are good readers and great writers are great readers), rereading as I write essays and articles as well as reviews.

But a lifetime—yours, mine—with books has to begin somewhere. And while talking with James over our plates of turkey at the literacy party, I kept on trying to recall exactly when it was I first learned how to read. James could pinpoint his own beginning with the printed word: on a certain night in June, in Washington, at a restaurant where he had first met his tutor. Before that time, the printed language was a mystery to him, a cipher used by the rest of the world to keep him constantly on his toes. On the job he devised elaborate formulas to keep up with his work. In the supermarket he often depended on the kindness of strangers to tell him where certain foods were located. And as he was talking about his own pre-literate life as an adult, I got carried back to one of the few pre-literate scenes in my own memory.

Once upon a time a young boy—he must have been about three years old—crawled into bed with his mother and father. It was a Sunday morning, in spring, probably, because even though it was light outside the window, his father still lay in bed rather than having gone to work. While his mother created a space between them where the boy burrow beneath the covers, his father reached over to the night table and picked up a rectangular object about six by nine inches—it had an orange and sepia cover, an abstract decision that suggested not quite formed stars and crescents—that he said he had just found in his old trunk from a place he called *Roosh*-a. The boy loved the sound of the word and asked his father to say it again: *Roosh*-a. There was a smell to the object too, this thing made of paper and bound in stiff board, the odor of dust and oranges that had been lying long in the hot sun.

When his father opened the front of it, the boy noticed strange designs stretched out in rows. The only thing he recognized was a drawing, that of a golden rooster-like bird. *The Tale of the golden cockerel,* his father announced as he fixed his eye on the page and began to speak in a strange and incomprehensible fashion, making a series of globlike and skidding sounds, with a lot of phushes and ticks and bubblelike slurs and pauses.

The boy was me, of course, and the man was my father reading to me in Russian, a language I've never learned, from a book of fairy tales that has long ago been lost in the flood of years rushing through a family's life. And he of course is gone, too, and I'm old enough now to have a while ago put aside such fairy tales and think instead about what novels to give as gifts to my children for Christmas and other occasions. But I still recall the way my father opened to the first page of that now lost volume and began to make those sounds with his mouth and tongue, interpreting the odd designs in front of him as if it were the easiest thing in the world. It was from this day on that I decided, I believe—if "deciding" is what children at that age I was then ever do—that I would learn to read for myself.

I don't actually remember when I first mastered this basic intellectual aptitude. As Roger Shattuck has pointed out in a recent essay, few of us do. "Most minds," he says, "bury those early faltering steps under recollections of later rewards—the fairy tales or comic books on which we perfected our new skill." But some writers have tried to remember. Novelist Nicholas Delbanco describes a wonderful example of this when he writes of a transatlantic crossing, from England to America, at the age of six. On the third day out, he recalls, he received his first pair of long pants and he taught himself to read using a book about boats. Suddenly "the alphabet's tumblers went click." I remember the feel of it, the pride in it, the pleasure, the way the world made sense." Only as a middle-aged adult did he find a copy of a book called *Henry's Green Wagon,* inscribed to him from his kindergarten teacher in London for being "the best reader in Miss Jamaica's Kindergarten Class" in the year before his voyage.

I don't recollect beyond my one tantalizing session with the book of Russian fairy tales that my father ever read to me again. Or my mother. Though I suppose they must have. I certainly hope that my children recall the time that I read to them. If Delbanco can't recall winning his award from Miss Jamaica' s kindergarten class, I probably shouldn't expect my son or daughters to keep in mind the hours we spent going over *The Little Engine that Could* or the "Ant and Bee" stories. If we do teach our children to read we can never forget the first few times that they skate off across the page on their own, a thrill in life something like the first time we sail away on our bikes without the use of training wheels.

An industry now supports this hope-filled activity. The middle class is urged to prep its children in advance of school. "Improved reading skills begin at home," say headlines in the "Parent and Child" columns of the *New York Times*. You can buy books, take courses. And you can hook your child up to your computer and plug in such programs as the Disney-made "Mickey's ABCs" and "Follow the Reader." You can learn tips about how to encourage your children to read. And read to them yourself. In a statement of what seems to be the Original Sin of illiteracy Dr. Michael Presslev, a professor of educational psychology at the University of Maryland, is quoted as saying, "The kids who have the most trouble tend to have parents who didn't read to them when they were younger . . . and didn't see their parents or other people reading and writing."

But just as I have only that single memory of being read to, and in Russian besides, I don't recall seeing my parents read much at all. I do have the faint recollection of watching my father sit in a small alcove of a second-floor apartment on lower State Street in Perth Amboy, New Jersey, tapping on the keys of a small black, typewriter trying to write stories in English in the manner of the Russian satirists Ilf and Petrov. But I never saw him read anything other than the newspaper or a beat-up old copy of Richard Halliburton's *The Nine Wonders of the World* the texture of whose cover and quality of photographs—waterfalls, drawings of statues—I recall rather than any text. My mother might have read the front page of the newspaper. I never saw her hold any book in her hand.

But I grew up reading, reading like a bandit. And no fairy tales for me. I went straight to comic books. *Archie Comics* at first, and then the superheros, *Superman* and *Batman, Plastic Man, Wonder Woman* and then on to the horror comics, *EC Stories* and *The Heap,* building a collection that rivaled just about any in the neighborhood. Of a Saturday you could see us comic fans, pushing baby carriages left over from our younger siblings' infancies filled with our collections on our way to trade meets at someone's house. After a while a quest for something more than Archie, etc. sent me onward to better reading, which meant, of course, *Classics Illustrated*. The western world's greatest poems and stories turned into comic books, from *The Iliad* and *The Odyssey* on through the centuries all the way to Poe, that was my reading for years of early adolescence.

Some educators these days are encouraging parents to allow their kids to cut their first reading teeth on *Classics Illustrated,* then watch them go on to more complicated books. I watched myself graduate to the serialized Christmas story that appeared in our local newspaper each December, and then to the sea adventures of C. S. Forester, his Captain Horatio Hornblower series, to years and years of science-fiction novels and short stories. Although we "read" *Silas Marner* in junior high school I don't remember a thing about it. It was always the adventure stories and speculative fiction that captured me. Proust's Marcel writes of his afternoons with novels in the fabled Combray:

On the sort of screen dappled with different states and impressions which my consciousness would simultaneously unfold while I was reading, my innermost impulse, the lever whose incessant movements controlled everything else, was my belief in the philosophic richness and beauty of the book I was reading, and my desire to appropriate them for myself, whatever the book might be. . . . Next to this central belief which while I was reading, would be constantly reaching out from my inner self to the outer world, towards the discovery of truth, came the emotions roused in me by the action in which I was taking part, for these afternoons were crammed with more dramatic events than occur, often, in a whole lifetime. These were the events taking place in the book I was reading. . . .

How many summer afternoons and long winter evenings this Jersey Marcel, yours truly, spent lost in this fashion! As you all have been lost, discovering and deepening your imaginative life in such a way as to change your ordinary waking physical life forever.

Except for those math geniuses who are probably anomalies when it comes to the quality of their minds, most of us find this period in which we encounter the mental adventures of reading the most important part of our maturation. Though to try to watch it happen is to see nothing. Last spring, for example, I spent a few days behind one-way glass observing an eighth-grade reading class at a middle school in Huntsville, Texas. I'm not sure what I expected to find, but this was what I saw: several dozen kids from around ages eleven to thirteen seated at their desks or sprawled on large cushions on the floor holding books open in front of them. They moved their limbs and twitched their eyes as they might have in sleep. Scarcely any of them did more than change position on the cushions or cross or extend their legs beneath their desks. Yet the internal processes in their minds, no more visible than coal changing under pressure into diamond, would change their lives. It will help them discover the world in a way like no other, to learn of history and philosophy and science and art, to acquire an awareness of God and insects, of water and the nature of life in a mining town in Belgium in 1900, to study Buddhism and physics, or merely to keep boredom at arm's length on an autumn evening in Great Falls, Montana: to become army captains and sales managers and priests and cotton farmers, and to ponder, if they are so inclined, the relation, between their hometown, in this case, Huntsville, Texas, and the rest of the state, the country, the continent, the world, the solar system, galaxy, and cosmos.

However, you have only to observe a lower-level reading class in order to be reminded, if you need such an elemental tip, that this skill is not part of what we would call human nature. Kids study the shape of the letters and learn to sound each letter group of letters, then make words. We've sounded letters, vowels and consonants resounding and, popping for our own kids. To watch a whole batch of them at once get this training is like witnessing the first hatch of tree frogs in a warm climate in early spring. The entire air fairly sings and squeaks with the wondering noise of it all. But despite the illusion of the naturalness of reading, an activity as everyday as breathing this skill is, in the history of western culture, a relatively new invention. For the majority of humanity in Europe and the West verbal art was spoken or sung. And what we now call illiteracy was once the normal condition of culture in what we also name the Golden Age of Greece.

The thousand years or more prior to the sixth century B.C. in Athens was the time of the Homeric rhetors or rhapsodes, who chanted and sang the great poems of the culture to devoted audiences. It was only with the faltering of the Homeric tradition, when it seemed as though the transmission of the poems in memory from one generation to the next was in danger of dying out, that Pisistratus, the Greek tyrant, ordered that scribes record the performance of the two great epics, *The Iliad* and *The Odyssey*,—on papyrus lest they be lost for all time.

Maybe that's when Paradise was truly lost, when it became necessary to read the great songs that had formerly been sung. Is it C. M. Ciorian who describes this transition as the culture's "fall into language?" Prior to this time no one read because there was no written language, but a hunger was present—present, it seems, from the beginnings of human culture—the hunger for story, for narrative, for the arrangement of incidents into an action, even an action that might move the listener to feel pity and fear. This craving for order with emotional resonance was satisfied during the pre-classical period in the Mediterranean only by oral epic.

Drama arose during the fifth century B.C. and filled, among its other functions, the traditional need for a public gathering at which poetry was performed over an extended period of time. But by the first century A.D. poetry and drama were as often as not read on papyrus as performed. Prose narratives were composed as well, but these, like the *Satyricon* seemed to take second place to the more engaging works of history in the mind of an audience looking, apparently, for a way both to restore a certain order to a life from which the formerly awesome power of the old gods had faded and for exciting and interesting stories that spoke to their own daily round.

Between the decline of Greece and Rome and the withering away of the Christendom that arose to take their place most westerners had to settle for one book, the Bible, with its multitudes of stories, as the storehouse of narrative. It wasn't really until the fourteenth century and the creation of *The Decameron* that secular stories came to prominence as literary art—folk narratives were as plentiful as trees—in Europe. As every school kid used to know, the invention of movable type eventually made it possible for the wide dissemination of texts of all varieties, not just the Bible for which the printing press was first widely used. After Luther's revolt against Rome's authority as the prime interpreter of the Holy Book, literacy became a necessity in his part of Europe for the religious man, and soon evolved into a means of power among the rising merchant class, and reading became a sign that a person was wholly civilized.

Consider for a moment what this meant in existential terms for European society. In the great Homeric age of Greece, any citizen of Athens who could attend the performances of the epics—at four seasonal renderings each year in the great amphitheater of the city could apprehend them merely by listening attentively. To be a citizen thus meant among other things to be a listener, collectively, with all the other citizens of Athens. You listened and the words of the gods, through the conduit of the poet, went directly to your ears, telling of the great heroes and heroines, gods and goddesses, engaged in the straightening out, or messing up, of epic affairs in heaven, earth, and the underworld.

With the breakup of this oral culture and the rise of scriptural authority, reading became a prized activity, not just for the priesthood but for the elite of the continent's court and fief. The book became a metaphor for the world, and reading emerged as a method for interpreting God's creation. To be illiterate meant one stood several stages removed from a knowledge of sacred reality. The idea that one listened to the words of the epic poet and thus heard the language of the muses directly in one's ears became, in this thousand-year interregnum between the demise of oral poetry and the establishment of a secular reading culture, static and sterile when the priest, rather than the poet, served as conduit between holy work and worshiper. With the secularization of storytelling, from Boccaccio forward, the printed word became even further detached from its sacred origins in theodicic poetry, telling stories of the death of kings and then barons and then squires, so that by the time of Balzac, say, readers learned of the lives, loves, and sorrows of the denizens of a great secular city, which is to say, themselves.

As the story evolves—some might want to say descends—from scripture to secular tales of middle-class life, the relation of text to reader evolves as well. Christian theology demanded a singular oath from its worshippers, the acceptance of Christ on the part of the individual as his savior. Eighteen hundred years later the individual picks up a copy of *Tom Jones* and finds that the story illuminates part of his or her daily round, a far cry from any hint of salvation. In fact, quite the opposite, if you consider the distance between the hope of heaven and the worlds in contemporary fiction. To pass one's eyes across the lines of the Holy Writ was an act of prayer. What is it then to read modern fiction?

Proust's Marcel has—again—a pretty good way of seeing it. A real person, he asserts, because he is known to us only through our senses, remains opaque to us:

If some misfortune comes to him, it is only in one small section of the complete idea we have of him that we are capable of feeling any emotion: indeed it is only in one small section of the complete idea he has of himself that he is capable of feeling any emotion either. The novelist's happy discovery was to think of substituting for those opaque sections, impenetrable to the human soul, their equivalent in immaterial sections, things, that is which one's soul can assimilate. After which it matters not that the actions, the feelings of this new order of creatures appears to us in the guise of truth, since we have made them our own, since it is in ourselves that they are happening, that they are holding in thrall, as we feverishly turn over the pages of the book; our quickened breath and staring eyes. And once the novelist has brought us to this state, in which, as in all purely mental states, every emotion is multiplied tenfold, into which his book comes to disturb us as might a dream, but a dream more lucid and more abiding than those which come to us in sleep, why then, for the space of an hour he sets free within us all the joys and sorrows in the world, a few of which only we should have to spend years of our actual life in getting to know, and the most intense of which would never be revealed to us because the slow course of their development prevents us from perceiving them. . . .

So we read for pleasure? And for a glimpse of what a coherent vision of the world might be like? It may well be that putting together in our own minds a lifetime of novel reading is close to knowing what it must be like in the mind of God. From these simple stories, of a foolish hidalgo in search of a phantom lover, of the way the past rises up against the present in an English village called Middlemarch, of a Jewish advertising salesman wandering about Dublin looking for sympathy, of a Mississippi family plagued by alcoholism, madness, and imagined incest, of a woman named Maria who aimlessly drives the L.A. freeways, we make up a cosmos.

Think of reading then as an act of praise, of prayer, even, in which individuals reassert their devotion to creation and to the immanent world in which we reside, a world in which every aspect of life, from old used tires piled high in a trash heap to the multiform patterns of snowflakes on a day in high winter, from the sickness of murder to the charity of parenthood, all make up part of a larger pattern. And when we read, we reenact that pattern, an activity that may be as close to serious prayer as most of us will get. Or want to. The organized modern religions hold no patent on expressing devotion to the universe. In fact, the pagan poets, the epic Homers of the oldest stories of the western Mediterranean, show a lot more imagination when it comes to creating great characters and overarching plots than the lyricists and lamenters of the Old and New Testaments. Some great poetry in the former, but nothing much in the latter unless you're spiritually bound to the text. Apply the test of narrative coherence and the pagan epics win hands down. And if the response of the reader, the immersion into a story that delights and instructs in the deepest fashion we know, is any test of the presence of godliness, there's no doubt in my mind which stories show the mark of real deity.

If there is such a thing, The great hype about our present epoch is that we've moved into a period of technology with exponential possibility. The computer has become the metaphor for God. Fine with me. I'm an old science-fiction fan from way back when I first started reading. Let's fly to Jupiter, let's shine our pen-lights into black holes. But on those long flights to the outer planets, or even the short hyper-space commuter hops between galaxies, there's going to be time that's free. Maybe some techno-hotshots will want to use those hours, or months or years, to play computer games or speak with voice-activated viewer-integrated videos. But most of the crew and/or passengers will probably want to read. And what will we do with our spare time once we move out beyond this current pioneering age of space exploration?

Imagine an engineer lying in his bunk in a space station at the outer reaches of our solar system with a peerless view of stars, to borrow a phrase, like dust. As people such as this have done for—what's the phrase here?—countless eons, he picks up a copy of a book, or punches out the text on his computer screen, and begins to read, or, if you will, scan the text. And what might it be? Anything from the stories of Louis, L'Amour to *Paradise Lost* or *Moby Dick,* no doubt. Consider how the poetry of Milton or the ocean scenes of Melville or the cowpokes and bandits of L'Amour would carry him back to earth-themes and earth-places. Even if he's never set foot on Earth, these are still the stories of the species' home place.

Reading—reading is home itself, the place where we go when we wish to be with ourselves and our own minds and our own hearts. It is, an act of the eye which, unlike the viewing of painting or film, has little to do with what the eye perceives before it. Theater and film are the imagination externalized, the created images of the mind or minds of other parties performed objectively before us. While viewing a dance or a play, our eye is captive. Narrative prose or poetry, like music, is a different and, I believe, higher form of representation. The words like musical notations, are mere potential art, waiting to be performed by the reader on the interior stage of the imagination. And just as nothing could be more public than the performance of a play, nothing could be more private than reading a novel or story. As novelist Laura Furman recently suggested, reading may in fact be the last private activity of merit in our culture.

Neurologically one can distinguish the act of reading from the perception of other art forms, such as dance and drama, and one can see how it has a social reality distinct from the external performance, and perception, of ancient oral poetry, medieval drama, and all the other theatrical and visual art that has come after. Unlike oral poetry, which presumed the presence of a community ethos and the absence of what we would call individual ego, prose on the page demands individual participation and, ever since the advent of the age of symbolism, individual interpretation. Everyone in the Homeric audience understood the explicit meaning of the poems— there was no implicit meaning—and celebrated these values and beliefs by means of listening. Since the middle of the eighteenth century, readers have pondered the implicit values of a work within the confines of their own imaginations, and sometimes despaired of a world in which such solitariness is the norm and values are determined by the situation of the individual.

It's no wonder then that we all know so many people who never dare venture seriously into the world of reading. For most people a functioning imagination can be a treacherous and even frightening possession, generating such trivial but annoying conditions as hypochondria on the one hand and much more dangerous situations such as jealousy, paranoia, and megalomania on the other. In this regard, we read *Don Quixote,* the first modern novel, as a book about the dangers of taking books literally. Logos detached from its divine origins is a symbol awaiting interpretation by the god within us, which is to say, our imaginative powers. Woe to him—look at poor Quixote—who takes it at face value.

But that woe, the woe of literalism in an age of symbolic interpretation, is exactly what many Americans rush to embrace, cheered on by McLuhanite theoreticians of the new media. The flat screen, the so-called interactive game, has become the new repository for the faith of tens of millions, the perfect altar for our neo-Puritanical faith in which efficacy is next to godliness, and poetry (which as Auden puts it in his elegy for Yeats) "makes nothing happen," and fiction is relegated to the dust-bin of the new age. There seem to be two kinds of citizens in this nation that produced *Moby Dick* either Ahabs or Ishmaels, and the former appear to be growing in direct proportion to the growth in population while the latter may be diminishing in number.

The figures on readership in America and the reading aptitude scores seem to suggest that this is so. More Ahabs, fewer Ishmaels. American students are reading less and less and watching more and more television every year. The majority of American students, it seems, read only to get along, most of them having been taken over by the games mentality of the new high-tech sales culture. So-called computer literacy has led to what we can only hope is a temporary rise in a new variety of illiteracy, the willful avoidance of narrative fiction and poetry as a means of knowledge and awareness. For the new exploding ranks of American students it seems to be Gameboy over C. S. Forester, and coming right up behind Gameboy, and as far and away from computer games today as they are from pinball, is the burgeoning new industry of virtual reality or VR. Probably within the next five years and certainly within the next ten, VR will become the distraction of choice for the majority of school kids and reading will be demoted even further down the line than where it is now, somewhere between violin lessons and learning a foreign language. In other words, it will become an activity for the few and elite, just as it was in Goethe's Germany where out of sixty million inhabitants only about sixty thousand could read.

That's one scenario, anyway, and not an impossible one, considering the current state of popular culture in which trash seems to have driven out the good. From Emerson to Donahue, from Twain to Robert Fulgham, it's been a bad long slide downward. There are some areas, of course, where we can see actual evolutionary forces at work to good ends, particularly in music. When you consider the way in which jazz has worked its way into the majority consciousness—and radio programming—or the rise of bluegrass, there's cause for celebration.

But in literary culture, things look bleak. For a century that started out with such wise and valuable critics as Van Wyck Brooks and Edmund Wilson and Suzanne Langer and saw its mid-age in the wonderful company of Alfred Kazin and John W. Aldridge, the prospects for the next century seem less plausible. Great literature demands great critics, and though it may well be that all of us who are writing fiction today truly deserve the company of the myopic—and at the same time megalomaniac—crew of neo-Marxists and femsters and post-post-modern academic culture vultures, to have to live with them is not thrilling, to say the least.

On the one hand they puff up second- and third-rate work because it serves their theses, rather than, as the great critics have always done, discovering their values in the great work of the time. On the other, they ignore entire areas of creation because it does not suit their already decided upon values. But more important for the situation of the reader is the fact that none of these critics writes well enough to have much appeal for the lay person. This leaves the playing field to the contest between the reviewers and the publicists. And since many of the best reviewers are novelists (the best of these is John Updike), and put their best efforts as they should into writing fiction rather than just writing about it, the formation of public taste is usually worked on full-time only by the publicists.

I don't mean to attack publicists, They do what they're supposed to do, which is bring the books to the public attention. God help writers these days who don't have a good one working on their behalf. But with hundreds of novels published each year and a limited number of dollars in the pockets of potential readers, someone has to try to do more than merely assert that whatever book they're touting at the moment is the best book of the moment. Yet fewer and fewer voices are speaking with critical authority, style, and intelligence in an effort to help the reading public sort things out.

The results are paradoxical and, for serious readers, not to mention serious writers, somewhat demoralizing. On the one hand we have limited, what we might call "pocket," successes. American versions of the European art novel, that find a small but devoted audience—novels by, say, Joyce Carol Oates or Jayne Anne Phillips. And then there is the work put forward in certain academic circles because it stands as evidence of a particular presentation of American culture (I'm using the word *culture* rather than *life* because this sort of book, for me, at least, never really lives except as part of a larger argument about society), the work of Don DeLillo and Paul Auster coming to mind here. At the other extreme is the big-seller list, which is by and large pretty awful stuff, with Stephen King and Tom Clancy standing at the top of the pile. Now and then a movie tie-in or some ethnic predilection will kick a serious book up on the list, a novel by Doctorow or Edith Wharton or Amy Tan or Toni Morrison. But for the most part mainstream readers elevate the awful to stardom. It's been that way since the creation of the best-seller list just before World War One, and it will certainly not get better for a while, if at all.

For the past few seasons, for example, the novels of Mississippi lawyer John Grisham have been all the rage. When I picked up a copy of *The Firm*—having been surrounded at family occasions by relatives urging me to do it—out of the hope for some fast-paced reading pleasure, the kind I used to look for in those sea stories of Forester and in science fiction and for the past few decades have found in a select band of spy novelists and thriller writers from John Le Carré to Thomas Harris, I was terribly disappointed. But not surprised. The same thing happened years before when I tried out of desperation to fend off the Robert Ludlum crowd. It's all mediocre fare, with no real sense of language or psychology or plot beyond the melodramatic. Danielle Steel and the other romance writers are no better. "He entered her and they made love all night." That sentence of Steel's has stayed with me since I first read it. You can't get much worse and still be writing published fiction. But anything this woman touches turns to money. So that's the good news and bad news about the American reading public, as John Gardner used to say: "The good news is that in actual numbers more people are reading today than ever before in the history of the planet. The bad news is that they're reading mostly shit."

Commercial publishers don't offer all that much optimism. Even as they produce sales figures slightly above last year's, you notice that the dreck makes up most of the sales. Perhaps it's always been so, but lately it seems more so than usual. As the late publisher Sol Stein once put it so ironically and truly, "It's only those books that transmit the culture from one generation to the next" that are being left off the lists these days. And so called "midlist" writers, wonderfully entertaining and serious all in one, find themselves driven out of the marketplace for—where? If the trend keeps moving in this direction, an entire generation of gifted but non-best-selling American fiction writers are headed towards oblivion long before death.

"But look at all the book clubs just here in Washington," a friend pointed out to me the other day when I presented him with this portrait of literary culture and readership in chaos. "There are readers all over the place." And it's true. This is a city of book clubs, and I'm sure there are many, many cities like it across the country. And in the schools across the country there's no dearth of bright readers. Those kids lying on cushions in that classroom in Huntsville, Texas, for example. Or the Jane Austen fans at the private girls school in Troy, New York, where I visited one afternoon to witness a discussion of *Mansfield Park* that was as heated and intense as any gents' squash game. Or the Washington, D.C., public school classes where the PEN/Faulkner Foundation sends visiting fiction writers to discuss their work with interested students.

It's not that we're sliding back into some dark age of total illiteracy. But as we lurch towards the millennium the news for the future of the American readership is growing exceedingly strange. McLuhanite doomsayers are appearing on all sides. Ivan Illich, for example, argues in his new book *In the Vineyard of the Text* that "the age of the bookish text seems to be passing." The advent of the personal computer and the electronic era, Illich goes on, has irrevocably undermined the primacy of the book and altered our way of pursuing knowledge. Such faddish visions make the writer's heart sink.

But it's the reader in me more than the writer that takes the greatest offense. Having grown up in the time of the Big Talk about the Death of the Novel and now finding myself on the verge of an epoch in which the Big Talk focuses on the Death of Literature and possibly even the Death of the Book itself, all the Jersey rises up in me and wants to spit on the Reeboks of whatever current theologian of culture makes this argument. And there's no help from the academy either. In exactly that quarter where you'd think you might find people professing their love of literature and the importance, if not the primacy, of the art of fiction and poetry, you meet instead theory-taught ideologues, waving foreign paradigms about in place of scripture, telling us of every reason under the sun for spending time with a book except the necessary ones.

To know another mind. To know another life. To feel oneself in the heart of another age, in the heart of another human being. To live out the entire trajectory of a human motivation and understand its fullness in time. To move out of ourselves, lifted into another scene, another action, another destiny, so that we might gain a better sense of our own. To warm our spirits by the heat of a fine story, to help us keep the vision (even if illusion) of order in a world constantly on the verge of chaos. Bored theoreticians, losing hold of their own humanity, turn away from these blessings that the novel offers in order to further their own pallid fantasies of the modern spirit. And by shirking their responsibility towards the very humanist tradition that spawned them, they show their contempt not only for their own best (now sadly blighted) tendencies as readers but also for the new generations of potential readers to come who even now in the elementary schools of urban America are doing their best to prepare themselves—sounding their vowels, making out their letters, clumping them together into stumbling words on the page—to partake of the riches of our culture from Homer to Virginia Woolf to John Edgar Wideman. And for the potential new readers among our immigrant populations. And for the newly educated adults, born here but not born free enough to learn to read as children, new readers such as James the truck driver, my companion at the literacy council Christmas supper.

"TV gets to you after a while," James said to me as we were finishing up our turkey, "And let me tell you, life is tough enough without finding out a way to see it a little better. I learned the hard way, by not learning until now. My Mama told us good stories when we were children, but she couldn't write them down. I'm missing a good story like in the old days. So when I get good enough with my reading, that's what I'm going to do."

"Write them down?" I said.

James laughed and chewed a bite of food.

"I don't know if I'd ever get that good. But I could like to read one."

"Talking here with you," I told him, "made me remember the first time I ever heard a story, the first time I ever thought about learning how to read."

"Tell me the story," he said.

I explained that I couldn't because it had been in Russian and all these years I had never found the English version of that tale.

"Well, that's a story by itself," he said. "Remembering it, trying to find it, not finding it. Write that one down. And maybe sometime when I get good enough, I'll see it on a page."

So this is what I've done.

The Writer in the Family

E. L. Doctorow

*I*n 1955 my father died with his ancient mother still alive in a nursing home. The old lady was ninety and hadn't even known he was ill. Thinking the shock might kill her, my aunts told her that he had moved to Arizona for his bronchitis. To the immigrant generation of my grandmother, Arizona was the American equivalent of the Alps, it was where you went for your health. More accurately, it was where you went if you had the money. Since my father had failed in all the business enterprises of his life, this was the aspect of the news my grandmother dwelled on, that he had finally had some success. And so it came about that as we mourned him at home in our stocking feet, my grandmother was bragging to her cronies about her son's new life in the dry air of the desert.

My aunts had decided on their course of action without consulting us. It meant neither my mother nor my brother nor I could visit Grandma because we were supposed to have moved west too, a family, after all. My brother Harold and I didn't mind—it was always a nightmare at the old people's home, where they all sat around staring at us while we tried to make conversation with Grandma. She looked terrible, had numbers of ailments, and her mind wandered. Not seeing her was no disappointment either for my mother, who had never gotten along with the old woman and did not visit when she could have. But what was disturbing was that my aunts had acted in the manner of that side of the family of making govern- ment on everyone's behalf, the true citizens by blood and the lesser citizens by marriage. It was exactly this attitude that had tormented my mother all her married life. She claimed Jack's family had never accepted her. She had battled them for twenty-five years as an outsider.

A few weeks after the end of our ritual mourning, my Aunt Frances phoned us from her home in Larchmont. Aunt Frances was the wealthier of my father's sisters. Her husband was a lawyer, and both her sons were at Amherst. She had called to say that Grandma was asking why she didn't hear from Jack. I had answered the phone. "You're the writer in the family," my aunt said. "Your father had so much faith in you. Would you mind making up something? Send it to me and I'll read it to her. She won't know the difference."

"That evening, at the kitchen table, I pushed my homework aside and composed a letter. I tried to imagine my father's response to his new life. He had never been west. He had never traveled anywhere. In his generation the great journey was from the working class to the professional class. He hadn't managed that either. But he loved New York, where he had been born and lived his life, and he was always discovering new things about it. He especially loved the old parts of the city below Canal Street, where he would find ships' chandlers or firms that wholesaled in spices and teas. He was a salesman for an appliance jobber with accounts all over the city. He liked to bring home rare cheeses or exotic foreign vegetables that were sold only in certain neighborhoods. Once he brought home a barometer, another time an antique ship's telescope in a wooden case with a brass snap.

"Dear Mama," I wrote. "Arizona is beautiful. The sun shines all day and the air is warm and I feel better than I have in years. The desert is not as barren as you would expect, but filled with wildflowers and cactus plants and peculiar crooked trees that look like men holding their arms out. You can see great distances in whatever direction you turn and to the west is a range of mountains maybe fifty miles from here, but in the morning with the sun on them you can see the snow on their crests."

My aunt called some days later and told me it was when she read this letter aloud to the old lady that the full effect of Jack's death came over her. She had to excuse herself and went out in the parking lot to cry. "I wept so," she said. "I felt such terrible longing for him. You're so right, he loved to go places, he loved life, he loved everything."

We began trying to organize our lives. My father had borrowed money against his insurance and there was very little left. Some commissions were still due but it didn't look as if his firm would honor them. There was a couple of thousand dollars in a savings bank that had to be maintained there until the estate was settled. The lawyer involved was Aunt Frances's husband and he was very proper. "The estate!" my mother muttered, gesturing as if to pull out her hair. "The estate!" She applied for a job part-time in the admissions office of the hospital where my father's terminal illness had been diagnosed, and where he had spent some months until they had sent him home to die. She knew a lot of the doctors and staff and she had learned "from bitter experience," as she told them, about the hospital routine. She was hired.

I hated that hospital, it was dark and grim and full of tortured people. I thought it was masochistic of my mother to seek out a job there but did not tell her so.

We lived in an apartment on the corner of 175th Street and the Grand Concourse, one flight up. Three rooms. I shared the bedroom with my brother. It was jammed with furniture because when my father had required a hospital bed in the last weeks of his illness we had moved some of the living-room pieces into the bedroom and made over the living room for him. We had to navigate bookcases, beds, a gateleg table, bureaus, a record player and radio console, stacks of 78 albums, my brother's trombone and music stand, and so on. My mother continued to sleep on the convertible sofa in the living room that had been their bed before his illness. The two rooms were connected by a narrow hall made even narrower by bookcases along the wall. Off the hall were a small kitchen and dinette and a bathroom. There were lots of appliances in the kitchen—broiler, toaster, pressure cooker, counter-top dishwasher, blender—that my father had gotten through his job, at cost. A treasured phrase in our house: *at cost*. But most of these fixtures went unused because my mother did not care for them. Chromium devices with timers or gauges that required the reading of elaborate instructions were not for her. They were in part responsible for the awful clutter of our lives and now she wanted to get rid of them. "We're being buried," she said. "Who needs them!"

So we agreed to throw out or sell anything inessential. While I found boxes for the appliances and my brother tied the boxes with twine, my mother opened my father's closet and took out his clothes. He had several suits because as a salesman he needed to look his best. My mother wanted us to try on his suits to see which of them could be altered and used. My brother refused to try them on. I tried on one jacket, which was too large for me. The lining inside the sleeves chilled my arms and the vaguest scent of my father's being came to me.

"This is way too big," I said.

"Don't worry," my mother said. "I had it cleaned. Would I let you wear it if I hadn't?"

It was the evening, the end of winter, and snow was coming down on the windowsill and melting as it settled. The ceiling bulb glared on a pile of my father's suits and trousers on hangers flung across the bed in the shape of a dead man. We refused to try on anything more, and my mother began to cry.

"What are you crying for?" my brother shouted. "You wanted to get rid of things, didn't you?"

A few weeks later my aunt phoned again and said she thought it would be necessary to have another letter from Jack. Grandma had fallen out of her chair and bruised herself and was very depressed.

"How long does this go on?" my mother said.

"It's not so terrible," my aunt said, "for the little time left to make things easier for her."

My mother slammed down the phone. "He can't even die when he wants to!" she cried. "Even death comes second to Mama! What are they afraid of, the shock will kill her? Nothing can kill her. She's indestructible! A stake through the heart couldn't kill her!"

When I sat down in the kitchen to write the letter I found it more difficult than the first one. "Don't watch me," I said to my brother. "It's hard enough."

"You don't have to do something just because someone wants you to," Harold said. He was two years older than me and had started at City College; but when my father became ill he had switched to night school and gotten a job in a record store.

"Dear Mama," I wrote. "I hope you're feeling well. We're all fit as a fiddle. The life here is good and the people are very friendly and informal. Nobody wears suits and ties here. Just a pair of slacks and a short-sleeved shirt. Perhaps a sweater in the evening. I have bought into a very successful radio and record business and I'm doing very well. You remember Jack's Electric, my old place on Forty-third Street? Well, now it's Jack's Arizona Electric and we have a line of television sets as well."

I sent that letter off to my Aunt Frances, and as we all knew she would, she phoned soon after. My brother held his hand over the mouthpiece. "It's Frances with her latest review," he said.

"Jonathan? You're a very talented young man. I just wanted to tell you what a blessing your letter was. Her whole face lit up when I read the part about Jack's store. That would be an excellent way to continue."

"Well, I hope I don't have to do this anymore, Aunt Frances. It's not very honest."

Her tone changed. "Is your mother there? Let me talk to her."

"She's not here," I said.

"Tell her not to worry," my aunt said. "A poor old lady who has never wished anything but the best for her will soon die."

I did not repeat this to my mother, for whom it would have been one more in the family anthology of unforgivable remarks. But then I had to suffer it myself for the possible truth it might embody. Each side defended its position with rhetoric, but I, who wanted peace, rationalized the snubs and rebuffs each inflicted on the other, taking no stands, like my father himself.

Years ago his life had fallen into a pattern of business failures and missed opportunities. The great debate between his family on the one side, and my mother Ruth on the other, was this: who was responsible for the fact that he had not lived up to anyone's expectations?

As to the prophecies, when spring came my mother's prevailed. Grandma was still alive.

One balmy Sunday my mother and brother and I took the bus to the Beth El cemetery in New Jersey to visit my father's grave. It was situated on a slight rise. We stood looking over rolling fields embedded with monuments. Here and there processions of black cars wound their way through the lanes, or clusters of people stood at open graves. My father's grave was planted with tiny shoots of evergreen but it lacked a headstone. We had chosen one and paid for it and then the stone-cutters had gone on strike. Without a headstone my father did not seem to be honorably dead. He didn't seem to me properly buried.

My mother gazed at the plot beside his, reserved for her coffin. "They were always too fine for other people," she said. "Even in the old days on Stanton Street. They put on airs. Nobody was ever good enough for them. Finally Jack himself was not good enough for them. Except to get them things wholesale. Then he was good enough for them."

"Mom, please," my brother said.

"If I had known. Before I ever met him he was tied to his mama's apron strings. And Essie's apron strings were like chains, let me tell you. We had to live where we could be near them for the Sunday visits. Every Sunday, that was my life, a visit to mamaleh. Whatever she knew I wanted, a better apartment, a stick of furniture, a summer camp for the boys, she spoke against it. You know your father, every decision had to be considered and reconsidered. And nothing changed. Nothing ever changed."

She began to cry. We sat her down on a nearby bench. My brother walked off and read the names on stones. I looked at my mother, who was crying, and I went off after my brother.

"Mom's still crying," I said. "Shouldn't we do something?"

"It's all right," he said. "It's what she came here for."

"Yes," I said, and then a sob escaped from my throat. "But I feel like crying too."

My brother Harold put his arm around me. "Look at this old black stone here," he said. "The way it's carved. You can see the changing fashion in monuments—just like everything else."

Somewhere in this time I began dreaming of my father. Not the robust father of my childhood, the handsome man with healthy pink skin and brown eyes and a mustache and the thinning hair parted in the middle. My dead father. We were taking him home from the hospital. It was understood that he had come back from death. This was amazing and joyous. On the other hand, he was terribly mysteriously damaged, or, more accurately, spoiled and unclean. He was very yellowed and debilitated by his death, and there were no guarantees that he wouldn't soon die again. He seemed aware of this and his entire personality was changed. He was angry and impatient with all of us. We were trying to help him in some way, struggling to get him home, but something prevented us, something we had to fix, a tattered suitcase that had sprung open, some mechanical thing: he had a car but it wouldn't start; or the car was made of wood; or his clothes, which had become too large for him, had caught in the door. In one version he was all bandaged and as we tried to lift him from his wheelchair into a taxi the bandage began to unroll and catch in the spokes of the wheelchair. This seemed to be some unreasonableness on his part. My mother looked on sadly and tried to get him to cooperate.

That was the dream. I shared it with no one. Once when I woke, crying out, my brother turned on the light. He wanted to know what I'd been dreaming but I pretended I didn't remember. The dream made me feel guilty. I felt guilty in the dream too because my enraged father knew we didn't want to live with him. The dream represented us taking him home, or trying to, but it was nevertheless understood by all of us that he was to live alone. He was this derelict back from death, but what we were doing was taking him to some place where he would live by himself without help from anyone until he died again.

At one point I became so fearful of this dream that I tried not to go to sleep. I tried to think of good things about my father and to remember him before his illness. He used to call me "matey." "Hello, matey," he would say when he came home from work. He always wanted us to go someplace—to the store, to the park, to a ball game. He loved to walk. When I went walking with him he would say: "Hold your shoulders back, don't slump. Hold your head up and look at the world. Walk as if you meant it!" As he strode down the street his shoulders moved from side to side, as if he was hearing some kind of cakewalk. He moved with a bounce. He was always eager to see what was around the corner.

The next request for a letter coincided with a special occasion in the house: My brother Harold had met a girl he liked and had gone out with her several times. Now she was coming to our house for dinner.

We had prepared for this for days, cleaning everything in sight, giving the house a going-over, washing the dust of disuse from the glasses and good dishes. My mother came home early from work to get the dinner going. We opened the gate-leg table in the living room and brought in the kitchen chairs. My mother spread the table with a laundered white cloth and put out her silver. It was the first family occasion since my father's illness.

I liked my brother's girlfriend a lot. She was a thin girl with very straight hair and she had a terrific smile. Her presence seemed to excite the air. It was amazing to have a living breathing girl in our house. She looked around and what she said was: "Oh, I've never seen so many books!" While she and my brother sat at the table my mother was in the kitchen putting the food into serving bowls and I was going from the kitchen to the living room, kidding around like a waiter, with a white cloth over my arm and a high style of service, placing the serving dish of green beans on the table with a flourish. In the kitchen my mother's eyes were sparkling. She looked at me and nodded and mimed the words: "She's adorable!"

My brother suffered himself to be waited on. He was wary of what we might say. He kept glancing at the girl—her name was Susan—to see if we met her approval. She worked in an insurance office and was taking a course in accounting at City College. Harold was under a terrible strain but he was excited and happy, too. He had bought a bottle of Concord-grape wine to go with the roast chicken. He held up his glass and proposed a toast. My mother said: "To good health and happiness," and we all drank, even I. At that moment the phone rang and I went into the bedroom to get it.

"Jonathan? This is your Aunt Frances. How is everyone?"

"Fine, thank you."

"I want to ask one last favor of you. I need a letter from Jack. Your grandma's very ill. Do you think you can?"

"Who is it?" my mother called from the living room.

"OK, Aunt Frances," I said quickly. "I have to go now, we're eating dinner." And I hung up the phone.

"It was my friend Louie," I said, sitting back down. "He didn't know the math pages to review."

The dinner was very fine. Harold and Susan washed the dishes and by the time they were done my mother and I had folded up the gateleg table and put it back against the wall and I had swept the crumbs up with the carpet sweeper. We all sat and talked and listened to records for a while and then my brother took Susan home. The evening had gone very well.

Once when my mother wasn't home, my brother had pointed out something: the letters from Jack weren't really necessary.

"What is this ritual?" he said, holding his palms up. "Grandma is almost totally blind, she is half dead and crippled. Does the situation really call for a literary composition? Does it need verisimilitude? Would the old lady know the difference if she was read the phone book?"

"Then why did Aunt Frances ask me?"

"That is the question, Jonathan. Why did she? After all, she could write the letter herself—what difference would it make? And if not Frances, why not Frances's sons, the Amherst students? They should have learned to write."

"But they're not Jack's sons," I said.

"That's exactly the point," my brother said. "The idea is service. Dad used to bust his balls getting them things wholesale, getting them deals on things. Frances of Westchester really needed things at cost. And Aunt Molly. And Aunt Molly's husband, and Aunt Molly's ex-husband. Grandma, if she needed an errand done. He was always on the hook for something. They never thought his time was important. They never thought every favor he got was one to pay back. Appliances, records, watches, china, opera tickets, any goddamn thing. Call Jack."

"It was a matter of pride to him to be able to do things for them," I said. "To have connections."

"Yeah, I wonder why," my brother said. He looked out the window. Then suddenly it dawned on me that I was being implicated.

"You should use your head more," my brother said.

Yet I had agreed once again to write a letter from the desert and so I did. I mailed it off to Aunt Frances. A few days later, when I came home from school, I thought I saw her sitting in her car in front of our house. She drove a black Buick Roadmaster, a very large clean car with whitewall tires. It was Aunt Frances all right. She blew the horn when she saw me. I went over and leaned in at the window.

"Hello, Jonathan," she said. "I haven't long. Can you get in the car?"

"Mom's not home," I said. "She's working."

"I know that. I came to talk to you."

"Would you like to come upstairs?"

"I can't, I have to get back to Larchmont. Can you get in for a moment, please?"

I got in the car. My Aunt Frances was a very pretty white-haired woman, very elegant, and she wore tasteful clothes. I had always liked her and from the time I was a child she had enjoyed pointing out to everyone that I looked more like her son than Jack's. She wore white gloves and held the steering wheel and looked straight ahead as she talked, as if the car was in traffic and not sitting at the curb.

"Jonathan," she said, "there is your letter on the seat. Needless to say I didn't read it to Grandma. I'm giving it back to you and I won't ever say a word to anyone. This is just between us. I never expected cruelty from you. I never thought you were capable of doing something so deliberately cruel and perverse."

I said nothing.

"Your mother has very bitter feelings and now I see she has poisoned you with them. She has always resented the family. She is a very strong-willed, selfish person."

"No she isn't," I said.

"I wouldn't expect you to agree. She drove poor Jack crazy with her demands. She always had the highest aspirations and he could never fulfill them to her satisfaction. When he still had his store he kept your mother's brother, who drank, on salary. After the war when he began to make a little money he had to buy Ruth a mink jacket because she was so desperate to have one. He had debts to pay but she wanted a mink. He was a very special person, my brother, he should have accomplished something special, but he loved your mother and devoted his life to her. And all she ever thought about was keeping up with the Joneses."

I watched the traffic going up the Grand Concourse. A bunch of kids were waiting at the bus stop at the corner. They had put their books on the ground and were horsing around.

"I'm sorry I have to descend to this," Aunt Frances said. "I don't like talking about people this way. If I have nothing good to say about someone, I'd rather not say anything. How is Harold?"

"Fine."

"Did he help you write this marvelous letter?"

"No."

After a moment she said more softly: "How are you all getting along?"

"Fine."

"I would invite you up for Passover if I thought your mother would accept."

I didn't answer.

She turned on the engine. "I'll say good-bye now, Jonathan. Take your letter. I hope you give some time to thinking about what you've done."

That evening when my mother came home from work I saw that she wasn't as pretty as my Aunt Frances. I usually thought my mother was a good-looking woman, but I saw now that she was too heavy and that her hair was undistinguished.

"Why are you looking at me?" she said.

"I'm not."

"I learned something interesting today," my mother said. "We may be eligible for a VA pension because of the time your father spent in the navy."

That took me by surprise. Nobody had ever told me my father was in the navy.

"In World War I," she said, "he went to Webb's Naval Academy on the Harlem River. He was training to be an ensign. But the war ended and he never got his commission."

After dinner the three of us went through the closets looking for my father's papers, hoping to find some proof that could be filed with the Veterans Administration. We came up with two things, a Victory medal, which my brother said everyone got for being in the service during the Great War, and an astounding sepia photograph of my father and his shipmates on the deck of a ship. They were dressed in bell-bottoms and T-shirts and armed with mops and pails, brooms and brushes.

"I never knew this," I found myself saying. "I never knew this."

"You just don't remember," my brother said.

I was able to pick out my father. He stood at the end of the row, a thin, handsome boy with a full head of hair, a mustache, and an intelligent smiling countenance.

"He had a joke," my mother said. "They called their training ship the SS *Constipation* because it never moved."

Neither the picture nor the medal was proof of anything, but my brother thought a duplicate of my father's service record had to be in Washington somewhere and that it was just a matter of learning how to go about finding it.

"The pension wouldn't amount to much," my mother said. "Twenty or thirty dollars. But it would certainly help."

I took the picture of my father and his shipmates and propped it against the lamp at my bedside. I looked into his youthful face and tried to relate it to the father I knew. I looked at the picture a long time. Only gradually did my eye connect it to the set of Great Sea Novels in the bottom shelf of the bookcase a few feet away. My father had given that set to me: it was uniformly bound in green with gilt lettering and it included works by Melville, Conrad, Victor Hugo, and Captain Marryat. And lying across the top of the books, jammed in under the sagging shelf above, was his old ship's telescope in its wooden case with the brass snap.

I thought how stupid, and imperceptive, and self-centered I had been never to have understood while he was alive what my father's dream for his life had been.

On the other hand, I had written in my last letter from Arizona—the one that had so angered Aunt Frances something that might allow me, the writer in the family, to soften my judgment of myself. I will conclude by giving the letter here in its entirety.

Dear Mama, This will be my final letter to you since I have been told by the doctors that I am dying. I have sold my store at a very fine profit and am sending Frances a check for five thousand dollars to be deposited in your account. My present to you, Mamaleh. Let Frances show you the passbook. As for the nature of my ailment, the doctors haven't told me what it is, but I know that I am simply dying of the wrong life. I should never have come to the desert. It wasn't the place for me. I have asked Ruth and the boys to have my body cremated and the ashes scattered in the ocean.

Your loving son,
Jack

Edie: A Life

Harriet Doerr

In the middle of an April night in 1919, a plain woman named Edith Fisk, lifted from England to California on a tide of world peace, arrived at the Ransom house to raise five half-orphaned children.

A few hours later, at seven in the morning, this Edith, more widely called Edie, invited the three eldest to her room for tea. They were James, seven; Eliza, six; and Jenny, four. Being handed cups of tea, no matter how reduced by milk, made them believe that they had grown up overnight.

"Have some sugar," said Edie, and spooned it in. Moments later she said, "Have another cup." But her *h*'s went unspoken and became the first of hundreds, then thousands, that would accumulate in the corners of the house and thicken in the air like sighs.

In an adjoining room the twins, entirely responsible for their mother's death, had finished their bottles and fallen back into guiltless sleep. At the far end of the house, the widower, Thomas Ransom, who had spent the night aching for his truant wife, lay across his bed, half awake, half asleep, and dreaming.

The three children sat in silence at Edie's table. She had grizzled hair pulled up in a knot, heavy brows, high cheeks, and two long hairs in her chin. She was bony and flat and looked starched, like the apron she had tied around her. Her teeth were large and white and even, her eyes an uncompromising blue.

She talked to the children as if they were her age, forty-one. "My father was an ostler," she told them, and they listened without comprehension. "My youngest brother died at Wipers," she said. "My nephew was gassed at Verdun."

These were places the children had never heard of. But all three of them, even Jenny, understood the word "died."

"Our mother died," said James.

Edie nodded.

"I was born, the oldest of eight, in Atherleigh, a town in Devon. I've lived in five English counties," she told them, without saying what a county was. "And taken care of thirty children, a few of them best forgotten."

"Which ones?" said James.

But Edie talked only of her latest charges, the girls she had left to come to America.

"Lady Alice and Lady Anne," said Edie, and described two paragons of quietness and clean knees, who lived in a castle in Kent. Edie didn't say "castle," she said "big brick house." She didn't say "lake," she said "pond." But the children, dazzled by illustrations in Cinderella and King Arthur, assumed princesses. And after that, they assumed castle, tower, moat, lake, lily, swan.

Lady Alice was seven and Lady Anne was eight when last seen immaculately crayoning with their ankles crossed in the tower overlooking the lake.

Eliza touched Edie's arm. "What is gassed?" she said.

Edie explained.

Jenny lifted her spoon for attention. "I saw Father cry," she said. "Twice."

"Oh, be quiet," said James.

With Edie, they could say anything.

After that morning, they would love tea forever, all their lives, in sitting rooms and restaurants, on terraces and balconies, at sidewalk cafes and whistle stops, even under awnings in the rain. They would drink it indiscriminately, careless of flavor, out of paper cups or Spode, with lemon, honey, milk, or cream, with spices or with rum.

Before Edie came to the Ransom house, signs of orphanhood were everywhere—in the twins' colic, in Eliza's aggravated impulse to pinch Jenny, in the state of James's sheets every morning. Their father, recognizing symptoms of grief, brought home wrapped packages in his overcoat pockets. He gave the children a Victrola and Harry Lauder records.

"Shall we read?" he would ask in the evening, and take Edward Lear from the shelf. "'There was an Old Man with a beard,'" read Thomas Ransom, and he and his children listened solemnly to the unaccustomed voice speaking the familiar words.

While the twins baffled everyone by episodes of weight loss and angry tears, various efforts to please were directed toward the other three. The cook baked cakes and frosted their names into the icing. The sympathetic gardener packed them into his wheelbarrow and pushed them at high speeds down sloping paths. Two aunts, the dead mother's sisters, improvised weekly outings—to the ostrich farm, the alligator farm, the lion farm, to a picnic in the mountains, a shell hunt at the beach. These contrived entertainments failed. None substituted for what was needed: the reappearance at the piano or on the stairs of a young woman with freckles, green eyes, and a ribbon around her waist. Edie came to the rescue of the Ransoms through the intervention of the aunts' English friend, Cissy. When hope for joy in any degree was almost lost, Cissy wrote and produced the remedy. The aunts brought her letter to Thomas Ransom in his study on a February afternoon. Outside the window, a young sycamore, planted by his wife the year before, cast its sparse shadow on a patch of grass.

Cissy wrote that all her friends lost sons and brothers in the war and she was happy she had none to offer up. Wherever one went in London, wounded veterans, wearing their military medals, were performing for money. She saw a legless man in uniform playing an accordion outside Harrods. Others, on Piccadilly, had harmonicas wired in front of their faces so they could play without hands. Blind men, dressed for parade, sang in the rain for theater queues.

And the weather, wrote Cissy. Winter seemed to be a state of life and not a season. How lucky one was to be living, untouched by it all, in America, particularly California. Oh, to wake up to sunshine every morning, to spend one's days warm and dry.

Now she arrived at the point of her letter. Did anyone they knew want Edith Fisk, who had taken care of children for twenty-five years and was personally known to Cissy? Edie intended to live near a cousin in Texas. California might be just the place.

The reading of the letter ended.

"Who is Cissy?" said Thomas Ransom, unable to foresee that within a dozen years he would marry her.

James, who had been listening at the door, heard only the first part of the letter. Long before Cissy proposed Edie, he was upstairs in his room, trying to attach a harmonica to his mouth with kite string.

Edie was there within two months. The aunts and Thomas Ransom began to witness change.

Within weeks the teasing stopped. Within months the nighttime sheets stayed dry. The twins, male and identical, fattened and pulled toys apart. Edie bestowed on each of the five children equal shares of attention and concern. She hung their drawings in her room, even the ones of moles in traps and inhabited houses burning to the ground. Samples of the twins' scribblings remained on permanent display. The children's pictures eventually occupied almost all one wall and surrounded a framed photograph of Lady Alice and Lady Anne, two small light-haired girls sitting straight-backed on dappled ponies.

"Can we have ponies?" Eliza and Jenny asked their father. But he had fallen in love with a woman named Trish and, distracted, brought home a cage of canaries instead.

Edie and the Ransom children suited each other. It seemed right to them all that she had come to braid hair, turn hems, push swings, take walks; to apply iodine to cuts and embrace the cry that followed, to pinch her fingers between the muddy rubber and the shoe. Edie stopped nightmares almost before they started. At a child's first gasp she would be in the doorway, uncombed and minus her false teeth, tying on her wrapper, a glass of water in her hand.

The older children repaid this bounty with torments of their own devising. They would rush at her in a trio, shout, "We've 'idden your 'at in the 'all," and run shrieking with laughter, out of her sight. They crept into her room at night, found the pink gums and big white teeth where they lay floating in a mug, and, in a frenzy of bad manners, hid them in a hatbox or behind the books.

Edie never reported these lapses of deportment to Thomas Ransom. Instead, she would invoke the names and virtues of Lady Alice and Lady Anne.

"They didn't talk like roustabouts," said Edie. "They slept like angels through the night."

Between spring and fall the nonsense ceased. Edie grew into the Ransoms' lives and was accepted there, like air and water and the food they ate. From the start, the children saw her as a refuge. Flounder as they might in the choppy sea where orphans and half-orphans drown, they trusted her to save them.

Later on, when their father emerged from mourning, Edie was the mast they clung to in a squall of stepmothers.

Within a period of twelve years Thomas Ransom, grasping at the outer fringe of happiness, brought three wives in close succession to the matrimonial bed he first shared with the children's now sainted mother. He chose women he believed were like her, and it was true that all three, Trish, Irene, and Cissy, were smallboned and energetic. But they were brown-eyed and, on the whole, not musical.

The first to come was Trish, nineteen years old and porcelain-skinned. Before her arrival Thomas Ransom asked the children not to come knocking at his bedroom door day and night, as they had in the past. Once she was there, other things changed. The children heard him humming at his desk in the study. They noticed that he often left in midmorning, instead of at eight, for the office where he practiced law.

Eliza asked questions at early-morning tea. "Why are they always in their room, with the door locked?"

And Jenny said, "Yes. Even before dinner."

"Don't you know anything?" said James.

Edie poured more pale tea. "Hold your cups properly. Don't spill," she told them, and the lost *h* floated into the steam rising from the pot.

Trish, at nineteen, was neither mother nor sister to the children. Given their priorities of blood and birth and previous residence, they inevitably outdistanced her. They knew to the oldest steamer trunk and the latest cookie the contents of the attic and larder. They walked oblivious across rugs stained with their spilled ink. The hall banister shone with the years of their sliding. Long ago they had enlisted the cook and the gardener as allies. Three of them remembered their mother. The other two thought they did. Trish said good morning at noon and drove off with friends. Later she paused to say good night in a rustle of taffeta on Thomas Ransom's arm as they left for a dinner or a dance.

James made computations. "She's nine years older than I am," he said, "and eighteen years younger than Father."

"He keeps staring at her," said Eliza.

"And kissing her hand," said Jenny.

Edie opened a door on a sliver of her past. "I knew a girl once with curly red hair like that, in Atherleigh."

"What was her name?" James asked, as if for solid evidence.

Edie bit off her darning thread. She looked backward with her inward eye. Finally she said, "Lily Stiles. The day I went into service in Dorset, Lily went to work at the Rose and Plough."

"The Rose and Plough," repeated Eliza. "What's that?"

"It's a pub," said Edie, and she explained what a public house was. Immediately, this establishment, with its gleaming bar and its game of darts, was elevated in the children's minds to the mysterious realm of Lady Alice and Lady Anne and set in place a stone's throw from their castle. At home, Trish's encounters with her husband's children were brief. In passing, she waved to them all and patted the twins on their dark heads. She saw more of the three eldest on those Saturday afternoons when she took them, along with Edie, to the movies.

Together they sat in the close, expectant dark of the Rivoli Theater, watched the shimmering curtains part, shivered to the organist's opening chords, and, at the appearance of an image on the screen, cast off their everyday lives to be periled, rescued, rejected, and adored. They sat spellbound through the film and when the words "The End" came on, rose depleted and blinking from their seats to face the hot sidewalk and full sun outside.

Trish selected the pictures, and though they occasionally included Fairbanks films and ones that starred the Gishes, these were not her favorites. She detested comedies. To avoid Harold Lloyd, they saw Rudolph Valentino in *The Sheik*. Rather than endure Buster Keaton, they went to *Gypsy Blood,* starring Pola Negri.

"I should speak to your father," Edie would say later on at home. But she never did. Instead, she only remarked at bedtime, "It's a nice change, going to the pictures."

Trish left at the end of two years, during which the children, according to individual predispositions, grew taller and developed the hands and feet and faces they would always keep. They learned more about words and numbers, they began to like oysters, they swam the Australian crawl. They survived crises. These included scarlet fever, which the twins contracted and recovered from, and James's near electrocution as a result of his tinkering with wires and sockets.

Eliza and Jenny, exposed to chicken pox on the same day, ran simultaneous fevers and began to scratch. Edie brought ice and invented games. She cleared the table between their beds and knotted a handkerchief into arms and legs and a smooth, round head. She made it face each invalid and bow.

"This is how my sister Frahnces likes to dahnce the fahncy dahnces," Edie said, and the knotted handkerchief waltzed and two-stepped back and forth across the table.

Mesmerized by each other, the twins made few demands. A mechanical walking bear occupied them for weeks, a wind-up train for months. They shared a rocking horse and crashed slowly into one another on tricycles. James, at eleven, sat in headphones by the hour in front of a crystal radio set. Sometimes he invited Edie to scratch a chip of rock with wire and hear a human voice advance and recede in the distance.

"Where's he talking from?" Edie would ask, and James said, "Oak Bluff. Ten miles away."

Together they marveled.

The two aunts, after one of their frequent visits, tried to squeeze the children into categories. James is the experimenter, they agreed. Jenny, the romantic. The twins, at five, too young to pigeonhole. Eliza was the bookish one.

Single-minded child, she read while walking to school, in the car on mountain curves, on the train in tunnels, on her back on the beach at noon, in theaters under dimming lights, between the sheets by flashlight. Eliza saw all the world through thick lenses adjusted for fine print. On Saturdays, she would often desert her invited friend and choose to read by herself instead. At these times Edie would approach the bewildered visitor. Would she like to feed the canaries? Climb into the tree house?

"We'll make tiaras," she told one abandoned guest and, taking Jenny along, led the way to the orange grove. "We're brides," announced Jenny a few minutes later, and she and Eliza's friend, balancing circles of flowers on their heads, stalked in a barefoot procession of two through the trees.

That afternoon, Jenny, as though she had never seen it before, inquired about Edie's ring. "Are you engaged?"

"I was once," said Edie, and went on to expose another slit of her past. "To Alfred Trotter."

"Was he killed at Wipers?"

Edie shook her head. "The war came later. He worked for his father at the Rose and Plough."

In a field beyond the grove, Jenny saw a plough, ploughing roses. "Why didn't you get married?"

Edie looked at her watch and said it was five o'clock. She brushed off her skirt and got to her feet. "I wasn't the only girl in Atherleigh."

Jenny, peering into the past, caught a glimpse of Lily Stiles behind the bar at the Rose and Plough.

After Trish left, two more years went by before the children's father brought home his third wife. This was Irene, come to transplant herself in Ransom ground. Behind her she trailed a wake of friends, men with beards and women in batik scarves, who sat about the porch with big hats between them and the sun. In a circle of wicker chairs, they discussed Cubism, Freud, Proust, and Schoenberg's twelve-tone row. They passed perfumed candies to the children.

Irene changed all the lampshades in the house from white paper to red silk, threw a Persian prayer rug over the piano, and gave the children incense sticks for Christmas. She recited poems translated from the Sanskrit and wore saris to the grocery store. In spite of efforts on both sides, Irene remained an envoy from a foreign land.

One autumn day, not long before the end of her tenure as Thomas Ransom's wife, she took Edie and all five children to a fortune-teller at the county fair. A pale-eyed, wasted man sold them tickets outside Madame Zelma's tent and pointed to the curtained entrance. Crowding into the stale air of the interior, they gradually made out the fortune-teller's veiled head and jeweled neck behind two lighted candelabra on a desk.

"Have a seat," said Madame.

All found places on a bench or on hassocks, and rose, one by one, to approach the palmist as she beckoned them to a chair facing her. Madame Zelma, starting with the eldest, pointed to Edie.

"I see children," said the fortune-teller. She concentrated in silence for a moment. "You will cross the ocean. I see a handsome man."

Us, thought Jenny. Alfred Trotter.

Madame Zelma, having wound Edie's life backward from present to past, summoned Irene.

"I see a musical instrument," said Madame, as if she knew of Irene's guitar and the chords in minor keys that were its repertory. "Your flower is the poppy. Your fruit, the pear." The fortune-teller leaned closer to Irene's hand. "Expect a change of residence soon."

Edie and the children listened.

And so the fortunes went, the three eldest children's full of prizes and professions, talents and awards, happy marriages, big families, silver mines, and fame.

By the time Madame Zelma reached the twins, she had little left to predict. "Long lives," was all she told them. But what more could anyone divine from the trackless palms of seven-year-olds?

By the time Cissy, the next wife, came, James's voice had changed and his sisters had bobbed their hair. The twins had joined in painting an oversized panorama titled

"After the Earthquake." Edie hung it on her wall.

Cissy, the children's last stepmother, traveled all the way from England, like Edie. Introduced by the aunts through a letter, Thomas Ransom met her in London, rode with her in Hyde Park, drove with her to Windsor for the day, then took her boating on the upper reaches of the Thames. They were married in a registry, she for the third time, he for the fourth, and spent their honeymoon on the Isle of Skye in a long, gray drizzle.

"I can hardly wait for California," said Cissy.

Once there, she lay about in the sun until she blistered. "Darling, bring my parasol, bring my gloves," she entreated whichever child was near.

"Are the hills always this brown?" she asked, splashing rose water on her throat. "Has that stream dried up for good?"

Cissy climbed mountain paths looking for wildflowers and came back with toyon and sage. Twice a week on her horse, Sweet William, she rode trails into the countryside, flushing up rattlesnakes instead of grouse. On national holidays that celebrated American separation from Britain, Cissy felt some way historically at fault. On the day before Thanksgiving, she strung cranberries silently at Edie's side. On the Fourth of July they sat together holding sparklers six thousand miles from the counties where their roots, still green, were sunk in English soil.

During the dry season of the year, from April to December, the children sometimes watched Cissy as she stood at a corner of the terrace, her head turning from east to west, her eyes searching the implacable blue sky. But for what? An English bird? The smell of fog?

By now the children were half grown or more, and old enough to recognize utter misery.

"Cissy didn't know what to expect," they told each other.

"She's homesick for the Sussex Downs," said Edie, releasing the *h* into space.

"Are you homesick too, for Atherleigh?" asked Eliza.

"I am not."

"You knew what to expect," said Jenny.

Edie said, "Almost."

The children discussed with her the final departure of each stepmother.

"Well, she's gone," said James, who was usually called to help carry out bags. "Maybe we'll have some peace."

After Cissy left, he made calculations. "Between the three of them, they had six husbands," he told the others.

"And Father's had four wives," said one of the twins. "Six husbands and four wives make ten," said the other.

"Ten what?" said James.

"Poor souls," said Edie.

At last the children were as tall as they would ever be. The aunts could no longer say, "How are they ever to grow up?" For here they were, reasonably bright and reasonably healthy, survivors of a world war and a great depression, durable relics of their mother's premature and irreversible defection and their father's abrupt marriages.

They had got through it all—the removal of tonsils, the straightening of teeth, the first night at camp, the first dance, the good-byes waved from the rear platforms of trains that, like boats crossing the Styx, carried them away to college. This is not to say they were the same children they would have been if their mother had lived. They were not among the few who can suffer anything, loss or gain, without effect. But no one could point to a Ransom child's smile or frown or sleeping habits and reasonably comment, "No mother."

Edie stayed in the Ransom house until the twins left for college. By now, Eliza and Jenny were married, James married, divorced, and remarried. Edie went to all the graduations and weddings.

On these occasions the children hurried across playing fields and lawns to reach and embrace her.

"Edie!" they said. "You came!" They introduced their fellow graduates and the persons they had married. "This is Edie. Edie, this is Bill, Terry, Peter, Joan," and they were carried off in whirlwinds of friends.

As the Ransom house emptied of family, it began to expand. The bedrooms grew larger, the hall banister longer, the porch too wide for the wicker chairs. Edie took leave of the place for want of children in 1938. She was sixty years old.

She talked to Thomas Ransom in his study, where his first wife's portrait, painted in pastels, had been restored to its place on the wall facing his desk. Edie sat under the green-eyed young face, her unfaltering blue glance on her employer. Each tried to make the parting easy. It was clear, however, that they were dividing between them, top to bottom, a frail, towering structure of nineteen accumulated years, which was the time it had taken to turn five children, with their interminable questions, unfounded terrors, and destructive impulses, into mature adults who could vote, follow maps, make omelets, and reach an accord of sorts with life and death.

Thinking back over the intervening years, Thomas Ransom remembered Edie's cousin in Texas and inquired, only to find that Texas had been a disappointment, as had America itself. The cousin had returned to England twelve years ago.

"Would you like that?" he asked Edie. "To go back to England?"

She had grown used to California, she said. She had no one in Atherleigh. So in the end, prompted by the look in his first wife's eyes, Thomas Ransom offered Edie a cottage and a pension, to be hers for the rest of her life.

Edie's beach cottage was two blocks back from the sea and very small. On one wall she hung a few of the children's drawings, including the earthquake aftermath. Opposite them, by itself, she hung the framed photograph of Lady Alice and Lady Anne, fair and well-seated astride their ponies. Edie had become the repository of pets. The long-lived fish swam languidly in one corner of her sitting room, the last of the canaries molted in another. Each Ransom child came to her house once for tea, pulling in to the curb next to a mailbox marked Edith Fisk.

"Edie, you live so far away!"

On their first Christmas apart, the children sent five cards, the next year four, then two for several years, then one, or sometimes none.

During the first September of Edie's retirement, England declared war on Germany. She knitted socks for the British troops, and on one occasion four years after she left it, returned briefly to the Ransom house. This was when the twins were killed in Europe a month apart, at the age of twenty-four, one in a fighter plane over the Baltic, the other in a bomber over the Rhine. Two months later Thomas Ransom asked Edie to dispose of their things, and she came back for a week to her old, now anonymous, room.

She was unprepared for the mass of articles to be dealt with.

The older children had cleared away childhood possessions at the time of their marriages. But here were all the books the twins had ever read, from Dr. Dolittle to Hemingway, and all their entertainments, from a Ouija board to skis and kites. Years of their civilian trousers, coats, and shoes crowded the closets.

Edie first wrapped and packed the bulky objects, then folded into cartons the heaps of clothing, much of which she knew. A week was barely time enough to sort it all and reach decisions. Then, suddenly, as though it had been a matter of minutes, the boxes were packed and at the door. Edie marked each one with black crayon. Boys Club, she printed, Children's Hospital, Red Cross, Veterans.

That afternoon she stood for a moment with Thomas Ransom on the porch, the silent house behind them. The November air was cold and fresh, the sky cloudless.

"Lovely day," said Edie.

Thomas Ransom nodded, admiring the climate while his life thinned out.

If the three surviving children had written Edie during the years that followed, this is what she would have learned.

At thirty-five, James, instead of having become an electrical engineer or a master mechanic, was a junior partner in his father's law firm. Twice divorced and about to take a new wife, he had apparently learned nothing from Thomas Ransom, not even how to marry happily once. Each marriage had produced two children, four intended cures that failed. James's practice involved foreign corporations, and he was often abroad. He moved from executive offices to boardrooms and back, and made no attempt to diagnose his discontent. On vacations at home, he dismantled and reassembled heaters and fans and wired every room of his house for sound.

Whenever he visited England, he tried, and failed, to find time to send Edie a card.

Eliza had been carried off from her research library by an archaeologist ten years older and three inches shorter than she. He took her first to Guatemala, then to Mexico, where they lived in a series of jungle huts in Chiapas and Yucatan. It was hard to find native help, and the clothes Eliza washed often hung drying for days on the teeming underbrush. Her damp books, on shelves and still in boxes, began to mildew. She cooked food wrapped in leaves over a charcoal fire. On special days, like her birthday and Christmas, Eliza would stand under the thatch of her doorway and stare northwest through the rain and vegetation in the direction of the house where she was born and had first tasted tea.

Edie was still living in the house when Jenny, through a letter from her last step-mother, Cissy, met the Englishman she would marry. Thin as a pencil and pale as parchment, he had entered the local university as an exchange fellow. Jenny was immediately moved to take care of him, sew on his missing buttons, comb his sandy hair. His English speech enchanted her. "Tell about boating at Henley," she urged him. "Tell about climbing the Trossachs. Explain cricket." And while he described these things as fully as his inherent reserve would allow, the inflections of another voice fell across his. Jenny heard "fahncy dahnces." She heard "poor souls."

"Have you ever been to Atherleigh in Devon?" she asked him.

"That's Hatherleigh," he said.

If Jenny had written Edie, she would have said, "I love Massachusetts, I love my house, I can make scones, come and see us."

On a spring afternoon in 1948, Thomas Ransom called his children together in the same study where the aunts had read Cissy's letter of lament and recommendation. The tree his wife planted thirty years ago towered in green leaf outside the window.

The children had gathered from the outposts of the world—James from Paris, Eliza from the Mayan tropics, Jenny from snowed-in Boston. When he summoned them, they had assumed a crisis involving their father. Now they sat uneasily under the portrait of their mother, a girl years younger than themselves. Thomas Ransom offered them tea and sherry. He looked through the window at the tree.

At last he presented his news. "Edie is dying," he said. "She is in the hospital with cancer," as if cancer were a friend Edie had always longed to share a room with.

They visited her on a shining April morning, much like the one when they first met. With their first gray hairs and new lines at their eyes, they waited a moment on the hospital steps.

James took charge. "We'll go in one by one," he said.

So, as if they had rehearsed together, one after another they stood alone outside the door that had a sign, No Visitors, stood there while patients prepared for surgery or carts of half-eaten lunches were wheeled past, stood and collected their childhood until a nurse noticed and said, "Go in. She wants to see you." Then each one pushed the door open, went to the high narrow bed, and said, "Edie."

She may not have known they were there. She had started to be a skeleton. Her skull was pulling her eyes in. Once they had spoken her name, there was nothing more to say. Before leaving, they touched the familiar, unrecognizable hand of shoelaces and hair ribbons and knew it, for the first time, disengaged.

After their separate visits, they assembled again on the hospital steps. It was now they remembered Lady Alice and Lady Anne.

"Where was that castle?" Eliza asked.

"In Kent," said Jenny.

All at one time, they imagined the girls in their tower after tea. Below them, swans pulled lengthening reflections across the smooth surface of the lake. Lady Alice sat at her rosewood desk, Lady Anne at hers. They were still seven and eight years old. They wrote on thick paper with mother-of-pearl pens dipped into ivory inkwells.

"Dear Edie," wrote Lady Alice.

"Dear Edie," wrote Lady Anne.

"I am sorry to hear you are ill," they both wrote.

Then, as if they were performing an exercise in penmanship, they copied "I am sorry" over and over in flowing script until they reached the bottom of the page. When there was no more room, they signed one letter "Alice" and the other letter "Anne."

In the midst of all this, Edie died.

Book Codes: II

Carolyn Forche

a field tunneled by mice the same thought continually
like two hands indissolubly clasped to begin
as if in a coffin and can therefore think of nothing else
how incomplete a moment is human life

fragments together into a story before the shape of the whole
like a madman—time and again torn from my mouth
out of a nearby chimney each child's hand was taken
though this is not a fairy tale explained in advance

the sign of the cross on an invisible face with the calm of a butcher
as if it bore witness to some truth
with whom every connection had been severed
as if in a coffin and can therefore think of nothing else

an afternoon swallowing down whole years its every hour
troops marching by in the snow until they are transparent
from the woods through tall firs a wood with no apparent end
cathedrals at the tip of our tongues with countries not yet seen

whoever can cry should come here

Book Codes: III

stories no more substantial than the clouds or what had been his face
the view, the wind, the light disposing of the bodies
who walked in the realm of dreams but like everything else

for our having tried to cross the river caught between walls
one could hear a voice "Bear the unbearable"
and the broadcast was at an end

you might relay the message the rivers and mountains remained
the unseen figure of the enemy entirely covered
the central portion of their visual fields this blindness for names

the bone became black with flies again hatching in ruins
here were the black, burnt ceilings and boxes of flags
the walls covered with soot like a kitchen

smaller clouds spread out a golden screen
given the task of painting wounds
through the darkened town as though it had been light

at the moment of the birth of this cloud

The Testimony of Light

Our life is a fire dampened, or a fire shut up in stone.
—JACOB BOEHME, *De Incarnatione Verbi*

Outside everything visible and invisible a blazing maple.
Daybreak: a seam at the curve of the world. The trousered legs of the women
    shimmered.
They held their arms in front of them like ghosts.

The coal bones of the house clinked in a kimono of smoke.
An attention hovered over the dream where the world had been.

For if Hiroshima in the morning, after the bomb has fallen,
    is like a dream, one must ask whose dream it is.

Must understand how not to speak would carry it with us.
With bones put into rice bowls.
While the baby crawled over its dead mother seeking milk.

Muga-muchu: without self, without center. Thrown up in the sky by a wind.

The way back is lost, the one obsession.
The worst is over.
The worst is yet to come.

We must know *whether*
And if not: then what is the task
very much on the surface
by means of finite signs
when one is frightened of the truth
"Are there simple things?"
    What depends on my life?
would be possible for me to write
like the film on deep water
over too wide chasms of thought
the world does not change
the visual field has not a form like this
so many graces of fate
the boundary (not a part) of the world
mirrored in its use
nothing except what can be said

The Garden
Shukkei-en

By way of a vanished bridge we cross this river
as a cloud of lifted snow would ascend a mountain.

She has always been afraid to come here.

It is the river she most
remembers, the living
and the dead both crying for help.

A world that allowed neither tears nor lamentation.

The *matsu* trees brush her hair as she passes
beneath them, as do the shining strands of barbed wire.

Where this lake is, there was a lake,
where these black pine grow, there grew black pine.

Where there is no teahouse I see a wooden teahouse
and the corpses of those who slept in it.

On the opposite bank of the Ota, a weeping willow
etches its memory of their faces into the water.

Where light touches the face, the character for heart is written.

She strokes a burnt trunk wrapped in straw:
I was weak and my skin hung from my fingertips like cloth

Do you think for a moment we were human beings to them?

She comes to the stone angel holding paper cranes.
Not an angel, but a woman where she once had been,

who walks through the garden Shukkei-en
calling the carp to the surface by clapping her hands.

Do Americans think of us?

So she began as we squatted over the toilets:
If you want, I'll tell you, but nothing I say will be enough.

We tried to dress our burns with vegetable oil.

Her hair is the white froth of rice rising up kettlesides, her mind also.
In the postwar years she thought deeply about how to live.

The common greeting *dozo-yiroshku* is please take care of me.
All *hibakusha* still alive were children then.

A cemetery seen from the air is a child's city.

I don't like this particular red flower because
it reminds me of a woman's brain crushed under a roof.

Perhaps my language is too precise, and therefore difficult to understand?

We have not, all these years, felt what you call happiness.
But at times, with good fortune, we experience something close.
As our life resembles life, and this garden the garden.
And in the silence surrounding what happened to us

it is the bell to awaken God that we've heard ringing.

Elegy

The page opens to snow on a field: boot-holed month, black hour
the bottle in your coat half vodka half winter light.
To what and to whom does one say *yes?*
If God were the uncertain, would you cling to him?

Beneath a tattoo of stars the gate opens, so silent so like a tomb.
This is the city you most loved, an empty stairwell
where the next rain lifts invisibly from the Seine.

With solitude, your coat open, you walk
steadily as if the railings were there and your hands weren't passing through
    them.

"When things were ready, they poured on fuel and touched off the fire.
They waited for a high wind. It was very fine, that powdered bone.
It was put into sacks, and when there were enough we went to a bridge on the Narew
    River."

And even less explicit phrases survived:
"To make charcoal.
For laundry irons."
And so we revolt against silence with a bit of speaking.
The page is a charred field where the dead would have written
We went on. And it was like living through something again one could not live through
    again.

The soul behind you no longer inhabits your life: the unlit house
with its breathless windows and a chimney of ruined wings
where wind becomes an aria, your name, voices from a field,
And you, smoke, dissonance, a psalm, a stairwell.

Optimists

Richard Ford

All of this that I am about to tell happened when I was only fifteen years old, in 1959, the year my parents were divorced, the year when my father killed a man and went to prison for it, the year I left home and school, told a lie about my age to fool the army, and then did not come back. The year, in other words, when life changed for all of us and forever—ended, really, in a way none of us could ever have imagined in our most brilliant dreams of life.

My father was named Roy Brinson, and he worked on the Great Northern Railway, in Great Falls, Montana. He was a switch-engine fireman, and when he could not hold that job on the seniority list, he worked the extra-board as a hostler, or as a hostler's helper, shunting engines through the yard, onto and off the freight trains that went south and east. He was thirty-seven or thirty-eight years old in 1959, a small, young-appearing man, with dark blue eyes. The railroad was a job he liked, because it paid high wages and the work was not hard, and because you could take off days when you wanted to, or even months, and have no one to ask you questions. It was a union shop, and there were people who looked out for you when your back was turned. "It's a workingman's paradise," my father would say, and then laugh.

My mother did not work then, though she *had* worked—at waitressing and in the bars in town—and she had liked working. My father thought, though, that Great Falls was coming to be a rougher town than it had been when he grew up there, a town going downhill, like its name, and that my mother should be at home more, because I was at an age when trouble came easily. We lived in a rented two-story house on Edith Street, close to the freight yards and the Missouri River, a house where from my window at night I could hear the engines as they sat throbbing, could see their lights move along the dark rails. My mother was at home most of her time, reading or watching television or cooking meals, though sometimes she would go out to movies in the afternoon, or would go to the YWCA and swim in the indoor pool. Where she was from—in Havre, Montana, much farther north—there was never such a thing as a pool indoors, and she thought that to swim in the winter, with snow on the ground and the wind howling, was the greatest luxury. And she would come home late in the afternoon, with her brown hair wet and her face flushed, and in high spirits, saying she felt freer.

The night that I want to tell about happened in November. It was not then a good time for railroads—not in Montana especially—and for firemen not at all, anywhere. It was the featherbed time, and everyone knew, including my father, that they would eventually lose their jobs, though no one knew exactly when, or who would go first, or, clearly, what the future would be. My father had been hired out ten years, and had worked on coal-burners and oilburners out of Forsythe, Montana, on the Sheridan spur. But he was still young in the job and low on the list, and he felt that when the cut came young heads would go first. "They'll do something for us, but it might not be enough," he said, and I had heard him say that other times—in the kitchen, with my mother, or out in front, working on his motorcycle, or with me, fishing the whitefish flats up the Missouri. But I do not know if he truly thought that or in fact had any reason to think it. He was an optimist. Both of them were optimists, I think.

I know that by the end of summer in that year he had stopped taking days off to fish, had stopped going out along the coulee rims to spot deer. He worked more then and was gone more, and he talked more about work when he was home: about what the union said on this subject and that, about court cases in Washington, D.C., a place I knew nothing of, and about injuries and illnesses to men he knew, that threatened their livelihoods, and by association with them, threatened his own—threatened, he must've felt, our whole life.

Because my mother swam at the YWCA she had met people there and made friends. One was a large woman named Esther, who came home with her once and drank coffee in the kitchen and talked about her boyfriend and laughed out loud for a long time, but who I never saw again. And another was a woman named Penny Mitchell whose husband, Boyd, worked for the Red Cross in Great Falls and had an office upstairs in the building with the YWCA, and who my mother would sometimes play canasta with on the nights my father worked late. They would set up a card table in the living room, the three of them, and drink and eat sandwiches until midnight. And I would lie in bed with my radio tuned low to the Calgary station, listening to a hockey match beamed out over the great empty prairie, and could hear the cards snap and laughter downstairs, and later I would hear footsteps leaving, hear the door shut, the dishes rattle in the sink, cabinets close. And in a while the door to my room would open and the light would fall inside, and my mother would set a chair back in. I could see her silhouette. She would always say, "Go back to sleep, Frank." And then the door would shut again, and I would almost always go to sleep in a minute.

It was on a night that Penny and Boyd Mitchell were in our house that trouble came about. My father had been working his regular bid-in job on the switch engine, plus a helper's job off the extra-board—a practice that was illegal by the railroad's rules, but ignored by the union, who could see bad times coming and knew there would be nothing to help it when they came, and so would let men work if they wanted to. I was in the kitchen, eating a sandwich alone at the table, and my mother was in the living room playing cards with Penny and Boyd Mitchell. They were drinking vodka and eating the other sandwiches my mother had made, when I heard my father's motorcycle outside in the dark. It was eight o'clock at night, and I knew he was not expected home until midnight.

"Roy's home," I heard my mother say. "I hear Roy. That's wonderful." I heard chairs scrape and glasses tap.

"Maybe he'll want to play," Penny Mitchell said. "We can play four-hands."

I went to the kitchen door and stood looking through the dining room at the front. I don't think I knew something was wrong, but I think I knew something was unusual, something I would want to know about firsthand.

My mother was standing beside the card table when my father came inside. She was smiling. But I have never seen a look on a man's face that was like the look on my father's face at that moment. He looked wild. His eyes were wild. His whole face was. It was cold outside, and the wind was coming up, and he had ridden home from the train yard in only his flannel shirt. His face was red, and his hair was strewn around his bare head, and I remember his fists were clenched white, as if there was no blood in them at all.

"My God," my mother said. "What is it, Roy? You look crazy." She turned and looked for me, and I knew she was thinking that this was something I might not need to see. But she didn't say anything. She just looked back at my father, stepped toward him and touched his hand, where he must've been coldest. Penny and Boyd Mitchell sat at the card table, looking up. Boyd Mitchell was smiling for some reason.

"Something awful happened," my father said. He reached and took a corduroy jacket off the coat nail and put it on, right in the living room, then sat down on the couch and hugged his arms. His face seemed to get redder then. He was wearing black steel-toe boots, the boots he wore every day, and I stared at them and felt how cold he must be, even in his own house. I did not come any closer.

"Roy, what is it?" my mother said, and she sat down beside him on the couch and held his hand in both of hers.

My father looked at Boyd Mitchell and at his wife, as if he hadn't known they were in the room until then. He did not know them very well, and I thought he might tell them to get out, but he didn't.

"I saw a man be killed tonight," he said to my mother, then shook his head and looked down. He said, "We were pushing into that old hump yard on Ninth Avenue. A cut of coal cars. It wasn't even an hour ago. I was looking out my side, the way you do when you push out a curve. And I could see this one open boxcar in the cut, which isn't unusual. Only this guy was in it and was trying to get off, sitting in the door, scooting. I guess he was a hobo. Those cars had come in from Glasgow tonight. And just the second he started to go off, the whole cut buckled up. It's a thing that'll happen. But he lost his balance just when he hit the gravel, and he fell backwards underneath. I looked right at him. And one set of trucks rolled right over his foot." My father looked at my mother then. "It hit his foot," he said.

"My God," my mother said and looked down at her lap.

My father squinted. "But then he moved, he sort of bucked himself like he was trying to get away. He didn't yell, and I could see his face. I'll never forget that. He didn't look scared, he just looked like a man doing something that was hard for him to do. He looked like he was concentrating on something. But when he bucked he pushed back, and the other trucks caught his hand." My father looked at his own hands then, and made fists out of them and squeezed them.

"What did you do?" my mother said. She looked terrified.

"I yelled out. And Sherman stopped pushing. But it wasn't that fast."

"Did you do anything then," Boyd Mitchell said.

"I got down," my father said, "and I went up there. But here's a man cut in three pieces in front of me. What can you do? You can't do very much. I squatted down and touched his good hand. And it was like ice. His eyes were open and roaming all up in the sky."

"Did he say anything?" my mother said.

"He said, 'Where am I today?' And I said to him, 'It's all right, bud, you're in Montana. You'll be all right.' Though, my God, he wasn't. I took my jacket off and put it over him. I didn't want him to see what had happened."

"You should've put tourniquets on," Boyd Mitchell said gruffly. "That could've helped. That could've saved his life."

My father looked at Boyd Mitchell then as if he had forgotten he was there and was surprised that he spoke. "Don't know about that," my father said. "I don't know anything about those things. He was already dead. A boxcar had run over him. He was breathing, but he was already dead to me."

"That's only for a licensed doctor to decide," Boyd Mitchell said. "You're morally obligated to do all you can." And I could tell from his tone of voice that he did not like my father. He hardly knew him, but he did not like him. I had no idea why. Boyd Mitchell was a big, husky, red-faced man with curly hair—handsome in a way, but with a big belly—and I knew only that he worked for the Red Cross, and that my mother was a friend of his wife's, and maybe of his, and that they played cards when my father was gone.

My father looked at my mother in a way I knew was angry. "Why have you got these people over here now, Dorothy? They don't have any business here."

"Maybe that's right," Penny Mitchell said, and she put down her hand of cards and stood up at the table. My mother looked around the room as though an odd noise had occurred inside of it and she couldn't find the source.

"Somebody definitely should've done something," Boyd Mitchell said, and he leaned forward on the table toward my father. "That's all there is to say." He was shaking his head *no*. "That man didn't have to die." Boyd Mitchell clasped his big hands on top of his playing cards and stared at my father. "The unions'll cover this up, too, I guess, won't they? That's what happens in these things."

My father stood up then, and his face looked wide, though it looked young, still. He looked like a young man who had been scolded and wasn't sure how he should act. "You get out of here," he said in a loud voice. "My God. What a thing to say. I don't even know you."

"I know you, though," Boyd Mitchell said angrily. "You're another featherbedder. You aren't good to do anything. You can't even help a dying man. You're bad for this country, and you won't last."

"Boyd, my goodness," Penny Mitchell said. "Don't say that. Don't say that to him."

Boyd Mitchell glared up at his wife. "I'll say anything I want to," he said. "And he'll listen, because he's helpless. He can't do anything."

"Stand up," my father said. "Just stand up on your feet." His fists were clenched again.

"All right, I will," Boyd Mitchell said. He glanced up at his wife. And I realized that Boyd Mitchell was drunk, and it was possible that he did not even know what he was saying, or what had happened, and that words just got loose from him this way, and anybody who knew him knew it. Only my father didn't. He only knew what had been said.

Boyd Mitchell stood up and put his hands in his pockets. He was much taller than my father. He had on a white Western shirt and whipcords and cowboy boots and was wearing a big silver wristwatch. "All right," he said. "Now I'm standing up. What's supposed to happen?" He weaved a little. I saw that.

And my father hit Boyd Mitchell then, hit him from across the card table—hit him with his right hand, square into the chest, not a lunging blow, just a hard, hitting blow that threw my father off balance and made him make a *chuffing* sound with his mouth. Boyd Mitchell groaned, "Oh," and fell down immediately, his big, thick, heavy body hitting the floor already doubled over. And the sound of him hitting the floor in our house was like no sound I had ever heard before. It was the sound of a man's body hitting a floor, and it was only that. In my life I have heard it other places, in hotel rooms and in bars, and it is one you do not want to hear.

You can hit a man in a lot of ways, I know that, and I knew that then, because my father had told me. You can hit a man to insult him, or you can hit a man to bloody him, or to knock him down, or lay him out. Or you can hit a man to kill him. Hit him that hard. And that is how my father hit Boyd Mitchell—as hard as he could, in the chest and not in the face, the way someone might think who didn't know about it.

"Oh my God," Penny Mitchell said. Boyd Mitchell was lying on his side in front of the TV, and she had gotten down on her knees beside him. "Boyd," she said. "Are you hurt? Oh, look at this. Stay where you are, Boyd. Stay on the floor."

"Now then. All right," my father said. "Now. All right." He was standing against the wall, over to the side of where he had been when he hit Boyd Mitchell from across the card table. Light was bright in the room, and my father's eyes were wide and touring around. He seemed out of breath and both his fists were clenched, and I could feel his heart beating in my own chest. "All right, now, you son of a bitch," my father said, and loudly. I don't think he was even talking to Boyd Mitchell. He was just saying words that came out of him.

"Roy," my mother said calmly. "Boyd's hurt now. He's hurt." She was just looking down at Boyd Mitchell. I don't think she knew what to do.

"Oh, no," Penny Mitchell said in an excited voice. "Look up, Boyd. Look up at Penny. You've been hurt." She had her hands flat on Boyd Mitchell's chest, and her skinny shoulders close to him. She wasn't crying, but I think she was hysterical and couldn't cry.

All this had taken only five minutes, maybe even less time. I had never even left the kitchen door. And for that reason I walked out into the room where my father and mother were, and where Boyd and Penny Mitchell were both of them on the floor. I looked down at Boyd Mitchell, at his face. I wanted to see what happened to him. His eyes had cast back into their sockets. His mouth was open, and I could see his big pink tongue inside. He was breathing heavy breaths, and his fingers—the fingers on both his hands—were moving, moving in the way a man would move them if he was nervous or anxious about something. I think he was dead then, and I think Penny Mitchell knew he was dead, because she was saying, "Oh please, please, please, Boyd."

That is when my mother called the police, and I think when my father opened the front door and stepped out into the night.

All that happened next is what you would expect to happen. Boyd Mitchell's chest quit breathing in a minute, and he turned pale and cold and began to look dead right on our living-room floor. He made a noise in his throat once, and Penny Mitchell cried out, and my mother got down on her knees and held Penny's shoulders while she cried. Then my mother made Penny get up and go into the bedroom—hers and my father's—and lie on the bed. Then she and I sat in the brightly lit living room, with Boyd Mitchell dead on the floor, and simply looked at each other—maybe for ten minutes, maybe for twenty. I don't know what my mother could've been thinking during that time, because she did not say. She did not ask about my father. She did not tell me to leave the room. Maybe she thought about the rest of her life then and what that might be like after tonight. Or maybe she thought this: that people can do the worst things they are capable of doing and in the end the world comes back to normal. Possibly, she was just waiting for something normal to begin to happen again. That would make sense, given her particular character.

Though what I thought myself, sitting in that room with Boyd Mitchell dead, I remember very well, because I have thought it other times, and to a degree I began to date my life from that moment and that thought. It is this: that situations have possibilities to them, and we have only to be present to be involved. Tonight was a very bad one. But how were we to know that it would turn out that way until it was too late and we had all been changed forever? I realized though, that trouble, real trouble, was something to be avoided, inasmuch as once it has passed by, you have only yourself to answer to, even if, as I was, you are the cause of nothing.

In a little while the police arrived to our house. First one and then two more cars with their red lights turning in the street. Lights were on in the neighbors' houses—people came out and stood in the cold in their front yards watching, people I didn't know and who didn't know us. "It's a circus now," my mother said to me when we looked through the window. "We'll have to move somewhere else. They won't let us alone."

An ambulance came, and Boyd Mitchell was taken away on a stretcher, under a sheet. Penny Mitchell came out of the bedroom and went with them, though she did not say anything to my mother, or to anybody, just got in the police car and left into the dark.

Two policemen came inside, and one asked my mother some questions in the living room, while the other one asked me questions in the kitchen. He wanted to know what I had seen, and I told him. I said Boyd Mitchell had cursed at my father for some reason I didn't know, then had pushed Boyd, and that was all. He asked if my father was a violent man, and I said no. He asked if my father had a girlfriend, and I said no. He asked if my mother and father had ever fought, and I said no. He asked if I loved my mother and my father, and I said that I did. And then that was all.

I went out into the living room then, and my mother was there, and when the police left we stood at the front door, and there was my father outside, standing by the open door of a police car. He had on handcuffs. And for some reason he wasn't wearing a shirt or his corduroy jacket but was bare-chested in the cold night, holding his shirt behind him. His hair looked wet to me. I heard a policeman say, "Roy, you're going to catch cold," and then my father say, "I wish I was a long way from here right now. China maybe." He smiled at the policeman. I don't think he ever saw us watching, or if he did he didn't want to admit it. And neither of us did anything, because the police had him, and when that is the case, there is nothing you can do to help.

All this happened by ten o'clock. At midnight my mother and I drove down to the city jail and got my father out. I stayed in the car while my mother went in—sat and watched the high windows of the jail, which were behind wire mesh and bars. Yellow lights were on there, and I could hear voices and see figures move past the lights, and twice someone called out, "Hello, hello. Marie, are you with me?" And then it was quiet, except for the cars that drove slowly past ours.

On the ride home, my mother drove and my father sat and stared out at the big electrical stacks by the river, and the lights of houses on the other side, in Black Eagle. He had on a checked shirt someone inside had given him, and his hair was neatly combed. No one said anything, but I did not understand why the police would put anyone in jail because he had killed a man and in two hours let him out again. It was a mystery to me, even though I wanted him to be out and for our life to resume, and even though I did not see any way it could and, in fact, knew it never would.

Inside our house, all the lights were burning when we got back. It was one o'clock and there were still lights in some neighbors' houses. I could see a man at the window across the street, both his hands to the glass, watching out, watching us.

My mother went into the kitchen, and I could hear her running water for coffee and taking down cups. My father stood in the middle of the living room and looked around, looking at the chairs, at the card table with cards still on it, at the open doorways to the other rooms. It was as if he had forgotten his own house and now saw it again and didn't like it.

"I don't feel I know what he had against me," my father said. He said this to me, but he said it to anyone, too. "You'd think you'd know what a man had against you, wouldn't you, Frank?"

"Yes," I said. "I would." We were both just standing together, my father and I, in the lighted room there. We were not about to do anything.

"I want us to be happy here now," my father said. "I want us to enjoy life. I don't hold anything against anybody. Do you believe that?"

"I believe that," I said. My father looked at me with his dark blue eyes and frowned. And for the first time I wished my father had not done what he did but had gone about things differently. I saw him as a man who made mistakes, as a man who could hurt people, ruin lives, risk their happiness. A man who did not understand enough. He was like a gambler, though I did not even know what it meant to be a gambler then.

"It's such a quickly changing time now," my father said. My mother, who had come into the kitchen doorway, stood looking at us. She had on a flowered pink apron, and was standing where I had stood earlier that night. She was looking at my father and at me as if we were one person. "Don't you think it is, Dorothy?" he said. "All this turmoil. Everything just flying by. Look what's happened here."

159

My mother seemed very certain about things then, very precise. "You should've controlled yourself more," she said. "That's all."

"I know that," my father said. "I'm sorry. I lost control over my mind. I didn't expect to ruin things, but now I think I have. It was all wrong." My father picked up the vodka bottle, unscrewed the cap and took a big swallow, then put the bottle back down. He had seen two men killed tonight. Who could've blamed him?

"When I was in jail tonight," he said, staring at a picture on the wall, a picture by the door to the hallway. He was just talking again. "There was a man in the cell with me. And I've never been in jail before, not even when I was a kid. But this man said to me tonight, 'I can tell you've never been in jail before just by the way you stand up straight. Other people don't stand that way. They stoop. You don't belong in jail. You stand up too straight.'

"My father looked back at the vodka bottle as if he wanted to drink more out of it, but he only looked at it. "Bad things happen," he said, and he let his open hands tap against his legs like clappers against a bell. "Maybe he was in love with you, Dorothy," he said. "Maybe that's what the trouble was."

And what I did then was stare at the picture on the wall, the picture my father had been staring at, a picture I had seen every day. Probably I had seen it a thousand times. It was two people with a baby on a beach. A man and a woman sitting in the sand with an ocean behind. They were smiling at the camera, wearing bathing suits. In all the times I had seen it I'd thought that it was a picture in which I was the baby, and the two people were my parents. But I realized as I stood there, that it was not me at all; it was my father who was the child in the picture, and the parents there were his parents, two people I'd never known, and who were dead—and the picture was so much older than I had thought it was. I wondered why I hadn't known that before, hadn't understood it for myself, hadn't always known it. Not even that it mattered. What mattered was, I felt, that my father had fallen down now, as much as the man he had watched fall beneath the train just hours before. And I was as helpless to do anything as he had been. I wanted to tell him that I loved him, but for some reason I did not.

Later in the night I lay in my bed with the radio playing, listening to news that was far away, in Calgary and in Saskatoon, and even farther, in Regina and Winnipeg—cold, dark cities I knew I would never see in my life. My window was raised above the sill, and for a long time I had sat and looked out, hearing my parents talk softly down below, hearing their footsteps, hearing my father's steel-toed boots strike the floor, and then their bedsprings squeeze and then be quiet. From out across the sliding river I could hear trucks—stock trucks and grain trucks heading toward Idaho, or down toward Helena, or into the train yards where my father hostled engines. The neighborhood houses were dark again. My father's motorcycle sat in the yard, and out in the night air I felt I could hear even the falls themselves, could hear every sound of them, sounds that found me and whirled and filled my room—could even feel them, cold and wintry, so that warmth seemed like a possibility I would never know again.

My father went to Deer Lodge Prison and stayed five months for killing Boyd Mitchell by accident, for using too much force to hit him. In Montana you cannot simply kill a man in your living room and walk off free from it, and what I remember is that my father pleaded no contest, the same as guilty.

My mother and I lived in our house for the months he was gone. But when he came out and went back on the railroad as a switchman the two of them argued about things, about her wanting us to go someplace else to live—California or Seattle were mentioned. And then they separated, and she moved out. And after that I moved out by joining the army and adding years to my age, which was sixteen.

I know about my father only that after a time he began to live a life he himself would never have believed. He fell off the railroad, divorced my mother, who would now and then resurface in his life. Drinking was involved in that, and gambling, embezzling money, even carrying a pistol, is what I heard. I was apart from all of it. And when you are the age I was then, and loose on the world and alone, you can get along better than at almost any other time, because it's a novelty, and you can act for what you want, and you can think that being alone will not last forever. All I know of my father, finally, is that he was once in Laramie, Wyoming, and not in good shape, and then he simply disappeared from view.

A month ago I saw my mother. I was buying groceries at a drive-in store by the interstate in Anaconda, Montana, not far from Deer Lodge itself, where my father had been. It had been fifteen years, I think, since I had seen her, though I am forty-three years old now, and possibly it was longer. But when I saw her I walked across the store to where she was and I said, "Hello, Dorothy. It's Frank."

She looked at me and smiled and said, "Oh, Frank. How are you? I haven't seen you in a long time. I'm glad to see you now, though." She was dressed in blue jeans and boots and a Western shirt, and she looked like a woman who could be sixty years old. Her hair was tied back and she looked pretty, though I think she had been drinking. It was ten o'clock in the morning.

There was a man standing near her, holding a basket of groceries, and she turned to him and said, "Dick, come here and meet my son, Frank. We haven't seen each other in a long time. This is Dick Spivey, Frank."

I shook hands with Dick Spivey, who was a man younger than my mother but older than me—a tall, thin-faced man with coarse blue-black hair—and who was wearing Western boots like hers. "Let me say a word to Frank, Dick," my mother said, and she put her hand on Dick's wrist and squeezed it and smiled at him. And he walked up toward the checkout to pay for his groceries.

"So. What are you doing now, Frank," my mother asked, and put her hand on my wrist the way she had on Dick Spivey's, but held it there. "These years," she said.

"I've been down in Rock Springs, on the coal boom," I said. "I'll probably go back down there."

"And I guess you're married, too."

"I was," I said. "But not right now."

"That's fine," she said. "You look fine." She smiled at me. "You'll never get anything fixed just right. That's your mother's word. Your father and I had a marriage made in Havre—that was our joke about us. We used to laugh about it. You didn't know that, of course. You were too young. A lot of it was just wrong."

"It's a long time ago," I said. "I don't know about that."

"I remember those times very well," my mother said. "They were happy enough times. I guess something was in the air, wasn't there? Your father was so jumpy. And Boyd got so mad, just all of a sudden. There was some hopelessness to it, I suppose. All that union business. We were the last to understand any of it, of course. We were trying to be decent people."

"That's right," I said. And I believed that was true of them.

"I still like to swim," my mother said. She ran her fingers back through her hair as if it were wet. She smiled at me again. "It still makes me feel freer."

"Good," I said. "I'm happy to hear that."

"Do you ever see your dad?"

"No," I said. "I never do."

"I don't either," my mother said. "You just reminded me of him." She looked at Dick Spivey, who was standing at the front window, holding a sack of groceries, looking out at the parking lot. It was March, and some small bits of snow were falling onto the cars in the lot. He didn't seem in any hurry. "Maybe I didn't appreciate your father enough," she said. "Who knows? Maybe we weren't even made for each other. Losing your love is the worst thing, and that's what we did." I didn't answer her, but I knew what she meant, and that it was true. "I wish we knew each other better, Frank," my mother said to me. She looked down, and I think she may have blushed. "We have our deep feelings, though, don't we? Both of us."

"Yes," I said. "We do."

"So. I'm going out now," my mother said. "Frank." She squeezed my wrist, and walked away through the checkout and into the parking lot, with Dick Spivey carrying their groceries beside her.

But when I had bought my own groceries and paid, and gone out to my car and started up, I saw Dick Spivey's green Chevrolet drive back into the lot and stop, and watched my mother get out and hurry across the snow to where I was, so that for a moment we faced each other through the open window.

"Did you ever think," my mother said, snow freezing in her hair. "Did you ever think back then that I was in love with Boyd Mitchell? Anything like that? Did you ever?"

"No," I said. "I didn't."

"No, well, I wasn't," she said. "Boyd was in love with Penny. I was in love with Roy. That's how things were. I want you to know it. You have to believe that. Do you?"

"Yes," I said. "I believe you."

And she bent down and kissed my cheek through the open window and touched my face with both her hands, held me for a moment that seemed like a long time before she turned away, finally, and left me there alone.

First Things First: One more writer's beginnings

t my particular age, forty-four (neither exactly young nor exactly old is how that feels), most partisan arguments aimed at proving some general truth about the world resolve themselves—in my mind anyway—into what I think of as nice, existential equilibrium: almost nothing seems to be generally true, almost nothing generally false, so that the best anyone can do is find his own way, reveal it as such, and go on hopefully. Counsel, real counsel, in the way Walter Benjamin meant it—useful words about human life—is and always has been very hard to come by. Benjamin believed counsel was the great virtue of told stories, those spoken in the human voice by wise travelers, and that in them the righteous man might encounter himself in the person of the storyteller.

Which was all very well when we had plenty of those tellers, whose faces we knew, out and around visiting homes without TVs, where people passed their evenings weaving and spinning. Now storytelling itself is a brisk cottage industry. Slews of young writers stay up nights, letting no one in, trying their best to write well and be read, at a time when books are popularly conceived of as cordless miniseries, and getting read is hard. Both giving and taking counsel require adapting, I guess. The human voice must be listened for more freely and also more acutely. The righteous man, *whoever he is,* needs to take consolation more willingly, and be ready to encounter himself less in the person of the storyteller or even in the tale told properly, and more in the fabric of a life which might simply be like his. After all, even Benjamin admits that counsel is "less an answer to a question than a proposal concerning the continuation of a story which is just unfolding."

When I got out of school, in 1970, ready to begin being a writer, there seemed to hold sway in the country a kind of conventional wisdom regarding writing, and particularly getting started writing; a protocol for getting work (stories, in my case) published into the world and eventually read by real readers. I'm no longer sure that such a protocol exists in the minds of young writers today. I do not even know why we thought what we thought. But we thought it, acted on it. And for some people it worked out fine, while for others—me—it didn't.

Wisdom was that for young writers there was a particular "publishing world" out there, a world divided into hemispheres. One hemisphere was the sub-world of small presses, literary magazines, university reviews. And the other, more brilliant upper half was the world of large-circulation, widely read, money-paying, famous-making magazines printed on slick pages, and not in Baton Rouge or Bowling Green, but in New York and Boston. The Big Time this was.

What we—or at least I—understood about this whole world was that I needed to "break into it." There was a "level" I could empirically find by sending my stories out—literary magazines were where one started—and either getting them back or having them approved and published. Good stories were to be found there, it was alleged, and mine would stand a chance. Once I'd done that, broken into print, I could try to "move up" to better, more widely read and distributed magazines—there was a floating sense of which were better than others. My work, my name would begin to get around. I would see some action. Acceptance would be a word I'd hear more. Money would rarely change hands, but I was not in this for money (and, truly, I wasn't). All this would go along for a while, years perhaps, while I got better, while I had more work published, while my name on a manuscript began to be associated with good writing; until, by some act of providence, a story of mine would get "taken" upwards by an editor from the other world, the one where all the bright lights were turned on. And then I would be someplace. That would be the it heard often in the phrase "You've made it."

The trouble was, this progression didn't work for me. Oh, it worked for others well enough. Some of the finest, most admirable writers writing today have gone up through these ranks, their good stories published, their readership solidly banked by their earliest admirers. And some writers, of course, simply ignored this whole ladder-and-rung business altogether, sent stories to the *New Yorker* or the *Atlantic,* got the good word straight away, hit the ground running, and have never looked back. Much maligned now by spoilsports, such early and great success must've been very sweet. I'd have handled mine admirably, I'm sure. In any case, all formulas for creating one's writing life break down once the first term—*I write a story*—is put into place.

I, however, could not get my stories published. I sent them to many—very many—of the magazines that were on everyone's checklists. (Actual, mimeographed lists were eventually compiled by who-knows-what mysterious Samaritan using the *Writer's Digest* and some unverifiable word-of-mouth about publications generously, if inexplicably, courting unpublished writers.) I kept a log, a little notebook in which I had lined off little boxes, inside which I wrote where this story was sent and when, when it came back, where it went next. Somebody—I forget who now—told me this is what I should do. I needed to be orderly. Systematic. It was serious business I was up to. The strangling horror that a story would be accepted at two or perhaps three magazines at once, the embarrassment, and bad editorial blood this would cause to flow, could all be avoided this way. Meanwhile, the system, my logging in dates and destinations like a shipping clerk, would give me something to do while I awaited my own good news, offer solace when there wasn't good news. And there wasn't.

I was persistent. I kept my stories out. I furrowed my brow over levels. Maybe the *Cimarron Review* was just too good for me at this point; I should send a story to a magazine with a less resolute name. I remember one called the *Fur-Bearing Trout,* where I was chattily turned down by an editor who said he didn't like short stories longer than eight pages, though they need not be about fish.

I pulled strings—any ones I thought I had. To *Sumac,* a magazine in Michigan, I wrote that I was a graduate of Michigan State. That seemed cagey. To a magazine in Mississippi I bragged I was a native. No dice. I got my friend whom the *Cimarron Review* firmly admired and regularly published to recommend me. No again. I even got an old teacher who had once taught Willie Morris at Texas to middleman a story to *Harper's Magazine*—shooting, just once, for the moon. No.

Once a man named Nick Crome (I hope he's happy, wherever he is) asked me to revise a story I'd sent to his magazine, *TransPacifc*. Though when I eagerly did and returned it to him, he ignored my new version, but asked me to badger my local library (which happened to be the Chicago Public Library) into subscribing and inserting his magazine onto its shelves. I admit it—I wrote him promptly and suggested where he ought best insert his magazine, whereupon he dispatched to me a three-page, single-spaced letter full of invective and threat in which he periodically used the red half of his ribbon for emphasis, and in which he called me "sonny," "sport," "ace," "junior," a "simpleton," a "sorry, petulant fool," and an "ignorant motherfucker." To his credit, though, he also wrote this to me: "I devote most of my waking hours to the attempt to promote the careers of people like you, ace. I do this not only by publishing them—but by writing every one personally, so they know there's a real person here, who knows who they are and who does read what they write. . . . My wife, who is acting now as the business manager, tells me you're not a subscriber. That's okay—relatively few care about preserving the means by which young writers in America find publication—shit now, junior, they just want to get PUBLISHED! ! ! ! !" "Published" was one of those words typed in red.

Seasoning, I think this is called. Dues paying. Learning the ropes. Getting my feet wet. Starting at the bottom. I was doing this. Only nobody liked my stories.

Finally a call came from a friend in California. A magazine, he said, in New Zealand was interested in new American writing. Maybe I could send something there. New Zealand, I thought, gazing out my window at an unpromising winter sky. A nice place. English spoken there. New Zealand. Yes. I would. And sure enough the editors took my story, even asked for another, which I sent and they agreed to publish soon. And for a time in the winter of 1971, I thought very, very fondly about New Zealand, about what good people were there. Readers. People willing to give you a chance. Careless of trends, vogues, reputations. It was summer there, then. I thought of Mr. Peggotty in David Copperfield, sailing off to Australia: "We will begin a new life over theer," is how he put it. Exuberant. Valiant. I considered a move.

First, though, I fastidiously entered the titles of my two stories and their new "homes" into my logbook beside the word "accepted," and into the heretofore empty space on my curriculum vitae reserved for publications. New Zealand. It seemed farther away there on that page than when the happy letters had arrived. I wondered for a moment what someone would think who saw these entries, what sort of writer they'd think I was, what form of giggly desperation inhabited me that I needed to send my stories all the way there. Would they realize the North American serial rights for each story were still intact, and I could still publish the stories stateside if I wanted to? Or if someone else wanted to? And who would ever read these stories? The editors—all good fellows—liked them, paid them compliments. But no one else ever weighed in with praise or complaint or notice of any kind. All was quiet. And in a month I decided not to move to New Zealand. Not yet. It wasn't going anyplace, after all.

Though neither was I.

I went back to circulating my stories. *Epoch, North American Review, Red Clay*

Reader, New American Review—where I'd read some writers whose names I knew. Philip Roth, William Gass, Robert Coover. I quit writing cagey cover letters. My own "production," however, was beginning to slow. I'd written eight or so stories, I was twenty-seven years old, and I felt I was becoming confused about my "style." My log-book was filled up. A student journal at a small Ohio college agreed to print a story, but one I'd written three years ago! When I was just starting school! The editor loved it: "If you can write like this," I remember his letter saying, "you should be writing for the slicks." Only I couldn't write like that anymore. I'd "developed" beyond this. Maybe I shouldn't have. What did he know?

It all got me down. That much I can tell you. Stories would whistle back into my mailbox just ahead of a dark mistral. I'd read the enclosed letters, check to see if the story was still clean and enough undented by paper clips to send out again, gulp down some bearable bitterness, and then just quit for the day. Usually I'd have a drink about 10:45 in the morning and take a long walk until my wife got off work and there was something new to take heart from.

And then, unsuddenly, I quit writing stories, "gagged by the silence of others," as Sartre says. I was discouraged. But I do not think I was disillusioned. Even then I knew that a life, even a short one like mine, once dedicated to literature was not a wasted life. I was merely a failure at what I was doing, and along with failure's other dull commissions comes—as should be—the opportunity to think things over. Failure may not always inspire one's best decisions, but one's profoundest convictions do often arise nearby.

And so, in the late winter of 1971, in Chicago, I took an account of the world and, as it says in Dickens, my "personal history, adventures, experience, and observation" of it.

There is a koan often overheard among avant-gardists and inside the better, more progressive graduate writing programs, which asks: Is it not almost always the case that you can tell a good story by the fact that very few people like it? Considering, however, who were the few who liked my stories, I did not feel I had the full comfort of even that befuddling wisdom. And, in any case, I wanted people to like my stories. More importantly, I wanted people to *read* them, even if they couldn't like them. I believed—or I came to believe that winter—that writers, the ones I cared about, and even myself, wrote to be read; not to aggrandize themselves in cringing elitism, not to please or psychoanalyze themselves by getting closer to their feelings, and not, indeed, just to be published and to fill that empty space on a resume. Writers wrote, I concluded, not even to appeal to a particular readership, but to discover and bring to precious language the most important things they were capable of, and to reveal this to others with the hope that it will commit an effect on them—please them, teach them, console them. Reach them.

I, it was plain, wasn't succeeding here. Nobody was reading my stories because, I decided, they simply weren't very good—not good enough, anyway. Maybe I knew it in my backbrain; maybe I just trusted the editors who sent them all back to me. But I knew it. It's true I've always trusted rejection more than acceptance (at the time I'd had more experience with rejection). But it's also true that I came to believe that no good writing would go unpublished. Perhaps this was just the original, free, and blind act of writer's faith, but if so, it seemed to me collateralized by the lavish evidence of so much awful writing—even if not mine—routinely finding its "home" in print.

Beyond these first principles of belief, certain practical matters became apparent to me. I did not write very fast. I wrote hard, but at my pace I would never get the proper amount of low-level publishing experience to move up through the ranks. Too few at bats, you could say. Moreover, I didn't like the whole major league/minor league premise of that conventional wisdom I'd inherited. I read the magazines I'd been submitting to, as well as the ones I wished I could, and I couldn't see evidence that the premise worked very well. Plenty of terrible stories were popping up in both leagues. There was reason to believe, in fact, that not a whole lot of really excellent writing got done, or probably ever did. That, of course, is still the case, though it doesn't discourage anyone, nor should it.

Even more to the point, I began to resent what seemed to me the unprovable premise that there existed any useful structure or scheme of ascendable rungs whose rule was that my stories weren't good enough at first but might be better later on; and that I should have patience and go on surrendering myself to its clankings. What I felt was that I wanted my stories to be great stories, as good as could be written. And now. And if they weren't (and they weren't) that was my own business, my problem, not the concern of some system for orderly advancement in the literary arts, some wisdom kept presumptuously active by wretched, gradstudent magisters sitting before piles of mss., or else some already belly-up writer who'd changed boats middlecourse and fallen into being an "editor." I had hard thoughts that winter. But I meant my failings to be my own affair.

Some people, I guess, thrive by deferring to unknown and presumably higher authority, to the benevolence of vast, indistinct institutions. And, of course, it's never a simple matter when your life requires submitting to the judgment of others. We all accommodate that. But most of the writers I have respected and still respect seem to me not so adept at discerning and respecting underlying design, but at trying to invent designs anew. What was out there, I thought eighteen years ago, and think even more this minute, is not a structure for writers to surrender to, but fidgety, dodgy chaos. And our privileged task is to force it, calm it to our wills.

What I did, then, with all this fresh in mind, was put my stories away in their tabbed folders, fattened by the various drafts and revisions and rejection notices that lodged with them, and dedicate myself to writing a novel, which I assumed would take years, and did. Not that I propose this strategy for anyone else. My belief about starting novels, and particularly the first one, is that you treat the impulse like the impulse to marry: solemnly, and with the proviso that if you can talk yourself out of it you should. And if you can't, then there's no advice to give you.

But I needed to get better—much, much better at what I was doing, and in ways I don't even want to think about now. A novel would take those years; I could go more slowly; there was more to work on, get better at. No demoralizing rejections would crash into my mailbox every morning. One might eventually come, but it was far off. And in trade for this easement, this slow-going, this sumptuous usage of my time and youth, I'd have a novel, maybe, when all was over—a not inconsiderable achievement. It was a bargain I was only too happy to enter.

Thinking back on 1971, I am even more convinced now than I could've been then. Not that a commanding philosophy of the writer's life was forged on this one decision. I still wanted my work published—that was the only way it would ever get read. This was simply a matter of practical protocol: I decided I could do my best at a distance from the preoccupations and the institutions and the thin solaces and the misfires of publication. Said another way, failure at publishing stories where I wanted and tried vigorously to publish them turned me back to my work, which is what's important. "Success," which I still calibrate in readers, was withheld, and I somehow was encouraged—even if it felt different at the time. And it did feel different.

I dignify my decision now by believing that publication of those first stories might've just plain shot me in the foot by conferring approval—of some kind—on work I wanted to be good but that wasn't very good. When I look around in literary bookstores now, and in the back ad pages of magazines, it seems that with patience and resourcefulness *every* writer can find a publisher for everything that's written—good, bad, mediocre. And while I won't wag a finger at publishing too fast or publishing your buddies or publishing the famous because they're thought to be "lightning rods of the culture" (as a famous editor recently admitted) or even just publishing a magazine that nobody but the editors and their parents will ever read—a young Joyce might always be lurking, and who cares, anyway—I have written enough stories myself that "aren't right for us" or that "showed promise" or that "would surely find a home elsewhere" so as to feel sovereignty over this one opinion: publishing work that's no good probably isn't a very good idea for writers and publishers, either one, no matter where along the literary ladder they happen to be clinging. For writers, it's hard when no one likes your work, and hard in another way when things begin finally to break for you, but it's best to try and set your own high standards for what's good and what isn't—even if, God knows, you happen to have written the stuff yourself.

Finally, small presses, literary magazines, university reviews, do still have a place in my writing life. On occasion they have been willing to publish what—by my own standards—have been stories as good as I can write after years of trying. I do not, however, believe that small presses or literary journals are "where it's at" for writing in this country, any more than I believe the *New Yorker* or *Esquire* are. I've never been convinced or seen evidence that the audiences for quarterlies with 1,800 readers are any more perceptive or appreciative or forgiving than other putative audiences, or that their editors are any more open-minded, generally willing to take risks, less capricious, less victims of cronyism, or had their ears more finely tuned to excellent writing than anybody else who sets up as a public literary arbiter. True, those slick magazines are run to the tune of profits. Money. But one fellow's profit is likely to be another man's principle. Who's to say whose god is meaner, coarser?

Where it's at for literature in this country is where it's always been, of course—with writers, and what they write. Writing is dark and lonely work, and no one has to do it. No one will even care much if it doesn't get done at all, so that choosing to do it and to try to do it well is enough of an existential errand, enough of a first step, and for whatever my money and counsel's worth, enough of a last step, too.

Corpse Cradle

Tess Gallagher

Nothing hurts her like the extravagance
of questions, because to ask is
to come near, to be humbled at the clotted nucleus.
One persistent cry bruises her cheekbones and she lets
it, lets the open chapel of her childhood brighten over
her with tree-light. Gray-white future
of alder, hypnosis of cedar as when
too much scent-of-nectar combs
her breathing. Rain on rain
like an upsurge in his sudden need to graze her
memory, bareheaded at the quayside
where he dreamily smoked a cigarette and guided her,
the satin shell of her stillness, toward
that same whiteness at the top of rain, swollen
and gradual. How lucid she is,
blurred edgeless, like listening
to be more wide awake, that music she pressed into him
in order to fascinate what beautifully
he had begun. All bird and no recall, she
thinks, and lives in his birdness, no burden
but strange lightness so she wants to be up at dawn,
the mountains fogged with snow, a world
that sleeps as if it were
all the world and, being so, able to be seen
at its beginning, freshly
given as sleep is, bleak fertility of sleep when
she thinks far into his last resting
wherein she drifted, drifts, slow and white,
deeply asking, deep with its dark below.

Those pages he turned down in peaks
at the corners are kerchiefs now, tied
to the last light of each favorite tree
where he paused, marking my path
as surely as if he'd ordered squads
of birds to rustle leaves overhead.

And I do look up often, musing into
his warmed-over nests or letting
a thrum of recognition pulsate *koto*-like
as if his head were over my shoulder
in a cool fog allowed to think its way
down a marble staircase shorn
of its footfalls. In a child's crude
pea-pod canoe my amber beads float seaward
like a cargo meant to be lost.

How often I am held alive by half-a-matchstick,
remembering his voice across rooms
and going when called to hear some line
of poetry read aloud in our two-minded way
like adding a wing for ballast and
discovering flight.

So much of love is curved there
where his pen bracketed
the couplet mid-page, that my unused

trousseau seems to beckon deeply
like a forehead pressed into paradox
by too much invitation.

Now That I Am Never Alone

In the bath I look up and see the brown moth
pressed like a pair of unpredictable lips
against the white wall. I heat up
the water, running as much hot in as I can stand.
These handfuls over my shoulder—how once
he pulled my head against his thigh and dipped
a rivulet down my neck of coldest water from the spring
we were drinking from. Beautiful mischief
that stills a moment so I can never look
back. Only now, brightest now, and the water
never hot enough to drive that shiver out.

But I remember solitude—no other
presence and each thing what it was. Not this raw
fluttering I make of you as you have made of me
your watch-fire, your killing light.

Moon Crossing Bridge

If I stand a long time by the river
when the moon is high
don't mistake my attention
for the merely aesthetic, though
that saves in daylight.
Only what we once called worship
has feet light enough to carry
the living on that span of brightness.
And who's to say I didn't cross
just because I used the bridge in its witnessing,
to let the water stay the water
and the incongruities of the moon to chart
that joining I was certain of.

Black Valentine

I run the comb through his lush hair,
letting it think into my wrist
the way the wrist whispers to the cards
with punctuation and savvy in a game of solitaire.
So much not to be said the scissors
are saying in the hasp and sheer
of the morning. Eleven years I've cut
his hair and even now, this last time, we hide
fear to save pleasure
as bulwark. *My dearest*—the hair says as it brushes my
thighs—*my only*—on the way to the floor. If the hair
is a soul-sign, the soul obeys our gravity, piles up
in animal mounds and worships the feet. We're
silent so peace rays over us like Bernice's hair
shaken out across the heavens. If there were gods
we are to believe they animated her shorn locks
with more darkness than light, and harm
was put by after the Syrian campaign, and
harm was put by as you tipped the cards
from the table like a child bored
with losing. I spread my hair like a tent over us
to make safety wear its twin heads, one to face death,
the other blasted so piteously by love
you throw the lantern of the moment against
the wall and take me in with our old joke, the one
that marks my northern skies, "Hey, babe," you say
like a man who knows how to live on earth. "Hey,"
with your arm around my hips, "what you doing
after work?" Silly to ask now if the hair
she put on the altar, imagining her power over
his passage, was dead or living.

We're All Pharaohs When We Die

Our friends die with us
    and the sky too
        in huge swatches, and lakes, and places
           we walked past, just going and
              coming.
The spoons we ate with look dim, a little deadened
    in the drawer. Their trips to the mouth
        forlorn, and the breath caught there
           fogged to a pewtery smudge.

   Our friends die with us and are thrown in because we
used them so well.
But they also stay on earth awhile like the abandoned
      huts of the Sherpas on a mountain that doesn't know
        it's being climbed. They don't fall down all at once.
          Not like his heart
    fell down, dragging
the whole gliding eternity of him out of sight.

Guttural and aslant, I chew the leather sleeve
      of his jacket, teething like a child on the unknown pressure
        budding near its tongue. But the tongue
          is thrown in too, everyone's who said his name
    as he used to be called
    in our waking and sleeping,
      dreaming and telling the dreams.
        Yes, the dreams are thrown in
    so the mystery
      breaks through still wearing its lid, and I am never
        to be seen again
          out of his muslin striding.

If this is my lid then, with its eyebrows painted on, with
its stylized eyes glazed open above the yet-to-be-dead ones, even so
          a dead-aliveness looks through
             as trees are thrown in
                 and clouds and the meadows under the orchards
          the deer like to enter-those returning souls
             who agree to be seen
                gazing out of their forest-eyes
          with our faint world painted over them.

Northwest by Northwest

Our stones are subtle here, a lavender that is
almost gray, a covert green
a step shy of its blue.
For eating, as with loneliness, we prefer
the bowl to the plate, for its
heaping up, its shapeliness of offering
what it half encloses. Just
when it seems the day has gone to sleep, the eagle
drops suddenly from its black chambers.

The silks of drowsy weddings sham the horizon and ecstasy
is a slow mirage we drift towards, voyaging in
some eternal orient whose seasons
ache, serenely inhabit, but disdain
to yield. The *she* who rules here leans
across the void to reward our perpetual suspension
with an ongoing tomb—"If," she says, "you
existed." Requiring pleasure to revolve
outside its answer.

Picking Bones

Emiko here from Tokyo in her red dress
and voice like a porcelain hand
on silk. We carry roses to the grave
under the tilt of gulls. Some have
walked their hieroglyphics across the poem
carved there, to make sure we comprehend
this stopping off to flight. Small tasks

prepare another silence, kinship of pouring
water, fallen petals brushed across granite.
Gradually we come there after we've
come there. Hard to light candles
in the breeze from the strait. His delight
flickers and gusts. We are steady
and erased a little more. Finally we talk quietly,

the presence palpable as we crouch there.
That overlay too of new sound Emiko has given
his poems in Japanese. Our voices nudge closer
on the cliffside. Pungency and sweetness
of joss sticks, Emiko says, in Japanese cemeteries,
and smoke curling up. After cremation of the loved one,
working in pairs, the relatives join in the ritual

of "picking bones." Two by two with chopsticks lifting
each bone from the ashes, dropping it
into an urn. Her friend, Yoshi, who said he had
much feeling and grief on viewing

his father's body, but who saw and felt,
in lifting shards of a father—the lightness, the necessary

While I Sit in a Sunny Place

Tame love that remembers a birthday
but scorns the every-moment,
how you robbed the pit from the cherry,
that wooden pearl I was carrying
under my tongue. Talisman
of silence wedged between the poet's words
when I say, "Don't you know
I'm the joyful girl inside
the woman with the forever-melting ghost
on her lips?" If the word "happy"
has a future it's mine because
I don't exist in the favored shell
of what I'm meagerly given. Isn't
there enough sky? Isn't there
laughter and running? Can't the ardor
of one smiling face make a deer leap,
even when to leap could mean
an alternate calamity?

I have only these hot-cold widow's hands
to touch the world back with.
You know that and it doesn't stop you.
Something sacred, a vast accord between
my ghosted-love and how it could
convey the shadow-selves of some happiest
surrender—was this what brought you?

Be equal to it then, like a deer that chooses
to leap over a rose. Like a rose with its leaping
above it.

Thieves at the Grave

Now snow has fallen I have been to you
in all weather, especially lovebird weather,
a valence throughout, thanks to
the viewpoint at the cliff edge
where teenagers park to rehearse in daylight
certain suppressions of desire
so as to repeal them more aggressively
at dark. Their glances along the shore below
and farther out at the fishing boats reflect a gauze
of homecoming as when your patina of green
wears through me. Purposeful

then to bury you above our fishing grounds.
Purposeful as fish locked in their fluidity,
as we are. Location, says the snow,
is what you do to me, what I record briefly
and change into second nature. My knee-marks
are two bald companion moons where we glide
grassily in place. I leave things
to test your company—the two potted plants
so tempting in August bees were a fever
in goldenrod and I could think, "He loves
their industry." By September someone
had hefted them away into a secret garden.
That simple desecration, the thief's prerogative,

joined you back to my living, and we are benefactors
to shepherds, blind walkers, a braille of winds.
What the bees took they gave again

My Father's Love Letters

I t's two days before Christmas and I have checked myself into the Dewitt Ranch Motel. "We don't ask questions here," says the manager, handing me the key to number 66. I let him think what he thinks.

The room is what I need, what I've been imagining for the past two days—a place with much passing and no record. I feel guilty about spending the money, but I've trusted my instincts about what it will take to get this writing done. For the past week I've been absorbed with student manuscripts and term papers. At the finish, I discover I have all but vanished. Coming to the motel is a way to trick myself out of anonymity, to urge my identity to rise like cream to the top again.

I had known from the first moments of being asked to write about my influences as a writer that I would want to get back to the child in me. For to talk of influences for a writer is essentially to trace the development of a psychic and spiritual history, to go back to where it keeps starting as you think about it, as an invention of who you are becoming. The history which has left its deepest imprint on me has been an oral and actual history and so involves my willingness at a very personal level. It involves people no one will ever know again. People like the motel room I write this in, full of passing and no record. The "no record" part is where I come in. I must try to interrupt their silence. Articulate it and so resurrect them so that homage can be paid.

To speak of influences, then, is not to say "Here, try this," only "This happened and this is what I think of it at this moment of writing."

I want to begin with rain. A closeness, a need for rain. It is the climate of my psyche, and I would not fully have known this if I had not spent a year in Arizona, where it rained only three glorious times during my entire stay there. I begin with rain also because it is a way of introducing my birthplace on the Olympic peninsula in Washington State, the town of Port Angeles. The rain forest is a few miles west. The rain is more violent and insistent there. Port Angeles lies along the strait of Juan de Fuca and behind the town are the Olympic Mountains. The Japanese current brings in warm air, striking the mountains, which are snow-covered into June.

It is a faithful rain. You feel it has some allegiance to the trees and the people, to the little harbor with its long arm of land which makes a band of calm for the fishing boats and for the rafts of logs soon to be herded to the mills. Inside or outside the wood-framed houses, the rain pervades the temperament of the people. It brings an ongoing thoughtfulness to their faces, a meditativeness that causes them to fall silent for long periods, to stand at their windows looking out at nothing in particular. The people don't mind getting wet. Galoshes, umbrellas—there isn't a market for them here. The people walk in the rain as within some spirit they wish not to offend with resistance. Most of them have not been to Arizona. They know the rain is a reason for not living where they live, but they live there anyway. They work hard in the logging camps, in the pulp mills and lumberyards. Everything has a wetness over it, glistening quietly as though it were still in the womb, waiting to be born.

Sudden Journey

Maybe I'm seven in the open field—
the straw-grass so high
only the top of my head makes a curve
of brown in the yellow. Rain then.
First a little. A few drops on my
wrist, the right wrist. More rain.
My shoulders, my chin. Until I'm looking up
to let my eyes take the bliss.
I open my face.
Let the teeth show. I
pull my shirt down past the collar-bones.
I'm still a boy under my breast spots.
I can drink anywhere. The rain. My
skin shattering. Up suddenly, needing
to gulp, turning with my tongue, my arms out
running, running in the hard, cold plenitude
of all those who reach earth by falling.

Growing up there, I thought the moss-light that lived with us lived everywhere. It was a sleepy predawn light that muted the landscape and made the trees come close. I always went outside with my eyes wide, no need to shield them from sun bursts or the steady assault of skies I was to know later in El Paso or Tucson. The colors of green and gray are what bind me to the will to write poems.

Along with rain and a subdued quality of light, I have needed the nearness of water. I said once in an interview that if Napoleon had stolen his battle plans from the dreams of his sleeping men, then maybe I had stolen my poems from the gray presence of water.

The house I grew up in overlooks the eighteen-mile stretch of water between Canada and America at its far northwest reach. The freighters, tankers, tugs, and small fishing boats pass daily; and even at night a water star, the light on a mast, might mark a vessel's passage through the strait. My father was a longshoreman for many of these years, and he knew the names of the ships and what they were carrying and where they came from: the *Kenyo Maru* (Japanese), the *Eastern Grace* (Liberian), the *Bright Hope* (Taiwanese), the *Brilliant Star* (Panamanian), the *Shoshei Maru* (Japanese)—pulp for paper, logs for plywood, lumber for California. He explained that *maru* was a word that meant that the ship would make its return home. I have been like these ships, always pointed on a course of return to this town and its waters.

On Saturdays my father would drive my mother and my three brothers and me into town to shop and then to wait for him while he drank in what we called the "beer joints." We would sit for hours in the car, watching the townspeople pass. I noticed what they carried, how they walked, their gestures as they looked into the store windows. In other cars were women and families waiting as we were, for men in taverns. In the life of a child, these periods of stillness in parked cars were small eternities. The only release or amusement was to see things, and to wonder about them. Since the making of images is for me perhaps 90 percent seeing and 10 percent word power, this car seeing and the stillness it enforced contributed to a patience and a curiosity that heightened my ability to see. The things to be seen from a parked car were not spectacular, but they were what we had—and they promoted a fascination with the ordinary. My mother was an expert at this: "See that little girl with the pigtails. I bet she's never had her hair cut. Look there, her father's taking her in there where the men get their hair cut." And sure enough, the little girl would emerge twenty minutes later, eyes red from crying, one hand in her father's and the other clutching a small paper sack. "The pigtails are in there."

Every hour or so my mother would send me on a round of the taverns to try for a sighting of my father. I would peck on the windows and the barmaid would shake her head *no* or motion down the dim aisle of faces to where my father would be sitting on his stool, forgetting, forgetting us all for a while.

My father's drinking, and the quarrels he had with my mother because of it, terrorized my childhood. There is no other way to put it. And if coping with terror and anxiety are necessary to the psychic stamina of a poet, I had them in steady doses—just as inevitably as I had the rain. I learned that the world was not just, that any balance was temporary, that unreasonableness could descend at any minute, thrashing aside everything and everyone in its path.

Emotional and physical vulnerability was a constant. Yet the heart began to take shelter, to build understandings out of words. It seems that a poet is one who must be strong enough to live in the unprotected openness, yet not so strong that the heart enters what the Russian poet Akhmatova calls "the icy calm of unloving." Passion and forgiveness, emotional fortitude—these were the lessons of the heart I had no choice but to learn in my childhood. I wonder now what kept me from the calm of not loving. Perhaps it was the unspoken knowledge that love, my parents' love, through all was constant, though its blows could rake the quick of my being.

I was sixteen when I had my last lesson from the belt and my father's arm. I stood still in the yard, in full view of the neighbors. I looked steadily ahead, without tears or cries, as a tree must look while the saw bites in, then deepens to the core. I felt my spirit reach its full defiance. I stood somehow in the power of my womanhood that day and knew I had passed beyond humiliation. I felt my father's arm begin to know I had outleaped the pain. It came down harder. If pain could not find me, what then would enforce control and fear?

I say I entered my womanhood because I connect womanhood with a strong, enduring aspect of my being. I am aware, looking back, that women even more than children often serve a long apprenticeship to physically and psychically inflicted threat and pain. Perhaps because of this they learn more readily what the slave, the hostage, the prisoner, also know—the ultimate freedom of the spirit. They learn how unreasonable treatment and physical pain may be turned aside by an act of will. This freedom of spirit is what has enabled poets down through the ages to record the courage and hopes of entire peoples even in times of oppression. That women have not had a larger share in the history of such poetry has always seemed a mystery to me, considering the wealth of spiritual power that suffering often brings when it does not kill or maim the spirit. I can only assume that words have been slow in coming to women because their days have, until recently, been given over so wholly to acts, to doing and caring for.

During these periods of abuse, I did not stop loving. It was our hurt not to have another way to settle these things. For my father and I had no language between us in those numb years of my changing. All through my attempts in the poems, I have needed to forge a language that would give these dead and living lives a way to speak. There was often the feeling that the language might come too late, might even do damage, might not be equal to the love. All these fears. Finally no choice.

The images of these two primal figures, mother and father, condense now into a vision of my father's work-thickened hands, and my mother's back, turned in hopeless anger at the stove where she fixed eggs for my father in silence. My father gets up from the table, shows me the open palms of his hands. "Threasie," he says, "get an education. Don't get hands like these."

Out of this moment and others like it I think I began to make a formula which translates roughly: words = more than physical power = freedom from enslavement to job-life = power to direct and make meaning in your own life.

There were few examples of my parents' having used words to transcend the daily. The only example was perhaps my father's love letters. They were kept in a cedar chest at the foot of my bed. One day I came across them, under a heap of hand-embroidered pillowcases. There were other treasures there, like the deer horn used to call the hounds when my father had hunted as a young man. The letters were written on lined tablet paper with a yellow cast to it. Written with a pencil in a consistently erratic hand, signed "Les" for Leslie and punctuated with a brigade of XXXXXs. I would stare at these Xs, as though they contained some impenetrable clue as to why this man and woman had come together. The letters were mainly informational—he had worked here, was going there, had seen so-and-so, would be coming back to Missouri at such and such a time. But also there was humor, harmless jokes some workman had told him, and little teasings that only my mother could have interpreted.

My mother's side of the correspondence was missing, probably because my father had thrown her letters away or lost them during the Depression years when he crossed the country, riding the rails, working in the cotton fields, the oil fields, and the coal mines. My mother's lost letters are as important to remember as those I found from my father. They were the now invisible lifeline that answered and provoked my father's heart-scrawl across the miles and days of their long courtship.

I might easily have called this essay "My Mother's Love Letters," for they would have represented the most articulate half of the correspondence, had they been saved. That they are now irrevocably lost, except to the imagination, moves them into the realm of speculation. The very fact that my mother had saved my father's love letters became a sign to me as a child that love *had* existed between my parents, no matter what acts and denials had come after.

As with my parents, invisible love has been an undercurrent in my poems, in the tone of them, perhaps. They have, when I can manage it, what Marianne Moore called iodine and what I call turpentine. A rawness of impulse, a sharpness, a tension, that complicates the emotion, that withholds even as it gives. This is a proclivity of being, the signature of a nature that had learned perhaps wrongheadedly that love too openly seen becomes somehow inauthentic, unrealized.

My father's love letters were then the only surviving record of my parents' courtship and, indeed, the only record that they ever loved each other, for they never showed affection for one another in front of us. On a fishing trip years after I'd left home, my father was to remark that they had written to each other for over ten years before they married in 1941.

My father's sleep was like the rain. It permeated the household. When he was home he seemed always to be sleeping. We saw him come home and we saw him leave. We saw him during the evening meal. The talk then was of the ILWU long-shoremen's union and of the men he worked with. He worked hard. It could be said that he never missed a day's work. It was a fact I used in his defense when I thought my mother was too hard on him after a drinking bout.

Stanley Kunitz has seen the archetypal search for the father as a frequent driving force for some poets, his own father having committed suicide before his birth. It occurs to me that in my own case, the father was among the living dead, and this made my situation all the more urgent. It was as if I had set myself the task of waking him before it was too late. I seemed to need to tell him who he was and that what was happening to him mattered and was witnessed by at least one other. This is why he has been so much at the center of my best efforts in the poems.

The first poem I wrote that reached him was called "Black Money," this image taken from the way shoveling sulfur at the pulp mills had turned his money black. He had come to visit me in the Seattle apartment where I lived as a student and I remember telling him I'd written this poem for his birthday. I had typed it and sealed it into an envelope like a secret message. He seemed embarrassed, as if about to be left out of something. Then he tore the envelope open and unfolded the poem. He handed it back to me. "You read it to me," he said. I read the poem to him and as I read I could feel the need in his listening. I had finally reached him. "Now that's something," he said when I'd finished. "I'm going to show that to the boys down on the dock."

Black Money

His lungs heaving all day in a sulphur mist,
then dusk, the lunch pail torn from him
before he reaches the house, his children
a cloud of swallows about him.
At the stove in the tumbled rooms, the wife,

her back the wall he fights most, and she
with no weapon but silence and to keep him from the bed.

In their sleep the mill hums and turns
at the edge of water. Blue smoke
swells the night and they drift
from the graves they have made for each other,
float out from the open-mouthed sleep
of their children, past banks and businesses,
the used car lots, liquor store, the swings in the park.

The mill burns on, now a burst of cinders,
now whistles screaming down the bay, saws jagged
in half light. Then like a whip
the sun across the bed, windows high with mountains
and the sleepers fallen to pillows
as gulls fall, tilting
against their shadows on the log booms.
Again the trucks shudder the wood framed houses
passing to the mill. My father
snorts, splashes in the bathroom,
throws open our doors to cowboy music
on the radio, hearts are cheating,
somebody is alone, there's blood in Tulsa.
Out the back yard the night-shift men rattle
the gravel in the alley going home.
My father fits goggles to his head.

From his pocket he takes anything metal,
the pearl-handled jack knife, a ring of keys,
and for us, black money shoveled
from the sulphur pyramids heaped in the distance
like yellow gold. Coffee bottle tucked in his armpit
he swaggers past the chicken coop,
a pack of cards at his breast.
In a fan of light beyond him
the *Kino Maru* pulls out for Seattle,
some black star climbing
the deep globe of his eye.

As the oldest child, I seemed to serve my parents' lives in an ambassadorial capacity. But I was an ambassador without a country, for the household was perpetually
on the verge of dissolving. I cannot say how many times I watched my father go
down the walk to the picket fence, leaving us forever, pausing long enough at the

gate to look back at us huddled on the porch. "Who's coming with me?" he would ask. No one moved. Again and again we abandoned each other.

Maybe this was the making of my refugee mentality. And perhaps when you are an emotional refugee you learn to be industrious toward the prospect of love and shelter. You know both are fragile and that stability must lie with you or it is nowhere. You make a home of yourself. Words for me and later poems were the tools of that home-making.

Even when you think you are only a child and have nothing, there are things you have, and as Sartre has already told us, one of these things is words. When I saw I had words and that these could affect what happened to me and those I loved, I felt less powerless, as through these might win through, might at least mediate in a life ruled as much by chance as by intention.

These ambassadorial skills I was learning as a child were an odd kind of training for the writing of poems, perhaps, but they were just that. For in the writing of the poem you must represent both sides of the question. If not in fact, then in understanding. You must bring them into dialogue with one another fairly, without the bias of causes or indignation or needing too much to be right. It requires a widening of perspective, away from oversimplification—the strict good or bad, wrong or rightness of a situation. The sensibility I've been attempting to write out of wants to represent the spectrum of awareness. In this way the life is accounted for in its fullness, when I am able.

I have spoken of words as a stay against unreasonableness, and they are often this— though more to one's solitude than to the actual life. My father came to his own words late, but in time. I was to discover that at seventy he could entertain my poet friends and would be spoken of afterward as someone exceptional in their experience. He told stories, was witty, liked to laugh. But in those early days, my father was not a man you could talk with. He would drive me to my piano lessons, the family's one luxury, without speaking. He smoked cigarettes, one after the other. He was thinking and driving. If he had had anything to drink during these times it was best to give him a wide berth. I was often afraid of him, of the violence in him, though like the rain, tenderness was there, unspoken and with a fiber that strangely informed even the unreasonable. If to be a poet is to balance contraries, to see how seemingly opposite qualities partake of, in fact penetrate, each other, I learned this from my combative parents.

3 A.M. *Kitchen: My Father Talking*

For years it was land working me, oil fields,
cotton fields, then I got some land. I
worked it. Them days you could just about
make a living. I was logging.

Then I sent to Missouri. Momma
come out. We got married.
We got some kids. Five kids.
That kept us going.

186

We bought some land near the water.
It was cheap then. The water
was right there. You just looked out
the window. It never left the window.

I bought a boat. Fourteen footer.
There was fish out there then.
You remember, we used to catch
six, eight fish, clean them right
out in the yard. I could of fished to China.

I quit the woods. One day just
walked out, took off my corks, said that's
it. I went to the docks.
I was driving winch. You had to watch
to see nothing fell out of the sling. If
you killed somebody you'd
never forget it. All
those years I was just working
I was on edge, every day. Just working.

You kids. I could tell you
a lot. But I won't.

It's winter. I play a lot of cards
down at the tavern. Your mother.
I have to think of excuses
to get out of the house. You're
wasting your time, she says. You're wasting
your money.

You don't have no idea, Threasie.
I run out of things
to work for. Hell, why shouldn't I
play cards? Threasie,
some days now I just don't know.

This long childhood period of living without surety contributed in another way to my urge to write poetry. If I had to give one word which serves my poetry more than any other, it might be "uncertainty." Uncertainty which leads to exploration, to the articulation of fears, to the loss of the kind of confidence that provides answers too quickly, too superficially. It is the poet's uncertainty which leaves her continually in an openness to the possibilities of being and saying. The true materials of poetry are essentially invisible—a capacity for the constant emptying of the house of the word, turning it out homeless and humbled to search its way toward meaning again. Maybe "poem" for me is the act of a prolonged beginning, one without resolution except perhaps musically, rhythmically—the word "again" engraved on the fiery hammer.

After my youngest brother's death when I was twenty, I began to recognize the ability of poetry to extend the lives of those not present except as memory. My brother's death was the official beginning of my mortality. It filled my life, all our lives, with the sense of an unspoken bond, a pain which traveled with us in memory. It was as though memory were a kind of flickering shadow left behind by those who died. This caused me to connect memory firmly to the life of the spirit and finally to write poems which formalized the sharing of that memory.

I have been writing about my progress toward a life in words and poems, but my first love was actually paint. As a child I took great pleasure in the smell of linseed, the oil of it on my fingers, the tubes of oil paint with their bands of approximate color near the caps, the long-handled brushes. I had heard somewhere that artists taught themselves by copying other painters. But the only paintings we had in the house were those in some Bible books a salesman had sold my mother. I began to copy these with oil colors onto some rough paper I'd found in a boxcar near the paper mill below our house. I remember especially my painting of Jacob sleeping at the foot of a heavenly stairway, with several angels descending. They each had a pair of huge wings, and I wondered at the time why they didn't just fly down, instead of using the stairs. The faces of these angels occupied a great deal of my efforts. And I think it is some help to being a poet to paint the faces of angels when you are ten.

I finished the Jacob painting and sent it to my grandfather in Missouri. He was a farmer and owned a thousand-acre farm of scrub oak, farmland, and riverbed in the Ozarks. My mother had been raised there. Often when she had a faraway look about her, I imagined she was visiting there in her thoughts.

My Mother Remembers That She Was Beautiful

The falling snow has made her thoughtful
and young in the privacy
of our table with its netted candle
and thick white plates. The serious faces
of the lights breathe on the pine boards
behind her. She is visiting
the daughter never close
or far enough away to come to.

She keeps her coat on, called into
her girlhood by such forgetting
I am gone or yet
to happen. She sees herself
among the townspeople, the country glances
slow with fields and sky

as she passes or waits
with a brother in the hot animal smell
of the auction stand: sunlight,
straw hats, a dog's tail
brushing her bare leg.

"There are things you know.
I didn't have to beg," she said, "for anything."

The beautiful one speaks to me
from the changed, proud face and I see
how little I've let her know
of what she becomes. Years
were never the trouble, or the white hair
I braided near the sea
on a summer day. Who
she must have been
is lost to me through some fault
in my own reflection and we will have to go on
as we think we are, walking for no one's sake
from the empty restaurant into the one color
of the snow—before us, the close houses,
the brave and wondering lights of the houses.

Children sometimes adopt a second father or mother when they are cut off from the natural parent. Porter Morris, my uncle, was the father I could speak with. He lived with my grandparents on the farm in Windyville, Missouri, where I spent many of my childhood summers. He never married, but stayed with the farm even after my grandparents died. He'd been a mule trainer during the Second World War, the only time he had ever left home. He loved horses and raised and gentled one for me, which he named Angel Foot because she was black except for one white foot.

I continued to visit my grandfather and my uncle during the five years of my first marriage. My husband was a jet pilot in the Marine Corps. We were stationed in the South, so I would go to cook for my uncle during the haying and I would also help stack the hay in the barn. My uncle and I took salt to the cattle. We sowed a field with barley and went to market in Springfield with a truckload of pigs. There were visits with neighbors, Cleydeth and Joe Stefter or Jule Elliot, when we sat for hours telling stories and gossiping. Many images from my uncle's stories and from these visits to the farm got into the long poem "Songs of the Runaway Bride" in my first book.

My uncle lived alone at the farm after my grandfather's death, but soon he met a woman who lived with her elderly parents. He began to remodel an old house on the farm. There was talk of marriage. One day my mother called to say there had been a fire at the farm. The house had burned to the ground and my uncle could not be found. She returned to the farm, what remained of her childhood home. After the ashes had cooled, she searched with the sheriff and found my uncle's skeleton where it had burned into the mattress springs of the bed.

My mother would not accept the coroner's verdict that the fire had been caused by an electrical short-circuit, or a fire in the chimney. It was summer and no fire would have been laid. She combed the ashes looking for the shotgun my uncle always kept near his bed and the other gun, a rifle, he hunted with. They were not to be found. My mother believed her brother had been murdered and she set about proving it. She offered a reward and soon after, a young boy walking along the roadside picked my uncle's billfold out of the ditch, his name stamped in gold on the flap.

Three men were eventually brought to trial. I journeyed to Bolivar, Missouri, to meet my parents for the trial. We watched as the accused killer was released and the other two men, who had confessed to being his accomplices, were sentenced to five years in the penitentiary for manslaughter. Parole would be possible for them in two to three years. The motive had been money, although one of the men had held a grudge against my uncle for having been ordered to move out of a house he'd been renting from my uncle some three years before. They had taken forty dollars from my uncle, then shot him when he could not give them more. My parents and I came away from the trial stunned with disbelief and anger.

Two Stories

to the author of a story taken from the death of
my uncle, Porter Morris, killed June 7, 1972

You kept the names, the flies
of who they were, mine
gone carnival, ugly Tessie.
It got wilder but nothing
personal. The plot had me
an easy lay for a buck.
My uncle came to life
as my lover. At 16
the murderer stabbed cows
and mutilated chickens. Grown,
you gave him a crowbar that happened
to be handy twice. Then you made him
do it alone. For me
it took three drunks, a gun, the house
on fire. There was a black space
between trees where I told you.

The shape of my uncle
spread its arms on the wire springs
in the yard and the neighbors

came to look at his shadow
caught there under the nose
of his dog. They left that angel
to you. Your killer never
mentioned money. Like us he wanted
to outlive his hand in the sure blood
of another. The veins of my uncle streaked
where the house had been. They watched
until morning. Your man found a faucet
in an old man's side. His pants
were stiff with it for days. He left
the crowbar on Tessie's porch like a bone.

My weapon was never found.
The murderers drove a white
stationwagon and puked
as they went. They hoped
for 100 dollar bills stuffed
in a lard can. But a farmer
keeps his money in cattle
and land. They threw his billfold
into the ditch like an empty
bird. One ran away. Two stayed
with women. I kept the news
blind. You took it from my mouth,
shaped it for the market, still
a dream worse than I remembered.

Now there is the story of me
reading your story and the one
of you saying it
doesn't deserve such care.
I say it matters
that the dog stays by the chimney
for months, and a rain
soft as the sleep of cats
enters the land, emptied
of its cows, its wire gates pulled down
by hands that never dug
the single well, this whitened field.

I tried to write it out, to investigate the nature of vengeance, to disarm myself of
the anger I carried. I wrote two poems about this event: "Two Stories" and "The
Absence." Images from my uncle's death also appeared in "Stepping Outside," the

title poem of my first, limited-edition collection. I began to see poems as a way of settling scores with the self. I felt I had reached the only possible justice for my uncle in the writing out of my anger and the honoring of the life that had been taken so brutally. The *In Cold Blood* aspect of my uncle's murder has caused violence to haunt my vision of what it is to live in America. Sometimes, with my eyes wide open, I still see the wall behind my grandfather's empty bed, and on it, the fiery angels and Jacob burning.

I felt if my uncle, the proverbial honest man, could be murdered in the middle of the night, then anything was possible. The intermittent hardships of my childhood were nothing compared to this. I saw how easily I could go into a state of fear and anger which would mar the energy of my life and consequently my poems for good. I think I began, in a steady way, to move toward accepting my own death, so that whenever it would come before me as a thought, I would release myself toward it. In the poems I've written that please me most, I seem able to see the experience with dead-living eyes, with a dead-living heart.

My own sense of time in poems approximates what I experience in my life—that important time junctures of past and present events via memory and actual presences are always inviting new meanings, revisions of old meanings, and speculation about things still in the future. These time shifts are a special province of poems because they can happen there more quickly, economically, and convincingly than in any other art form, including film. Film is still struggling to develop a language of interiority using the corporeal image, while even words like *drum* or *grief* in poems can borrow inflection from the overlap of words in context, can form whole new entities, as in a line from Louise Bogan's poem "Summer Wish": "the drum pitched deep as grief."

Since my intention here has been to emphasize experiential influences rather than literary ones, I must speak of the Vietnam War, for it was the war that finally caused me to take up my life as a poet. For the first time since I had left home for college, I was thrown back on my own resources. My husband and I had met when I was eighteen and married when I was twenty-one. I was twenty-six when he left to fly missions in Vietnam. I'd had very little life on my own. It became a time to test my strengths. I began working as a ward clerk in a hospital, on the medical floor. I did this for about five months, while the news of the war arrived daily in my mailbox. I was approaching what a friend of that time called an "eclipse." He urged me to leave the country. It was the best decision I could have made, as I look back now.

My time in Ireland and Europe during the Vietnam War put me firmly in possession of my own life. But in doing this, it made my life in that former time seem fraudulent. The returning veterans, my husband among them, had the hardship of realizing that many Americans felt the war to be wrong. This pervasive judgment was a burden to us both and one that eventually contributed to the dissolution of our marriage.

I began to experience a kind of psychic suffocation which expressed itself in poems that I copied fully composed from my dreams. For a while, this disassociation of dream material from my life caused the messages to go unheeded. But gradually my movement out of the marriage began to enact the images of dissolution in the poems. It was a parting that gave me unresolvable grief, yet at the same time allowed my life its first true joys as I began a full commitment to my writing. I think partings have often informed my poems with a backward longing, and it was especially so with this one.

I returned to Seattle in 1969 and began to study poetry with David Wagoner and Mark Strand at the University of Washington. My family did not understand what I was doing. Why should I divorce and then go back to college to learn to write poetry? It was beyond them. What was going to become of me now? Who would take care of me?

Trees have always been an important support to the solitude I connect with the writing of poetry. I suspect my affection and need of them began in those days in my childhood when I was logging with my parents. There was a coolness in the forest, a feeling of light filtering down from the arrow-shaped tops of the evergreens. The smell of pitch comes back. The chain-saw snarl and a spray of wood chips. Sawdust in the cuffs of my jeans. My brothers and I are again the woodcutter's children. We play under the trees, but even our play is a likeness to work. We construct shelters of rotten logs, thatch them with fireweed, and then invite our parents into the shelters to eat their lunches. We eat Spam sandwiches and smoked fish, with a Mountain Bar for dessert. After a time, my parents give me a little hatchet and a marking stick so I can work with them, notching the logs to be cut up into pulpwood to be made into paper. My brothers and I strip cones from the fallen trees, milking the hard pellets with our bare hands into gunnysacks, which are sold to the Forestry Department for ten dollars a bag. There is a living to be made and all of us are expected to do our share.

When I think of it now, it is not far from the building of those makeshift shelters to the making of poems. You take what you find, what comes naturally to the hand and mind. There was the sense with these shelters that they wouldn't last, but that they were exactly what could be done at the time. There were great gaps between the logs because we couldn't notch them into each other, but this allowed us to see the greater forest between them. It was a house that remembered its forest. And for me, the best poems, no matter how much order they make, have an undercurrent of forest, of the larger unknown.

To spend one's earliest days in a forest with a minimum of supervision gave a lot of time for exploring. I also had some practice in being lost. Both exploring and being lost are, it seems now, the best kind of training for a poet. When I think of those times I was lost, they come back with a strange exhilaration as though I had died yet had the possibility of coming back to life. The act of writing a poem is like that. It is that sense of aloneness which is trying to locate the world again, but not too soon, not until the voice has made its cry, "Here here, over here," and the answering voices have called back, "Where are you?"

My mother and father started logging together in 1941, the year my mother traveled from Missouri by bus to marry my father. As far as she knows, she was the only woman who worked in the woods, doing the same work the men did. She was mainly the choker-setter and haul-back. She hauled the heavy steel cable, used to yard the logs into the landing, out over the underbrush to be hooked around the fallen trees My mother's job was a dangerous one because the trees, like any dying thing, would often thrash up unexpectedly or release underbrush which could take out an eye or lodge in one's side. She also lifted and stacked the pulpwood onto the truck and helped in the trimming of the branches. She did this work for seven years.

There is a photograph of my mother sitting atop two gigantic logs in her puffed-sleeve blouse and black work pants. It has always inspired me with a pride in my sex. I think I grew up with the idea that whatever the rest of the world said about women, the woman my mother was stood equal to any man and maybe one better. Her labor was not an effort to prove anything to anyone. It was what had to be done for the living. I did not think of her as unusual until I was about fourteen. I realized then that she was a wonderful mechanic. She could fix machines, could take them apart and reassemble them. None of the mothers of my friends had such faith in their own abilities. She was curious and she taught herself She liked to tinker, to shift a situation or an object around. She had an eye for possibilities and a faculty for intuitive decision-making that afterward looked like knowledge. I feel I've transferred to the writing of poems many of my mother's explorative methods, even a similar audacity toward my materials.

"What happened to those letters?" I ask my mother over the telephone. I don't tell her I'm at the Dewitt Ranch Motel writing this essay. I don't tell her I'm trying to understand why I keep remembering my father's love letters as having an importance to my own writing.

"Well, a lot of them were sent to the draft board," she says. "Your dad and I were married November of forty-one. Pearl Harbor hit December seventh, so they were going to draft your father. A lot of men was just jumping up to get married to avoid the draft. We had to prove we'd been courting. The only way was to send the letters, so they could see for themselves."

"But what happened to the letters?"

"There was only about three of them left. You kids got into them, so I burnt them."

"You burnt them? Why? Why'd you do that?"

"They wasn't nothing in them."

"But you kept them," I say. "You saved them."

"I don't know why I did," she says. "They didn't amount to anything."

I hang up. I sit on one of the two beds and stare out at an identical arm of the motel which parallels the unit I'm in. I think of my father's love letters being perused by the members of the draft board. They become convinced that the courtship is authentic. They decide not to draft him into the war. As a result of his having written love letters, he does not go to his death, and my birth takes place. It is an intricate chain of events, about which I had no idea at the start of this essay.

I think of my father's love letters burning, of how they might never have come into their true importance had I not returned to them here in my own writing. I sit in the motel room, a place of much passage and no record, and feel I have made an important assault on the Great Nothing, though the letters are gone, though they did not truly exist until this writing, even for my parents, who wrote and received them.

My father's love letters are the sign of a long courtship and I pay homage to that, the idea of writing as proof of the courtship—the same blind, persistent hopefulness that carries me again and again into poems.

Envy

George Garrett

Calls itself injustice.
Calls itself the grim, appropriate answer
to a swarm of bitter questions.
Lies heavy, heavy on my heart.

Names me fool at first sight.
Makes me fool of the feast of the dead.
Serves me ditch water and moldy bread.
Winks at me with your green eyes.

Tide Turning

(for John Ciardi)

Even as, inch by living inch,
I contrive to chip and cut and carve
myself into various and sundry parts—

first, of course, the fingers
and the toes, then ears and nose,
these offered, as it were, in the words

of *The Book of Common Prayer,* to be
"a reasonable, holy and living sacrifice."
Eyes before sex, arms before legs;

next the thin peeled skin and last
a bloody mess of muscles and meat,
fat and lonely internal organs. . . .

Must we be universal donors, John?

Much too much to hope for.
Better (and you knew it and said so,
well and so many times)

to spend our skin and bones, to pay
out blood and breath upon
a wholly unimportant poem,

something reasonably simple and simply
(while memory still burns) unforgettable:
you and I, one time, late on my front porch

in York Harbor, Maine, drinking
stone fences—your special favorite
apple jack and apple cider, all

the fumes and essences of Eden;
two old guys feeling no pain
underneath the brightly reeling stars,

while nearby, shiny and smooth
as a black snake, the river is rising
to high tide, inch by living inch.

Figure of Speech

"It's a doggie dog world."
—student paper

For years my litter of wounds
moved quietly, obedient and gentle,
well-trained, eager to please.
Loved my quick heels and a tight leash,
begged cutely, fetched and rolled over
and licked the fingers that fed them.

Now they return, a gaunt and feral pack,
each and every one presenting
a noisy mouth, rich with cruel teeth
and drooling tongue. See their red eyes,
how the hair stands up as they turn against
each other, killing for my choicest parts.

A Postcard to My Old Friends, the Poets

One of these days soon
I, too, will have another day
blank as a new pillow case
or a field of fresh snow.
And then and there once again
I'll lay down my head, I will
make angels in the wet snow.
I will write words, words, words
as you do and sign my name,
naming my new poems like children,
calling them home from the dark.

Abraham's Knife

Where hills are hard and bare,
rocks like thrown dice, heat
and glare that's clean and pitiless,
a shadow dogs my heels, limp
as a drowned man washed ashore.
True sacrifice is secret, none
to applaud the ceremony, nor
witness to be moved to tears.
No one to see. God alone
knows, Whose great eye winks not,
from Whom no secrets are hid.

My father, I have loved you,
love you now, dead so many years.
Your ghost shadows me home.
Your laughter and your anger still
trouble my scarecrow head like wings.
My own children, sons and daughter,
study my stranger's face. Their flesh,
bones frail as a small bird's,
is strange, too, in my hands.
What will become of us?
I read my murder in their eyes.

And you, old father, Abraham,
my judge and executioner, I pray
bear witness for me now. I ask
a measure of your faith. Forgive
us, Jew and Gentile, all
your children, all your victims.
In naked country of no shadow
you raise your hand in shining arc.
And we are fountains of foolish tears
to flood and green the world again.
Strike for my heart. Your blade is light.

Main Currents of American Political Thought

Gone then the chipped demitasse cups
at dawn, rich with fresh cream and coffee,
a fire on the hearth, winter and summer,
a silk dandy's bathrobe, the black Havana cigar.

Gone the pet turkey gobbler, the dogs and geese,
a yard full of chickens fleeing the shadow of a hawk,
the tall barn with cows and a plough horse, with corn,
with hay spilling out of the loft, festooning the dead
    Pierce Arrow.

Gone the chipped oak sideboards and table,
heavy with aplenty of dented, dusty silverware.
Gone the service pistol and the elephant rifle
and the great bland moosehead on the wall.

"Two things," you told me once, "will keep
the democratic spirit of this country alive—
the free public schools and the petit jury."
Both of these things are going, too, now, Grandfather.

You had five sons and three daughters,
and they are all dead or dying slow and sure.
Even the grandchildren are riddled with casualties.
You would not believe these bitter, shiny times.

What became of all that energy and swagger?
At ninety you went out and campaigned for Adlai
    Stevenson
    in South Carolina. Half that age and I have to force
myself to vote, choosing among scoundrels.

Early Thaw

A little sun a light south wind
and all of a sudden we're in the big middle
of mud season O long time yet before the lilacs
or anything else even first green leaves
my loud proud black and tan hound dog
stands to bark at a lone crow high in the dead
limbs of the dying elm next door
Crow shrugs as only crows can
if crows can he's lonesome up there all alone
I'm richer owning my own hound dog and also
today all that wrinkling of dazzling gold
on the windy river as well as
all the fresh thick mud my boots can
gorge and carry Crow he's a whole lot lighter
if poorer He can shrug and flap
ragged wings to rise out of the branches
Shrug and flap and fly away black
as my best thought a piece of burnt paper
one moody poem too muddy to believe

Some Snapshots

I. Italian Lesson

When I hear of the death of another major poet these days,
I remember Rome, *1958,* myself standing alongside an
    enormous priest
by a newspaper kiosk in Trastevere, staring at headlines—
IL PAPA E MORTO! As the priest turns away a voice from
    the crowd
(all too poor to buy a paper) calls out: "Is it true the Holy
    Father is dead?"
The priest nods, then shrugs hugely and answers in the
    local dialect:
"Better him than us, eh? Better him than us." And walks
    off to his chores
among the poor who are always with us even until the
    end of the world.

Buzzard

I've heard that holy madness is a state
not to be trifled with, not to be taken
lightly by jest or vow, by lover's token
or any green wreath for a public place. Flash
in the eyes of madmen precious fountains,
whose flesh is wholly thirst, insatiate.

I see this graceful bird begin to wheel,
glide in God's fingerprint, a whorl
of night, in light a thing burnt black,
unhurried. Somewhere something on its back
has caught his eye. Wide-winged he descends
like angels to the business of this world.

I've heard that saintly hermits, frail, obscene
in rags, slack-fleshed, eyes like jewels, kneel
in dry sand among the tortured mountains, feel
at last the tumult of their prayers take shape,
take wings, assume the brutal rush of grace.
This bird comes then and picks those thin bones clean.

Rice University

I was already in Houston, working at the Alley Theater and, as it happened, living only a few blocks from Rice in the little enclave of West University, when Rice needed somebody to teach a couple of English courses on very short notice. I think somebody or other had quit just before the fall term got under way. But I don't really know what happened to create a job for me. I never asked.

Rice seemed like a wonderful little school. Small-college atmosphere in the big middle of a city. I would walk over from my house three days a week pick up any mail at the English office, teach my classes, and meet with students for tutorials and conferences in the student center. The kids were overworked and tired most of the time. The whole thing was free in those days, but a student could be expelled (there was a waiting list for every place and slot) for falling behind or low grades. They came and went. Sometimes I would cut through the campus coming back from a play or a concert or the movies or a party in downtown Houston. And at two o'clock in the morning all the lights in all the dorms would be burning. They studied all the time.

But the students were good (not *adventurous,* but good) and my colleagues left me happily alone. And the schedule was easy, really no more than an interruption in my writing day.

Best of all Rice seemed to have next to no bureaucracy, almost no paperwork. Every other school I knew of was a blizzard of papers, memos to read and answer, forms to fill out, reports to make or to comment on. There was hardly ever anything in my departmental mailbox.

I told my colleagues, whenever we did get together over coffee or something, how lucky they were to work at a university that was not smothering American education.

They smiled and shrugged and looked a little odd. Of course, they didn't really have anything to compare it with. They probably couldn't appreciate how remarkably free they were.

Things were so loose and casual that at the end of the first semester, I didn't receive any grade sheets from the registrar's office. I went there and checked in, explaining my problem. They assured me that they had sent out some grade sheets for my classes, but maybe they had been lost or something. They were very polite and considerate (amazingly so for academic administrators, who tend to cultivate rudeness to faculty as a perk of their jobs, part of their job descriptions), and I left convinced that Rice was unique in the simplicity and decency of its administration. A model for every other college and university in America. I said this to my colleagues also. And, as before, they smiled oddly and shrugged.

Came the end of the year. Last class. I taught it, then dropped by the English department to see if there was anything—final grade sheets maybe—in my mailbox.

Nothing much. I turned and encountered the chairman, whom I had actually seen in person about twice during the whole academic year.

We exchanged idle pleasantries, indulged in small talk.

Then he said: "I do hope you and your wife are going to come to our party on Thursday night."

"Well, sir," I told him, "we would certainly like to and we will if we can. This is the first I've heard about it."

"That can't be," he said. "I sent you at least three notices about the party."

"Well, I'm sorry. I never got any of them."

"That's strange."

I was getting mildly annoyed at the whole thing.

"I come here regularly Monday, Wednesday, and Friday to teach my classes. I always come here to the department and check the mailbox. And I never got anything about any kind of a departmental party."

"Oh," he said. "I wouldn't have sent it here. I sent it to your office."

"My office? I don't have an office."

"Sure you do," he said. "Everybody has an office."

"I don't."

After a little more of this he got a key and led me over to the library then down to the basement.

Pretty soon we were standing in front of a door with my name stenciled on it. He opened the door, and we pushed our way inside. Pushed, had to, because the whole room was a huge pyramid of paper. Official letters, memos, forms to be filled out, reports to be made. Piles and piles. Copies of copies. Some stamped Final Notice. Others bearing savage warnings of what I might expect if I did not reply at once and forthwith.

I stood and laughed awhile. He gave me the smile and the shrug. Closed and locked the door. We walked outside together.

By the time we were in sunlight and shade I had time to think a couple of things about all this.

First thing I realized was that I had failed not just occasionally, but completely. In terms of the bureaucracy and paperwork I had done nothing, *zero,* right all year long. So? Nothing had happened to me or my students or the school. All was well.

Next thought I had was to picture it from their point of view. There's this guy, this one fella over there in the English department, who is absolutely and completely uncooperative. He won't do anything right. Or wrong, either. Won't do anything except teach his classes. What's wrong with him? What the fuck is he trying to prove? Must be crazy. Send him a memo. Send him another warning.

The Right Thing to
Do at the Time

*T*his is a true story about my father, a true story with the shape of a piece of fiction. Well, why not? Where do you suppose all the shapes and forms of fiction came from in the first place? And what's the purpose of fiction anyway, whether it's carved out of the knotty hardwood of personal experience or spun out of the slick thin air like soap bubbles? "What's the purpose of the bayonet?" they used to yell when I was a soldier years ago. The correct answer was: *"To kill, to kill,* TO KILL!"

The purpose of fiction is simply to tell the truth.

My father was a small-town southern lawyer, not a writer, but he was a truth-teller. And he would tell the truth, come what may, hell or high water. And since he loved the truth and would gladly risk his life (and ours, the whole family's) for the sake of it, he would fight without stint, withholding nothing, offering no pity or quarter against what he took to be wrong—that is, against the untruth. He would go to any length he had to. And that is what this story is all about—how far one man would go to fight for the truth and against what was and is wrong.

We were living in the cow town of Kissimmee, Florida, in the early years of the Great Depression. Disney World is near there now, and it looks pretty much like every place else. But it was a hard, tough place then, a place where life was hard for many decent people, black and white. And it was a place where some not-so-decent people had managed to seize power and to hold power and were extremely unlikely to be dislodged from power. Among the people in power in those days were the Ku Klux Klan, not a sad little bunch of ignorant racists in bedsheets but a real clan, a native-grown kind of organized crime family.

My father and his law partner were fighting against the Klan in court and in public with the promise that they would (as they, in fact, did) represent free of charge any person at all who chose to resist the Klan and wanted a lawyer.

This exposed position led to a whole lot of trouble, believe me. And in the end it led to the demise of the Klan as a power of any kind in central Florida. But the big trouble came later. This happened early on as the lines were being drawn and the fight was just getting under way.

Sometimes in the early evening we would go together, my mother and father and the other children, into town for an ice-cream cone: a great treat in those days. One evening we piled into our old car and drove into the center of town and parked in front of the drugstore. Went inside and sat on tall swivel chairs at the counter eating our ice-cream cones. We were all sitting there in a row when a young policeman walked in. Try as I will, I can't remember his name anymore. Just that he was very young and that my mother, who was a teacher then, had taught him in high school. He greeted her politely at first. He seemed a little awkward and embarrassed.

"Mr. Garrett," he said to my father, "I'm afraid I'm going to have to give you a red ticket."

"Oh, really?" my father said, still licking his ice-cream cone. "What for?"

"Well, sir, your taillights don't work."

"They did when I came down here."

"Well, sir, they sure don't now."

"Let's us have a look."

So we all trooped outside and looked at the taillights. They didn't work, all right, because they were broken and there was shattered red glass all over the street right behind the back bumper.

"I wonder who would do a thing like that," my father said, giving the young cop a hard look.

"Well, I wouldn't know, sir," he said. "I just work for the city and I do what I'm told. And I have to write you a ticket."

"Fine," my father said. "I understand that."

Then he surprised the cop and us too by asking if he could pay for the ticket right then and there. And the cop said yes, that was his legal right, and he said it would cost five dollars.

Now that was considerable money in those days when grown men with some skills were earning eight or ten dollars a week. Nobody had any money in those days, nobody we knew or knew of. Most of my father's clients, those who could pay at all, paid him in produce and fresh eggs, things like that.

My father peeled off five one-dollar bills. The cop wrote him a receipt. Then my father told my mother to drive us on home when we had finished our ice cream. He had to go somewhere right away.

He whistled loudly and waved his arm for a taxi. One came right over from the Atlantic Coastline depot directly across the way. He kissed my mother on the cheek and said he would be back just as soon as he could. Gave her the keys to our car and hopped into the cab.

None of us heard what he told the driver: "Let's go to Tallahassee."

Tallahassee was and is the state capital, a good three hundred or so miles away by bad, narrow roads in those days.

Much later we learned what happened. They arrived very late. Slept in the cab. First thing in the morning he got himself a shave in the barbershop. Then went to the legislature. Where, exercising a constitutional right to speak on this kind of matter, he quickly established that the town charter for Kissimmee, Florida, was completely illegal and unconstitutional. In a technical, legal sense that town did not exist and never had. It would require a special action of the state legislature to give the town a new charter and a legal existence. Having made his point, he thanked the legislators kindly and left the capitol. Woke the snoring taxi driver and said, "Let's go back home."

It probably cost him a hundred dollars for that ride. Maybe more. He never told us, and nobody, not even my mother, ever dared ask him.

By the time he arrived home there was a delegation waiting to see him at our house: the mayor, the chief of police, the judge, pretty much the whole gang. Legislators had been on the phone all day to them, and they were deeply worried. Because, you see, everything they had ever done, in the absence of a valid town charter, including collecting taxes, had been illegal. You can imagine what that could mean if people got it in mind to be litigious about things.

Everybody came into our living room. And the whole family, too, because, he said, we saw the beginning of it and deserved to see the end.

Before the mayor or any of them said a word, he explained to them exactly what he had done. And he told them that, under the state constitution, establishing a town was a very tricky legal business. He said the chances were a hundred to one that they would mess it up again. He wished them good luck, promising that if they ever bothered him or us anymore, he would go to Tallahassee again and close them down for keeps.

There was a lot of silence. Finally the mayor spoke.

"What do you want from us, Garrett?"

"Ah," said my father. "I knew it would come down to that. And I'm glad it did, because there is something I do want from you all."

They were all looking and waiting. I reckon they were ready to do or pay most anything. That's how things were handled.

"Damn it!" he said. "I want my five dollars back from that phony traffic ticket."

Long pause.

"That's all?"

"That's all. You give me my five dollars back and I'll give you back your receipt."

So they paid him the five dollars and he tore the receipt in two and they filed out of our house.

"You beat them, Daddy," I said. "You won!"

"That's right, boy," he told me. "And I taught them a very important lesson."

"What's that?" my mother asked, nervously.

"If they want to stop me now," he said, "they're going to have to kill me. And I don't think they've got the guts for it."

Then he laughed out loud. And so did I, not because it was funny, but because it seemed like the right thing to do at the time.

Faith

James Houston

M aybe it happened as the first long earth-wave rolled through
our town. Maybe it was later. We had aftershocks all night.
Faith, my wife, wouldn't sleep inside. No one would but me.
Everyone spent the night in the driveways on cots, or on the
lawns in sleeping bags, as if this were a neighborhood slumber party. I think I had to
prove to myself that if all else failed I could still believe in my own house. If that first
shaker had not torn it to pieces, I reasoned, why should I be pushed around and bul-
lied by these aftershocks rated so much lower on the Richter scale?

When the second big one hit us, just before dawn, I was alone and sleeping fit-
fully, pinned to my bed, dozing like a corporal in the combat zone waiting for the
next burst of mortar fire. I sat up and listened to rafters groaning, calling out for
mercy. I heard dishes leap and rattle in the kitchen. I listened to the seismic roar that
comes rushing toward you like a mighty wind. I should have run for the doorjamb. I
couldn't. I could not move, gripped by the cold truth of my own helplessness.

I sat there with the quilt thrown back and rode the tremor until the house settled
down. Outside I heard voices. They rose in a long murmur of anxiety laced with
relief, as children called to their parents, as neighbor talked to neighbor from lawn to
lawn, from driveway to driveway. Eventually the voices subsided, and I was aware for
the first time of a hollow place within, a small place I could almost put my finger on.
Describing it now, I can say it felt as if a narrow hole had been scooped out, or
drilled, right behind my sternum, toward the lower end of it, where the lowermost
ribs come together.

At the time I had no words for this, nor did I try to find any. From the rising of the
sun we had to take things one hour at a time. We were out of water. Sewage lines had
burst, contaminating the mains. Phone lines were down. Power was out all over the
county, and many roads were cut off. Long sections of roadbed had split. In the central shopping district, several older buildings, made of brick and never retrofitted,
were in ruins. They'd been built on flood plain. As the tremor passed through it, the
subsoil liquified. Faith and I live in a part of town built on solider stuff. No one's
house jumped the foundation. But indoors, everything loose had landed on the
floor—dishes, pictures, mirrors, lamps. Half our chimney fell into the yard. Every
other house had a square hole in the roof or a chimney-shaped outline up one wall
where the bricks once stood.

The next day I was working side by side with neighbors I had not talked with for
weeks, in some cases, months. As we swapped stories and considered the losses,
the costs, the federal help that might be coming in, I would often see in their eyes a

startled and questioning fear that would send me inward to the place where whatever was now missing had once resided. I found myself wondering whether it was
something new, or an old emptiness that had gone unnoticed for who knows how
long. I'm still not sure.

By the third morning we had electricity again. We could boil water without building a campfire outside or cranking up the Coleman. I sat down at the kitchen table
with a cup of coffee and I guess I just forgot to drink it. Faith sat down across from
me and said, "What's the matter, Harry?"

"Nothing."

"Are you all right?"

"No, I'm not all right. Are you?"

"You've been sitting here for an hour."

"I don't know what to do. I can't figure out what to do next."

"Let's sell this place. Let's get out of here while we're still alive."

She looked like I felt. Along with everything else we were getting three or four
aftershocks a day. It kept you on the ragged edge.

I said, "Where can we go?"

"Inland. Nevada. Arizona. I don't care."

"You said you could never live in Arizona."

"That was last year."

"The desert would drive you bananas, you said."

Halfway through that sentence, my voice broke. My eyes had filled with water. It
would have been the easiest thing in the world to break into heaving sobs right there
at the table.

"It's too hard," she said, "trying to clean up this mess and never know when
another one's going to hit us. Who can live this way?"

"What does it feel like to have a nervous breakdown?" I said.

"Maybe all we need is a trip. I don't care where. Let's give ourselves a week,
Harry, while we talk things over."

"That's not it."

"What's not it?"

I didn't answer. She waited and asked again, her voice on the rise, "What's not it?
What's the matter, Harry? What's happening to us?"

Her eyes were blazing. Her mouth was stretched wide in a way I have learned to
be wary of. It was not a smile. Faith has a kind of chiseled beauty. As the years go by,
her nose, her cheeks, her black brows get sharper, especially when she's pushed. We
were both ready to start shouting. Thirty more seconds we would be saying things
we didn't mean. I didn't need a shouting match just then. Somehow she always pre-
vails. Her background happens to be Irish and Mexican, a formidable combination
when it's time to sling the words around.

Thankfully the phone rang. We hadn't heard it for so long, the jangle shocked us
both. It was her mother, who had been trying to get through. Once they knew the
houses were standing and no one had been injured, they talked on for half an hour
or so, the mother mostly, repeating all the stories she'd been hearing, among them

210

the story of a cousin with some acreage here in the county, where he grows lettuce and other row crops. Some men on the cousin's crew had recently come up from central Mexico on labor contracts, and one of them had asked for a morning off to take his wife to a local healer. During the quake the wife's soul had left her body, or so she feared, and this healer had ways to bring a soul back. Faith's mother reminded her that after the big one in Mexico City back in 1987, numerous stories had drifted north, stories of people who found themselves alive and walking around among the ruins, while inside something had disappeared.

I still have to wonder why the mother called when she did. Whether it was by chance or by design, I still can't say. Probably a little of both. She claims to have rare intuitive powers. This healer, the *curandera,* happened to be a woman she knew by name and had been visiting for a year or so, ever since her husband had passed away. Faith had been visiting her, too. Her skills, they said, remedied much more than ailments of the flesh.

As soon as her mother hung up, Faith repeated the story of the field worker's wife. It came with an odd sort of pressure, as if she were testing my ability to grasp its importance. I don't know. I'm still piecing that day together. Maybe Faith, too, was feeling some form of inexpressible loss, and maybe she, too, was groping for a way to voice it.

"This healer," I said, "what does she do?"

"It's hard to explain."

"Is it some kind of Catholic thing? The devil creeping in to steal your soul away?"

She shook her head. "I don't think it's like good spirits and evil spirits or anything along those lines."

"What is it, then?"

"Maybe it's like the door of your life springs open for a second."

"Why do you say that?"

"Maybe your soul flies out and the door slams shut again."

"You think that can happen?"

"I'm just thinking out loud."

"It's a hell of a thing to say."

"Don't look at me that way."

"Just tell me if you believe something like that could happen."

"You hear people talk about it."

"When are you going down there again?"

"Sometime soon, I hope. It would be a good time for a treatment."

"Is that what they call it?"

"You can call it whatever you want."

"A treatment? That sounds like . . ."

"Like what?"

"Some kind of medical deal."

"Please, Harry. If you're going to get defensive, I don't want to talk about it."

"I'm not defensive."

"Your guard goes up."

"Gimme a goddamn break, Faith!"

"I can feel it, Harry! You know I can!"

My guard goes up. What guard, I was thinking. I had no guards left. That was the problem. Everything I had ever used to defend myself or support myself was gone. I was skidding. That's how I felt. Supportless. I had to get out of there. I had to think. Or perhaps I had to get out of there and not think.

I took off for the hardware store, to pick up some new brackets for the bookshelves. I switched on one of the talk shows out of San Francisco. The guest was a trauma counselor. The theme was, "Living With the Fault Line." Someone had just called in a question about betrayal.

"Can you give me an example?" the counselor said.

"Maybe that isn't the right word," the caller said.

"You feel like something has been taken away from you." It wasn't a question.

"It's almost like my body opened up and something escaped."

A long chill prickled my arms, my neck. I had just reached the hardware store. I pulled into the parking lot, switched off the engine, and turned up the sound.

"That's big," the talk show host said. "That's major."

"Hey," said the counselor, "let's think about it together for a minute."

"Think about what?" the host said. "Betrayal?"

"The earth. Think about the umbilical tie. From your mother, to your grandmother, and on down the line. On back through the generations to whatever life forms preceded ours. Sooner or later we all have to trace our ancestry to this nurturing earth, and meanwhile we have laid out these roads and trails and highways and conduit pipes and bridges and so forth in full faith that she is stable and can be relied upon. You follow me? Then when she all of a sudden gives way, splits open, lets off this destructive power without even the little advance notice you get for a hurricane or a killer blizzard, why, it's like your ground wire disconnects. It's so random . . . you realize how we're all just hanging out here in empty space. Believe me, folks, you're not alone. I've been feeling this way myself for days . . ."

He had a low, compelling voice that sent buzzes through me. I was tingling almost to the point of nausea. The tears I had not been able to release in the kitchen now began to flow. I sat in the hardware store parking lot weeping the way a young child lost on a city street might weep for missing parents.

When my tears subsided, I tried to call the house. The line was busy. I started driving south, sticking to roads I knew were open, more or less following a route I'd followed once before, on a day when Faith's car was in the shop and she needed a ride. It only takes twenty minutes, but you enter another world. Down at that end of the county it's still mostly fertile delta land. From the highway you look for a Burger King and a Stop-N-Go. Past a tract of duplexes you enter an older neighborhood of bungalows and windblown frame houses from the 1920s and earlier. The street leading to her cottage was semi-paved. Beyond the yard, row crops went for a mile across broad, flat bottomland—lettuce, chard, broccoli, onions. The grass in the yard was pale and dry. Low cactus had been planted next to the porch.

The fellow who answered my knock said he was her son, Arnoldo, lean and swarthy and watchful. He wore jeans and dusty boots, as if he might have just walked in by another door. When I mentioned my wife's name he did not seem impressed. Anglos never came to see this woman. In his eyes I could have been an infiltrator from County Health, or from Immigration, or someone shaking them down for a license. When I mentioned my mother-in-law's family name, he softened a little. Dredging up some high school Spanish, I tried to describe my symptoms. Arnoldo spoke a little English, but not much. I touched my chest.

"*Mi alma,*" I said. "*Despues del temblor, tengo mucho miedo. Es posible que mi alma . . .*"

"*Ha volado?*" he said. Has flown away?

"*Si. Comprende?*"

He looked at me for quite a while, making up his mind. He looked beyond me toward the curb, checking out the car. At last he stepped aside and admitted me into a small living room where a young mother and her son were sitting on a well-worn sofa. There was a TV set, a low table with some Spanish-language magazines, a sideboard with three or four generations of family photos framed. In one corner, votive candles flickered in front of an image of the blue-robed, brown-faced Virgin of Guadalupe. Between this room and a kitchen there was a short hallway where a door now opened. A moment later a pregnant woman appeared, followed by an older woman, short and round and very dark. She stopped and looked at me while Arnoldo explained the family tie. The names seemed to light her face with a tiny smile of recognition. I heard him mutter, "*Susto.*" A scare. She nodded and said to me, "*Bienvenidos.*" Welcome. Please make yourself at home.

She beckoned to the woman on the sofa and the son, who limped as he started down the hallway. The rear door closed, and Arnoldo offered me a chair. I couldn't sit. I was shivering. I made him nervous. I was sure he regretted letting me inside. He pointed to a long, jagged lightning streak of a crack across the sheetrock wall behind the TV set. "*El temblor,*" he said. The earthquake.

Again, I pointed at my chest. "*El temblor.*"

We both laughed quiet, courteous laughs and looked away. I sat down then, though I could not bear the thought of waiting. This was crazy. I was out of control. What was I doing? What did I think would happen? I remembered the day I'd driven over there with Faith and parked at the curb. I remembered the glow on her face and how I had extinguished the glow. She had wanted me to come inside with her. "What for?" I said. "There's nothing wrong with me." The idea filled me with resentment. "It's not a lot of money, Harry," she had said. "She doesn't charge. You just leave something on the table, whatever you feel like leaving."

It wasn't the money. It was the strangeness of being there with her. Faith has these dramatic, mixed-blood looks that have kept people guessing, and have kept me guessing, too, I suppose. Greek? they ask. Portuguese? Italian? Black Irish? Mexico has always been somewhere on that list, but when we first started dating she would never have emphasized it. Her Spanish was no better than mine. Faith McCarthy was her maiden name. Suddenly I did not know this woman. Mexican on her mother's side, that was one thing. Going into the barrio to visit healers, that was something else. I wasn't ready for that. When did it start? Where would it lead? I remembered the rush of dread that day in the car as I realized I was looking at a complete stranger who was inviting me to some place I had never been.

Sitting there with Arnoldo I felt it again, the dread of strangeness. Who was he, after all, with his boots and his lidded eyes? Her son? He could be anyone. What if this was the wrong house?

I heard voices from the hallway. Then the young mother and the limping boy passed through the living room, out the front door, and the healer was beckoning to me. I, too, was limping, crippled with doubt. I had no will. I followed her to another room, with a backyard view across the fields, once a bedroom, now furnished with a chest of drawers, a couple of chairs, a long couch with a raised headrest. She didn't speak for quite some time. She just looked at me. She was no more than five feet tall, her hair silver, pulled back in a short braid. I guessed she was in her sixties, her body thick and sturdy, covered by a plain dress with short sleeves that left her arms free. Her face was neutral, neither smiling nor frowning. Her eyes seemed to enter me, black eyes, the kind that go back in time, channels of memory. She knew my fear. She knew everything about me.

She asked me to take off my shoes and my shirt, nodding toward a chair before she turned away, as if occupied with some small preparation on top of the chest. My panic welled up. It was mad to be doing this, stripping down at the edge of a broccoli field, inside the house of people I'd never seen before. I imagined the old woman asking me to swallow something terrible. Above the chest a shelf was lined with jars and small pouches. Who knew what they contained? My panic turned to fury. I could have taken the old woman by the throat. I wanted to. She knew too much. Maybe I began to understand hysteria just then, how a person can start to spin around and fly to pieces. Why didn't I spin? Why didn't I run? I stood there swearing that if she tried to give me something, I would not swallow it. That was the little contract I made with myself as I lay down on the long couch.

She covered me to my neck with a sheet. From a pouch tied around her waist she withdrew a clump of leafy fragrant stems and waved it up and down the length of my body. Her lips moved but made no sound. She leaned in close, pushing her thumbs across my forehead, digging into the furrows there, digging in close to my eyes. She began to speak, a soft murmur of words that were not Spanish. Later on, Faith's mother would tell me these may have been Yaqui words, a Yaqui incantation. There is something to be said for not knowing the literal meaning of words. If you trust the speaker to be using them in the proper way, it makes it easier to surrender. You can surrender to the sound. Is that what was happening? Did I trust the sound of the *curandera's* voice? Let's say I wanted to. Let's say my need to trust her outweighed my fear. Who else could I have turned to? In her hands I began to drift. I would not say she put me to sleep. I was not asleep. I did not feel asleep. I just wasn't entirely awake. My eyes weren't open. But I was still aware of being in the room. I was outside the room, yet in it, too, listening to her gentle voice.

While her hands worked on my forehead, my temples, my eyes, my nose and cheeks, her voice became the voice of wings, large and black and wide as the couch, as wide as the room, as wide as the house, sheets of darkness moving toward me, undulating, until I saw that these were the wings of an enormous bird, a dark eagle or a condor hovering. It finally settled on my chest, its feet on my skin so I could feel the talons. They held me as if in the grip of two great hands. They dug in. They were on my chest and inside my chest. From the talon grip I understood some things about this bird. I knew its solitary drifting on the high thermal currents, soaring, waiting. I knew its hunger. I knew the power of the beak. When the flapping of the wings increased, I wasn't surprised. They made a flapping thunder that sent a quiver through me, then a long shudder, then a shaking as sudden and as terrifying as the shaking of the earth, with a sound somewhere inside it, the slap of a ship's sails exploding in a gale. I was held by the chest and shaken by this huge bird until my body went slack, exhausted by the effort to resist. In that same moment the wings relaxed. The hold upon my chest relaxed. I watched the bird lift without any motion of the wings, as if riding an updraft. It hovered awhile, and I had never felt so calm. A way had been cleared at last, that's how it felt. Everything had been rattled loose again and somehow shaken into place. A rim of light edged the silhouette of dusky feathers. I saw the fierce beak open as if about to speak. Its piercing cry almost stopped my heart.

My eyes sprang wide. The woman's dark brown face was very close. The heel of her hand had just landed on my forehead with a whack. Her black eyes were fixed on mine. What did I see there? Who did I see?

When I got back home Faith met me at the door. She, too, had been crying. I'd been gone maybe three hours. She stood close and put her arms around me. We didn't speak. We looked at each other. In her face I recognized something I would not, until that afternoon, have been able to identify. Her eyes were like the old woman's eyes, that same fierce and penetrating tenderness. It swept me away. We kissed as if we had not seen each other in weeks, as if we had had the fight that nearly happened and we were finally making up. It was a great kiss, the best in years. It sent us lunging for the bedroom where we made love for the first time in many days.

In our haste we forgot to pull the curtains. Afternoon light was pouring through the windows. At first she was bathed in light, though as we thrashed and rolled she seemed to be moving in and out of shadow. Then she was above me and so close she blocked the light. As she rose and fell and rose and fell I could only see her out-line. When she abruptly reared back, her arms were wings spread wide against the brightness, while she called out words I could scarcely hear. A roaring had filled my ears. A thousand creatures were swarming towards the house, or a storm-driven wind. Maybe it was another aftershock. Maybe it was the pounding of my own blood.

"Oh! Oh! Harry!" Her voice came through the roar. "Harry! Harry!" as if I were heading out the door again. Had I been able to speak I would have called to her. Maybe I did call. I know I heard my voice. "I'm here!" I cried. "I'm here! I'm here!"

O Furo (The Bath)

Jeanne Houston

Snow fell in sheets of lace, a translucent curtain swirling and fluttering with the wind. Through the barracks window, Yuki watched in wonderment. She had not seen snow for forty years, not since leaving Japan. Unused to the glare, she blinked, hoping it was not cataracts that caused her eyes to sting. Many elders in camp had developed cataracts, invisible films that grew over the dark part of the eye. She didn't want any veil to soften her view of the desert's harsh landscape.

The room felt cold. She turned up the oil heater and set a pan of water on top. It was still too early to retire. The thought of bundling up in blankets and sleeping the day away was tempting. But Dixon would soon be bringing dinner. She sat down and rubbed her cold stockinged feet. Should she worry about frostbite?

How good a *furo* would feel. She had not taken a hot bath since coming to internment camp a year ago. The communal showers and toilets were one of the more distasteful necessities she had to endure in this crowded settlement of strangers. When she first arrived, she had refused to shower in the dark cement room where a dozen metal nozzles sprayed water over huddled figures, who covered their privates with a towel in one hand, and with the other—and another towel—washed themselves. Such humiliation! Wasn't it bad enough for one family to live all in one small room! But to bathe with strangers—and not even in a tub—was too much to expect. Now she showered in the middle of the night when others slept.

Yuki was seventy-three. She was proud of her youthful looks. Most people were surprised she was over sixty and often asked what she did to stay so young. "Dance and sing a lot," she'd say, "and take *o furo* every night." She would like to say, "and please yourself as much as you can." But that sounded selfish, especially from an elder, a grandmother who should reflect ideals of martyrdom and self-sacrifice.

Remembering her warm apartment in east Los Angeles, the large three rooms above Nishio's Shoe Store, Yuki often wondered what bad karma she had earned to end up in such a place. Dust, tumbleweeds, wind and heat! She welcomed the snow, how it blanketed the bleakness with white, giving an illusion of space, so that when she looked out, she could imagine herself back in Japan, back in the farmhouse surrounded by fields, large fields that spread up to pine forests bordering the land. She didn't think of Japan often. There were years when it seemed she never had lived there. She did play the *shamisen* and also taught dancing and singing. But sometimes it seemed she had created the art herself in America.

Yuki contemplated the snow. Did it have meaning? Her first thought was its purity. Its cleansing and purifying powers. But she also could look at the truth. She could accept the fact that winter had arrived, and she was now in the winter of her life, the time when tree limbs turned barren, just as her own limbs felt stripped of flesh. She had not seen snow for so many years. Was this a sign? An omen? Was she to die in this camp? What calamity! To die in an infertile desert, where she had not seen one bright flower! Even the rocks looked tired and jagged, chipped away by tumbleweeds smashing against them. No, she would not die here. Instead, she read it to be a gift from the snow-god, a gentle covering of ugliness, a reminder of beauty and innocence.

As the snow had transformed the desert, Yuki realized she too must transform her spirit. With this illumination, she felt a lightness in her heart she had not felt since the war began. It somehow gave meaning to the true purpose of her imprisonment. She now had a goal, a reason to create new rituals and ceremonies. Singing and playing the *shamisen* were not enough.

When Dixon brought dinner from the messhall, she ate with rare gusto. Even the dry rice and rubbery Vienna sausages seemed tasty. Noticing his grandmother's new zest, Dixon asked, "What's up, Ba-chan?"

The chopsticks gently gripping a sausage stopped midair. Yuki looked at him with mock startled eyes. "What you mean?"

"Come on, Ba-chan, I know you. What's cooking?"

She studied his face before biting the sausage. She liked the square jawline and swarthy complexion, double-lidded eyes beneath feathery eyebrows that lifted at the outer corners like eagle wings. Her own complexion was pale, with pink-tinged cheeks, a complexion coveted by both men and women in Japan. Lucky she was born into a family of Niigata, a Japanese province known for its ivory-skinned women. Dixon had inherited dark skin from his mother whose parents came from Kagoshima, the southernmost part of Kyushu. Yuki knew her grandson was intelligent, a fact revealed by his high forehead and steady gaze. He sensed things, felt thoughts, especially hers.

Yuki wisely had chosen him early, the middle son, a quiet, gentle child lost in the shuffle of a hectic brood. A widow such as herself would need a devoted grandchild to champion her causes, a defender and willing helper to depend upon in old age. She had raised Dixon to fit that role. He was her favorite and, even though the special treatment brought cruel teasing from his siblings and a coolness from his mother, he seemed to love *obachan* despite it all.

Yuki and Dixon now lived by themselves away from the family. It had been hard living with noisy teenagers, and she never had approved of her daughter-in-law, Rose, either. Too much like the *hakujin,* not teaching the children Japanese ways and letting them run wild like coyotes.

A few months earlier, Yuki's sense had been bombarded to the flash point. Clifford's clarinet whined in concert with the grating voices of Dolly, Frances and Mary as they attempted to imitate a singing trio called The Andrew Sisters. She had crawled under one of the iron cots, refusing to talk to anyone—even Dixon, who tried coaxing her with food and promises of walks by the creek outside the barbed wire. But she had remained silent, curled like an old cat taking refuge from a pack of savage dogs.

After three days, her son and Rosie became concerned, worried they might have to report this strange behavior. What would the authorities do to someone gone crazy? The whole family tried to cajole her, lying on their stomachs, baby-talking and patting her like she was a petulant pet. But she withdrew further, hiding her head under the army blanket Dixon draped over her.

On the fourth day, when Dixon brought food, she accepted it.

"Why are you doing this?" he whispered as he shoved the tray of rice and stew toward her.

"So we have place alone," she whispered back.

"Oh . . . ," his eyes round, finally understanding her antics. "But there aren't any empties on the block. They're all full, Grandma."

She smiled, eyes crinkling into slits of light beaming from the dark lair. "Go to other block! Think big, Dixie-chan." Her voice was strong. "Tell papa *ba-chan* crazy because too much people. You me live someplace away. Okay?"

"*Obachan* is not used to so much noise, Pop," Dixon said. "Shouldn't we find another place for her?"

"Is that what she wants?" His father was surprised. Why hadn't she just asked? he thought. "But there aren't any empty rooms in this block."

Dixon answered quickly . . . too quickly. "There's one small room in the next block . . . block 30. I can stay with her."

"Oh, you've already checked?"

"No . . . I didn't check with anyone. I just noticed one of the end compartments was empty. When I was over at Lincoln Takata's place."

His father mulled the situation. Dixon had spent most of his life at his mother's apartment in Japantown. It would not seem odd for the two to stay together in the next block. In fact, it was logical, he rationalized.

Feeling a tinge of guilt for the relief he knew his wife and other children would savor with his mother's departure, he, nevertheless, agreed to talk to the next block's manager and request the empty room for medical reasons.

The new cubicle was located at the end of a barrack, smaller than others, but with the advantage of double doors. They could be swung open, allowing air and light into the dark interior of rough-hewn boards, shaggy and knot-holed and smelling of tar.

Yuki had kept the room stark and sparsely furnished. Even the iron cots were missing. With extra army blankets procured by Dixon, she had fashioned some thick futons upon which they slept at night and rolled up during the day. She stored her clothes—mostly kimonos—folded in the wicker trunk she had brought from home. Dixon's were stacked in an upended wooden box that served as a closet, its opening covered by a maroon curtain splashed with pink and white flowers. A shrine rested on a low shelf along with a picture of her deceased husband, Jun, and an incense burner and small plate for food.

Dixon asked his grandmother again, "*Ba-chan,* what are you thinking about?"

"No know yet, Dixie. I thinking too much. But, no worry. I not going to die this place."

"Ba-chan! What are you doing thinking about dying!" Wasn't her act about going crazy enough? What was this about dying!

"The snow, Dixie-chan. The snow. Something tells me. Soon I know."

Dixon gathered up the dishes to return to the messhall. It sobered him to think of *Obachan* dying. He knew it would happen someday, but he pushed those thoughts away, clinging to the hope that when that time came, he would be a grown man and blessed with the love of another woman.

That night Yuki meditated and chanted before the picture of her long-deceased husband. She lit the last of the incense she had brought from Los Angeles. She prayed to the *kamisama* of the desert, of the rocks, of the mountains, and even of the tumbleweeds. When she finally lay down to sleep, her last conscious image was herself as a child in Japan, walking in snow, her bare feet elevated by tall *getas* (wooden clogs). Gliding like a skater on ice, she seemed to float, skimming the snow to a destination she did not yet know.

She awoke at dawn. Her last thoughts before sleep had continued into a dream she remembered in clear detail. Instead of being a child, she was a young girl of fifteen. Dressed in a cotton *yukata* (kimono) and no longer wearing *getas* she trudged up a narrow rocky path on the side of a mountain. It was winter, cold and windy, and her bare feet ached against the steely granite. Still she persevered, knowing there was a purposeful end to her journey. She rounded a bend. On the side of the mountain, a grotto appeared. It seemed carved into the rocks. Inside, steam hissed over a bubbling pool. It was a hot spring.

She knew the dream's meaning. Gratefully, she prayed an extra strong mantra and left more food than usual before the shrine.

"Dixie! Dixie-chan, get up." She shook her sleeping grandson.

His eyes snapped open. He was beginning to wonder if Ba-chan really had suffered a nervous breakdown or stroke. Her actions were so strange lately.

"We make *o furo*. Real kind. Japan style."

"*O furo!* What's that?"

"Bath . . . bath. Lots hot water."

"What's the matter with the showers?"

"Not same same, Dixie. Ba-chan have to clean heart, spirit." She pointed to her chest. "Just like snow. That's why we have snow in desert."

"Can't you take a pail or bucket into the latrines? I see other ladies doing that."

She was filled with a sense of urgency and felt impatient with Dixon's lack of enthusiasm.

"No." She almost shouted. "I teach you make *furo*. Help Ba-chan, OK?"

Dixon sat up and yawned. He saw his grandmother wrinkle her nose and wave a hand in front of her face.

"Phew . . . bad smell, Dixie. You need clean soul, too."

The first thing to decide was where to put it. The space between barracks was too public, so the only choice was in front of their apartment, beyond the double doors. It meant they would have to extend a fenced-in area that would jut out past the other barracks. Yuki disregarded what the neighbors might think of this. She was tired on thinking of others. After all, her age entitled her to some self-indulgence.

Dixon scavenged some posts and plywood boards from the edge of camp where new barracks were under construction. He built a square fence about six feet high. Inside the enclosure, Yuki shoveled snow away and raked the sand underneath. She instructed Dixon to dig a shallow hole and place around it large flat boulders he had retrieved from the creek. But the most important item was missing. The tub. It was impossible to build a water-tight tub of wood. And no metal could be found for flooring, which had to withstand the heat of a fire underneath.

For several days, Yuki was depressed. Like her mood, the weather became ominously darker. The wind howled, tearing at the new fence and rattling windows. It was a blizzard, a fierce storm that brought cold she could not remember, even in the long winters of her childhood in northern Japan.

She knelt beside the oil stove, playing *shamisen* and singing old love ballads. Perhaps the gods heard and enjoyed her plaintive songs, for it was during an especially intense rendition that she thought of the solution. Or maybe it was the smell of burning oil. Suddenly she saw her *o furo*. . . an oil drum! The perfect tub!

"Dixie!" she shouted. "Tomorrow we go find empty drum! We make *o furo* from oil drum!"

Fortunately the storm passed enabling Yuki and Dixon to search the maintenance area, where stacks of grey barrels, some streaked with tar, were mounded behind a large warehouse. Brushing away snow, he searched the pile until he found one that had contained laundry detergent. About the size of a large wine cask, it was shiny and clean and smelled sweetly of pine. A perfect tub, too narrow for one to recline in, but wide enough for someone Yuki's size to sit comfortably on a stool.

They waited until dusk to build a fire. Yuki estimated the water would be hot enough by nightfall and hoped darkness would discourage nosey neighbors from peering into the yard. Already gossipy Ikeda and self-appointed block security officer Goto had paid uninvited visits, bringing *omiyage* (gifts) of old Japanese magazines and raisins. She knew they only wanted to see what she was up to and was smugly amused at their questioning eyes scanning the stark space cleared of snow with only a shallow pit surrounded by rocks.

"Dixie-chan and I are making a wishing pool," she had said in Japanese.

Their faces stony, they bowed stiffly, uncertain how they should assess the situation. Yuki knew they thought her strange. She had heard gossip she "wasn't all there," that the camp had driven her mad.

"Gentlemen! Tell me your wishes and I will ask the water-god for you when our pool is finished!" she shouted as they left the yard.

Dixon had fashioned a wooden stool from scrap lumber and also had made a platform of slatted wood to set on the metal bottom for protection from the heat. He put them in the tub, raising the water level up to three-fourths full. Outside, he had piled three boxes—like stairs—so Yuki could climb in. He was anxious, worried she might fall or even be boiled. The tub looked like a witch's cauldron to him. But his grandmother was shuffling around the yard, a busy pigeon checking the temperature and stoking the fire. He knew she, more than anybody, could take care of herself.

"*O furo* ready, Dixie-chan. Go now. I take bath."

Yuki took off the *yukata* and hung it on a peg attached to the fence. The air cut into her naked body. Sucking in her breath, she quickly discarded the *getas* and stepped up on the boxes, grasping the tub's metal edge. She swung one leg over the rim and felt for the stool with her foot. Finding it stable, she stepped down and brought the other leg into the tub, raising the water level to her breasts, barely reaching the nipples. Gingerly she seated herself on the stool and slid her feet across the slatted raft. The water was hot, very hot and in the seated position reached up to her neck. Already she felt pimples of perspiration erupting on her forehead and upper lip.

Her head rested below the rim. She was encased in blackness and savored the solitude, a canopy of blinking diamonds overhead the only source of light. The stars seemed to hang so close, she felt she could pluck them like cherries from a tree. Not even the steamy wooden *o furo* of her childhood in Japan could match this.

Yuki stroked her arms under water, softly massaging her bony elbows and hairless armpits. She rolled the flesh of her narrow haunches and thighs, noticing how easily she could grasp a handful of skin. Even the flat breasts, once taut and round with desire and then milk, felt like deflated balloons. Heart twinging at the remembrance of her sensuality, the succulence of youth, she closed her eyes.

Her first bath in America came to mind. It was her wedding night, the first night she would sleep with her husband, a stranger she had met only a few days before. She had been a picture bride, married by proxy to Shimizu Jun, youngest son of a stone cutter from a neighboring village. Already immigrated to America seven years earlier, he had earned enough money to pay for a bride's passage.

He had met her at the dock in San Francisco, and after a day of travel by wagon, they finally had arrived at the compound of bachelors in San Jose where he had been living. She had worn a kimono for the entire trip, arriving grimy and exhausted and grateful for the *o furo* the bachelors had fired up. They had anticipated the newlyweds would appreciate a hot soak.

Yuki recalled the bath ritual. While Jun poured buckets of boiling water into a large wooden tub partially filled with cold water, she washed her face, scrubbing away white rice powder. He removed his cotton *yukata* and began soaping himself. She had kept eyes downcast, trying not to look directly at him. He was her husband but still a stranger. She had scarcely seen his face, and now she would be sharing *o furo* with him.

Steam and smoke clouded the night air. He sat down on a small wooden stool to wash his feet. Hesitantly, she had moved next to him and washed his back with a cotton cloth. His muscled, yet smooth back, felt hard. With a small basin, she scooped water from the tub and poured it over him, rinsing away the soap

They didn't speak. He stood up and stepped into the tub, his cool body sending hisses of steam as he sat down in the hot water. He beckoned for Yuki to join him. She took off her *yukata* and sat on the stool he had just left and scrubbed herself with a strong smelling yellow soap and cloth. She was shivering.

Water spilled over the sides and onto pebbles covering the ground as she slipped into the tub. She sat down, facing him with legs bent. Their legs pressed against each other, and she could feel his taut calves and hairless skin. Through the mist, she saw sweat roll down his cheeks and drip into the water. Her own sweat slipped down her forehead and stung her eyes. Afraid and excited, she felt her heart thumping against her chest. She wondered if Jun could feel its throb through the water.

A cool wind whistled into the drum. Her eyes snapped open. Slightly embarrassed by the sensual reminiscence, she stood up and peered over the edge into the yard. Where was Dixon? Another gust forced her to sit down again. Gathering clouds had not yet covered the moon, but the stars had lost their brilliance. She stared at the milky disc, imagining its rays stroking her body like a masseuse's hand. The light engulfed her whole body . . . the tub . . . then the yard and barracks. She saw it envelop the block, the fire-break, the camp . . . the country . . . even the world!

Softly and quietly, snow began falling. Delicate flakes floated from the now dark sky. Yuki studied an intricate flake as it descended, following the wafer of ice—so full of its own life and beauty, so unaware of the imminent end when its freefalling journey from heaven would finish in a metal drum filled with hot water. She watched the flake flutter close to her face. It seemed to dance and jump, almost mischievously. Then it fell into the water near her breasts.

"*Obachan!*" Dixon shouted through the open door. "Are you Okay?"

"Me Okay," she shouted back. "I get out. Your turn *o furo*. This bath number one bath, Dixie-chan. Best *o furo* in camp."

Dixon closed the door, allowing privacy for his tiny grandmother, who was rising up through the steam.

Introducing the Fathers

Maxine Kumin

For Anne Carpenter

Yours lugs shopping bags of sweet corn
via parlor car to enhance the lunches
of his fellow lawyers at the Century Club.
Sundays he sneaks from church to stretch a net
across the Nissequegue River
and catches shad as they swim up to spawn.

Mine locks up the store six nights at seven,
cracks coconuts apart on the brick hearth,
forces lobsters down in the boiling pot.
Sundays he lolls in silk pajamas,
and swaggers out at nightfall to play pinochle.

In our middle age we bring them back, these despots,
mine in shirtsleeves, yours in summer flannels,
whose war cry was: the best of everything!
and place them side by side, inflatable
Macy daddies ready for the big parade.

We open a friendship between them, sweetly posthumous,
and watch them bulge out twirling Malacca canes
into the simple future of straight losses,
still matching net worths, winning big at blackjack,
our golden warriors rising toward the Big Crash.

Expatriate

Today from a paint-spattered ladder I pick the last
of the five thousand Kentucky Wonders that have embellished
the teepee with green pencils since you planted them in May,
you and the child, four pale seeds circling each pole.
In June you were still with us, although at arm's length always.
We watched hummingbirds suck sugar water from a bowl.

Today I am going up in the sky with these tendrils,
these snakelets that reach, reach, double back, and respell
ever ad astra the names of Bombay, Hong Kong, Singapore
and droplets of Indonesia called Sumba, Flores, Timor.

Sprung loose by the thrust of a beanstalk, victim
of wretched excess, of superabundance, today I am
going up to cross over and seize you, you and the little boy
who belong to us, although at arm's length always.
Down the broad green stem I will bear you home
in the numinous light of late summer to the brown loam.

The Poet Visits Egypt and Israel

Sand, sand. In the university the halls,
seats, table tops, sills, are gritty with it.
Birds fly in and out at the open windows.
During the lecture an elderly porter
splendid in turban and djellaba,
shuffles in, opens a cabinet on the apron,
plugs in a microphone, spits into it twice,
and plumps it down on the lectern.
She continues to speak, amplified,

on American women poets since World War One
to an audience familiar with Dickinson,
Poe, and at a safe remove, Walt Whitman.
Afterward, thick coffee in thimbles. Sticky cakes
with the faculty. In this polite fortress
a floating unease causes her hands to shake
although nothing is said that could trespass
on her status as guest from another, unveiled, life.
She is a goddess, rich, white, American,

and a Jew. It says so in some of her poems.
There are no visible Jews in the American
Embassy, nor at the Cultural Center, and none
turns up in Cairo or Alexandria
although an itinerant rabbi is rumored
to cross from the other side once a fortnight
and serve the remaining congregants. The one
synagogue, a beige stucco Parthenon,
sleeps in the Sabbath sun, shuttered tight
and guarded by languid soldiers with bayonets.

All that she cannot say aloud she holds
hostage in her head: the congruities

of bayonets and whips; starved donkeys
and skeletal horses pulling impossible loads;
the small, indomitable Egyptian flies
that perch on lips, settle around the eyes
and will not be waved away. Like traffic
in Cairo, they persist, closing the margin
between life and death to a line so thin

as to become imperceptible.
Transported between lectures, she is tuned
to the rich variety of auto horns, each one
shriller, more cacophonous, peremptory
than its abutter. The decibel level
means everyone drives with windows closed,
tapedeck on full, airconditioning at maximum.
Thus conveyed, fender nudging fender,
she comes to ancient Heliopolis

where the Sheraton sits apart in an oasis.
Gaudier than Las Vegas, she thinks, checking in.
Behind her in the lobby, two BMWs,
several sheiks, exotic birds in cages,
and plumbing fixtures of alabaster
ornament this nouveau riche heaven.
Backlighted to enhance their translucency,
the toilet tank and bidet bowl are radiant,
the kind of kitsch she wishes she didn't notice.

Outdoors in the sports enclave, pool attendants
in monogrammed turtlenecks, like prep-school athletes,
carry iced salvers from bar to umbrellaed table,
proffer thick towels, reposition chaise longues
for the oiled, bikini-ed, all-but-naked bodies
of salesmen's wives and hostesses on holdover.
What do they think about, the poet wonders,
as they glide among the infidels, these men
whose own wives wrap up head to toe in public,

whose cousins' cousins creep from day to day
in a state of chronic lowgrade emergency.
Anonymous again in transit,
the poet leaves for Tel Aviv at night.
She watches a pride of pregnant tabbies stalk
cockroaches in the threadbare airport lounge
for protein enough to give a litter suck.
Always the Saving Remnant learns to scrounge

to stay alive. Could she now name the ten

plagues God sent? Uneasy truce exists
between these two antagonists.
El Al's flight, a frail umbilicus
that loops three times a week to the Holy Land,
is never posted on the Departures Board.
Security's intensè. Shepherded
by an Israeli packing two guns,
she's bused with a poor handful to the tarmac.
The takeoff's dodgy, as if in fear of flak,

as if God might turn aside and harden
Pharaoh's heart, again fill up the sea.
Once down, she knows the desert by its gardens,
the beachfront by its senior citizens
assembled for calisthenics on the sand.
An hour later in the Old City
she sees a dozen small white donkeys,
descendants of the one that Jesus straddled,
trot docilely beside Volkswagen Beetles,

Mercedes cabs, tour buses full of young
camera-strapped, light-metered Japanese.
She peers into archaeological digs that reach
down through limestone to the days of Babylon,
pridefully down to the first tribes of Yahweh
sacrificing scapegoats on a stone.
Down through the rubble of bones and matter
—Constantinian, Herodian, Hasmonean—
that hold up the contemporary clutter.

At the Western Wall, Sephardic Jews,
their genders separated by a grill,
clap for the bar mitzvah boy with spit curls
who struggles to lift a gold-encrusted Torah
that proclaims today he is a man.
The poet polkas, dancing to tambourine
and bongo drums with other passersby.
Behind her, dinosaurs against the sky,
two Hapag-Lloyd Ltd. cranes

raise massive stacks of facing stones,
the eighth or ninth or tenth civilization
to go up on the same fought-over bedrock.
Near the Via Dolorosa, among the schlock
for sale—amber beads, prayer rugs, camel saddles—
lamb legs are offered, always with one testicle
attached. Ubiquitous sweet figs, olive trees botanically certified to be sprouts from
the sacred roots of Gethsemane.

She tries to haggle for a sheepskin coat
but lacks the swagger needed for cheerful insult.
A man whose concentration-camp tattoo
announces he was zero six nine eight
picks through a tangle of ripe kumquats
beside a Bedouin, her hands and face daubed blue,
who could as easily have been a Druid,
the poet thinks, and she an early Christian.
In a restored Burnt House from 70 A.D.,

the year the Romans sacked the second Temple,
she dutifully clambers down to view
scorch marks, gouged walls, some human bones, amid
a troop of new recruits in green fatigues.
Girls the shape and gawk of girls back home.
Boys whose bony wrists have overshot
their cuffs already. Not yet on alert
but destined to serve on one front or another,
eye contact in this shrine says: Jews together.

Meanwhile, clusters of Hasidic zealots
(most of them recent Brooklyn imports)
in bobbing dreadlocks and black stovepipe hats
pedal breakneck along the claustral streets
of the Arab Quarter on ten-speed bikes to await
the messianic moment any minute
now. Look for a pillar of fire and in it
the one true Blessed-be-He, whose very name
cannot be spoken in the waiting game.

The one true Blessed-be-He, who still is hidden.
The poet sees a film on television,
news clips of shock troops: Syrian women
soldiers holding live snakes, biting them
on command, chewing and spitting out
the raw flesh. *In this way we will chew
and spit out the enemy*. Guess who.
Parental discretion was advised for viewing.
As if the young in these geographies

had not yet heard of torture, frag bombs, the crying
out at night that is silenced by garrote.
Another clip, the commentator said,
closeups of Assad's crack soldiers ordered
to strangle puppies and squeeze out blood
to drink as he reviewed the troops, was censored.
Judged too depraved for any audience.
How much is propaganda, how
much real? How did we get here,

the poet wonders, in the name of God,
in the name of all gods revving up their motors
to this high-pitched hum, like tripwire
stretched taut before the spark ignites the fuse
fragmenting life for life, blood running
in the dust to mingle Shiite, Druse,
Israeli, French, American. *If I forget thee,
O Jerusalem, may my right hand forget its cunning.*

In the Absence of Bliss

Museum of the Diaspora, Tel Aviv

The roasting alive of rabbis
in the ardor of the Crusades
went unremarked in Europe from
the *Holy Roman Empire* to 1918,
open without prerequisite
when I was an undergraduate.

While reciting the Sh'ma in full
expectation that their souls
would waft up to the bosom
of the Almighty the rabbis burned,
pious past the humming extremes
of pain. And their loved ones with them.
Whole communities tortured and set aflame
in Christ's name
while chanting Hear, O Israel.

Why?
Why couldn't the rabbis recant,
kiss the Cross, pretend?
Is God so simple that He can't
sort out real from sham?
Did He want
these fanatic autos-da-fé, admire
the eyeballs popping,
the corpses shrinking in the fire?

We live in an orderly
universe of discoverable laws,
writes an intelligent alumna
in *Harvard Magazine*.
Bliss is belief,
agnostics always say
a little condescendingly
as befits mandarins who function
on a higher moral plane.

230

Consider our contemporary
Muslim kamikazes
hurling their explosives-
packed trucks through barriers.
Isn't it all the same?
They too die cherishing the fond
certitude of a better life beyond.

We walk away from twenty-two
graphic centuries of kill-the-jew
and hail, of all things, a Mercedes
taxi. The driver is Yemeni,
loves rock music and hangs
each son's picture—three so far—
on tassels from his rearview mirror.

I do not tell him that in Yemen
Jewish men, like women, were forbidden
to ride their donkeys astride,
having just seen this humiliation
illustrated on the Museum screen.

When his parents came
to the Promised Land, they entered
the belly of an enormous
silver bird, not knowing whether
they would live or die.
No matter. As it was written,
the Messiah had drawn nigh.

I do not ask, who tied
the leaping ram inside the thicket?
Who polished, then blighted the apple?
Who loosed pigs in the Temple,
set tribe against tribe
and nailed man in His pocket?

But ask myself, what would
I die for and reciting what?
Not for Yahweh, Allah, Christ,
those patriarchal fists
in the face. But would
I die to save a child?
Rescue my lover? Would
I run into the fiery barn
to release animals,
singed and panicked, from their stalls?

Bliss is belief, but where's
the higher moral plane I roost on?
This narrow plank given to splinters.
No answers. Only questions.

Visiting Professor

At MIT on the oval
my students stretch out like corpses
this day of budded maples.
Like the dead of Beirut in the sun.

Here everything is hopeful
because unconsidered. Fierce in
their indolence my students
turn themselves over sunning.

This evening under fluorescent lights
in a cooling classroom we will discuss
poems of the apocalypse
which serenely never happens

in their dreams. In mine, that one
Poseidon submarine carrying
like the fish, its eggs enough
to flood the pond, warheads enough

to level every medium
every large city in
the Soviet Union, that one
Poseidon sub sticks up its snub nose.

Diogenes at ninety held his breath
until he suffocated, so goes the myth
that says how much we want to be in charge.
My students will colonize

outer space. They will
domesticate the solar cell.
Syzygy and the molecular
cloning of genes will not overpower

their odes to the 21st century
their love poems and elegies.
Meanwhile their illegal puppies
wrestle among them on the oval

in springtime in Cambridge again
in a world where all, all is possible.
The chrome of new dandelions
assaults the sun.

How to Survive Nuclear War

After reading Ibuse's Black Rain

Brought low in Kyoto,
too sick with chills and fever
to take the bullet train to Hiroshima,
I am jolted out of this geography,
pursued by Nazis, kidnapped, stranded
when the dam bursts, my life
always in someone else's hands.
Room service brings me tea and aspirin.

This week the Holy Radish
Festival, pure white daikons
one foot long grace all the city's shrines.
Earlier, a celebration for the souls
of insects farmers may have trampled on
while bringing in the harvest.
Now shall I repent?
I kill to keep whatever
pleases me. Last summer
to save the raspberries
I immolated hundreds of coppery
Japanese beetles.

In some respects,
Ibuse tells me,
radiation sickness is less
terrible than cancer. The hair
comes out in patches. Teeth
break off like matchsticks
at the gum line but the loss
is painless. Burned skin itches,
peels away in strips.
Everywhere the black rain fell
it stains the flesh like a tattoo
but weeks later, when
survivors must expel
day by day in little pisses
the membrane lining the bladder
pain becomes an extreme grammar.

234

I understand we did this.
I understand
we may do this again
before it is done to us.
In case it is thought of
to do to us.

Just now, the homage that
I could not pay the irradiated dead
gives rise to a dream.
In it, a festival to mourn
the ritual maiming of the ginkgo,
pollarding that lops
all natural growth
from the tumorous stump
years of pruning creates.
I note that these faggots
are burned. I observe that the smoke
is swallowed with great ceremony.
Thereupon every severed shoot
comes back, takes on
a human form, fan-shaped,
ancient, all-knowing,
tattered like us.

This means
we are all to be rescued.

Though we eat animals
and wear their skins,
though we crack mountains
and insert rockets in them

this signifies
we will burn and go up.
We will be burned and come back.

I wake naked, parched,
my skin striped by sunlight.
Under my window
a line of old ginkgos hunkers down.
The new sprouts that break from
their armless shoulders
are the enemies of despair.

A New England Gardener Gets Personal

Kale
curls. Laughs at cold rain.
Survives
leaf-snapping hail.
Under snow, stays green.
Comes crisp as a handclap
to the bowl,
then lies meekly down
with lettuces and cole.

Willynilly
after years of no-peppers
a glut of them
perfect as Peter Piper's.
Only piccalilli
will get shut of them.
None grow riper
none redden in this clime
but such sublime
pectorals! Such green hips!
No Greek torso could be
more nobly equipped.

What ails you, cherry tomato?
Why do you blossom and never bear?
Is it acid rain you're prey to
or nicotine in the air?

Are you determinate or not,
wanting trellises,
strings to cling to from the pot?
What evil spell is this?

Apple on a stalk
kohlrabi
grows fronds in its ears.
Stands stiff as a bobby
when the Queen appears.
Quoth she: my dears,
eat this pale knob when small
or not at all.

Winters, like money in the bank,
that dull gargantuan, the swede,
yellow, thick, and faintly rank,
is eaten by cattle and people in need.

Carrot
wants company in bed.
Presses
to be held on either side
by purslane, chickweed
and coarser grasses.
Meanwhile puts down deep alone
its secret orange cone.

The Long Approach

In the eel-thin belly of the Metro Swearingen
banking in late afternoon over Boston Harbor,
the islands eleven lily pads, my life loose as a frog's,
I try to decipher the meaning of hope rising up again
making music in me all the way from Scranton
where the slag heaps stand like sentries shot dead
at their posts. Hope rising up in my Saab hatchback,
one hundred thousand honest miles on it as I speed
due north from LaBell's cut-rate autopark
to my spiny hillside farm in New Hampshire.

March 21st. Snow still frosts the manure heap
and flurries lace the horses' ample rumps
but in here it's Stephen Foster coming back to me
unexpurgated, guileless, all by heart.
'Tis summer, the darkies are gay, we sang in Miss Dupree's
fifth grade in a suburb that I fled long ago.
Gone are my friends from the cotton fields away
to—an allusion that escaped me—a better land I know.
O the melancholia as I too longed to depart.
Now I belt out Massa's in de cold cold ground
and all the darkies are a'weepin on route I-93
but what I think of are the french-pastel mornings
daylit at five in my own hills in June when I may
leap up naked, happy, with no more premonition
than the mother of the Pope had. How the same
old pump of joy restarts for me, going home!

What I understand from travel is how luck
hangs in the lefthand lane fifteen miles
over the limit and no cop, no drunk, no ice slick.
Only the lightweight ghosts of racist lyrics
soaring from my throat in common time.
Last week leaving Orlando in a steep climb
my seatmate told me flying horses must be loaded
facing the tail of the plane so they may brace
themselves at takeoff. Otherwise you run
the risk they'll panic, pitch over backwards,
smash their hocks. Landing, said the groom,
there is little we can do for them except
pray for calm winds and ask the pilot
to make a long approach.

O brace me, my groom. Pray for calm winds.
Carry me back safely where the snow stands deep in March.
I'm going home the old way with a light hand on the reins
making the long approach.

Ode of Sevenths to Thirst and Hunger

Howard McCord

I.

No
not a word, but
a density,
     the word working
like a magnet,
mass
       in the continuum
of the poem
       stars
from any position.
Rushing.

II.

To clarify
the magic without diminishing it
      Recall
       the cloud
flinging lightning
at the cliffs,
      all she screamed
was your emptiness to her
The light, the roar
of the fire,
      the heat
   inaudible.

Language public land
waiting
    but not for settlers

Out of flow,
                not this time
quiet, a few birds
above the sand.

III.
Lava
      the simplest analogue
to thought:
          stuff
boiled up from under the surface.

      On the map,
    that sort of land
        is blue
and is held in common
    by an
abstraction.
    What kind of
taxes can be assessed
on an acre of malpais?

Value is use,
        and the poem?
          Her azure eyes?
   The wet roar of the arroyo
astonished
       by
         water.

IV.

The prime meridian
of the dictionary is midway
between
        the average word
and the mean.
        The moon breathes
in
   and
      out

The cusp tilts
in winter,
       the letters shift,
swell.
     She says nothing
comfortably, sensual
as
      (not a conjunction).
O, that it burn
like a rose rubbed
in the cut, that
it burn
      like a petal.

V.

At the edge of philosophy
an old man chatters his teeth
in the cold
and knows
       he speaks truth.

The woman and the blind
watchmaker
     metabolists of dark
       conspire
in her dream/
        her melodic
line of words
drawn against,
   absorbing
the flickering
      dark.

VI.

The white dots on the mountain
are
     goats.
          The black dots
on the glacier
     are not
          bears.

Certain simplicities
assert themselves.

A word does not have the nervous
system of
     the eyelash mite,
  nor the solidity
of ash.

The ghost meridian
     lies sweetly against my
forehead,
     cool as a rifle barrel.

VII.

Dry rivers are best,
crabbed corners
     choked with tumbleweeds
the long
arm of buffalo gourd
a green sword careless
  on the rocks.

What can you want
when you are without water?
Nothing else.

     All
     a wild
       fevered
         Blur.

Attending
the Forest

for Eva Schaff, M.D.

Seeing through the trees
is flicker business
a tiny patch of fur
a movement
stealthy as a pulse
hidden in a sick wrist
or the glint of madness
in the old man's eye

There's not much to see
sight is so overburdened
with still or rustling
green going into brown
all broken in random
mechanics which bewilder
in spite of their implacable
logic, as listening
to the wheeze and rumble
in a chest divines the contents

Something is blossoming
beyond the sound, and deft
fingers bending dogwood to the nose, filling,
then brushing the cheek
like a sentence in the old
language remembered
assert the unknown through
the familiar

The sky beyond the leaves
an entrance to the depths
we walk into the forest.
All is tangle, greenbriar,
the heart's uncertainties,

the mind is a brush-filled
hollow impenetrable and dark.
No wild thing our size
can travel there.
But there are scales of knowing
which translate us beyond
ourselves, the palpitation
of the abdomen which reveals
a swollen spleen, the thwack
with a cruising axe
that makes a game tree drum
and the squirrel family inside
go sharp with terror.

What is without?
Who's there?
Mites out of mites' eggs
on a spider's leg ask this as the universe
eases more open in diminishing
awareness, cools.

Like cures like, or does
bitter taint the sweet?
At our feet, Goldseal
for fever, ginseng
for life, mint, balomy
(or white turtlehead)
to set worms free of the body.
There at the edge of the run,
Sampson's Snakeroot, the marsh
gentian, for gout and nervous
distress. Who knows what other
simples wait in the shadows,
knots of molecules threaded in
petals and bark?

"The unknown by the more unknown"
alchemists claimed, "the obscure
by the even more obscure."
We understand their fear that all the
light they brought revealed new dark.
The forest is a body, hidden
and before us plain.
What the wind does, or
the beat of rain,
the meaning of the deer musk's addendum
to the air, or why anything
is precisely as it is just now
beyond even faith's ability
to gather in, and knowledge
is a chip from the mind's veneer.

Let us be ignorant.
Fire still warms us,
and the comfort of easing back
against a tree to lose ourselves
in a distant turkey's gobble
is self-evident, and bit by
tiny bit we learn
what we put our hands upon
and what it is our eyes
have tried to see.

Waiting for the Elf

When an old person is not far from death, an
elf will sometimes approach him, and ask to
sit inside his body a while, promising in return
that the old one may look through an elf's eyes
while the elf sits. Many an old person thinks
this is a fine trade, for their bodies are not
much, and there is plenty of room for an elf
inside. And perhaps, they think, seeing with
an elf's eyes will help make sense of all this.
The elf, no bigger than the dream of a pea,
enters easily, lets his eyes slip behind those of
the old one, and then sightless himself, begins
to feel his way through the mysteries of the
old, dying body. The old one smiles when he
first sees like an elf, and often laughs. This
indeed explains most things. Meanwhile, the
elf, his tiny hands outstretched, each foot
tentative on the way, moves through, the old
man or woman as though he were a house
holder at midnight the lights, gone, and an
errand to run. Where did he leave it? Can he
find it after so long? Where was his seat he
had left so many years ago? Each elf is born
sitting on a three-legged ivory stool inside
a baby. The first laugh of the infant expels the
elf, and he must wander a human earth,
fraught with fierce dangers to someone so
small, until the infant's body is old, old
to death. Then he may return and find his ivory
seat. The old one hardly notices the footsteps
of the elf inside, for the world he sees through
the elf's eyes is such that he will wonder what
is the glory of a butterfly to a wolf? Or how
alike in every way, an apple and Mozart's
music is. Elven eyes do not see things so much
as the connection of things. When the elf
stumbles on his ivory stool somewhere deep
in the pancreas, or tucked behind a kneecap,
he sits down, his eyes return, and the old one
dies.

August Storm on the Jornada del Muerto

for David Burwell

Evening's larkspur blue
edges the black mass
of the San Mateos. North
toward the twisting Magdalenas
the storm cooks the darkness
after sunset, and if
there are stars to the south,
the dark-churning northwest
sucks the flickering
bolts down below black
in the spectrum.

Behind us, another ground
popping cannonade of rain
reaches out of the Oscuras.

We have no tent.
Who would carry such a crazy
weight on the Jornada's waterless
miles?

I wrap in a plastic tarp
and ready for sleep.

David sits in his poncho, his face
gaunt grey in the lightning,
stolid as ten years' humping
with the Marines
can make it.

It only rains till midnight,
and the nearest lightning strike
was a hundred yards away.

At dawn, the antelope
are still, careless, and
grazing much closer than
the lightning did.

248

Buffalo Girls

(chapter 7)

Larry McMurtry

*N*o Ears finally persuaded Sitting Bull and several of the older Indians to go to the zoo with him so they could take information about some of the unusual animals back to their tribes. No Ears felt strongly that as many tribes as possible should know about such beasts as the great mudpig, the anteater, and the ostrich; also the large cats and the even larger white bear. Even if the people in the tribes never saw a mudpig or the great white bear, the information might still be important. The animals might appear to them in dreams; it was simply good policy to learn as much as possible about such animals and pass the information on.

Sitting Bull became very angry while walking around the zoo. He was very much annoyed that the whites had collected such ugly animals—and not merely ugly—many of the animals were clearly quite dangerous; only people as stupid as the whites could collect such animals and pasture them near their homes.

Sitting Bull took a particular dislike to the warthog—not only was it extremely ugly, it was also quite clearly ferocious. Sitting Bull wanted to go back to camp, get his rifle, and come back and shoot the warthog before it broke loose and began to kill people.

By the time they actually returned to camp, Sitting Bull's anger had increased. He immediately began to try to persuade the young braves to steal some real ammunition from Cody's wagon and come back to the zoo with him. They would have a fine hunt and rid the world of many dangerous and obnoxious animals. The young braves, who were rather tired of shooting off false bullets in the Wild West show, were perfectly willing to accompany the old chief on a hunt.

No Ears and Two Hawks, a sensible Brule Sioux, tried their best to put a stop to the notion of a hunt in the London zoo. The whites would be very disturbed—it was necessary to point out how outnumbered the Indians were, should war result. Also, there was the ocean to get back across—even if they fought their way out of London, they still didn't know how to run a boat.

Sitting Bull was not convinced. He wanted to go back and shoot the warthog before he started to have bad dreams about it—the great white bear was also worrisome. It was just the kind of animal likely to cause troublesome dreams; he thought they ought to get on their horses, ride through the zoo, and wipe out as many of the bad animals as they could. As for the ocean, it was only a big lake. If they followed its shoreline they would eventually get around it and make their way home.

Sitting Bull's opinion about the ocean was popular with quite a few of the Indians, none of whom was looking forward to getting back on the great boat. Most considered that they had been very lucky to make it across the ocean the first time. Two Hawks himself had been very uncomfortable on the ocean; he had spent much of the voyage singing his death song. He reminded everyone of the great whale fish. What if a herd of whale fish tried to attack? The thought of a herd of whale fish did not improve Sitting Bull's mood—or anyone else's mood, either.

Fortunately Cody appeared in time to keep everyone's mood from getting any worse. Cody wanted Sitting Bull and a few chiefs to go with him to something he called a wax museum. It seemed to be a place where they kept wax carvings of great chiefs of various tribes. Cody told Sitting Bull and Red Shirt and one or two others that the Queen particularly hoped they would let the carvers of the wax museum make statues of them; that way the Queen could visit the museum once in a while and be reminded of the visit they had all made to her country.

No Ears decided to go along. He thought he might enjoy seeing a few carvings. Even if the carvings were ugly, he might enjoy seeing the buildings along the way. It was a puzzle why whites felt they had to put their buildings so close together.

As they clumped along the river, he saw that there were even little tribes of people who lived in boats. Cody was doing his best to keep Sitting Bull in a good mood, telling him several times what a great honor it was that the Queen wanted him to have his statue carved so she could remember his visit. Despite Cody's efforts, Sitting Bull remained in a surly temper. As a guest, he felt it was incumbent on him to do what the Queen requested, but what he really wanted to do was go back and shoot the warthog.

The first thing they saw when they got to the museum was a statue of Cody, and another of Annie Oakley—they had only been finished the day before. Sitting Bull was very taken with the statue of his little sure shot and began to ask if he could buy it. He was told he couldn't, which didn't improve his mood. He grew annoyed when the man who was going to make his statue began to measure him, but Cody finally got him to behave.

No Ears was not particularly interested in the statues; he felt it might be more interesting to go back and study the tribes who lived on boats. Of course it was odd that the whites had filled a whole building with statues of dead chiefs or their women, but he didn't take much interest in the proceedings until he happened to see one of the men who worked in the museum sticking a pair of ears on the head of a tiny statue.

Jack Omohundro, who stood beside No Ears, saw the point immediately. He looked at No Ears, he looked at the statue that was having its ears fixed, and he walked over to the workman and got right down to business.

"Is that a statue of a midget?" he asked.

"Yes, Tom Thumb," the man said irritably; he seemed to be in the kind of mood Sitting Bull was in.

"A nasty little brat pulled his ears off," he added. "It's happened before and it will happen again."

The man had a sizable goiter on his neck, but he knew his business; he quickly worked the ears back onto the statue.

"The point is I've got a friend here who needs a pair of ears," Jack said. "How much to make him a pair?"

The workman had quite a start when he looked around and saw that No Ears indeed lacked ears.

"Lord Gad!" he said. "Who pulled this old fellow's off?"

Once his professional curiosity was aroused he quickly became more friendly; he came over and gave No Ears's head a close inspection. "Whoever sawed 'em off should have sharpened his saw," the man remarked. "They done a rough job. Let's go down and see what we can find."

They went down some stairs until they were quite a distance under the earth; to No Ears's astonishment they were taken into a large room filled with parts of people. One whole shelf, the length of the room, contained heads—but the heads had no features. There was a shelf of hands, and a shelf of feet—even a shelf of torsos. Smaller shelves were covered with ears and noses. The workman studied the shelf of ears for a while and then held up two that seemed about right for No Ears. He rummaged in a drawer and found a mirror so No Ears could look at himself and take part in the selection.

No Ears began to get the shakes. He had seen whites go in stores and try on hats and other garments, but he had never supposed that the hour would come when he would be trying on ears. The workman had become very friendly; he seemed ready to spend all day seeing that No Ears got exactly the ears he desired.

The selection wasn't easy, either. No Ears had the shakes so badly he could hardly keep the various ears shoved up against his head long enough to consider which looked best. He changed his mind several times; he felt upset and could not remember to talk in English. He began to express his opinions in Sioux. Jack knew a little Sioux but not enough to follow No Ears's discussion, which was rather particular; he ran upstairs to get an Indian who could help, and soon, to the workman's amazement, the whole party was down in his workroom, helping No Ears pick out ears.

When so many eyes fixed upon him, No Ears grew even more shaky—he began to despair of making up his mind. One set of ears would seem correct for a few seconds; then he would see another that seemed better. Everyone else had an opinion, too—one would argue for one pair, someone else for another. A young brave named Plenty Horses, who seemed to dislike his own ears, wanted someone to cut them off for him so he could have a new pair. Several people wanted to buy a spare set of hands or feet in case they lost theirs in battle.

Fortunately Cody finally showed up and solved the problem by buying No Ears a dozen pairs of ears.

"They're wax, they might wear out," Cody told him. "Let's get a supply while we're here."

The workman with the goiter, who turned out to be a patient fellow, gave No Ears some special glue to help him fix the ears to his head; he carefully explained how the glue was to be put on and taken off.

"Now these won't do for every day," the man cautioned. "If a brat grabs one, it'll spoil it. If I was you I'd just save them for weddings or maybe funerals—they'll do fine for special occasions."

He gave No Ears a nice wooden box to keep his ears in. Of course, when they got back to camp everyone wanted to see them; two or three pair were badly smudged before curiosity diminished. Fortunately the workman at the museum had given the party a sackful of wax limbs, arms and legs mostly, that had been broken off statues and were no longer deemed useful. These kept most of the crew amused.

For the first few days No Ears did nothing but guard his ears from all comers. Sitting Bull was jealous because he had not been given any ears; he demanded that No Ears present him with a set. No Ears resisted and fortunately his understanding friend Cody came to his aid. Cody gave him a fine box, lined in velvet, to keep the ears in. The box even had a lock and key so that No Ears could lock up his ears whenever he wanted to.

The box with the lock and key reassured him for a while, but not for long—it was all too obvious that virtually everyone in the troupe envied him his wax ears. Sitting Bull was far from being the only one who coveted them—even his old friend Two Hawks, who had two perfectly good ears of his own, pestered No Ears for a look and even asked if he could borrow a pair for a few days.

No Ears soon came to feel quite resentful of the fact that everyone coveted his new ears. All the people who envied him had real ears of their own and had had real ears their whole lives, whereas he had spent nearly seventy years without ears of any kind. It annoyed him that people couldn't simply have the good manners to let him enjoy his ears in his own way.

No Ears told Calamity of his disappointment in the manners of his friends while the two of them stood at the rear of the great boat as it sailed away from England. No Ears felt a little sad; he had not liked England, yet it had to be admitted that the English were ingenious. No Sioux had ever ever thought of making him wax ears; no American had, either.

Calamity did not look well. She had taken to drinking and fighting with sailors almost every night. The police had taken her pistol away; without her pistol she could not scare the sailors, and thus got regularly pummeled. She looked so battered that she refused to have her picture taken with the troupe before departure. Cody, after one look at her face, had not insisted.

"It's good riddance to England," she said, as she and No Ears watched the gray shore fade into the gray sea.

She was in such a warlike mood that No Ears was rather fearful about what might happen once they returned to America. What if she didn't want him to travel with her anymore? Where would he go?

"I can't wait to see Dora," Calamity said. "Do you reckon we'll be there in a month?"

"I'm afraid someone will steal my new ears while we're on this boat," No Ears said. It had become his darkest fear.

"I'll keep 'em for you," Calamity suggested. "They'll be safe with me. Nobody wants to get near me now. I've even got too rough for Sitting Bull."

No Ears adopted this suggestion. He hid his box of ears under Calamity's bunk; he visited her cabin several times a day to make sure they were still there.

On the sixth day out from England No Ears saw something as impressive as the whale fish; he saw a great mountain of ice floating in the sea. The ice mountain was so large that it took the ship all day to leave it behind. No Ears watched it as long as he could see it. A sailor informed him that there were thousands of ice mountains in the northern seas.

Before No Ears could think too much about the ice mountain, a storm struck the ship. The storm continued for three days, and long before the third day everyone on board was sick. The one exception was Annie Oakley, who was unaffected by the storm, though she did have to interrupt her shooting practice. Most of the Indians began to sing their death songs again, but No Ears felt too sick even to do that. Calamity decided she should sing a death song too, and she sang "Buffalo Girls." Her voice was too weak for the singing to be heard over the crash of the storm.

"I'm never leaving the shore again if I get out of this," she said after each spell of vomiting.

Sitting Bull got so sick that he wanted to shoot the captain of the ship, a man he had never liked. One of the elk got loose somehow and rushed around the deck frantically before jumping into the sea. No Ears watched it happen. The great sea immediately swallowed the foolish elk.

In the agony of the storm and the long fatigue that followed it, the box of ears was gradually forgotten. No Ears unlocked the box and looked at the ears only when no one was around. He fixed them to his head when he was alone. After some reflection he decided it was far too late to present himself in public as a man with ears. For seventy years he had been No Ears; everyone in the West knew him by that name. If he were to suddenly appear wearing ears, it would only confuse everyone. Some of his friends might think he had become a bad spirit and refuse to speak to him.

In private, though, when everyone was asleep, No Ears often opened his box and quietly fixed a pair of ears to his head for an hour or two. With ears on, he could sit and smoke and peacefully dream his way through a different life. He dreamed himself as he would have been as a young man like others—that is, with ears. He saw himself taking many more wives and becoming much more prosperous than he had been. He saw himself as a leader in battle, helped by his keen ears; he saw himself as a chief of his people, though in truth he had been something of an outcast.

Most pleasing of all to No Ears was an ability he acquired, thanks to his fine ears, to dream back the conversations he had missed in life due to the whistly and uncertain nature of his hearing. The voices of old-time people began to float back to him in his dreams. He heard again his lively young wife Pretty Moons; he heard his friend Sits On The Water describing the best tactic for catching angry turtles; he even dreamed back a conversation he had once had with Crazy Horse, an abrupt man who didn't have too many conversations. Crazy Horse had been in the mood to kill some soldiers that day, but whether he had done it had never been clear to No Ears. In the dream memory, though, he saw Crazy Horse coming back with three scalps, indicating that he had followed his mood.

All the way across the great ocean, No Ears attached his ears in private and listened to voices from the old times. It occurred to him that the sea must be very old; he had been taught to believe that the sky was the First Place and the Last Place, but as he sat and looked at the endless sea he began to wonder if perhaps the belief was wrong. Perhaps the ocean was the First Place; perhaps it was also the Last Place. Perhaps it was to the sea that souls went; the story about the hole in the sky could well be wrong. The very fact that he could hear so clearly the voices of people long dead made him wonder if perhaps the sea was not the Last Place; its great depths might contain all the dead and all their memories, too.

Sometimes Jim Ragg came on deck while No Ears was dreaming back voices. Occasionally they would sit and share a smoke. No Ears knew there was no need to hide his ears from Jim—Jim had no interest in ears. He knew that Jim had long been an angry man—it seemed that he was angry with his own people for having killed all the beaver. In London, though, he had discovered that all the beaver were not gone; they just lived in zoos now, where their life was easier, since no one was allowed to trap them. The discovery had changed Jim a lot. He didn't seem angry anymore. Even the fact that Bartle had taken a young wife didn't bother him.

Most people found Jim a more pleasant companion now that his anger was gone; No Ears had to admit that he was more pleasant, and yet he found Jim disquieting to be with for some reason. No Ears thought the matter over for several days without being able to decide what bothered him about Jim. The mountain man was perfectly friendly, and once or twice had even helped him adjust his ears when he hadn't got them fitted on quite right. And yet, something was troubling about the man.

While he was dreaming back the brief conversation with Crazy Horse, Jim Ragg walked by, and No Ears suddenly realized what was bothering him: Jim Ragg wasn't really there anymore. His spirit had been an angry spirit, like Crazy Horse's. Now it had gone. The realization made No Ears shiver a little. If Jim's spirit had gone, his body was not going to last too long. That was why conversations with him were rather disturbing: his voice came from the Last Place, just as Crazy Horse's had.

This realization shocked him so much that he confided it to Calamity next time she came on deck. Calamity's stomach had been slow to settle down after the passing of the storm. She spent a good deal of time at the rail, vomiting; No Ears watched her closely at such times. People who were ill often did foolish things; he didn't want Calamity to make the same kind of mistake the elk had made when it became so sick with fear that it jumped into the sea.

When Calamity recovered enough to sit down with him and accept a smoke, No Ears told her of his conviction that Jim Ragg's spirit had left him.

"I think he's gone where Crazy Horse is," No Ears said. "He is on a road he doesn't see."

"Sometimes I think you must get drunk in secret," Calamity said. "Then you stick on your new ears and think you know things you don't really know."

No Ears didn't press the point. It was obvious that Calamity was not feeling well; she had not been feeling well for most of the trip. It was hard enough to talk to whites about the spirit world when they were healthy; if they happened to be unhealthy, as Calamity was, the effort was a waste of time.

"What do you hear when you sit there with your ears on?" she asked.

"I hear some old-time people," No Ears said.

"You're doing better than me then," Calamity said. "I don't hear nothing but this old howling wind."

No Ears said nothing; he didn't want to argue about his dream conversations.

"Well, say hello to Wild Bill for me, if you happen to be speaking to him," Calamity said, as she got up to make her unsteady way downstairs.

Darling Jane,

This will be the saddest letter I have written you yet, Jim Ragg is dead. It happened in Chicago by the lake, so sudden neither Bartle nor me even saw it, Pansy didn't either though we were all not ten feet away. We had gone there to do one last show, they were having a big fair by the lake. Billy had been so nice we felt we couldn't refuse—he allowed us ample money to get home. I am sure he can afford it but many that can afford it wouldn't do it.

I know that will strike you as odd, here I am writing about Billy Cody's fortunes, the truth is I would rather write about anything other than the death of Jim Ragg. I didn't expect it, none of us did. Well, No Ears did, I should have listened to him, but what good would it have done?

A man they call an anarchist stabbed Jim in the ribs, the knife was so small no one saw it, Jim didn't, he just thought the man bumped into him. He sat down on a bench and died before he even realized he was stabbed. He bled to death inside, at least he didn't suffer. He just said he was a little tired and we decided to sit and eat some spun candy, while we were eating it Bartle said he thought Jim didn't look right, of course he didn't, he was dead.

I have never heard of an anarchist Janey, they say there are many of them in Chicago and also London, I didn't see any in England though. We saw the little man that stabbed Jim, he was a very small man, I think he was loco or crazy, he thought Jim was the Emperor of Austria that's why he stabbed him. You would have to be crazy to mistake Jim Ragg for the emperor of anywhere, Jim bore no resemblance to an emperor. The man was raving and screaming by the time they drug him away. I have never seen Bartle so stunned—of course it is hard to believe that a man could just walk up and stab Jim and Jim not even know he was stabbed. Bartle blames it on crowds, he says in a crowd it's so crowded you don't even notice your own death, he's right, too, Jim Ragg didn't, and he has witnessed hundreds of deaths.

Later Bartle wanted to go to the jail to make sure the killer would be hung promptly. At the police station they told us he is too insane to hang. Bartle was disgusted—out West no one is too insane to hang.

Billy Cody was nice as usual, he too was shocked at Jim's death, but not as shocked as Bartle. Billy made all the arrangements for Jim to be buried but at the last minute Bartle balked, he said Jim ought to be buried in the West. Now they are going to put his body on a steamer with us at Dubuque, he will be buried as soon as we reach the Missouri—anywhere along the Missouri would suit Jim fine, Bartle thought.

Of course we are all grieved, but Bartle is the most grieved. He partnered with Jim more than thirty years. Bartle has seen sudden death before, we all have, still, Bartle is having trouble adjusting to the fact that Jim is gone. It is a good thing Bartle has Pansy for a wife. I don't like her much but Bartle does—she cannot make up for Jim Ragg, nobody can, I will miss the man too. I was thinking of Jim last night—what I wish is he had been more of a talker. If I scratch my memory I can remember many things that Bartle said over the years, also things Dora said or even Blue—Blue's are easy to remember because they're mostly too raw to repeat—but it is hard now for me to remember one thing that Jim Ragg said, he has only been dead a week too. Perhaps it is my fault, Jim only liked to talk about beaver, they never interested me, they're just animals with big teeth.

The question is, what will Bartle do? He has never done anything really, he just followed Jim around the West. Jim did most of the work, Bartle provided the conversation. At one time they guided wagon trains, later on they scouted for the soldiers—neither of them liked that, but they did it. In those days, knowing the country, knowing where the water holes were, and where you could get across rivers was a skill you could sell. Even I sold it, and I never knew the West half as well as Bartle and Jim. Half the people out there in those days earned a living showing newcomers around, wagon trains, or whoever wanted help getting somewhere.

Now there's no need for scouts—the steamers or the railroads will get you close enough. I don't know what old scouts like Bartle and me will do, I guess we could work for Billy but the show only tours part of the year and he probably wouldn't want to hire me again anyway—all I did was fall off the stagecoach and embarrass him in front of the Queen. If I could shoot like Annie I'd have a job forever, but I can't—nobody else can either, she beat the English gun by forty-nine birds.

I thought I might get some money out of Buntline, but Buntline is hard to pin down—he might do this, he might do that. About the best I could get out of him is that he is planning to take a look at Montana pretty soon. When he does, he will stop by and write down a few of my tales. Billy Cody laughed when I told him that, he says Buntline never writes down anything, he just makes up tales. He thinks Buntline will write me up in dime novels and make me an outlaw worse than Belle Starr. If he does he's in for trouble, your mother has never been an outlaw, Janey. It's true I took food for the miners during the smallpox horrors—I paid for it later, though, it was not much food anyway. Even people who don't like me, there are plenty that don't, will admit that I'm honest—if I don't leave you anything else Janey at least I will leave you a good name.

Your mother,
Martha Jane

Lumumba Lives

Peter Matthiessen

1

*H*E COMES BY TRAIN out of the wilderness of cities, he has come from abroad this very day. At mid-life he has returned to a hometown where he knows no one.

The train tugs softly, slides away, no iron jolt and bang as in his childhood, no buck and yank of couplings, only a gathering clickety-click away along the glinting track, away along the river woods, the dull shine of the water, north and away toward the great bend in the Hudson.

Looking north, he thinks, The river has lost color. The track is empty, the soft late summer sunshine fills the bend, the day is isolate.

He is the one passenger left on the platform, exposed to the bare windows of Arcadia. He might be the one survivor of a cataclysm, emerging into the flat sun of the river street at the foot of this steep decrepit town fetched up against the railroad tracks on the east slope of the Hudson River Valley. What he hasn't remembered in the years he has been gone is the hard bad colors of its houses, the dirtied brick and fire bruises of the abandoned factory, the unbeloved dogs, the emptiness.

On this railroad street, a solitary figure with a suitcase might attract attention. To show that his business is forthright, he crosses the old cobbles quickly to the salesmen's hotel at the bottom of the downhill slide of human habitation. The dependent saloon has a boarded-up side door marked "Ladies Entrance," and the lobby reminds him, not agreeably, of looted colonial hotels in the new Africa that he supposes he will never see again.

The stranger's soft voice and quiet suit, his discreet manner, excite the suspicion of the clerk, who puts down a mop to shuffle behind the desk and slap out a registration form. This dog-eared old man spies on the name as it is being written. "We got a park here by that name," he says.

The man shakes his head as if shaking off the question. Asked where he's from, he says he has lived abroad. The foreign service. Africa.

"Africa," the clerk says, licking a forefinger and flicking the sports pages of a New York daily. "You'll feel right at home, then." He reads a while as if anticipating protest. "Goddam Afros overflowing right out of the city. Come up this way from Yonkers, come up at night along the river."

Nodding at his own words, the clerk looks up. "You have a wife?"

"I saw them," the stranger says. At Spuyten Duyvil, where the tracks emerged from the East River and turned north up the Hudson, black men had watched his train from the track sidings. The stranger's fingertips lie flat upon the counter as if he meant to spring into the air. "They were fishing," he says.

He is a well-made man of early middle age and good appearance, controlled and quiet in his movements. Dry blond hair is combed across a sun-scarred bald spot.

"Fishing," the clerk says, shaking his head. "I guess you learned to like 'em over there."

The man says nothing. He has shallow and excited eyes. He awaits his key.

Irritable and jittery under that gaze, the clerk picks out a key with yellowed fingers. "How many nights?"

The man shrugs. Who knows? Asked if he wishes to see the room, he shrugs again. He will see it soon enough. When he produces a thick roll of bills to pay the cash deposit in advance, the old man inspects the bills, lip curled, checking the stranger's face at the same time. Still holding the cash as if in evidence, he leans over the desk to glare at the large old-fashioned leather suitcase.

The stranger says, "I'll take it up. It's heavy."

"I'll bet," says the clerk, shaking his head over the weight he had almost been asked to hump up the steep stair. He snaps open the next page of his paper. "Bathroom down the hall."

On the floor above, the man listens a moment, wondering briefly why he sets people on edge even before trouble occurs. Their eyes reflect the distemper he is feeling.

He opens, closes, bolts the transomed door.

THE ROOM IS PENITENTIAL, it is high-ceilinged and skinny, with defunct fire pipes, no pictures, a cold-water sink, a scrawny radiator, a ruined mirror on the wall. The water-marked walls are the color of blue milk. The bedside table is so small that there is no room for a lamp. The Gideon Bible sits in the chipped washbasin. A rococo ceiling fixture overhead, a heavy dark armoire, an iron bed with a stained spread of slick green nylon.

The pieces stand in stiff relation, like spare mourners at a funeral whom no one is concerned to introduce.

His reflected face in the pocked mirror is unforgiving.

The room has no telephone, and there will be no visitors. He has no contacts in this place, which is as it should be. Checking carefully for surveillance devices, he realizes the precaution is absurd, desists, feels incomplete, finishes anyway.

Big lonesome autumn flies buzz on the windowsill. The high bare window over-looks the street, the empty railroad station, the river with its sour burden of industrial filth carried down from bleak ruined upstate valleys. Across the river the dark cliffs of the Palisades wall off the sky.

HIS MOTHER had not felt well enough to see him off, nor had his father driven him down to the station. The Assistant Secretary for African Affairs had wished to walk his English setter, and had walked his son while he was at it.

We want you to gain the Prime Minister's confidence. He may trust you simply because you are my son.

258

Unfortunately the more . . . boyish? . . . elements in our government want another sort of prime minister entirely. They are sure to find some brutal flunky who, for a price, will protect Western interests.

The Assistant Secretary had not waited for the train.

Make the most of this opportunity, young man.

By which he meant, You *have this chance to redeem yourself thanks to my influence.*

The gardener had brought the leather suitcase. From the empty platform they watched his father stride away. At the north end of the street, the tall straight figure passed through the iron gate into the park.

The gardener cried, *So it's off to Africa ye are! And what will ye be findin there, I'm askin?*

TURNING FROM the window, he removes his jacket, drapes it on a chair; he does not remove the shoulder holster, which is empty. He contemplates the Assistant Secretary's ancient suitcase as if the solution to his life were bundled up in it.

He unpacks his clothes, takes out a slim chain, locks and binds the suitcase, chains it to the radiator.

On the bed edge he sits upright for a long time as if expecting something. He has trained himself to wait immobile hour after hour, like a sniper, like a roadside African, like a poised hawk, ready for its chance, thinking of nothing.

A dying fly comes to his face. It wanders. Its touch is weak and damp. He does not brush it away.

BY THE RIVER at the north end of town is a public park established by his grand-father, at one time a part of the old Harkness estate. His father's great-uncle, in the nineteenth century, had bought a large tract of valleyside and constructed a great ark of a house with an uplifting view of the magnificent Palisades across the river, and his descendants had built lesser houses in the park, in one of which, as an only child, he had spent the first years of his life.

Not wishing to hurry, he does not go there on the first day, contenting himself with climbing the uphill street and buying a new address book. He must make sure that each day has its errand, that there is a point to every day, day after day.

Soon he visits the real-estate agent's office. The agent, a big man with silver hair slicked hard and puffy dimpled chin, concludes that the old Harkness property will have just the "estate" that Mr. . . . ? might be looking for.

"Call me Ed," the agent says, sticking out his hand. The client shakes it after a brief pause but does not offer his name.

All but the river park presented to the village was sold off for development, the agent explains, when the last Harkness moved away some years before. But the big trees and the big stone houses—the "manor houses," the agent calls them—are still there, lending "class" to the growing neighborhood.

Mother says you are obliged to sell the house. I'd like to buy it.

Absolutely not!

259

THE NARROW ROAD between high ivied walls was formerly the service drive-way, and the property the realtor has in mind is the gardener's brick cottage, which shares the river prospect with "the big house" on the other side of an old stand of oak and hickory.

As a child he fled his grandmother's cambric tea to take refuge in this cottage full of cooking smells. His nurse was married to the gardener, and he knows at once that he will buy the cottage even if the price is quite unreasonable. So gleeful is he in this harmony of fate that his fingers work in his coat pockets.

He has no wish to see the rooms until all intervening life has been cleaned out of them. Before the agent can locate the keys, he says, "I'll take it."

When the agent protests—"You don't want to look inside?"—he counts off five thousand dollars as a deposit and walks back to the car, slipping into the passenger seat, shutting the door.

Not daring to count or pocket so much cash, the agent touches the magic bricks in disbelief. He pats the house as he might pat a horse and stands back proudly. "Nosir, they don't make 'em like this, not anymore."

The one thing missing here is burglar lights, the agent says—a popular precaution these days, he assures his client, climbing back into the car. Like the man at the hotel, he evokes the human swarm emerging from the slums and coming up along the river woods at night. "Engage in criminal activity," he emphasizes when the other man, by his silence, seems to question this.

"Ready to go?" the client says, looking out the window.

On the way home he inquires about New York State law in regard to shooting burglars, and the agent laughs. "Depends on his color," he says, and nudges his client, and wishes he had not. "Don't get me wrong," he says.

BACK AT THE OFFICE the agent obtains the buyer's name to prepare the con-tract. "You've come to the right place, all right! Any relation, Mr. Harkness?"

The man from Africa ignores the question. He will reveal that he belongs here in his own good time. First he wants everything to be in place, the little house, its fur-nishings, his history. The place will be redone in the style of the big house across the hedge, with English wallpapers, old walnut furniture, big thick towels and linen sheets, crystal and porcelain, such as his parents might have left him, setting off the few good pieces he had put in storage after their deaths. The inside walls will be painted ivory, as the house was, and the atmosphere will be sunny and cheerful, with an aura of fresh mornings in the spring.

Once the cottage is ready, his new life will commence, and the names of new friends will flower in his address book.

TO HIS CHILDHOOD HOUSE he wishes to return alone, on foot. Since he means to break in, he makes sure that he leaves the hotel unobserved, that he is not followed. Not that there is anyone to follow him, it is simply a good habit, sound procedure.

He enters the park by the iron gate beyond the railroad station, climbing trans-versely across a field, then skirting an old boxwood border so as not to be seen by the unknown people who have taken over his uncle's house. He trusts the feel of things and not his sight, for nothing about this shrunken house looks quite familiar. It was always a formal, remote house, steep-roofed and angular, but now it has the dark of rottenness, of waterlogged wood.

He hurries on, descending past the stables (no longer appended to his uncle's house or frequented by horses, to judge from the trim suburban cars parked at the front). In the old pines stands a grotesque disc of the sort recommended to him by his would-be friend the agent, drawing a phantasmagoria of color from the heavens.

He is seeking a childhood path down through the wood, across the brook, and uphill through the meadow.

From the trees come whacks and pounding, human cries.

A PADDLE-TENNIS COURT has spoiled the brook, which is now no more than an old shadow line of rocks and broken brush. Wary of his abrupt appearance, his unplayful air—or perhaps of a stranger not in country togs, wearing unsuitable shoes for a country weekend—the players challenge him. Can they be of help?

He says he is looking for the Harkness house.

"Who?" one man says.

Calling the name—*Harkness!*—through the trees, hearing his own name in his own voice, makes him feel vulnerable as well as foolish, and his voice is thickened by a flash of anger. He thinks, I have lost my life while soft and sheltered men like these dance at their tennis.

He manages a sort of smile, which fails to reassure them. They look at each other, they look back at him. They do not resume playing.

"Harkness," one man says finally, cocking his head. "That was long ago. My grandfather knew your father. Something like that."

Dammit, he thinks. Who said that was my name!

Now the players bat the ball, rally a little. He knows they watch him as he skirts the court and leaves the trees and climbs the lawn toward the stone house set against the hillside at the ridge top.

His father's house has a flagstone terrace with a broad prospect of the Hudson. It is a good-sized stone house, with large cellar rooms, a downstairs, upstairs, and a third story with servants' rooms and attic. Yet even more than his uncle's place it seems diminished since his childhood. Only the great red oak at this south end of the house seems the right size, which confuses him until he realizes that in the decades he has been away it has grown larger.

In a snapshot of himself beneath this tree, in baggy shorts, he brandishes a green garden stake shoved through the hole of a small flower pot, used as a hand guard. He is challenging to a duel the Great Dane, Inga.

The oak stands outside the old "sun room," with its player piano and long boxes of keyed scrolls, and a bare parquet floor for children's games and tea dancing. The world has changed since a private house had a room designed for sun and dancing.

The weather-greened cannon are gone from the front circle. Once this staid

261

house stood alone, but now low dwellings can be seen, crowding forward like voyeurs through what is left of the thin woods farther uphill.

Completing the circuit of the house, he arrives at the formal garden—"the autumn garden," his mother called it, with its brick wall and flowered gate, its view down across the lawn to the woods and river. The garden is neglected, gone to weeds. Though most are fallen, his mother's little faded signs that identified the herb species still peep from a coarse growth of goldenrod, late summer asters.

In other days, running away, he had hidden past the dusk in the autumn garden, peering out at the oncoming dark, waiting for a voice to call him into the warm house. They knew his ways, and no one ever called. Choked with self-pity, a dull yearning in his chest, he would sneak up the back stairs without his supper.

The boiler room has an outside entrance under the broad terrace, on the downhill side. He draws on gloves to remove a pane, lever the lock. He crosses the spider-shrouded light to the cellar stair and enters the cold house from below, turning the latch at the top of the stair, edging the door open to listen. He steps into the hall. The house feels hollow, and white sheets hide the unsold furniture. In the kitchen he surprises an old cockroach, which scuttles beneath the pipes under the sink.

The silence follows him around the rooms. On his last visit before his father sold the house, faint grease spots still shone through the new paint on the ceiling of his former bedroom. Sometimes, sent up to his room for supper, he had used a banged spoon as catapult to stick the ceiling with rolled butter pats and peanut-butter balls.

From his parents' bedroom, from the naked windows, he gazes down over the lawn, standing back a little to make sure he is unseen. The court is empty. He is still annoyed that the paddle-tennis players have his name. Possibly they are calling the police. To be arrested would reflect badly on his judgment, just when he has asked if there might be an assignment for him someplace else.

Hearing a car, he slips downstairs and out through the cellar doors.

"Looking for somebody?"

The caretaker stands in the service driveway by the corner of the house. He wears a muscle-tight black T-shirt and big sideburns. He is wary, set for trouble, for he comes no closer.

Had this man seen him leave the house?

He holds the man's eye, keeping both hands in his coat pockets, standing motionless, dead silent, until uneasiness seeps into the man's face.

"I got a call. The party said there was somebody lookin for someone."

"Can't help you, I'm afraid." Casually he shrugs and keeps on going, down across the lawn toward the brook.

"Never seen them signs?" the man calls after him, when the stranger is a safe distance away. "What do you want around here, mister?"

2

WITH SOME IDEA of returning to the hotel by walking south beside the tracks, he makes his way down along the brook, his street shoes slipping on the aqueous green and sunshined leaves.

Whenever, in Africa, he thought of home, what he recalled most clearly was this brook below the house and a sandy eddy where the idle flow was slowed by his rock dam. Below this pool, the brook descended through dark river woods to a culvert that ran beneath the tracks into the Hudson. Lit by a swift sun that passed over the trees, the water crossed the golden sand—the long green hair of algae twined on bobbing stems, the clean frogs and quick fishes and striped ribbon snakes—the flow so clear that the diadem of a water skater's shadow would be etched on the sunny sand glinting below. One morning a snake seized a small frog—still a tadpole, really, a queer thing with newsprouted legs and a thick tail—and swallowed it with awful gulps of its unhinged jaws. Another day, another year, perhaps, peering into the turmoil in a puff of sunlit sand of the stream bottom, he saw a minnow in the mouth and claws of a mud-colored dragon. The dragonfly nymph loomed in his dreams for years thereafter, and he hated the light-filled creature it became, the crazy sizzle of the dragonfly's glass wings, the unnatural hardness of this thing when it struck the skin.

For hours he would hunch upon a rock, knees to his ears, staring at the passages and deaths. Sometimes he thought he would like to study animals. How remote this dark brook was from the Smiling Pool in his Peter Rabbit book up in the nursery, a meadow pool all set about with daffodils and roses, birds, fat bumblebees, where mirthful frogs, fun-loving fish, and philosophical turtles fulfilled their life on earth without a care.

Even then he knew that Peter Rabbit was a mock-up of the world, meant to fool children.

NEARING THE RAILROAD, the old brook trickles free from the detritus, but the flow is a mere seepage, draining into a black pool filled with oil drums. An ancient car, glass-shattered, rust-colored, squats low in the thick Indian summer undergrowth where once—or so his father said— an Algonkin band had lived in a log village.

In the sun and silence of the river, he sits on the warm trunk of a fallen willow, pulling mean burrs from his city trousers. From here he can see across the tracks to the water and the Palisades beyond. Perhaps, he thinks, those sugarmaple yellows and hot hickory reds along the cliffs welcomed Henry Hudson, exploring upriver with the tide four centuries before, in the days when this gray flood—at that time blue—swirled with silver fishes.

Hudson's ship—or so his father always claimed—had an elephant chained on the foredeck, an imposing present for the anticipated Lord of the Indies. Turned back at last by the narrowing river from his quest for the Northwest Passage, fed up with the task of gathering two hundred pounds of daily fodder for an animal that daily burdened the small foredeck with fifteen to twenty mighty shits—his father's word, in its stiff effort at camaraderie, had astonished and delighted him—Henry the Navigator had ordered the elephant set free in the environs of present-day Poughkeepsie. Strewing its immense sign through the woods, blaring its longing for baobab trees to the rigid pines, the great beast surely took its place in Algonkin legend.

Misreading his son's eager smile, his father checked himself, sighed crossly, and stood up. *A vigorous Anglo-Saxon term, not necessarily a dirty word to be leered and giggled at. You should have outgrown all that by now.* He left the room before the boy found words to undo such awful damage.

BEYOND THE MISTED TREES, upriver, lies Tarrytown—Had someone tarried there? his mother asked his father, purling demurely. Why his father smiled at this he did not know. From Tarrytown one might see across the water to the cliffs where Rip Van Winkle had slept for twenty years. As a child he imagined a deep warm cleft full of autumn light, sheltered from the northeast storms and northwest winds. He peers across the mile of water, as if that shelter high up in clean mountains were still there.

In the Indian summer mist the river prospect looks much as he remembered it— indeed, much as it had been portrayed by the Hudson River School of painters so admired by his maternal grandmother. *Atrocious painters, all of them,* his father said. The small landscape of this stretch of river—was that in the crate of family things he had in storage? How much he has lost track of, in those years away.

He places a penny on the railroad track.

He longs to reassemble things—well, not "things" so much as continuity, that was his mother's word. Her mother had been raised on the west banks of the Hudson, and she could recall, from her own childhood, her great-aunt relating how *her* grandmother had seen Alexander Hamilton sculling downriver one fine morning just below their house—"Good day, Mr. Hamilton!"—and how Mr. Hamilton had never returned, having lost his life that day to Mr. Burr in a duel at Weehawken.

His father loved this story, too, the more so because that reach of river cliff had changed so little in the centuries between. For both of them, the memory of Mr. Hamilton had an autumnal melancholy that reached far back across the nation's history, to the Founding Fathers.

It seemed he had not responded to it properly.

I suppose you find it merely quaint, his mother said.

AT ONE TIME he attended Sunday school here in Arcadia, and he thinks he will rejoin the Episcopal Church. On sunny Sundays in white shirt and sober suit he will find himself sustained and calmed by stained-glass windows and Bach organ preludes. Afterward he will return to the garden cottage with its antique furniture, blue flowers in white rooms, fine editions, rare music, and a stately dog thumping its tail on a warm rug. He envisions an esoteric text, a string quartet, a glass of sherry on a sunlit walnut table in the winter—his parents' tastes, he realizes, acquired tastes he is determined to acquire.

In this civilized setting, smoking a pipe, he will answer questions from young women about Africa, and the nature of Africans, and how to deal judiciously with these AfroAmericans, so-called. Those who imagine that Africans are inferior do not know Africans, he'll say. Africans have their own sort of intelligence, they are simply not interested in the same things we are. Once their nature is understood, he'll say, Africans are Africans, wherever you find them, never mind what these bleeding-hearts may tell you.

264

A TRAIN COMES from the north, clicketing by, no longer dull coal black, as in his childhood, but a tube of blue-and-silver cars, no light between. In his childhood he could make out faces, but with increased speed the human beings are pale blurs behind the glass, and nobody waves to the man on the dead tree by the railroad tracks.

The wind and buffet of the train, the sting of grit, intensify his sense of isolation. To his wave, the train responds with a shrill whistle that is only a signal to the station at Arcadia, a half mile south.

He gets up, stretching, hunts the penny. It glints at him among the cinders. Honest Abe, tarnished by commerce, has been wiped right off the copper, replaced by a fiery smooth shine.

Looking north and south, he picks his way across the tracks. The third rail—if such it is—is a sheathed cable between pairs of rails marked "Danger Zone 700 Volts." Has the voltage increased since his childhood? *If you so much as point at that third rail,* explained his mother, who worried about his solitary expeditions to the river, *you'll be electrocuted, like one of those ghastly criminals up at Sing-Sing!* He hesitates before he crosses, stepping over this rail higher than necessary.

The tracks nearest the river are abandoned, a waste of rusted rails and splintered oaken ties and hard dry weeds. Once across, he can see north to the broad bend where a shoulder of the Palisades juts out from the far shore into the Tappan Zee. A thick new bridge has been thrust across the water, cutting off the far blue northern mountains. In his childhood, a white steamer of the Hudson River Day Line might loom around that bend at any moment, or a barge of bright tomato-red being towed by a pea-green tug, both fresh as toys. His father would evoke the passage of Robert Fulton's steamship *Claremont,* and the river trade on this slow concourse, flowing south out of the far blue mountains.

In his own lifetime—is this really true?—the river has changed from blue to a dead gray-brown, so thickened with inorganic silt that a boy would not see his own feet in the shallows. The agent, not a local man but full of local lore, asserts that the Atlantic salmon have vanished from the Hudson, and that the striped bass and shad are so contaminated by the poisons dumped into these waters by the corporations that people are prohibited from eating them. Only the blacks, says he, come out to fish for them, prowling the no-man's-land of tracks and cinders.

A grit beach between concrete slabs of an old embankment is scattered with worn tires. He wonders, as his father had, at the sheer number of these tires, brought by forces unknown so very far from the roads and highways and dumped in low woods and spoiled sullen waters all across America, as if, in the ruined wake of the course of empire, the tires had spun away in millions down the highways and rolled off the bridges into the rivers and down into deep swamps of their own accord.

But the horizon is oblivious, the clouds are white, the world rolls on. Under the cliffs, the bend is yellow in the glow of maples, and the faraway water, reflecting the autumn sky, is gold and blue. Soiled though they are, the shining woods and glinting water and the bright steel tracks, the high golden cliffs across the river, seem far more welcoming than the valley slope above, with its tight driveways, smelly cars, vigilant houses.

For a long time, by the riverside, he sits on a drift log worn smooth by the flood, withdrawn into the dream of Henry Hudson's clear blue river, of that old America off to the north toward the primeval mountains, off to the west under the shining sky.

3

THE REAL-ESTATE AGENT has persuaded him to come to dinner, to celebrate his move into the cottage, and a van has delivered a large crate containing what is left of the family things. On a journey home after his father's death, he had got rid of everything else, glad to have Arcadia behind him. But when his years in Africa were ended, and he was faced with a return to the United States, where he knew no one, this crate, in his imagination, had overflowed with almost everything from childhood. However, all he finds are a few small antiques that could not be sold quickly yet had seemed too valuable to abandon. There are also a few unaccountable small scraps—a baby-blue bathroom rug with faded bears, the Peter Rabbit book, the photograph of his duel with the Great Dane Inga.

His grandmother's riverscape is jammed in carelessly, its gold frame chipped. Wrapped around his father's Hardy reels and .41Ø Purdy shotgun is the Assistant Secretary's worn-out hunting jacket, the silver brandy flask still in the pocket, the hard brown canvas and scuffed corduroy irrevocably stained with gun oil, bird blood, and the drool of setter dogs.

The riverscape is hung over the mantel, with the Purdy on oak dowel pins beneath. He likes the feel of the quick gun, with its walnut stock and blue-black finish, its fine chasing. He will keep it loaded, as a precaution against looters and marauders. Agent Ed has advised him to emulate the plump homes of his neighbors, which are walleyed with burglar lights, atremble with alarms.

However, he hates all that night glare, he feels less protected than exposed. As soon as his pistol permit is restored—he concocts this plan over his evening whiskeys—he'll use a silencer to extinguish every burglar light in the whole neighborhood.

Why scare off marauders, he asks Mrs. Ed at supper, when the death of one burglar at the hands of a private citizen would do more to prevent crime than all the floodlights in Westchester County? He has said this for fun, to alarm this upstate couple. Poor Ed loves this dangerous talk, having no idea that his guest means it, and as for the hostess, the woman is agog, her eyes loom huge and round behind her spectacles.

"You're such a . . . well, a *disturbing* man!" she says.

"Disturbed me from the very first day I met him!" Ed cries jovially to soften his wife's inadvertent candor. "I suppose you're waiting for a new foreign service job?"

"There won't be one," he says abruptly, as if admitting this to himself for the first time.

He drinks the whiskey he has carried to the table. That these folks want a Harkness for a friend is all too plain. He picks up the wine, sips it, blinks, pulls his head back from it, sets his glass down again. "A bit sweet," he explains, when her stare questions him.

Ed jars the table and his face goes red with a resentment that he has avoided showing until now. "Well, shit," he says. "You're a damn snob," he says.

"Oh my." The woman does not take her round eyes off their guest.

Ed scrapes his chair back and goes to the front door and opens it. "We just thought you might be kind of lonely," Mrs. Ed mourns.

"Probably likes it that way," the agent says.

Things are awry again. Afraid of something, he takes a large swallow of wine and nods approvingly. "Not bad at all," he says, with a poor smile.

"It's not just the wine," the agent warns his wife. The woman has crossed her bare arms on her chest in the cold draft that wanders through the opened door.

"I was hoping you'd call me Henry," he says, drinking more wine. "Very nice," he says. She turns her face away, as if unable to look upon his desperation. "Forgive me," he says.

"Nosir," the voice says from the door. "Nosir, I don't think we will."

4

NOT WANTING HIS NEW HOUSE to be finished, leaving things undone, he takes long walks along suburban roads and drives. People stare to let him know they have their eye on him. Bad dogs run out. Even so, the walks are dull and pointless. More and more often he returns to the low river woods, the endless iron stretch of tracks, the silent river, flickered over by migrating swallows.

One day in October, he crosses the tracks and sits on a dock piling with twisted bolts, wrenched free by some upriver devastation. The piling's faint creosote smell brings back some childhood boat excursion, upriver through the locks of Lake Champlain.

The breeze is out of the northwest, and has an edge to it. With a fire-blackened scrap of siding, he scrapes out a shelter under the old pilings, partly hidden from the woods by the pale sumac saplings that struggle upward from the cinders.

In the early autumn afternoon, out of the wind, he is warmed by the westering sun across the river. If the beach litter were piled in front of him, he thinks, he would be unseen even from the water. Not that there is anyone to see him, it is just the sheltered feeling it would give him. The freighters headed up to Albany, the tugs and barges, an occasional fat white motor cruiser with its nylon Old Glory flying from the stern, pass too far offshore to be aware of a hat-shadowed face in a pile of flotsam.

He hunches down a little, squinting out between his knees.

He is safe and secret, sheltered from the world, just as he had been long ago in his tree houses and attic hideouts, in the spruce hollow in the corner behind the lode of packages under the Christmas tree, in warm nests in the high summer grass, peeping out at the Algonkin Indians. Delawares, his father said. *Algonkin is the language family.* In the daytime, at least, no one comes along the tracks. He has the river kingdom to himself. As to whether he is content, he does not know.

He has packed dry sherry in his father's silver flask, a sandwich, a hard apple, and also a new bleeding-heart account of modern politics in the former Belgian Congo. His name receives harsh passing mention. He thinks, To hell with it. I did what was asked of me. I did my duty. Having the courage to dirty one's hands, without glory and at great risk of ingratitude, may become one's higher duty to one's country, wasn't that true?

The trouble was, he had not liked Lumumba. He had wondered if the Prime Minister might be unstable. Lumumba's hostility toward Europeans flared and shuddered like a fire in the wind but never died. He ate distractedly in small brief fits, growing thinner and thinner. He was moody, loud, self-contradictory, he smoked too much hemp, he drank a lot, he took one woman after another despite his devotion to his wife, he could not stop talking or stand still.

Wild ducks pass by within gun range, flaring away from his little cove with hard quacks of alarm. He swings his arms as if holding a gun, and they crumple and fall in a downward arc as he follows through. Watching them fly onward, he feels an exhilaration tinged with loss that wild fowl still tried to migrate south along this shore of poisoned mud and rust and cinders. On a northeast wind, in rain, his hiding place would serve well as a duck blind, for in order to land into the wind the birds would hook around over the open water and come straight in to the gun.

More ducks appear farther upriver where the black stumps of an old dock jut from the surface. The long rust heads and silver-white bodies are magically unsullied in the somber water. There are five.

Needing something to look forward to, he decides upon a sacramental hunt. A hunter's stiff whiskey by the fire, the wild-duck supper with wild rice, the red Bordeaux from his mother's old colonial crystal decanter—thus will he consecrate the return of the Harkness family to Arcadia. Since it will happen only once, he can't be bothered with decoys, waders, far less a retriever. The river is too swift and deep to wade in, and in the unlikely event that a duck falls, the current is bound to carry it ashore.

To acquire a license to kill ducks he goes to Yonkers, not wishing to excite local curiosity. It seems absurd to bother about a license for one bird, when to shoot on the railroad right-of-way will be illegal in the first place. He applies for the permit for the same reason that he would feel obliged to retrieve and eat any bird he shot, rather than waste it. His father had been strict about licenses, bag limits, and using what one killed, even in the days when ducks were plentiful. To offend this code would violate the hunt ceremony in some way, make the supper pointless.

He has no proof of U.S. residence in the previous year—in the previous two decades, if it comes to that. He does not say this, lest his very citizenship be challenged by the hostile young black woman, who says he will have to identify himself, submit proof of residence, proof of citizenship. But he has no driver's license or certificate of birth, and can't tell her that his passport has been confiscated.

"Next!"

As for the huge hunting license, it looks nothing like the duck-stamp badge his father had worn upon his fishing hat. The new license is worn on the back, to facilitate identification by the game warden. Though he knows it is foolish, he feels he is being tricked into the open. One might as well wear a bull's-eye on one's back.

"Next!"

268

Are the authorities suggesting, he inquires, that the duck hunter is stupid as well as lawless, that he will shoot over his limit and make off with his booty, yet neglect to remove this grotesque placard from his back?

"We ain't suggesting nothing. That's the law." She waves him aside. "Next!"

He is surprised that the man behind him in the line is black.

"Move along please! Next!"

His stalling has permitted him to fold a twenty-dollar bill into his application form and ease it back across the counter, at the same time requesting her to be more careful how she talks to him. Raising her eyebrows at his tone, then at the money, she heaves around as if to summon her superior, giving him a chance to withdraw the bill. He does so quickly, winking at the black man, asking this female if he really requires proof that he is an American—doesn't he look like one?

With the back of her hand, she brushes away his application form, which flutters to the floor.

"I could bust you, mister. You just watch your step."

She is already processing the next application.

"*Everybody* looks American," she is saying. "I look American. And you know what, mister?" She looks up at him. "I am American. More than you." She points at the incomplete form in his hand. "I haven't lived in Africa for half my life."

Please do not confuse your activities in Africa with the foreign service, far less true service to your country, less still an honorable career that would make you a credit to this family.

When he raised his eyes, his mother averted hers. He flipped his father's note back at her, in a kind of spasm. The letter struck her at the collarbone and fell into her lap. She looked down at it for a long moment, then picked it up between two fingers and set it on the table. Her eyes glistened.

You've changed so, Henry, dear. When you went off to war, you grew so hard. It wasn't your fault, of course. Seeing all those dreadful things—it's enough to confuse anyone, I'm sure!

Before he could protest, she had slipped away from him.

You were such a lonely boy. How I wish you'd found somebody. Or become a naturalist! she added brightly. *Animals are so much easier, aren't they?*

Inappropriately, she tried to smile, as if to soothe him.

We shall always love you, dear.

His rivals killed him! he insisted. *Mother?* He had wanted to seize her, to shake from her frail body some pledge of loyalty. *Patrice was the Soviets' little macaque!*

She opened her eyes wide in mock astonishment—Patrice?

And your little Mr. Mobutu, dear? The dictator? Whose macaque is he?

HE DECIDES he will need decoys after all. His father's hand-carved balsa ducks, close-etched with wild colors, had been rigged with cedar keels and fine-smelling tarred cod line and square lead anchors on which the line was wrapped, leaving just enough room in the open center so that line and weight fitted neatly over bill and head. But sturdy wood decoys are no longer available, or not, at least, in these seedy river towns.

What are offered instead are swollen plastic mallards, drake mallards only, with heads the dead green of zinc alloy and the rest a bad industrial brown fit to attract those mongrel ducks that inhabited the dirty waters of the city parks and the pilings of old river docks in Yonkers. By means of gaudy plastic twine that would cut the hands in winter weather each duck is rigged to a scrap of pig iron, sure to drag in any sort of wind.

He cannot bring himself to acquire more than three *(Always set an odd number, his father had said, in case of a lone bird),* since he would not harbor such horrors in his house, and does not intend to hunt ever again. So irritated is he by wasting money on such rubbish that he feels justified in commandeering a rain parka in its slim packet and also a handful of shotgun shells.

At the cottage he finds a burlap sack for carrying and concealing the decoys, the dismantled gun, the shells, and a thermos of coffee in its leather case. That evening, he rigs a treble-hooked surf-casting lure on a length of line—a makeshift retrieval gear of his own devising.

Within a few days comes a forecast of northeast wind, with rain. Since his days are his own—the one activity left to him, now that the house is finished, is phoning for groceries, which are delivered daily—he will go hunting with the first change in the weather.

BEARING HIS SACK over his shoulder like a burglar, he makes his way down toward the river. In the darkness, each house is fortified by its hard pool of light, and he half expects that his flashlight, spotted at the wood edge by some nosy oldster out of bed to pee, will bring police from all directions, filling the suburban night with whirling red, white, and blue beacons—the Nigger Hunters, as the hotel clerk referred to them, conveying contempt for cops and blacks alike.

In the woods he descends wet shadow paths, his sack catching and twisting in the thorns. At the track edge he peers north and south through a grim mist that hides him entirely from the world, then crosses the railroad to the river.

He lobs the decoys out upon the current, and the wind skids them quickly to the end of their strings, which swing too far inshore. In daybreak light, in choppy water, they in no way resemble three lorn ducks yearning for the companionship of a fourth.

He yanks his blind together, scrunching low as a train sweeps past toward the city. He feels clumsy, out of place, not nearly so well hidden as he had imagined. The upstate passengers, half-dozing in the fetid yellow light, cannot have seen him, though they stare straight at him through the grit-streaked windows. He breaks the light gun, loads two shells, and snaps it to, then sips his cup of coffee, peering outward.

As forecast, the wind is out of the northeast. Pale gulls sail past. But there is no rain, and the mist lifts, and the sun rises from the woods behind, filling the cliff faces across the river with a red-gold light.

The eerie windshine of the first day of a northeaster exposes the decoys for the poor things they are; the unnatural brightness of their anchor lines would flare a wild bird from five gunshots away. His folly is jeered at by clarion jays that cross back and forth among the yellow maples at the wood edge.

BANG

He has whirled and with a quick snap shot extinguished one of the jays, which flutters downward in the river woods like a blue leaf. He sinks back, strangely out of breath. And he is about to break his gun, retreat, slink home—he wants to drink—when there comes a small whispery sound, a small watery rush.

A black duck has landed just beyond the decoys. Struggling to make sense of its silent company, it quacks softly, turning back and forth. It rides the gray wavelets, wheat colored head held high in wariness.

He has one shell left and no time to reload.

The gentle head switches back and forth, one eye seeking, then the other. In the imminence of the morning sun, in the wild light, the bird's tension holds the earth together.

The duck springs from the surface with a downward buffet of the wings. In one jump it is ten feet in the air, drops of water falling, silver-lined wings stretched to the wind that will whirl it out of range.

BANG

The dark wings close. The crumpled thing falls humbly to the surface, scarcely a splash, as the echo caroms from the cliffs across the river.

In the ringing silence, the river morning is resplendent. Time resumes, and the earth breathes again.

The duck floats upside down, head underwater, red legs on the bronze-black feathers twitching.

Not a difficult shot, his father would have said. *The trigger is squeezed when the bird levels off at the top of the jump, for just at that moment it seems almost motionless, held taut by wires—not a difficult shot.*

How often in his boyhood he had missed it, turning away so as not to see his father's mouth set at the corners. Then one day he outshot his father, finishing up with a neat double, trying not to grin.

With that second barrel he had overshot his limit. He had known this but could not resist, his father's good opinion had seemed more important. The Assistant Secretary's nod acknowledged the fine shot, but his voice said, *You've always been good at things, Henry. No need to be greedy.* It was no use blustering that he had followed through the double as his father had taught him. His father had no patience with excuses.

Often his mother felt obliged to say, *Your father's standards are so high, you see.*

When he tried to ask just what she meant, she cut him off.

She smiled. *Sometimes what I think you lack is a sense of humor.*

He whirls his retrieval rig around his head and lets it go, looping the casting plug out beyond the duck, then tugging it back across the line of drift. On the third try it catches in the tail feathers and turns the bird around before pulling free. The next two tries are rushed, the last falls short.

The current has taken the diminished thing, it is moving more rapidly now, tending offshore.

Alone on the riverbank, peering about him, he takes a deep breath and regrets it, for the breath displaces his exhilaration, drawing into his lungs intuitions of final loneliness and waste and loss. That this black duck of the coasts and rivers should be reduced to a rotting tatter in the tidal flotsam, to be pulled at by the gulls, to be gnawed by rats, is not bearable, he cannot bear it, he veers from this bitter end of things with a grunt of pain. Or is it, he wonders, the waste that he cannot bear? Something else scares him: he dreads going home alone and empty-handed, to the life still to be lived in the finished cottage. If the hunt supper does not take place, nothing will follow.

Sooner or later, the black duck must enter an eddy and be brought ashore. Hiding the shells and thermos under the driftwood, abandoning the decoys to the river, he hurries down the tracks toward the city, gun across his shoulder.

The bird does not drift nearer, neither does it move out farther. Wind and current hold it in equilibrium, a dull dark thing like charred deadwood in the tidal water. Far ahead, the cliffs of both shores come together at the George Washington Bridge, and beyond the high arch, the sinking skyline of the river cities.

The world is littered with these puppet dictators of ours, protecting our rich businessmen and their filthy ruination of poor countries, making obscene fortunes off the misery of the most miserable people on this earth!

The old man shifted his bones for a better look at his impassive son, as if he had forgotten who he was. He considered him carefully in a long mean silence. *Who do you really work for these days, Henry? What is it that you do, exactly?*

I am the government liaison with the western corporations.

And it's your idea, I'm told, that these corporations pay these governments for the right to dump their toxic wastes in Africa.

When his son was silent, the old man nodded. *I gather they pay you well for what you do.*

Mother says you are obliged to sell the house. I'd like to buy it.

Absolutely not! I'd sooner sell it to Mobutu!

Didn't you warn me once against idealism? The Cold War is not going to be won by the polite and passive intrigues of your day—

Stop that at once! Don't talk as if you had standards of your own—you don't! You're some damn kind of moral dead man! You don't know who the hell you are, and I don't either! You probably should have been an undertaker!

The old man rummaged his newspaper. When his son sat down by him, he drew his dressing gown closer. Stricken, he said, *Forgive me. Perhaps you cannot help what you have become. I asked too much of you, your mother says, I was too*

272

harsh. He paused for a deep breath, then spoke shyly. *I'm sorry, Henry. Please don't come again.*

THE MIST has lifted, the sun rises.

Trudging south, he is overtaken by the heat, the early trains. In his rain parka with the stiff canvas beneath, lugging the gun, his body suffocates. It is his entire body, his whole being, that is growing angry. The trains roar past, they assail him with bad winds, faces stare stupidly. He waves them off, his curses lost in the trains' racketing. His jaw set in an iron rage, he concentrates on each railroad tie, tie after tie.

The dead bird is fifty yards offshore, bound for the sea. In the distance, the silver bridge glints in the mist. Nearer are the cliffs at Spuyten Duyvil, where the tracks turn eastward, following the East River. Once the bird had passed that channel mouth, he could only watch as it drifted down the west shore of Manhattan.

He trots a little. He can already see the rail yard and trestle where the tracks bend away under the cliffs.

5

THERE THEY ARE.

Perched on concrete slabs along the bank, thin darkskinned figures turn dark heads to see this white man coming with a gun. Though the day is warm, they are wearing purple sweatshirts with sharp, pointed hoods drawn tight, as in some archaic sect in Abyssinia.

They pretend to ignore him, he ignores them, too. "Hey," one says, more or less in greeting. Rock music goes loud then soft again as he moves past paper bags, curled orange peels.

In painted silver, the purple sweatshirts read:

Lumumba Lives

On a drift log lies a silver fish, twenty pounds or more, with lateral black stripes from gills to tail. In the autumn light, the silver scales glint with tints of brass. Should he tell these Africans that this shining New World fish carries cancer-causing poison in its gut?

Beyond the Africans, on the outside of the tracks between rails and river, is a small brick relay station. The wrecked windows are boarded up with plywood, and each plywood panel is marked with a single word scrawled in harsh black:

Nam Coke Rush

Crouched behind the station, he hides the gun under a board, slips his wallet into a crevice, then his shoulder holster. He fits a shard of brick.

The plaint of a train, from far upriver. The Africans teeter on their slabs, craning to see where he has gone. The sun disappears behind swift clouds.

He strips to his shorts and picks his way across dirtied weeds and rocks, down to the water edge.

Where an eddy has brought brown scud onto the shore lie tarred scrap wood and burnt insulation, women's devices in pink plastic, rusted syringes, a broken chair, a large filth-matted fake-fur toy, a beheaded cat, a spent condom, a half grapefruit.

Ah shit, he says aloud, as if the sound of his own voice might be of comfort. He forces his legs into the flood, flinching in anticipation of glass shards, metal, rusty nails through splintered wood.

The hooded figures shout, waving their arms. They yell again, come running down the bank.

His chest is hollowed out, his lungs yawn mortally. He hurls himself outward, gasping as the hard cold strikes his temples, as a soft underwater shape nudges his thigh. In his thrash, he gasps up a half mouthful of the bitter water, losing his breath as he coughs it out, fighting the panic.

Rippling along his ear, the autumn water whispers of cold deeps, green-turning boulders. The river is tugging at his arms, heavy as mercury, entreating him to let go, to sink away. Through the earth's ringing he can hear his arms splash, as the surface ear hears the far whistle of a train, as yells diminish.

Cold iron fills his chest, and desolation. It is over now— this apprehension of the end comes to him simply, as if body and soul were giving up together. The earth is taking him, he is far out on the edge, in the turning current.

The duck floats belly up, head underwater, droplets of Adirondack water pearled on the night blue of its speculum, drifting downriver from the sunny bend, from the blue mountains.

His cold hand is dull as wood on the stiffened duck.

The cold constricts him and his throw is clumsy. The effort of the throw takes too much strength. The duck slides away downstream. He swallows more water, coughs and spits, and overtakes it, rolling over on his back to get a breath.

A rock nudges him. He sees bare trees whirl on the sky. The point-head purple hoods loom up, dark faces break.

"Yo, man! Lookin good, man! You all right?"

From the shallows, he slings the duck onto the litter. He crawls onto the rocks, knocks away a hand.

"Easy, man! We trying to help!"

"Yay man? What's happenin? How come you jumpin in the river?"

"October, man! *Bad* river, man!"

"Never catch no *nigger* swimmin! Not out there!"

"*No,* man! Niggers *sink*! Any fool know *dat!*"

They yell with laughter.

"Goodbye cruel world, look like to me!"

"Cruel world!" another hoots, delighted. "That's about it!"

His wet underwear is transparent. He feels exposed, caught in the open. Rage grasps him, but he has no strength. He fights for breath.

"Hey man? You hearin me? Next time you need duck meat bad as that, you let me know. Go walkin in the park, toss me some crumbs, noose all you want! Two bucks apiece! Yeah man! Gone give you my card!"

They laugh some more. "Gone give the man his *card,* that nigger say!"

"Like to eat fish? We gone fry fish!"

He gazes from one black man to another, trying to bring the turmoil in his head under control. Four are middle-aged, in old suit trousers and broken street shoes. The fifth might be a son, and wears new running sneakers.

Lumumba Lives

They smile at him. He knows these Africans, he knows how well they feign subservience and admiration, laughing at someone when they have him at their mercy. He gets slowly to his feet.

"Who's Lumumba?" he inquires, playing for time.

"Who Lumumba is?"

This man looks down, he spreads his lettering with all eight fingers, then looks up at the younger man, who must be twenty.

"My boy Junius our Lumumba man. Who Lumumba, Junius?"

"Frag!"

"Who Lumumba, Frag?"

The white man coughs. Wasn't that the problem? That he had not liked Lumumba? Wasn't that it?

Ashamed of his elders, Frag rolls his eyes. Frag is feverish and skinny, wild-eyed, angry. "Have Lumumba on your fuckin shirt, don't know who he is?" He glares at the white man.

"Who he was, Lumumba Man. He's dead."

Frag shrieks, "You makin fun? You makin fun with me?"

The white man does a stiff shuffle, almost falling. "Wholumumba, wholumumba, wholumumba, WHO!" He is foot-numb, goosefleshed, shuddering with cold. Nothing seems real to him.

The faces in the purple hoods look mystified. He thinks, Come on, get it over with.

He starts out along the rail bed for the relay station, on the dead city stones and broken glass and metal litter.

At a sharp whistle he turns. Frag pitches the duck underhand, too hard, straight at his gut. He lets it fall.

"Shot it and swam for it, almost got drownded," one man says. "So why you *leavin* it? Ain't got no license?"

He points toward their fishing poles, upriver. They have no license, either. And possession of striped bass, he says, is against the law.

They exchange looks of comic disbelief. One raises both hands. "Whoo!" he says.

"Ol' fish washed up out of the river!"

"Yessir, that fish *all* washed up!"

They hoot, delighted, then frown and mutter when he will not laugh with them.

"Hey, we ain't *gone possess* that fish!"

"No, man! We gone *eat* him! You *invited!*"

When he tells them that their fish is poisoned, they stare back in mock outrage.

"Shit, man! Ain't niggers poisoned it!"

He goes on, knowing they will follow. They are after his wallet, and the gun.

"Where's that gun at, Whitey?"

There it is. They have come up fast, they are right behind him.

"None of your business, Blacky," he says, and keeps on going. He feels giddy.

"Blacky" is repeated, bandied about. He hears a whoop, a cry of warning, and he turns again.

An older man with silver grizzle at the temples, dark wet eyes, has his hand on Frag's arm. In Frag's hand is a large rock. The others jabber.

"What's happenin, man? What's up wit' you?"

"Come downriver see if we can help, and you just don't do right."

He resumes walking, paying no attention to the rock. Hauteur, he thinks, will always impress Africans. All the same, he feels confused, and tries to focus. On impulse he admits over his shoulder that he hid the gun, since they know this anyway.

"Scared we steal it, right?" Frag's voice is a near-screech.

"Seen niggers hangin around, right?" Frag bounces his big rock off a rail.

He wants to shout "Right!" but restrains himself.

An older voice says, "Easy, Junius, don't excite yourself."

"Frag!"

"Easy, Frag, don't excite yourself. You okay, Frag?"

At the relay station, his clothes are undisturbed. He sees the corner of his wallet in the crevice.

Nam Coke Rush

He pulls the pants on over his wet underwear, realizes that he does this out of modesty, stops himself, strips. They whoop and whistle. When he reaches for his pants a second time, Frag snaps them from his hand.

"Don't like niggers, right? Scared of 'em, right? We smell it! Oh, we *hate* that honky smell, man!"

His foot is right beside the board, he slides his toe beneath it.

"Mister? Frag excites hisself, okay?"

"Truth!" Frag yells. "Fuckin truth, man! We can take it! Don't like niggers, right?"

"Right," he says, because the timing is so satisfying. He doesn't care whether or not it's true. Five blacks, one white—a clear case of self-defense. He flips the board, stoops quick, brings up the gun.

"Let's have those pants," he says. "I'm tired of this."

The black men back away, form a loose circle neither out of range nor close enough to threaten him. Breathing raggedly, beside himself, Frag stays where he is, as if transfixed by the twin black holes of the gun muzzle.

"Don' point that mothafucka, man!" he gasps at last.

"Toss the man his damn pants, Junius! Go ahead, now!"

"Man might do it, Junius! See them eyes?"

"Fuck!" Frag yells, beside himself. "Li'l popgun!"

The father's soft voice is a plea. "Easy, mister, please, what's up wit' you? That boy can't help hisself."

He sees their fear of what they take to be his naked craziness.

At the train whistle, the black men look relieved. Frag jabs his finger, furious and scared. He keeps staring at the gun, he will not back off.

"Toss the man them pants now, Junius."

The train is coming down the track toward the city, loud as a riveting machine, as a machine gun.

"Train comin, man."

But he makes no move to hide himself. He steps farther out onto the tracks. What the engineer must see is a naked white man surrounded and beset by a gang of blacks.

The train blows three shrill whistles, lurches, and begins to slow.

"Junius? Trouble, boy! You got enough!"

"Shit!" the boy snarls. "Ain't us done nothin!"

He slings the pants. The older man grabs him from behind, spins him away. The boy curses in a vicious stream, angling out across the tracks toward the woods on the river slope behind the train, ready to run if anyone on the train starts to descend. He yells, "You ain't done with Frag yet, shithead! Honky mothafuck!"

The train eases to a stop. A hiss of steam. High cirrus clouds come out over the trees, over the river.

"Put them pants on, mister! Folks is *lookin* at you!"

"Back up," he says, lifting the gun. And right now, remembering that both shells in the gun have been expended, he feels a sharp tingle at the temples.

A voice from the train calls, "You all right?" He waves his hand, then lays the gun down and begins to dress.

Sullen and sad, the black men shake their heads. They mutter, but they do not speak, they will not meet the stares from the train windows. They watch him dress, watch him take his wallet from the crevice in the wall. When he straps on the empty shoulder holster, they groan and retreat farther.

The train departs. He starts away, walking upriver.

He wonders now if they meant him any harm, but he takes no chances. Every little while he turns to be sure he is not followed.

The figures stand in silhouette. Three wave and point as the fourth raises the wild duck, bill pointed against the city. They seem to entreat him, but it is too late. What are they calling?

The hurled duck arches on the sky, falls fast, and bounces, coming to rest in the junk along the river.

When he goes back for it, they scatter, abandoning their fish. He puts the gun down, raises both his arms. "Wait a minute!" he calls. "Listen!"

"Get outta here!" they holler back. "Jus' you get *outta* here!"

AT HIS BLIND he retrieves his equipment, leaving the three decoys to the river. With his burlap sack, he starts across the tracks toward the woods. Near the mouth of the old brook, he spins, recoiling from a clip of wind right past his ear.

A purple hood sinks back behind the auto body in the swamp. He circles the auto, crouching and running, but the rock-thrower has vanished, and the woods are silent.

He hunts quickly through the woods, chasing scared footfalls, then retreats half backward, swinging the gun. Moving slowly so that Frag can tail him without difficulty, he climbs the steep lawn below his father's house. Someone is shouting.

Inside, the cottage seems to enclose him. He listens to the clock tick. The house creaks. He pours himself a whiskey.

No one answers at the real-estate office. To the answering machine he whispers, "This is Henry Harkness. I have a wild duck here, and some wild rice and good wine. I was hoping you and . . ." He doesn't want to say "your wife," but he cannot recall the round-eyed woman's name. He puts the phone down. Somewhere his life took a turn without his knowledge.

The duck drips blood and water from its bill onto the white enamel of the kitchen table.

He slips out the back door and through the trees to the autumn garden. From here he can spot the purple hood coming up along the woods. The running, the game of it, the ambush are exhilarating, but the excitement dies quickly with the whiskey flush and does not return.

He settles down to wait behind the wall.

The light has gone wrong in some way. The sky is darkening in the noon sun, the dusk is waiting in the trees, and nowhere is there any shelter.

The African will come, perhaps at dark. Even now that face is peering from the trees. Neighbors will come to pay respects once it is over.

A police car comes and goes, lights flashing slowly, humping around the drive on its fat tires. The caretaker rides in the front seat.

No one comes up from the woods, the glinting river. Still he waits there in the autumn garden, cooling his forehead on the night-blue metal, in the haunted sunlight, in the dread of home.

In the Land of Men

Antonya Nelson

Since my attack last year, when I get off work at night one of my brothers is always waiting for me in our family car, the rusted boat, engine idling, double-parked on Halsted right outside Mizzi's, where I wait tables. No one asked them to do this and we don't talk about it, but when I emerge from the steamy restaurant into the biting, steel cold of Chicago, my heart offers up a grateful sigh at the presence of one or the other of my brothers' placid, safe faces.

Tonight they all three show. Sam, nineteen, the oldest boy but four years younger than me, sits on the hood with his pointed black ankle boots wedged between bumper and car. An inch of bare skin is exposed where the boots and pants cuffs don't quite meet, which is Sam's style. It is zero degrees out, according to the radio, factoring in wind chill, but Sam doesn't wear a coat.

"Too cool to feel cold?" I say.

He shells out a pittance of a smile. "Let's go." He hops off the hood to hold open the front door and presses my back with his palm. Sensing his eyes casting about protectively behind me, I catch my first whiff of something gone awry.

"I love a warm car," I say, settling in the passenger seat with my hands in front of the blowing heat vents. My other two brothers sit in the back the way the youngest always do. I say to them, "Hey."

Sam slams the driver's door and jerks us out of Park. He drives as if our transmission is not automatic, shifting into low or neutral frequently, keeping one hand active on the thin metal stick. Even as his older sister, I stay a certain nervous distance from Sam. Beneath his meticulously maintained smooth surface is a rage that can erupt and break windows or punch walls.

For a time I just ride along in the warmth, quietly losing my waitress aches. Lately I've found real comfort in these pocketlike moments of heat and peace, which can be as refreshing as deep, unconscious sleep. I breathe out, at last, hating to end it, but knowing I must. "So, what's the occasion?"

Sam grimly says nothing, flicking his eyes to the rearview. I turn, catty-corner, to Donald. Seventeen, the worrier, he looks alarmingly pale in the passing streetlights. His hand is in a fist under his nose as he bites a fingernail, staring desperately at the sidewalk and storefronts like a trapped dog. Donald has ulcers, migraines, all the ailments symptomatic of early adulthood. Beside him, Les, the family baby, seems more rosy-cheeked than usual, as if he's siphoned off Donald's color to top his own. But even happy Les has an uncertain smile on his face and watches Sam for cues. His teeth chatter, despite the car's abundant warmth.

Without taking his eyes off the panel van in front of him, Sam says tightly, "You got any plans tonight?"

I point at my chest. "Me? You're talking to me?"

"That's right. Anything you were going to do?"

"Is something wrong?" I ask, simultaneously anxious and annoyed that they are protecting me by withholding. "Is it Dad? Has something happened to Dad?"

"No," Donald says, looking at his watch. "Time for *WBN News at Nine*. Pistachios and beer."

From behind me, Les pats my arm soothingly. "Dad's cool," he assures me.

Sam catches my eye and we share an older siblings' smile, as if over Les's head. "He's fine," Sam says.

"And here you guys are. So what could it be?" I sit back, relieved: My family is alive. Lesser scenarios occur to me. A surprise party. An unexpected friend waiting at the airport. A trip to the police to clear up some minor infraction before my father discovers the offense. But here we are, enclosed and fine and balanced. I enjoy, for a second, suspense's tantalizing luxury. "So when do you tell me, guys?"

Sam stops uncharacteristically at a yellow light. We rock forward with inertia, rock back. Pedestrians, loaded down with afterwork, early Christmas shopping, plunge into the crosswalks, heads ducked in irritation against the cold. Telltale forest-green Marshall Field's sacks swing from their gloved fingers. It's late and they're homeward bound. A man carries a paper funnel of flowers, shielding it with his chest, turning his back to protect this gift for some woman. Ashy snow blows up in the six-way intersection, sings along the cracks in our car doors, and the taxi in front of us decides to turn left; a signal begins flashing. Generally, this draws a heavy lean on Sam's horn, but tonight he simply waits.

"You have a decision to make," he says.

Les adds excitedly, "A very *important* decision. Mega-important. Man, it's big, really big. Life and death, you could say."

Sam frowns into the rearview mirror at Les, his profile so sharp and grown-up I have a sudden moment of wonder: My brother's a man. I quickly look at Donald—has he, too, crossed the line? But no, Donald has no beard, no jutting jaw, no buried rage. He shakes his young head pessimistically, eyes still glued in appeal to the passing world.

The light changes.

"We got your perp," Sam says to me as we take off again and slide around the taxi. He shifts his eyes momentarily from the road to my face. He's a dangerously handsome man, the family heartbreaker, and his direct gaze has a life—volition, power—of its own.

"*My* perp?"

"Perpetrator!" Les shouts gleefully. "We got your perpetrator! That guy! He's in our trunk."

* * *

Last year on a night not unlike tonight—that is, a night in which one instant knifed the odds of my otherwise fair life—a man looped his bright red wool scarf over my head lasso-style and pulled me to his chest. Fast and easy. He was right behind me and I could feel the serious metal cylinder of gun at my back.

"Let's walk," he suggested, "and not make too much racket."

We'd been the only two people waiting for the bus and I hadn't looked closely at him. His red scarf had been woven around his neck, and his hair stood up comically in the back as a result. A cane hooked over his forearm. That's all I remembered. Innocuous. Maybe he wore a long camel's hair coat. Behind me, he matched his footsteps to mine so exactly that if I looked down I could see his right galoshes toe coming forward just behind my own. There weren't many people on Fullerton Avenue that night and those who were seemed to misread my frantic blinking eyes. What could our peculiar closeness have appeared to be? He took me as quickly as possible to an alley. I heard our bus pass without stopping, its upward-shifting gears, feeling furious with the driver, who knew my name, who knew I always rode home with him. . . .

"Got any money, baby?" the man asked as we hastened down the alley, leaning near enough to my ear for me to feel his eyelashes kiss it. I stumbled, but he led me through my clumsiness like an expert dancer. We were approaching the back of Mizzi's, and I prayed for one of the busboys, Danbo or Rudy, to be outside smoking a j. But it was too cold; they would be up above the walk-in refrigerator, in the airspace between floors. There wasn't a soul in the alley. I heard the muffled clatter of dishes and the motor of the Hobart, could easily imagine that lively, hot kitchen only a few crucial feet of space away from me.

"Money, babe?" he reminded me.

I nodded in my scarf sling. "I do. Take it, please, in my bag." I lifted my right shoulder carefully to draw attention to my purse hanging there.

He said, "Good girl. You a good girl? It would be in your interest to be a very good girl, you know." He had a precise British accent, cheerful and civilized-sounding. Could I have felt relief? We'd stopped and he positioned me face first against the rear wall of the empty storefront down the block from Mizzi's. It would be open in a month, its front windows claimed. A comedy club. I'd passed the sign a hundred times. Open mike on Wednesdays, no cover, two-drink minimum. He pushed me gently to the wall, nose to brick, and told me to grab on to the black window bars on either side.

"You hang on for dear life, do you hear me?"

I certainly did.

His gun, that metal erection, pressed into my lower spine, sending its insinuations to every part of me. Without lowering the gun, he dropped his cane to the ground and told me to put a foot on either end of it. I concentrated on the rubber tip and the curve of its worn handle. The worst thing that *could* happen, I told myself, was not going to. Then he drew my head back by the hair and slammed my forehead against the bricks. I tasted red wool.

Donald says, "He can probably hear us, you know. The trunk is right here." He pats

281

the seat behind him, leaning away from it. Les looks startled and also tips forward.

Even the remotest possibility of this man's presence has made me queasy and I clutch the door handle, as if waiting for the right moment to escape. "You can't be serious," I say hopefully.

"Serious as a heart attack, sweetheart," Sam says.

We're heading west on the Eisenhower. Magnificent, colorful Michigan Avenue has given way to gloomy industrial warehouses. Traffic is light and, for the second time in my city life, I wish it otherwise. Cars, humanity, witnesses—but to what?

I say, "How can you be positive it's him? I mean, did you ask him?"

"We didn't *talk* to him," Les says. "God, it was hard enough to find him. We've been watching him for a long time. We knew it was him. He had that England accent. Plus the cane."

My feet arch reflexively at the mention of the cane, the dry texture of scarf once more in my mouth. "What do you mean, you've been watching him? What are you talking about?"

Donald says, *"They*. These two have been staking out this guy since last winter. Not me. I was ready to let the police do it."

"The police," Sam scoffs. He shakes his head once.

"That's right!" Donald says. "The cops. You can't just go around being above the law."

Sam says, "Says who?"

"I thought about dressing up like a girl," Les tells me, and new images unreel before my eyes at a dizzying speed. "A decoy. But I would have looked like Bride of Frankenstein, and I kept thinking, what would Mom have thought?"

"Mom," Donald says, "would have wondered where you guys were all those nights. Mothers know where their kids are. With Dad, it's like, 'Oh, Sam and Les? Huh. Studying in their rooms, I guess.' Mom would never have let you out the door."

I say, "What are you saying?"

"They chased the guy," Donald explains.

"We *tailed* him," Les corrects. "There was no chasing. Chasing means running."

"Whatever. They *tailed* him. They—"

"We waited until he was alone," Les says. "We saw him at that same bus stop, you know. . . ." He clears his throat to indicate discretion in alluding to my rape.

"And?" I say.

"And we followed him home."

"On foot," Sam says pointedly. Since he's had his driver's license he's hardly walked anywhere.

Les bounces on the seat as he talks. "We know where he lives!"

"Pricey," Sam adds. "Yuppie."

"After we found out, we watched his walk-up, we saw him through the curtains. He's got those see-through kind, the ones Mom always said were a bad idea on the first floor. But we couldn't get him alone. He would walk out the door, and we'd start to get out of the car—here comes some people. Man, it was frustrating. I don't see how you could make a living doing it."

Sam says to me, "It is weird how hard it was to find him by himself."

The car is silent for a moment, all of us meditating on my rapist's extended good fortune. Then Donald says, "These two have been out asking for it, just asking for—"

"We had a gun," Les protests. *"He* didn't have a gun—"

"Luckily for you," Donald interrupts.

"—but we *did,* see, that's the whole point. We were in charge. Once we got some privacy, the rest was so easy you couldn't believe it. He comes out to get the paper, nobody around, and bang, Sam's there with the gun."

"Bang?" I ask. "Bang? Oh guys, you didn't shoot him?"

"Not bang like that, just bang, like, get in the car, bud, let's go for a cruise. We didn't even have to tie him up."

"But he had a gun," I say. "Last year, he had a gun."

Sam turns to me. "Nuh-uh. Piece of pipe. We've been watching, like Les said. We saw asswipe's weapon. Carries it in his coat. Jesus. Little six-inch pipe."

Donald, relinquishing his role as the voice of reason for a moment, giggles and says, "Saturday night plumber's special." They all three laugh, a frightening expulsion of breath.

"Please tell me you don't have a man in the trunk of this car."

"Sorry," Sam says. "No can do." His coldness, his assuredness—the way the thrust of his strong, righteous jaw seems to drive the very car—these things let me know they not only have a man in the trunk, but the right man. I now feel his weight, as if the back end of the automobile were notably lower to the road.

"Please," I say weakly, "could we think for a minute about going to the cops with this?"

"They'll turn him free," Sam says. "Right now we have him, he's ours, but they'll set him free."

"You know what the problem is?" Donald says speculatively. "The problem is over-crowding in jails. I've been thinking that they should just stick the smaller-crime guys in the army. You know how the army always needs recruits? Two birds with one—"

"Dumb," Sam says. "Put *that* guy in the army?"

"Not him. He's in prison for life. I said, *small-crime* guys get in the army."

"Dumb," Sam repeats.

"Why? It could work," Donald says, then adds, "But now it's too late to go to the cops. Now we'd be in trouble, even me, accessory after the fact. This is a no-win situation."

"We followed him on a date." Les leans against my seat, elbows on either side of me. "Movie at the Biograph, coffee at the French place. We could see him through one window, and you waiting tables right across the street through another window. Was that bizarre, or what?"

"We thought about getting him *and* his date," Sam says. "See how he'd feel about that."

"I can't believe we finally got him!" Les says in awe. "We waxed his ass. We showed him!"

Donald shakes his head at the sorriness of Les's logic. "Right. Let's talk counting chickens before they're hatched. He's still here." He indicates the trunk with his thumb. "We haven't shown him thing one."

For two weeks after the rape, I didn't go back to work. I didn't often leave the house, and, if I did, I was escorted to and from like a politician or criminal. I read the *Trib* every morning looking for other attacks. They seemed to be epidemic, but what doesn't, once it's happened to you? The cops told me my assailant sounded like one they'd been after for months. They liked to name their rapists; this one was Big Ben. He *did* have a British accent. He *did* speak in complete sentences. I saw a counselor. She'd been raped before, too. It was like a club. I prepared myself for nightmares, as instructed, but never had any directly related to that night. The signs in my dreams were more oblique. I would be pursuing a seemingly safe course on a road, then suddenly I would look around—where were the landmarks of civilization? Billboards, buildings, traffic lights? Surrounding me would be blank, cool air. High as an airplane, I would suddenly realize even my vehicle was gone. Nothing kept me from plummeting. The road, my world—all of it snatched out from under me, and it was then that horror would return.

I took sedatives. I slept like something dead.

And then two weeks later I was back at work. I'd been emptied but other things began inevitably to fill my life again, so that the attack was, soon enough, supplanted. Or, at least, shuffled into the deck. Still, it was the marked card, the one dividing before and after.

"I could kill him," Sam admits calmly, and I realize he's speaking the truth. He could. "If it was me, I'd kill him, but you decide." He turns to his brothers. "We'll do what she decides." We're parked a few yards from an off ramp, in front of the boarded windows of the Five Cents Germ-Free Cleaners. Inland from Lake Michigan, the snow falls more heavily and soon the car is its own late-model Ford igloo of isolation.

"I thought we were going to definitely kill him," Les whines. "I thought we had a plan. We had a lot of plans. Tell her about the Dumpster plan, Sam."

"Shut up," Donald says. "Really, just shut up. The right thing to do is turn around and go back to his house. We have to let him go. Otherwise we're all in trouble. Doesn't that make sense, Sam? He doesn't know us."

"We pull up, dump him, say, 'Hey, sorry, pal, just a joyride?'" Sam says this snidely, whirling in his seat to face Donald, behind him. "Who do you think is going to press charges at that point? We kidnapped him, basically."

Donald puts his finger to his lips. "He might be listening," he whispers. "You're giving him ideas."

"What about the drive-the-car-into-the-lake plan?" Les goes on. "That was good. We get a new car out of it, too, so it's a double good plan." His teeth, crooked and spotted with minuscule notches from his braces, chatter loud enough for us to hear over the sound of the wind. "Or castrating him. We talked about that."

"Jesus," Donald says.

"What if he's dead?" Les says suddenly, his teeth still. "What if he suffocated back there?"

Sam nods solemnly. "Back to the Dumpster plan. Dead, we don't have a problem."

284

"Man, if he's dead we have about ten million problems," Donald says, forgetting to whisper.

"But alive," Sam continues, "alive, I'm not sure what to do with him." He turns to me. "Like I said, it should be up to you. What do you want?"

"Shoot him," Les pleads. "Choose shooting."

"Shut up!" Donald orders. They all three look at me. The car has grown so cold I can see their breath. It would be colder still in the trunk. I review my options: Turn him loose, maim him, kill him, variations thereof. The moment I say the word, we all move into the future. For now, however, we're in one of those pockets.

Of course I have wanted this man punished, but I never went further than hoping he would *get what he deserved,* a concrete wish with only abstract underpinnings, one I would have been happy to let someone else make real. I never saw the man's face—maybe if I had I could have declared the correct retribution, hollowed the perfect scar—but as it was, he might have been any man, and any man might have been him.

"Maybe I should look at him," I say, stalling.

"Yeah?" Sam takes the keys from the ignition and spins them on his forefinger. "Yeah?"

"I want to see him," I decide.

Sam reaches across me and pokes the glove compartment open. A gun spills into his waiting hand. "Okey-doke," he says. "You want it, you got it."

"He's ugly," Les warns me as he clambers out.

From the outside, our car looks like one abandoned, the four swung-open doors leaving gaping holes in the storm. Feeling a curious and appealing sense of deja vu, I imagine our walking away, four children on a long winter trek. But, of course, passive as it is, even walking away is *doing* something.

Les whisks the snow off the trunk with his bare hand and raps on the metal. "Anyone home?"

"Listen," Donald says. "Okay, we don't let him go, that won't work. But . . ." He ticks off steps on his fingers. "We drive to the police station, we say Les and I got the guy—we're under eighteen, so it's a juvenile crime—we know he's the one, the cane, et cetera, and she"—he nods at me—"she identifies his voice. She makes him say what he said to her last year, he sounds like Prince Charles, they book him. It can happen. Okay?" He moves his head up and down as if he can coach us into agreement.

"Finished?" Sam asks.

Donald sighs. "You all are crazy, I swear."

Sam tries to hand me the gun.

"I don't want that."

"Yes," he says, "you do." He nudges my fingertips with the cold handle.

"I'll hold it," Les volunteers. "Let me hold it. I haven't gotten to hold it yet." This from my fourteen-year-old brother, the one who, until he was at least twelve, cried when he saw dead animals in the road.

"Give me that," I tell Sam. I use both hands and find myself with my knees bent like a TV cop.

"Ready?" he says, key to the trunk lock.

I shake my head no. It's funny, but even with a gun in my hands and the lid locked I don't feel at all invulnerable. Donald turns and begins walking away from us.

Sam yells to his back, "Keep a look out for cars."

Donald stops at the street, his shoulders drawn, as if trying to decide whether to step off the curb and keep on going.

"You watching?" Sam calls to him. A horn blows in the distance.

When Donald turns our way, I admire his loyalty to his brothers' bad cause. He nods to Sam. I aim the gun at the back of our car, quaking.

Then I say, "Now." Without taking my eyes off the bumper, I blink rapidly so I won't have to when the lid flies up.

The man lies fetuslike, filling our trunk, back to us. Expensive camel's hair coat. A cane thrown on top of him like an afterthought. The little light inside shows half his face, one closed eye, which, while I stare, opens.

"Shut it!" I yell at Sam. "Shut it! Shut it!"

Our mother died three years ago. We worried all along about the wrong things. We fretted about her recovery from cancer, chemotherapy, and the fluctuating number of months her doctors had thrown around as her life expectancy. But those things never turned out to be relevant. Some percentage of people slip away under anesthesia. It's a risk of every operation, a posted figure, like car accidents, like crimes. After my mother was gone, with only my brothers and my father and me, I thought, *Here you are in the land of men.* I never missed her more, I never felt more outnumbered, than when I came home from the police station last year. I told myself growing up meant losing things, but then it didn't feel so much like loss as it did theft.

"What do you want us to do?" my brother Sam asks me patiently. He must know that patience, or its illusion, is a grown-up virtue. Back in the driver's seat, he is tired, his duties in this territory of his own kind so mercilessly neverending.

"We can't just leave him there," Donald says. "For one thing, this is our car. What if we want to go somewhere? For another, it's cruel and unusual punishment."

Les, brave and savagely young, proclaims, "He could rot in there, for what he did to our sister!"

"That's true," Sam agrees. "He could rot . . . and he could not. You want him to rot?" he asks me.

I look out at the blanketed and beautified ugly buildings around us. Is there any wish made more often than the one for time to stop? But the snowdrift forming around our car has gotten deeper, and soon, if we let it, it will trap us, all five of us. What I want is for him to disappear, but I consider my real choices and also the mis-nomer *justice* in an unjust world. Soon I will insist on driving the car back into the city, back to the lights and signs and authorities created by mankind to keep us civilized.

Meanwhile, my brothers wait.

"I'm thinking," I tell them.

Go, Dog. Go!

ecently I was invited to Alaska as a visiting writer. Alaska! I always wanted to go to Alaska. Yes, I said, I'll come as your visitor. The university flew me and my husband, who is also a writer, and our two children to Fairbanks. They housed us in a log cabin in the woods. We did Alaska. We flew over Denali on a clear day, we dog sledded, we saw foraging—and ate dead moose, we soaked in hot springs, we attended an ice sculpture contest, we witnessed the aurora. My five-year-old daughter rode a plastic saucer down hills, my two-year-old son learned to link two words together he'd previously kept separate: Cold. Hurts.

Perhaps most of you have not given much thought to the process of creative writing. I'm sure most of you don't know much about my work. Who am I? But I think I could tell you something about the creation of fiction, whether it's my work you'd be reading or someone else's. I'm willing to bet that story writers have operated out of similar impulse for many years, and regardless of how famous or revered, I believe writers of the past would tell you something similar to what I'm going to attempt to explain.

A writer writes out of obsession, which can take the form of an image, a character, an anecdote, or even a persistent voice, yammering in the head. Something will not go away, like a bug, like an itch, like a disease, and the writer works to pull it from inside onto the page, a process of exorcism and relief: let's look at the creature. Let's explore. What does this image, or character, or nagging anecdote have to say to me? Why does it insist that I look at it, or listen to it, or lay it down and open it up, begin unpacking it?

Conceive of the material as a suitcase, one the writer hasn't exactly packed, but which has been packed for her, randomly, by a lifetime of varied impressions and experiences. Or think of the material as a large house, one you must investigate room by room, trying to discover why the place is a unified habitat, why doorways lead from one area to another. Why are all these particular items in a single suitcase? What family lives in this house and how do they like it?

After my trip to Alaska, two odd things stick with me, buzzing. Many other things were of interest to me, many astonishing and breathtaking. One cannot fly over the Alaska mountain range on a clear day without drawing in breath. But I want to talk about the two things that stayed uniquely with me.

The first is a large blood stain I saw on a frozen highway. The road was covered with ice, solid, and the blood stain was probably the size of a large tarp, frozen there in the ice, smooth and one-dimensional as a lake seen from the window of an airplane. We drove over it and it was gone. I didn't even mention its presence to my husband, who was scouring the surrounding woods for a view of moose. In the backseat the children were shouting, "Here, moosey moosey moosey."

We saw a moose, not long after that, an antlered fellow resting in a field, lying

287

peacefully in the snow, in the cold sunshine, calmly turning his head as I honked our car horn and slid on the ice. My daughter took a picture with her camera, a photograph destined to belong to the epic series of nature photos called Brown Dot Shots: see that brown dot there? That's a moose.

We did not find out until later that the moose "resting" in the field was undoubtedly wounded, dying. When we returned, three hours later, he was still there, still looking around at the white landscape, most likely dying. "Hello Moosey!" shouted the children, happy to recognize him. We protect them from the bad news of the world, though they will learn it, as we all do. They feel it more profoundly; it cannot be easily put aside by grander thoughts. A writer may write out of that childish, selfish need to understand her own fear.

The thing about writing is the thing poet Mary Oliver says: "If you notice anything / it leads you to notice / more / and more."

Why did I begin thinking about that blood stain on the road? Why did that image stay with me, even in the face of more brilliant and luminous sights? I would have to write about it to know. Writing is thinking. Consider the Northern Lights, the beautiful aurora borealis. My husband, also a writer of fiction, was most impressed by the aurora. When I asked him the prevalent image he'd brought home, he responded with it. I, on the other hand, can't let go of that blood. I don't think I even pointed it out to my husband as we drove over it. We have a little parental code that allows us to discuss unpleasant things in front of the children, a half-Spanish, half-spelled-out language. "Que es eso?" I could have said, pointing. "La B-L-O-O-D?"

But I wasn't thinking about the stain when I drove over it. I didn't even see it for very long. Yet it's stayed.

In Alaska, a large glass building has been built on the university campus, right into the side of a hill overlooking the idyllic barn and pens of the university lab farm. This structure looks like a huge food processor, or something out of Woody Allen's movie *Sleeper*. What's it for? To house the super computer recently purchased for the university with a mighty grant. Everyone gets hushed and giggly when they discuss the super computer, the way you do when you're ashamed of your childishness. Twenty-five million dollars: yipes. Right now the super computer is in Indiana, waiting for better weather in order to migrate to Alaska. When it arrives, it will be installed in its super building and super scientists will put it to work. What will it do? Work to harness the power of the aurora. The northern lights. People in Alaska snicker a little nervously about this; who knows? Maybe it'll work. Didn't we also harness the atom? And you can't even see an atom with the naked eye. But what would they use the aurora's power for? More lights? Is there some useful irony there? Trading one source of light for another? And so much less interesting light, but so controlled by us, the super humans.

In Alaska many of the graduate students in the writing program live without running water, some without central heat. No water? I ask. No toilet or tub? No thermostat? They use outhouses, unheated. Deep holes in the ground. They chop kindling; they know what a cord of wood looks like, how much of a truckbed it ought to occupy. They buy five-gallon bottles and fill them up with drinking water at the laun-

dromat, where they also shower while their clothes are spinning. I admire the sub-
terfuge and scavenging that characterizes these students, the practicality and layered
clothes. Maybe the aurora could be harnessed to provide them with heat. But they
seemed proud of their survival skills.

In Alaska, one thinks about survival. One doesn't seem to indulge in thoughts
about recycling, however. No one I met recycled. They didn't seem to feel guilty
about it, either. I thought maybe there was just so much space in Alaska you didn't
have to fret about running out of it for landfills. Here, wild animals must outnumber
the human population a thousand to one. Who was going to complain? Also, for
most of the year, you could toss your garbage from a moving vehicle and expect it to
sink deep down in the snow, disappear with a soft whuff.

It hides, that snow and ice. It also preserves. There was a red stain frozen solid on
the road.

In Alaska, people are unapologetic carnivores. They eat the typical meats, the
cows and chickens and pigs, and then they also eat the moose, the caribou, the bear,
the salmon, the halibut, the ptarmigon, the snowshoe hare. Their desert counterparts, my friends in New Mexico, are frequently vegetarians—at the very least, trying
to cut back. No such impulse in Alaska.

The beauty of travel, in this instance from the desert southwest to the arctic
north, is that it allows you to visit yourself in a different light, a northern light. I saw
in Alaska something other than what the people who'd been there a while could see.
They were adapted; I was a stranger who'd ridden into town. As a writer, one must
always look to defamiliarize the familiar world. Otherwise, you will see it in terms of
its symbolic rather than real meaning. You will hear "cold as ice" rather than, "Cold.
Hurts." You will revert to cliches: cliched emotions, cliched relationships, cliched
language. A cliche will deaden writing like nothing else. Cliches are like habits—your
life will pass by without your noticing it if you are too much a creature of habit. But
in Alaska, the landscape was startlingly unfamiliar, and I was a guest: I had no habits,
there. That's how I received the gift of raw vision, unrefined by expectation.

To write is, in a way, to return to childhood, to be occupied by things strange and
mysterious, to name worlds rudely, crudely, explicitly as they are rather than as they
might want to be named. Are we responsible for our childhoods? In a way, I would
argue we are. We teach our children manners, not to call the fat person fat. But I
think writers are sometimes rude folk, when they write. I think they'd be doing us a
disservice, as their audience, if they weren't willing to be impolite. They are leaving
records of our world for the one that follows; they need to feel free to tell the truth,
to let us know when the emperor is buck naked.

But the process of writing is like the process of having a nightmare: you go to a
strange world both familiar and unknown, taking place in your present life but hear-
kening back to your past life, stealing from different times and settings, the chain of
events having a perhaps unintelligible logic. You are not entirely responsible for your
nightmare, nor do I feel that writers are entirely responsible for the ideas that begin
lining up when they begin writing. In the end, of course, once you've had your nightmare and then tamed it, you are responsible for what is on the page. You have created

the beast and refined him before presenting him to the public. But you must be free to have your nightmare. And you must not be afraid of setting down the nightmare as it occurs to you, letting the subtle and mysterious process of association take place. The unconscious mind is wiser than the conscious one, and pseudo-scientific legend tells us that the human brain goes ninety percent unused. Your nightmare may be able to teach you something far more profound about yourself than, say, a daydream will.

You must learn to distinguish between a nightmare and a daydream; between art and entertainment.

One question I'm sure those of you engaged in the study of literature must hear asked in your classrooms is, "Did the author intend all this?" Meaning, of course, all the symbolism and thematic linkage that fill great works. My friend Judith Ortiz Cofer, a writer of poetry, fiction and non-fiction, claims that she meant all of it—*after the fact*. As if the subconscious part of your mind were something you could take credit for. As well as responsibility. There's always a gray cloud to that silver lining.

I thought of my friend Vicki during my stay in Alaska. Someone was saying that here it was late March, just about time for break up. The ice melts, the river flows, an errant driver falls through the suddenly mushy ice. Break up. But I thought, Alaska is like my friend Vicki: every spring she breaks up. And of course I entertained for all of three seconds a character who might begin a story with such a line: "Nancy's romantic life reminded her of Alaska: every spring she had to go through break up." But Nancy didn't take me far; her voice sounded sort of familiar, like somebody I'd already read or written about. She became an anecdote and nothing more than that, one I was happy to relay to Vicki the next time I saw her in the hot tub at my health club in New Mexico. "I thought of you," I said. She laughed, though over Spring Break she'd had a fling. She'd had sex on the hood of a Miata. Does it help you to know that Vicki's forty-five years old, a professor, mother of two teenagers? While she was making love on the hood of a Miata, she said cows were lowing all around her. That's the best part, isn't it? Those non-sequitous cows? Can you understand how the cows make her story about a hundred times more interesting than the sports-car does? And at least ten times more interesting than Nancy?

And aren't I a little like Alaska? Vast and only partially understood? Alaska as a human brain, nine-tenths unoccupied space?

Everyone told me, before I left my desert town in New Mexico for Alaska, "Watch *Northern Exposure*." I watched, but I'd already visited the site in Washington state where the show is shot. I already knew Hollywood had it wrong. Then I got to Alaska and heard how stupidly wrong they had it. For example, in *Northern Exposure* one night there were crickets chirping. No crickets in Alaska. Also, during a show set in the summer, it got dark outside. Doesn't happen in Alaska in the summer. There were sled dogs held by reins in *Northern Exposure*. In Alaska, sled dogs have rope harnesses and an understanding of a few important words. Then there's the big ice hook the musher can toss overboard like an anchor if the dogs have to be brought up short, slathering and whiplashed. And, of course, in Alaska there's the snow. The piles and heaps and loaded branches of it. The swaybacked trees sinking under it. The mattressed look of roofs, the sunken cars and buried road signs.

Think of how interesting *Northern Exposure* would be if, in winter, the sun refused to shine for days at a time. I believe the producers are missing out on the most fascinating part of the material they've created. But, as the writer Allan Gurganus says, "Stories don't happen to people who can't tell them."

In Alaska I met a couple who can't have children. My children were with me, a five-year-old and a two-year-old. This couple I met was composed of extraordinary people, warm and gracious and unpretentious and silly and funny and bright. They had cats instead of children. They were infertile, as a couple, and too old to adopt. Imagine: too old to adopt. The utter unfairness of that, as applied to two forty-year-olds. I felt immeasurably bad for them. My feeling bad translated itself into a desire to write fiction, as it frequently does. But what? Perhaps I would write straightforwardly about two good people to whom bad luck had happened. Surely that's the story of many people's lives. But that didn't sound too promising; I myself loathe fiction that makes use of victims as its central characters. Amos Oz said recently in a *Harpers'* piece, "Whenever I find that I agree with myself 100 percent, I don't write a story; I write an angry article telling my government what to do. But if I find more than just one argument in me, more than just one voice, it sometimes happens that the different voices develop into characters and then I know that I am pregnant with story."

So maybe this woman, my newly hatched character, had gotten her tubes tied when young and full of political verve. Maybe she believed the world was too bogged down with people anyway; maybe she believed she wasn't good enough to be a mother. Maybe she moved to Alaska because it was so empty of humans—yes, you see that's what I sensed about many people living in Alaska, a real desire to get away from the clutter of civilization—and now she was paying, ironically, for her youthful decision. Still, no story, but a more interesting premise than simple bad luck.

Of course that moose whose blood was all over the road was a victim of bad luck. What is it about the deaths of animals that draws me? They are our most frequent victims. We are so cavalier concerning their deaths. When I was a child, watching television, I understood that the humans who fell from buildings or were run over by cars were acting. They did not die. I had no such assurance about the animals. I felt certain that Hollywood would not bother to fake the deaths of dogs or horses. Even then, as a child, I understood the hierarchy we, as those making the hierarchy, assigned life forms on the earth.

I have said before that when the words, "It's not fair," first enter your mind and begin burning, that is when you have some inkling of what fiction is about. It is the driving force behind the desire to create art. It was not fair that whatever animal had died on the road had died there. But where is the story?

Let me begin again. The road was a highway from Fairbanks, first interstate, then slightly smaller highway, then smooth icy road that ended at the hot springs. Just plain stopped. Alaska went on, but the road didn't. We drove for an hour through a forest, nothing but an occasional passing car and Alaska's version of the Circle K: a trophy-laden wood structure selling everything from homemade pie to wolf pelts, chainlink to condoms. All along the outside of the building are mounds of snow, like igloos, though if you brush away the snow you find an abandoned automobile. It's quite eerie to see so many of these heaps, a great string of them like little rooms in the snow, little human fish bowls, frozen. In Mexico, every vaguely conical hill could reveal a primitive pyramid built to the gods. In Alaska, the hills were cars. It was as if they'd been left there by travelers who'd gone on, by other means, farther yet into the wilds. The only other operational vehicle in the parking lot is a huge dog-sled truck, sleds on top, dogs in compartments in the back panting and pacing. On the front, in the grill work, is the head of a caribou. Not just the skeleton, but the whole furry head, only slightly rotten, a big freshly dead hood ornament.

Or maybe not freshly dead. In Alaska, where it's cold, things preserve.

We ate pie, big sweet pieces. We returned to the car and children by yodeling for moose. One appeared, as if to our summons, resting peacefully in the snow, turning his heavy head as we honked at him. My daughter took his picture. Her brother took a picture of his own cheek as he held the camera backwards and sideways. He talked into it as if into a telephone: "Hello? Nuh uh, nuh uh, bye bye." We listened to the radio and heard foreign voices, far away in the snowy static. At the hot springs, we sat in a glass building wearing bathing suits while outside the snow was everywhere, thick on the ground and even falling, though the sky was blue. A small plane circled and then landed on the frozen surface of the Chena River. Break up, I thought. Mightn't the pilot go crashing through? Or just gently sink, like a tossed beer can in a snow drift?

My new collection of stories has in it a character I love dearly, a thirty-year-old incompetent man whose habit is to stop on the highway when he sees dead creatures and say a prayer over them as he buries them. He celebrates their life and death, saying over each, "God help those animals who must cross the road." He's comical, and near the end of the longest story about him he does something quite dastardly, but I still love him. He's like my brother, as many of my characters are, and in the way that stories are like nightmares, characters are like family: you don't choose them, you simply live trying to understand them. Allan Gurganus says: "Family: can't live with them, can't get born without them."

My character of the dead animal prayer is ill-suited to the world, the one where most of us drive right by dead animals, run right over their blood on the road. Another story in the same collection has as its central image a dead deer on the road whose head is being sawed off by a passing driver. He's taking home a trophy. That image always spoke to me of the worst of contemporary society: desiring the trophies of labor without the appropriate labor. Who could genuinely be proud of a rack of antlers gotten this way? That man symbolizes something pivotal in my vision of our world. It has everything to do with my fascination for the big frozen stain on the road.

In yet another of my stories, I have three desperate types drive by and witness a horrendous display of children tormenting another child. That particular story began with that image: three grown-ups who would simply drive by a child being brutalized. Who were these people? I asked myself. How did their guilt implicate me, their author? In what way am I the callous individual who cannot take action in the world when wrong is being done?

I did create a useful character while I was in Alaska, based on the woman whose house we stayed in. In fact, however, my character is nothing like our host. But something that happened made me come up with a very interesting passive-aggressive woman who will help in the writing of my novel. One day when we got home from our adventures—the day of the drive to Chena Hot Springs, the moose and blood day—our host was not home. Her front door was locked, although she'd told us she never locked the house. We had no key; it was probably all of seven degrees outside. We'd slid down the hill to her front door and then found it locked.

We got in by another route—through the basement, up the dark stairs—but I began to create a character. What kind of host locks her guests out? In our instance, it turned out that my son, the two-year-old, had spun the handle lock before we left. Our host hadn't been home since we'd seen her early in the morning. But what if it had been her? How interesting. A whole character came to me, a radicalized version of the person I thought, for a moment, our host was, a woman who locks out her guests, who gives them consistently bum directions for fun events in the town where they're visiting—always leaving off crucial turns or important landmarks—and, finally, a woman who, when she babysits their children, brings them back just slightly injured, accidents, but still.

This is how my fiction begins. I'm trying to give you the process straight. I do not yet know when that bloodstain will make an appearance in my work, or how it will function metaphorically. It remained on the road in the ice for anyone traveling over it who chose to first see it and then to pursue it, as a reminder of the harsh and unforgiving nature of life.

But I told you there were two things that stayed with me. The other, besides the blood, happened while dog sledding with my daughter. It was arranged by my host that we would sled with Knute, pronounced with a hard K like the publisher, Knopf, and his six-dog team. They were wild dogs, snapping and yelping and gnashing and peeing on everything in sight: the car, the snow, the sled, each other. They peed on the sleeping bag that was to be wrapped round my and my daughter's legs, leaving a damp warm spot that rested against my thigh the whole trip. The dogs yapped and barked and terrified my little son; when they finally raced away with me and his sister, he burst into tears in his father's arms: his mother, carried off by wild dogs. A primordial feral nightmare.

(Never mind that his favorite book in the world is *Go, Dog. Go!* Here is the gap that art must fill, in between entertainment and reality.)

Meanwhile, I was scared and exhilarated to be riding along behind these animals. After all, they were dogs. I don't like to ride in airplanes, and they're manned by reasonable beings. Go, dog, go, indeed. They threw up a fine spray of snow with their feet as they ran, and they ran so silently, just shushing along together, that I had to admire them. For a moment, holding tight to my little girl as she laughed at the sheer joy of it, as the icy mist hit my cheeks, under a blue sky in a luminous, white, alien landscape, I was removed from my life, simply flying along, happy as she was. It's rare, such happiness. As soon as you name it, it slides off to the left somewhere. But that's the second instant I preserved.

My fiction comes from two places as exemplified by those frozen moments in Alaska, snowmist and bloodstain: enraptured ecstasy and inexhaustible despair.

The Lives of the Dead

Tim O'Brien

*B*ut this too is true: stories can save us. I'm forty-three years old, and a writer now, and even still, right here, I keep dreaming Linda alive. And Ted Lavender, too, and Kiowa, and Curt Lemon, and a slim young man I killed, and an old man sprawled beside a pigpen, and several others whose bodies I once lifted and dumped into a truck. They're all dead. But in a story, which is a kind of dreaming, the dead sometimes smile and sit up and return to the world.

Start here: a body without a name. On an afternoon in 1969 the platoon took sniper fire from a filthy little village along the South China Sea. It lasted only a minute or two, and nobody was hurt, but even so Lieutenant Jimmy Cross got on the radio and ordered up an air strike. For the next half hour we watched the place burn. It was a cool bright morning, like early autumn, and the jets were glossy black against the sky. When it ended, we formed into a loose line and swept east through the village. It was all wreckage. I remember the smell of burnt straw; I remember broken fences and torn-up trees and heaps of stone and brick and pottery. The place was deserted—no people, no animals—and the only confirmed kill was an old man who lay face-up near a pigpen at the center of the village. His right arm was gone. At his face there were already many flies and gnats.

Dave Jensen went over and shook the old man's hand. "How-dee-doo," he said.

One by one the others did it too. They didn't disturb the body, they just grabbed the old man's hand and offered a few words and moved away.

Rat Kiley bent over the corpse. "Gimme five," he said. "A real honor."

"Pleased as punch," said Henry Dobbins.

I was brand-new to the war. It was my fourth day; I hadn't yet developed a sense of humor. Right away, as if I'd swallowed something, I felt a moist sickness rise up in my throat. I sat down beside the pigpen, closed my eyes, put my head between my knees.

After a moment Dave Jensen touched my shoulder.

"Be polite now," he said. "Go introduce yourself. Nothing to be afraid about, just a nice old man. Show a little respect for your elders."

"No way."

"Maybe it's too real for you?"

"That's right," I said. "Way too real."

Jensen kept after me, but I didn't go near the body. I didn't even look at it except by accident. For the rest of the day there was still that sickness inside me, but it wasn't the old man's corpse so much, it was that awesome act of greeting the dead. At one point, I remember, they sat the body up against a fence. They crossed his legs and talked to him. "The guest of honor," Mitchell Sanders said, and he placed a can of orange slices in the old man's lap. "Vitamin C," he said gently. "A guy's health, that's the most important thing."

They proposed toasts. They lifted their canteens and drank to the old man's family and ancestors, his many grandchildren, his newfound life after death. It was more than mockery. There was a formality to it, like a funeral without the sadness.

Dave Jensen flicked his eyes at me.

"Hey, O'Brien," he said, "you got a toast in mind? Never too late for manners."

I found things to do with my hands. I looked away and tried not to think.

Late in the afternoon, just before dusk, Kiowa came up and asked if he could sit at my foxhole for a minute. He offered me a Christmas cookie from a batch his father had sent him. It was February now, but the cookies tasted fine.

For a few moments Kiowa watched the sky.

"You did a good thing today," he said. "That shaking hands crap, it isn't decent. The guys'll hassle you for a while—especially Jensen—but just keep saying no. Should've done it myself. Takes guts, I know that."

"It wasn't guts. I was scared."

Kiowa shrugged. "Same difference."

"No, I couldn't *do* it. A mental block or something . . . I don't know, just creepy."

"Well, you're new here. You'll get used to it." He paused for a second, studying the green and red sprinkles on a cookie. "Today—I guess this was your first look at a real body?"

I shook my head. All day long I'd been picturing Linda's face, the way she smiled.

"It sounds funny," I said, "but that poor old man, he reminds me of . . . I mean, there's this girl I used to know. I took her to the movies once. My first date."

Kiowa looked at me for a long while. Then he leaned back and smiled.

"Man," he said, "that's a bad date."

* * *

Linda was nine then, as I was, but we were in love. And it was real. When I write about her now, three decades later, it's tempting to dismiss it as a crush, an infatuation of childhood, but I know for a fact that what we felt for each other was as deep and rich as love can ever get. It had all the shadings and complexities of mature adult love, and maybe more, because there were not yet words for it, and because it was not yet fixed to comparisons or chronologies or the ways by which adults measure things.

I just loved her.

She had poise and great dignity. Her eyes, I remember, were deep brown like her hair, and she was slender and very quiet and fragile-looking.

Even then, at nine years old, I wanted to live inside her body. I wanted to melt into her bones—*that* kind of love.

And so in the spring of 1956, when we were in the fourth grade, I took her out on the first real date of my life—a double date, actually, with my mother and father. Though I can't remember the exact sequence, my mother had somehow arranged it with Linda's parents, and on that damp spring night my dad did the driving while Linda and I sat in the backseat and stared out opposite windows, both of us trying to pretend it was nothing special. For me, though, it was very special. Down inside I had important things to tell her, big profound things, but I couldn't make any words come out. I had trouble breathing. Now and then I'd glance over at her, thinking how beautiful she was: her white skin and those dark brown eyes and the way she always smiled at the world—always, it seemed—as if her face had been designed that way. The smile never went away. That night, I remember, she wore a new red cap, which seemed to me very stylish and sophisticated, very unusual. It was a stocking cap, basically, except the tapered part at the top seemed extra long, almost too long, like a tail growing out of the back of her head. It made me think of the caps that Santa's elves wear, the same shape and color, the same fuzzy white tassel at the tip.

Sitting there in the backseat, I wanted to find some way to let her know how I felt, a compliment of some sort, but all I could manage was a stupid comment about the cap. "Jeez," I must've said, "what a *cap*."

Linda smiled at the window—she knew what I meant—but my mother turned and gave me a hard look. It surprised me. It was as if I'd brought up some horrible secret.

For the rest of the ride I kept my mouth shut. We parked in front of the Ben Franklin store and walked up Main Street toward the State Theater. My parents went first, side by side, and then Linda in her new red cap, and then me tailing along ten or twenty steps behind. I was nine years old; I didn't yet have the gift for small talk. Now and then my mother glanced back, making little motions with her hand to speed me up.

At the ticket booth, I remember, Linda stood off to one side. I moved over to the concession area, studying the candy, and both of us were very careful to avoid the awkwardness of eye contact. Which was how we knew about being in love. It was pure knowing. Neither of us, I suppose, would've thought to use that word, love, but by the fact of not looking at each other, and not talking, we understood with a clarity beyond language that we were sharing something huge and permanent.

Behind me, in the theater, I heard cartoon music.

"Hey, step it up," I said. I almost had the courage to look at her. "You want popcorn or *what?*"

The thing about a story is that you dream it as you tell it, hoping that others might then dream along with you, and in this way memory and imagination and language combine to make spirits in the head. There is the illusion of aliveness. In Vietnam, for instance, Ted Lavender had a habit of popping four or five tranquilizers every morning. It was his way of coping, just dealing with the realities, and the drugs helped to ease him through the days. I remember how peaceful his eyes were. Even in bad situations he had a soft, dreamy expression on his face, which was what he wanted, a kind of escape. "How's the war today?" somebody would ask, and Ted Lavender would give a little smile to the sky and say, "Mellow—a nice smooth war today." And then in April he was shot in the head outside the village of Than Khe. Kiowa and I and a couple of others were ordered to prepare his body for the dustoff. I remember squatting down, not wanting to look but then looking. Lavender's left cheekbone was gone. There was a swollen blackness around his eye. Quickly, trying not to feel anything, we went through the kid's pockets. I remember wishing I had gloves. It wasn't the blood I hated; it was the deadness. We put his personal effects in a plastic bag and tied the bag to his arm. We stripped off the canteens and ammo, all the heavy stuff, and wrapped him up in his own poncho and carried him out to a dry paddy and laid him down.

For a while nobody said much. Then Mitchell Sanders laughed and looked over at the green plastic poncho.

"Hey, Lavender," he said, "how's the war today?"

There was a short quiet.

"Mellow," somebody said.

"Well, that's good," Sanders murmured, "that's real, real good. Stay cool now."

"Hey, no sweat, I'm mellow."

"Just ease on back, then. Don't need no pills. We got this incredible chopper on call, this once in a lifetime mindtrip."

"Oh, yeah—mellow!"

Mitchell Sanders smiled. "There it is, my man, this chopper gonna take you up high and cool. Gonna relax you. Gonna alter your whole perspective on this sorry, sorry shit."

We could almost see Ted Lavender's dreamy blue eyes. We could almost hear him.

"Roger that," somebody said. "I'm ready to fly."

There was the sound of the wind, the sound of birds and the quiet afternoon, which was the world we were in.

That's what a story does. The bodies are animated. You make the dead talk. They sometimes say things like, "Roger that." Or they say, "Timmy, stop crying," which is what Linda said to me after she was dead.

Even now I can see her walking down the aisle of the old State Theater in Worthington, Minnesota. I can see her face in profile beside me, the cheeks softly lighted by coming attractions.

The movie that night was *The Man Who Never Was*. I remember the plot clearly, or at least the premise, because the main character was a corpse. That fact alone, I know, deeply impressed me. It was a World War Two film: the Allies devise a scheme to mislead Germany about the site of the upcoming landings in Europe. They get their hands on a body—a British soldier, I believe; they dress him up in an officer's uniform, plant fake documents in his pockets, then dump him in the sea and let the currents wash him onto a Nazi beach. The Germans find the documents; the deception wins the war. Even now, I can remember the awful splash as that corpse fell into the sea. I remember glancing over at Linda, thinking it might be too much for her, but in the dim gray light she seemed to be smiling at the screen. There were little crinkles at her eyes, her lips open and gently curving at the corners. I couldn't understand it. There was nothing to smile at. Once or twice, in fact, I had to close my eyes, but it didn't help much. Even then I kept seeing the soldier's body tumbling toward the water, splashing down hard, how inert and heavy it was, how completely dead.

It was a relief when the movie finally ended.

Afterward, we drove out to the Dairy Queen at the edge of town. The night had a quilted, weighted-down quality, as if somehow burdened, and all around us the Minnesota prairies reached out in long repetitive waves of corn and soybeans, everything flat, everything the same. I remember eating ice cream in the backseat of the Buick, and a long blank drive in the dark, and then pulling up in front of Linda's house. Things must've been said, but it's all gone now except for a few last images. I remember walking her to the front door. I remember the brass porch light with its fierce yellow glow, my own feet, the juniper bushes along the front steps, the wet grass, Linda close beside me. We were in love. Nine years old, yes, but it was real love, and now we were alone on those front steps. Finally we looked at each other.

"Bye," I said.

Linda nodded and said, "Bye."

Over the next few weeks Linda wore her new red cap to school every day. She never took it off, not even in the classroom, and so it was inevitable that she took some teasing about it. Most of it came from a kid named Nick Veenhof. Out on the playground, during recess, Nick would creep up behind her and make a grab for the cap, almost yanking it off, then scampering away. It went on like that for weeks: the girls giggling, the guys egging him on. Naturally I wanted to do something about it, but it just wasn't possible. I had my reputation to think about. I had my pride. And there was also the problem of Nick Veenhof. So I stood off to the side, just a spectator, wishing I could do things I couldn't do. I watched Linda clamp down the cap with the palm of her hand, holding it there, smiling over in Nick's direction as if none of it really mattered.

For me, though, it did matter. It still does. I should've stepped in; fourth grade is no excuse. Besides, it doesn't get easier with time, and twelve years later, when Vietnam presented much harder choices, some practice at being brave might've helped a little.

Also, too, I might've stopped what happened next. Maybe not, but at least it's possible.

Most of the details I've forgotten, or maybe blocked out, but I know it was an afternoon in late spring, and we were taking a spelling test, and halfway into it Nick Veenhof held up his hand and asked to use the pencil sharpener. Right away the kids laughed. No doubt he'd broken the pencil on purpose, but it wasn't something you could prove, and so the teacher nodded and told him to hustle it up. Which was a mistake. Out of nowhere Nick developed a terrible limp. He moved in slow motion, dragging himself up to the pencil sharpener and carefully slipping in his pencil and then grinding away forever. At the time, I suppose, it was funny. But on the way back to his seat Nick took a short detour. He squeezed between two desks, turned sharply right, and moved up the aisle toward Linda.

I saw him grin at one of his pals. In a way, I already knew what was coming.

As he passed Linda's desk, he dropped the pencil and squatted down to get it.

When he came up, his left hand slipped behind her back. There was a half-second hesitation. Maybe he was trying to stop himself; maybe then, just briefly, he felt some small approximation of guilt. But it wasn't enough. He took hold of the white tassel, stood up, and gently lifted off her cap.

Somebody must've laughed. I remember a short, tinny echo. I remember Nick Veenhof trying to smile. Somewhere behind me, a girl said, "Uh," or a sound like that.

Linda didn't move.

Even now, when I think back on it, I can still see the glossy whiteness of her scalp. She wasn't bald. Not quite. Not completely. There were some tufts of hair, little patches of grayish brown fuzz. But what I saw then, and keep seeing now, is all that whiteness. A smooth, pale, translucent white. I could see the bones and veins; I could see the exact structure of her skull. There was a large Band-Aid at the back of her head, a row of black stitches, a piece of gauze taped above her left ear.

Nick Veenhof took a step backward. He was still smiling, but the smile was doing strange things.

The whole time Linda stared straight ahead, her eyes locked on the blackboard, her hands loosely folded at her lap. She didn't say anything. After a time, though, she turned and looked at me across the room. It lasted only a moment, but I had the feeling that a whole conversation was happening between us. *Well?* she was saying, and I was saying, *Sure, okay.*

Later on, she cried for a while. The teacher helped her put the cap back on, then we finished the spelling test and did some fingerpainting, and after school that day Nick Veenhof and I walked her home.

It's now Iggo. I'm forty-three years old, which would've seemed impossible to a fourth grader, and yet when I look at photographs of myself as I was in 1956, I realize that in the important ways I haven't changed at all. I was Timmy then; now I'm Tim. But the essence remains the same. I'm not fooled by the baggy pants or the crewcut or the happy smile—I know my own eyes—and there is no doubt that the Timmy smiling at the camera is the Tim I am now. Inside the body, or beyond the body, there is something absolute and unchanging. The human life is all one thing, like a blade tracing loops on ice: a little kid, a twenty-three-year-old infantry sergeant, a middle-aged writer knowing guilt and sorrow.

And as a writer now, I want to save Linda's life. Not her body—her life.

She died, of course. Nine years old and she died. It was a brain tumor. She lived through the summer and into the first part of September, and then she was dead.

But in a story I can steal her soul. I can revive, at least briefly, that which is absolute and unchanging. It's not the surface that matters, it's the identity that lives inside. In a story, miracles can happen. Linda can smile and sit up. She can reach out, touch my wrist, and say, "Timmy, stop crying."

I needed that kind of miracle. At some point I had come to understand that Linda was sick, maybe even dying, but I loved her and just couldn't accept it. In the middle of the summer, I remember, my mother tried to explain to me about brain tumors. Now and then, she said, bad things start growing inside us. Sometimes you can cut them out and other times you can't, and for Linda it was one of the times when you can't.

I thought about it for several days. "All right," I finally said. "So will she get better now?"

"Well, no," my mother said, "I don't think so." She stared at a spot behind my shoulder. "Sometimes people don't ever get better. They die sometimes."

I shook my head.

"Not Linda," I said.

But on a September afternoon, during noon recess, Nick Veenhof came up to me on the school playground. "Your girlfriend," he said, "she kicked the bucket."

At first I didn't understand.

"She's dead," he said. "My mom told me at lunchtime. No lie, she actually kicked the goddang *bucket.*"

All I could do was nod. Somehow it didn't quite register. I turned away, glanced down at my hands for a second, then walked home without telling anyone.

It was a little after one o'clock, I remember, and the house was empty.

I drank some chocolate milk and then lay down on the sofa in the living room, not really sad, just floating, trying to imagine what it was to be dead. Nothing much came to me. I remember closing my eyes and whispering her name, almost begging, trying to make her come back. "Linda," I said, "please." And then I concentrated. I willed her alive. It was a dream, I suppose, or a daydream, but I made it happen. I saw her coming down the middle of Main Street, all alone. It was nearly dark and the street was deserted, no cars or people, and Linda wore a pink dress and shiny black shoes. I remember sitting down on the curb to watch. All her hair had grown back. The scars and stitches were gone. In the dream, if that's what it was, she was playing a game of some sort, laughing and running up the empty street, kicking a big aluminum water bucket.

Right then I started to cry. After a moment Linda stopped and carried her water bucket over to the curb and asked why I was so sad.

"Well, God," I said, "you're dead."

Linda nodded at me. She was standing under a yellow streetlight. A nine-year-old girl, just a kid, and yet there was something ageless in her eyes—not a child, not an adult—just a bright ongoing everness, that same pinprick of absolute lasting light that I see today in my own eyes as Timmy smiles at Tim from the graying photographs of that time.

"Dead," I said.

Linda smiled. It was a secret smile, as if she knew things nobody could ever know, and she reached out and touched my wrist and said, "Timmy, stop crying. It doesn't *matter.*"

In Vietnam, too, we had ways of making the dead seem not quite so dead. Shaking hands, that was one way. By slighting death, by acting, we pretended it was not the terrible thing it was. By our language, which was both hard and wistful, we transformed the bodies into piles of waste. Thus, when someone got killed, as Curt Lemon did, his body was not really a body, but rather one small bit of waste in the midst of a much wider wastage. I learned that words make a difference. It's easier to cope with a kicked bucket than a corpse; if it isn't human, it doesn't matter much if it's dead. And so a VC nurse, fried by napalm, was a crispy critter. A Vietnamese baby, which lay nearby, was a roasted peanut. "Just a crunchie munchie," Rat Kiley said as he stepped over the body.

We kept the dead alive with stories. When Ted Lavender was shot in the head, the men talked about how they'd never seen him so mellow, how tranquil he was, how it wasn't the bullet but the tranquilizers that blew his mind. He wasn't dead, just laid-back. There were Christians among us, like Kiowa, who believed in the New Testament stories of life after death. Other stories were passed down like legends from old-timer to newcomer. Mostly, though, we had to make up our own. Often they were exaggerated, or blatant lies, but it was a way of bringing body and soul back together, or a way of making new bodies for the souls to inhabit. There was a story, for instance, about how Curt Lemon had gone trick-or-treating on Halloween. A dark, spooky night, and so Lemon put on a ghost mask and painted up his body all different colors and crept across a paddy to a sleeping village—almost stark naked, the story went, just boots and balls and an M-16—and in the dark Lemon went from hootch to hootch—ringing doorbells, he called it—and a few hours later, when he slipped back into the perimeter, he had a whole sackful of goodies to share with his pals: candles and joss sticks and a pair of black pajamas and stat-uettes of the smiling Buddha. That was the story, anyway. Other versions were much more elaborate, full of descriptions and scraps of dialogue. Rat Kiley liked to spice it up with extra details: "See, what happens is, it's like four in the morning, and Lemon sneaks into a hootch with that weird ghost mask on. Everybody's asleep, right? So he wakes up this cute little mama-san. Tickles her foot. 'Hey, Mama-san,' he goes, real soft like. 'Hey, Mama-san—trick or treat!' Should've seen *her face*. About freaks. I mean, there's this buck naked ghost standing there, and he's got this M-16 up against her ear and he whispers, 'Hey, Mama-san, trick or fuckin' treat!' Then he takes off her pj's. Strips her right down. Sticks the pajamas in his sack and tucks her into bed and heads for the next hootch."

Pausing a moment, Rat Kiley would grin and shake his head. "Honest to God," he'd murmur. "Trick or treat. Lemon—there's one class act."

To listen to the story, especially as Rat Kiley told it, you'd never know that Curt Lemon was dead. He was still out there in the dark, naked and painted up, trick-or-treating, sliding from hootch to hootch in that crazy white ghost mask.

* * *

In September, the day after Linda died, I asked my father to take me down to Benson's Funeral Home to view the body. I was a fifth grader then; I was curious. On the drive downtown my father kept his eyes straight ahead. At one point, I remember, he made a scratchy sound in his throat. It took him a long time to light up a cigarette.

"Timmy," he said, "you're sure about this?"

I nodded at him. Down inside, of course, I wasn't sure, and yet I had to see her one more time. What I needed, I suppose, was some sort of final confirmation, something to carry with me after she was gone.

When we parked in front of the funeral home, my father turned and looked at me. "If this bothers you," he said, "just say the word. We'll make a quick getaway. Fair enough?"

"Okay," I said.

"Or if you start to feel sick or anything—"

"*I won't,*" I told him.

Inside, the first thing I noticed was the smell, thick and sweet, like something sprayed out of a can. The viewing room was empty except for Linda and my father and me. I felt a rush of panic as we walked up the aisle. The smell made me dizzy. I tried to fight it off, slowing down a little, taking short, shallow breaths through my mouth. But at the same time I felt a funny excitement. Anticipation, in a way—that same awkward feeling when I walked up the sidewalk to ring her doorbell on our first date. I wanted to impress her. I wanted something to happen between us, a secret signal of some sort. The room was dimly lighted, almost dark, but at the far end of the aisle Linda's white casket was illuminated by a row of spotlights up in the ceiling. Everything was quiet. My father put his hand on my shoulder, whispered something, and backed off. After a moment I edged forward a few steps, pushing up on my toes for a better look.

It didn't seem real. A mistake, I thought. The girl lying in the white casket wasn't Linda. There was a resemblance, maybe, but where Linda had always been very slender and fragile-looking, almost skinny, the body in that casket was fat and swollen. For a second I wondered if somebody had made a terrible blunder. A technical mistake: like they'd pumped her too full of formaldehyde or embalming fluid or whatever they used. Her arms and face were bloated. The skin at her cheeks was stretched out tight like the rubber skin on a balloon just before it pops open. Even her fingers seemed puffy. I turned and glanced behind me, where my father stood, thinking that maybe it was a joke—hoping it was a joke—almost believing that Linda would jump out from behind one of the curtains and laugh and yell out my name.

But she didn't. The room was silent. When I looked back at the casket, I felt dizzy again. In my heart, I'm sure, I knew this was Linda, but even so I couldn't find much to recognize. I tried to pretend she was taking a nap, her hands folded at her stomach, just sleeping away the afternoon. Except she didn't *look* asleep. She looked dead. She looked heavy and totally dead.

I remember closing my eyes. After a while my father stepped up beside me.

"Come on now," he said. "Let's go get some ice cream."

In the months after Ted Lavender died, there were many other bodies. I never shook hands—not that—but one afternoon I climbed a tree and threw down what was left of Curt Lemon. I watched my friend Kiowa sink into the muck along the Song Tra Bong. And in early July, after a battle in the mountains, I was assigned to a six-man detail to police up the enemy KIAs. There were twenty-seven bodies altogether, and parts of several others. The dead were everywhere. Some lay in piles. Some lay alone. One, I remember, seemed to kneel. Another was bent from the waist over a small boulder, the top of his head on the ground, his arms rigid, the eyes squinting in concentration as if he were about to perform a handstand or somersault. It was my worst day at the war. For three hours we carried the bodies down the mountain to a clearing alongside a narrow dirt road. We had lunch there, then a truck pulled up, and we worked in two-man teams to load the truck. I remember swinging the bodies up. Mitchell Sanders took a man's feet, I took the arms, and we counted to three, working up momentum, and then we tossed the body high and watched it bounce and come to rest among the other bodies. The dead had been dead for more than a day. They were all badly bloated. Their clothing was stretched tight like sausage skins, and when we picked them up, some made sharp burping sounds as the gases were released. They were heavy. Their feet were bluish green and cold. The smell was terrible. At one point Mitchell Sanders looked at me and said, "Hey, man, I just realized something."

"What?"

He wiped his eyes and spoke very quietly, as if awed by his own wisdom.

"Death sucks," he said.

Lying in bed at night, I made up elaborate stories to bring Linda alive in my sleep. I invented my own dreams. It sounds impossible, I know, but I did it. I'd picture somebody's birthday party—a crowded room, I'd think, and a big chocolate cake with pink candles—and then soon I'd be dreaming it, and after a while Linda would show up, as I knew she would, and in the dream we'd look at each other and not talk much, because we were shy, but then later I'd walk her home and we'd sit on her front steps and stare at the dark and just be together.

She'd say amazing things sometimes. "Once you're alive," she'd say, "you can't ever be dead."

Or she'd say: "Do I *look* dead?"

It was a kind of self-hypnosis. Partly willpower, partly faith, which is how stories arrive.

But back then it felt like a miracle. My dreams had become a secret meeting place, and in the weeks after she died I couldn't wait to fall asleep at night. I began going to bed earlier and earlier, sometimes even in bright daylight. My mother, I remember, finally asked about it at breakfast one morning. "Timmy, what's *wrong?*" she said, but all I could do was shrug and say, "Nothing. I just need sleep, that's all." I didn't dare tell the truth. It was embarrassing, I suppose, but it was also a precious secret, like a magic trick, where if I tried to explain it, or even talk about it, the thrill and mystery would be gone. I didn't want to lose Linda.

She was dead. I understood that. After all, I'd seen her body, and yet even as a nine-year-old I had begun to practice the magic of stories. Some I just dreamed up. Others I wrote down—the scenes and dialogue. And at nighttime I'd slide into sleep knowing that Linda would be there waiting for me. Once, I remember, we went ice skating late at night, tracing loops and circles under yellow floodlights. Later we sat by a wood stove in the warming house, all alone, and after a while I asked her what it was like to be dead. Apparently Linda thought it was a silly question. She smiled and said, "Do I *look* dead?"

I told her no, she looked terrific. I waited a moment, then asked again, and Linda made a soft little sigh. I could smell our wool mittens drying on the stove.

For a few seconds she was quiet.

"Well, right now," she said, "I'm *not* dead. But when I am, it's like . . . I don't know, I guess it's like being inside a book that nobody's reading."

"A book?" I said.

"An old one. It's up on a library shelf, so you're safe and everything, but the book hasn't been checked out for a long, long time. All you can do is wait. Just hope somebody'll pick it up and start reading."

Linda smiled at me.

"Anyhow, it's not so bad," she said. "I mean, when you're dead, you just have to be yourself." She stood up and put on her red stocking cap. "This is stupid. Let's go skate some more."

So I followed her down to the frozen pond. It was late, and nobody else was there, and we held hands and skated almost all night under the yellow lights.

And then it becomes 1990. I'm forty-three years old, and a writer now, still dreaming Linda alive in exactly the same way. She's not the embodied Linda; she's mostly made up, with a new identity and a new name, like the man who never was. Her real name doesn't matter. She was nine years old. I loved her and then she died. And yet right here, in the spell of memory and imagination, I can still see her as if through ice, as if I'm gazing into some other world, a place where there are no brain tumors and no funeral homes, where there are no bodies at all. I can see Kiowa, too, and Ted Lavender and Curt Lemon, and sometimes I can even see Timmy skating with Linda under the yellow floodlights. I'm young and happy. I'll never die. I'm skimming across the surface of my own history, moving fast, riding the melt beneath the blades, doing loops and spins, and when I take a high leap into the dark and come down thirty years later, I realize it is as Tim trying to save Timmy's life with a story.

To Find the Edge

Robert Stone

*B*rowne called the boat *Nona* after a boat of his father's. His father had named that boat after the sloop Hilaire Belloc sailed in the Irish Sea. After Nona, his father had acquired a schooner of twenty-four feet and fearlessly christened it Don Juan. The original Don Juan was the schooner that failed Shelley in the Gulf of Spezia. Shelley's boat had been a hot dog sheered for maximum speed. He and his friend had died running before the storm, billowing sails up, in imitation of the west wind. Browne's father, in his cups, could recite long bits of "Adonais." Browne himself supposed he knew more about Shelley's boat than about his prosody.

Just after sunrise, forty-eight hours and more than two hundred miles off the Ambrose Channel Lightship, Browne sat in *Nona's* open cockpit and looked at the western horizon. Astern, the last fat white clouds of home were falling away. A northwest wind whistled in the slot, force five and steady. Months before, on the night he'd agreed to sail *Nona* in the round-the-world Eglative solo, he had gone straight to the Admiralty charts and begun to plot his way around the globe. But he was not inclined now, watching the morning's white horses roll by, to lay lines or chart courses.

In the last hours of daylight he dozed off and awakened to find himself on a sunlit ocean of sultry blue—the Gulf Stream. For such a long time, he thought, he had been promising himself unfamiliar skies. Leaning over the side, he dipped his hand in the quarter wave and felt it warm. The sensation made him smile.

At some level he felt involved in an escape. His impulse was simply to head out and put the land behind him. Beyond that, it made sense to keep on easting while the wind held and get across the Stream as quickly as possible. The first weather fax had carried nothing but sweet assurance, there were no tropical storms on the prowl and no threatening northers.

Browne had slept very little after clearing The Narrows. Propped up in the cockpit against a stack of foul-weather gear, he had drifted in and out of consciousness, fighting to outlast darkness. His radar alarm was set for a fifteen-mile radius. Through three nights in the coastal shipping lanes, he had stayed on deck, scanning the dark horizons. A few hours on the Gulf Stream's sky bright waters inclined him to rest easy. In the afternoon, he went below, cleared the stacks of last-minute gear from his bunk, and stretched out.

When he went on deck again, the sun was low and the pastel water overlaid with a puritan October light. The wind was steady and he kept *Nona* eastward. In the last daylight, he checked the screws in the self-steering vane and eased the lines against chafing. According to his knot log, he had come 154 miles since the day before, a speed of close to seven knots.

For dinner he cooked a can of chicken broth and drank it from his usual coffee cup, a navy mug in the navy pattern. Anne had packed it for him in tissue with a blue ribbon. Inside was a note detailing the boat's stowage plan. He needed only to glance around the main cabin to realize how much of the stowage his wife had overseen. Tossing the homely red and white Campbell's soup can in the scraps gave him a momentary flash of incongruity. Home away from home.

On deck at dusk, he sipped his soup and listened to the accommodating wind. The loneliness he felt rather surprised him. Except for Anne's presence, he thought of himself as a solitary. In his deepest recollections, it seemed to him, he was always alone.

Browne's only previous solo passage over blue water had been five days spent between Florida and Cape Fear. It was a passage he had trouble remembering. One time at sea blended into another when things went well, and that one had gone well enough. Some of the time, mainly at night, his mind had played tricks. It had been easy to get the wind in tune and start it singing. On the open sea, the eye tended to impose form on random patterns of wave and light. The same thing happened in deep woods. It happened to everyone.

A clear sky burned overhead, appropriate to the west wind. Altair shone radiant over the continent behind him, Betelgeuse and Orion over the farther ocean. It was a childish pleasure to have the stars to himself again. Before midnight, he went below.

He awoke to a sound that cheered him. The sun was high in the sky and Morse code was coming over the Icom transceiver, loud and clear at more than thirty words a second. As a midshipman, in the autumn before he was commissioned, Browne had spent some months at the navy's radio school in Norfolk, Virginia. He had learned to type in radio school, and the typing of a letter still brought to his mind the ghostly echo of its Morse equivalent. It was early afternoon and he was hungry. Later, he decided, he would take a sighting.

He made himself a cheese omelet for breakfast and ate it with fried ham, and, as things did at sea, it tasted marvelous. When he had washed the dishes, he went on deck.

The day was fine, the wind steady and the ocean still as blue. As a bonus, four gray bottlenose dolphins were leaping with *Nona's* bow, as good an omen as could be.

At noon on November 20, Browne took a sun sighting and located himself northeast of the Cape Verde Islands. The fix did not conform well to his satellite reading. At the same time his compass was shifty, as though some countermagnetic force were in the air. The wind was moist and intermittent; he was riding the Canaries Current, making about two knots under the mainsail and a slack light drifter.

In midafternoon, he sighted an island off his starboard bow that was black but inlaid with a deep delicious green, a festive sight in the glare. A hill rose from it to a height he reckoned at 400 meters. Referring to the Admiralty sailing guide, he decided it was the island called Boa Vista. Later, a little boat painted in violent African colors went across his bow at a distance of a mile or so. Through binoculars he could make out a shirtless brown man with a red bandanna across his head standing behind the wheelhouse. The boat seemed top-heavy and tossed alarmingly in the mild sea. The name *Sao Martin da Porres* was stenciled across its stern.

At four o'clock, the marine operator broadcast a roll call of the entries. The stars of the race, the big boats, were already closing on Cape Agulhas. Browne's competition was spread westward over several hundred miles. Of the lot, only Preston Fowler was ahead of him, clearing the equatorial doldrums at latitude eleven south. When the broadcast ended, a weather fax arrived, announcing a tropical depression off the horn of Brazil.

Boa Vista passed out of sight before sunset. The moment the sun was down equatorial darkness closed around him, black on black under the cold stars. Worried about the current and the proximity of land, he stayed late on deck. His mind's eye refused to give up the image of the black and green island. Finally he played the game of refusing the image, trying to force it from his imagination. Eventually, he nodded off to sleep. Awakening with an odd but familiar sensation, he discovered himself in tears. The same thing had been happening all the way across the Atlantic. It was strange because his easting had been a particularly invigorating run, spinnaker set and westerlies across the port quarter at seventeen knots. Brilliant autumn weather. But night after night he would go to sleep in perfectly good spirits and wake to feel some old misery slinking away with an unremembered dream.

Finally he put on some Dorsey brothers music to guide himself through the darkness. For whatever reason, the old numbers sounded unreasonably sad. The image of the island stayed with him relentlessly until he could almost see it, glowing out on the dark ocean.

In one late dark hour, mysterious bibliolaters came in over the open transmitter.

"A false balance is abomination to the Lord," said a stern female voice, "but a just weight is His delight." The rest was static. Browne went to sleep on deck.

He opened his eyes to a peculiar amber light. There was sand on his eyelids and between his teeth. When he stood up, he felt a light salting of the stuff on the deck beneath his bare feet. From every quarter, the horizon seemed to be closing in, visibility eroding at a quarter of a mile or so. The sun was obscured but its glare was all around him. The wind was hot and comfortless. He checked the compass, then went aft to inspect the steering vane. Nona was on course in the strange fitful air. Each breeze lifted columns of spindrift from an oily, seamlessly rolling sea. Uneasy, heavy-handed, he went below and checked his radar scanner. The beam was reassuring. Half unwillingly, he climbed to his rack and went to sleep again.

His dreams were vivid and sweaty, incorporating a vaguely familiar noise that suggested telephone wires or nights in the country. Opening his eyes, he saw something in motion on the highest step of the companionway. The cabin was darker than usual; something was blotting out the fingers of light that usually penetrated the reinforced cabin windows. Then a moment came in which he connected the noise to what he was seeing and he stood up in terror.

Insects infested the wind. The companionway steps were covered with them.

They were spilling like a foul liquor from the higher to the lower steps and had covered the cabin windows. Charging up the ladder he crushed a million brittle carapaces underfoot. Once on deck, he refused the sight he saw. The things glided down singly like so many paratroopers and in writhing clusters that rolled like tumbleweed and skittered across the main hatch. Each shroud and stay was alive with them, the mainsail and mast crawling.

In his first active, waking moments, he felt the mass of fiddling legs and antennae cover his bare skin. Briefly, he was able to control his own panic. As he brushed them from his face, he became aware of the sound they made.

Browne ran headlong for cover, which the deck did not afford. Frantically, he tried to pry the insect bodies from his face. Their mandibles adhered. With his own shrill curses in his ears, he wrapped one arm around the boom, stared down at it, and saw it crawling.

All around the boat, as far into the murk as he could see, the surface of the water was smothered, as though the swarm had displaced the ocean. *Nona's* wake cut a swath through them, churning out creatures and soiled white water. Only when the noise stopped could he see that they had stopped falling. Teeth clenched, shuddering, he brushed himself off. He stamped as many as he could into the deck. Finally, more calmly, he took a hose to them, supplied from the bilges. He labored for hours to clean the decks and lines and brightwork. For weeks he would find them in unlikely places, sometimes in disgusting numbers. The insects were a little over an inch long, pale yellow and black, with delicate spotted wings folded against the thorax. Holding one spread-winged against a page of his log, he was reminded of a fantastic print he had seen reproduced long before. He thought he must have seen it in a book during his school days. Very distantly, he could remember the book as disturbing, showing things that were outside his experience then and of which he wanted no part.

In Vietnam, the battle-crazy Lurps who lived across the landing strip from Browne's Tactical Air Control base had made a legend of beetles that entered the brain and contaminated the mind. Some of the Lurps had believed so intensely in the beetles that they had succumbed to the infection. That evening, Browne entered the infestation in his log to bring the experience under control.

"1400 GMT, 1300 local, course 130 degrees, wind off the African coast. Khamsin or harmattan brought a cloud of insects, flying or airborne, covered *Nona* and the surrounding sea. Hours cleaning up." Beyond that he could think of nothing to write. Later, he thought, he might sit down to his journal and make a literary event out of it all.

Just before sundown the unwholesome mists cleared and a gentle breeze rose astern. Browne watched the passing of the light with a troubled mind.

Between Bahia and Trinidade, there were starry nights and glass and useless breezes too feeble to dry sweat or raise a hair. Each morning the sun came up on distant ghostly clouds that never changed their shape or bearing, the same clouds, it seemed, steaming on station, day after day. To coax what little air there was, Browne had raised a ghoster jenny, a big light sail with a Kevlar luff sheeted to the afterdeck.

He spent hours looking over the stern, watching the little millpond ripple of the current under his keel. The water was crazy blue, painted, Brazilian.

Once a stormy petrel settled safely on the boom to show him how little wind there was. When he approached it, it fixed him with a wise little eye but never shifted. Out of curiosity he reached his hand toward it. The bird made a quarter turn on its perch and pecked at him. Then it shot off, racing eastward an inch over the surface. As though there were anything for anyone out there.

Browne made a log entry: "Mother Carey's chicken on a fuck-you note."

A not too suitable reflection.

One night he turned on the radio and scanned the dial in search of a few sounds. The clown colors of the sunset had put him in mind of tropical riot, sambas, sibilant Portuguese. What he got was a religious lady on the customary band.

"Many of you have written in," said the grimly English religious lady, "to ask what is meant by God's covenant."

Browne opened a can of peaches and settled down to listen in spite of himself.

"By God's covenant," the lady said, "is meant the job that we are meant to do. If the boss gives you a job and you do it and are paid for it, then you have kept your covenant with the boss. But if you do not do the job, do not expect the boss to pay you.

"God has a job for all his creatures," the lady said, "for everyone in his kingdom. We must each do ours. For we are either covenant keepers or covenant breakers. Are you a covenant keeper or a covenant breaker? You must think about it.

"If you are not a covenant keeper," the lady said, "then you are in rebellion. I wonder how many of our listeners are covenant keepers. I hope it is very, very many. How lovely it would be if all our listeners were covenant keepers. I hope that none of our listeners are in rebellion."

"Not me," Browne said.

"To be in rebellion," the lady went on, "is to be alone. It is to be insane. For all reality belongs to God."

"I disagree," Browne said.

"We must all remember," the lady said, "what we are told in Hebrews 4: 'For the word of God is quick and powerful and sharper than any two-edged sword, piercing even to the dividing asunder of soul and spirit and of the joints and marrow and is a discerner of the thoughts and intents of the heart.

'Neither is there any creature that is not manifest in his sight, but all things are naked and opened unto the eyes of him with whom we have to do.'"

Browne found it curious to consider the dividing asunder of soul and spirit. The dividing asunder of joints and marrow was a sight he knew, familiar to him both from the dinner table and the aftermath of tactical air support. One might think of osso buco but also of someone's arm, impossibly bent, its boiling tubes exposed to flies, its red-mottled white bone to beetles. Hebrews 4, Browne thought, unquestionably had war and sacrifice on its bloody mind.

Overhead the stars were exquisite and, inviting reverence, featured the Southern Cross. Let him with whom we have to do, Browne thought by way of prayer, never sunder my spirit from my soul. It certainly did sound like insanity. Let him with whom we have to do have nothing to do with me.

When the fax with everyone's position came in, awakening him, he found himself disinclined to read it. It was as though he wanted not to be in a race. Which was not to say, he thought, that he wanted not to win one.

He actually left the fax unread, except for the section about the weather. Not checking it was a little stupid, but he was in his own house, in his own kingdom, and he supposed he would find out about the others soon enough. Is this self-confidence or cowardice? he had to ask himself. Independence or spite? The church lady's broadcast had put him in a vein of self-examination. He felt as though he might be in rebellion after all.

At dawn the next day, the same clouds were stretched out in convoy along the eastern horizon. The motionless sea changed with the sky from violet to smoky blue. Browne watched it close over his little wake. When the heat of the day came on, his rebellion took the form of a refusal to patiently endure another stifled day of calm. The silky glowing surface of the water, its cool blue promise, drove him to action.

He paid out a sheet to trail behind *Nona* as a safety line, its end wrapped around a belaying pin. The other end he secured to the mainmast. He left a bar of saltwater soap on the afterdeck. Then he stripped, went forward to the bow, and leaned against its aluminum rail for a moment to take a measure of the boat's faint forward motion. In the next instant he took a breath and dived over. The warm, still water closed welcomingly around him. Unresisted, he pushed deep and far. When he surfaced, his head was six feet from *Nona's* hull. He swam a stroke and put his hand against her skin; he could barely feel her sliding past. Turning over, he swam a few strokes aft, and when the sheet came by he seized it and pulled himself up to the boat's stern ladder. He soaped himself and did it all over again. The satin water, the rush of silence and surface in his ears, the salt on his lips—all made him feel renewed. When he had played the game for a while, he made himself a lunch of crackers, canned crabmeat and vegetable juice and went to sleep in the cockpit.

By late afternoon, only shifting light had changed the stock-still diagram of boat, attending clouds, and sea. He went swimming again; it was a drill with a rhythm, a good way of staying in shape. He decided he would keep at it through the calms.

Once he broke the surface of the water to find the upper world in unfamiliar shadow. From some quarter of the sky a cloud had come across the sun. Browne swam on his back, squinting at the sky. He felt himself rise on an invisible swell and, looking over his shoulder, saw the ghoster slowly filling, its contours darkening and curving as it puffed out. The boat began to groan; he saw it heave and slide forward, making a sound against the surface like rain in leaves. Then, before he knew it, the trailing line was rushing past him. He made an awkward overhand reach for the belaying pin at the end of the sheet and felt it slip through his fingers. In the growing distance, his future life, the *Nona* was sailing on alone, leaving him her new wake. Calmly, he swam after the line, in strong considered strokes that increased his speed with every kick. After fewer than a dozen he had caught the sheet; he wrapped it around his wrist and let the boat's sudden strength haul him for a while.

Back aboard, he stood looking back at the empty sea where he had made an object. Although the flow of the wake went on and the camber of the head sail suggested wind, he felt no breeze against his naked body. In the grip of a sudden notion, he hurried forward and dived ahead of the boat again. This time his heart raced, not with a true panic but with a safer, imagined one. All the same, he swam as hard as he could and when the sheet went by seized it with both hands and pulled himself home. He did the same thing again and again until he was almost exhausted. There was no sign of the cloud that obscured the sun before.

Afterward he lay down again on deck, half sleeping, half dreaming of the shore, childish days in the surf, summer birthdays, and his parents. In his single true dream, the sky had gone dark and he was swimming in warm water littered with floating straw. He opened his eyes to faded blue. The sun was low. Physically he felt very tired.

He had put his trunks on and was sitting in the cockpit when, on the edge of a vision, a shadow like that of a sail passed along *Nona's* bow. Leaning over the rail, he saw that it was an enormous shark just under the surface. The thing seemed unseeing and mechanical, barely animate. Once past the stern it swerved and came along the hull again. This time its dorsal fin broached slightly, silently sheering an inch or so of the breathing world. Browne crouched absolutely still to watch it pass. It was perfect, he thought. Worshipful. At home, unlike him.

When he tried, sitting at his navigation table, to describe for his journal what had happened—his swimming, missing the line, the thing coming—he could not make it turn out right. Nor could he quite manage the thing in memory. Remembering it, he felt both fear and longing, insulted and exalted.

In the middle of the night, when the next false breeze came up, Browne shivered and slaked his peculiar thirst with water.

He lazed against the mast reading. He had brought along some published memoirs by solitary sailors to reacquaint himself with the form. As it turned out, he found the books hard going. Except for Slocum, even books that had kept him reading through the night ashore seemed to lose pertinence at sea. The authors all sounded alike. He suspected them of cribbing from one another. The style was that of naval history, English and high-hearted.

They are writing about what cannot be fully described, Browne thought. They reduced things and provided no more than what they knew was expected. It was useless, Browne decided, to speculate about the men themselves. Who knew what they were really like? They seemed not much like him, but there was no way to tell. The books gave nothing away.

Browne was used to being where others were not like him. In the past, it had sometimes been possible to find a few kindred spirits. But not out here, he thought, inspecting the horizon. It looked untroubled, perfectly benign. No kindred here.

Seated atop the hatch, he leafed through the stack of books, inspecting the jacket photographs of his memoirists. They were all suitably lean and leathery. Well, he thought, I can do that. Things had their public side, and it was not altogether dishonorable to pose. He wanted a book or a cassette of his own. He was sure he could come up with the necessary posture and humorously tough-minded prose.

As the sun rose higher, Browne sought the shade of his mainsail with Francis Chichester. Half dozing, the thought struck him of what it might be like to record the reality of things, matched with the thoughts and impressions it brought forth. To find the edge on which the interior met the exterior space. It would not be something of general interest, Browne thought, only of a morbid fascination to certain minds. Something for private reflection that might or might not lend itself to very selective sharing. If he could keep some sense of how things really were, he might retain a little of it over time. The past was always disguising itself, disappearing into the needs of the moment. Whatever happened got replaced by the official story or competing fictions.

Once he had succumbed to the temptation to telephone home via the high-seas operator, in violation of his own instructions.

"I know what people expect," he had told her. "I've read the books and I know the lingo."

"Just be yourself, Owen."

Late in the day, the true trades rose behind him, preceded by their long blue swell. It was as though lies summoned forth the things themselves.

"Bandmaster," Browne said aloud, "a little music, if you please."

He put on an Elgar tape, *In the South*. Very grand it was.

When the wind looked like hanging on, he decided to rig the spinnaker. When that was done, he took a sponge bath and put on clean clothes in celebration of the bright brisk weather.

His face in the mirror showed a bad sunburn. He had not been shaving and had not seen his own face for some time. The sight of it gave him an odd thrill of fear. He stuck a Band-Aid on his nose, put on his windbreaker and a Tacron-26 squadron cap, and settled in the cockpit to wait for the next position reports. He kept a notebook by his side.

The wind was steady all through the afternoon, but Browne found no reflections worthy of his notebook. Voices from the false sea-stories he had been reading stayed with him. He could achieve neither the correct attitude nor the appropriate language. It was another case of things not being what they were supposed to be.

Around evening he had another great attack of desire for his wife.

After the lust was temporarily taken care of came loneliness.

She had told him not to perform so much. That people did not expect it. To be himself.

His father had been a professional authority on expectations. Browne lay back and watched the fluttering telltales.

"What about it, Dad?" he asked aloud. "Can I just be myself then? How about it?"

The very notion of such a question filled him with hilarity. He rolled in the cockpit laughing, imagining his father's voice gathering force for the reply.

"Yerself?"

It was too funny, Browne thought. First the mild and reasonable mode.

"Be yerself, you mean?"

That had been the time of terror, when the pitch changed and the voice ascended sweetly toward the thunderous heights on which it would charge itself with fury.

"Are you inquiring, my son, as to whether your private person will be deemed suitable for the station in life toward which you aspire?"

Browne clapped his hands and laughed harder. He could actually hear the old man's voice.

"Right, Dad. How about it?"

"You?"

A guy went slack, the wind changed, something caused a luffing in the main. He heard his father no longer enraged but cursing and weeping. That, of course, had been the other side of things.

In the last of the light he put on his safety harness, secured the spinnaker, and ran up an all-weather jib. His SatNav position located him at 36° 36' south and 27° 33' west, a formidable combination of treys. He sat up for a while taping preventers, listening to tangos. Eventually, he climbed in the rack for some proper zees.

If I have forgiven him, Browne wondered, nodding off on the wholesome swells, why is he out here, waiting for me?

The southern summer, Browne discovered, had light more radiant than that of autumn in Connecticut. Its shadows seemed darker and deeper. Day after day, the sky was luminous. The cool weather and the dry pure air aroused him to a faint excitement. Every night, the dazzle of stars overhead kept him awake and on deck.

He was tacking south, looking for the big winds below latitude forty. Since crossing the line, he had found no air heavier than twenty knots. Every day the fax reported a stationary front off Patagonia. After a while, the bright intensity of things gave him a headache. He felt as though his personal rhythms were a fraction too fast. He kept starting jobs and leaving them incomplete. The color of the water reminded him of something he could not bring to mind. It had grown a richer blue as he had gone farther south.

One evening, he was on deck listening to the radio when the sky filled with colored light. Curving bands in violet and dark green undulated across the dark blue sky. Bank after bank of purple light radiated from the southern horizon, in regular repeated patterns. So orderly were the emanations that they seemed to Browne to be a kind of signal. It was hard to believe that no unitary purpose was behind them.

The aurora reminded Browne of the night sky over the Song Chong valley in 1969. He had seen the most spectacular displays there, tracer rounds in red and green, parachute flares every night. Behind each illumination was some intention, it was being organized and coordinated, but to see it all was to know that things had gone beyond the compass of human will.

Over the radio, as the colored lights ranged across the sky, a man was explaining time.

"If we can speak of an absolute future and an absolute past," said the speaker, who had a brusque South African accent, "we can also make distinctions outside the continuum. What is outside and never to be intersected by our lines of event? We call it 'absolute elsewhere.'"

The aurora seemed somehow to interfere with the radio signal so that the lecturer's voice waxed and waned with the throbbing of the lights overhead. Eventually, it faded away. The lights were still shimmering when the stars came out. Browne looked up and saw his friends from home, Orion and Canis Major. Sirius burned away.

In the cabin, he tried, perversely, to find the missionary station. He had been listening to it with amusement almost every night since crossing latitude forty. This time it was not available.

At latitude fifty, although the skies were still clear and the air light, Browne secured the hemispheres of his cockpit bubble to the deck. To keep the Plexiglas clear, he washed it with the Clear Aid he used for his dive masks. He decided to leave the bubble open until the weather changed. The same evening he sought out the missionary station again. Instead there was more mere physics.

"What are we to say," asked the learned Boer, "of particle histories occurring in imaginary time? How can time be imaginary? Yet it can be. For imaginary time works its force on the continuum with the same degree of influence as so-called real time. How can we speak of histories occurring over imaginary time?"

The signal faded out. That night, lying in his bunk unable to sleep, he found rest in the notion of imaginary time. To consider it was like being reminded of something one had always known. It was as though things had a delicious secret side that had been inexplicably forgotten. The trick was to remember it in difficulty, so there was something at the worst of times. If we could experience that, Browne came to believe, we would understand a level of existence at which things were basically all right. He fondly remembered the sound of the broadcaster's voice, which seemed pregnant with that experience. Although the savor of the thing kept him from sleep, he could not quite bring it to bear.

He had stopped reading. In Vietnam, at the worst of times, he had been able to read himself clear out of the war, into history or else out of it, depending on the point of view. Now, with plenty of time, he somehow lacked the patience. And about music, he had found that it was necessary to be very careful. Certain music produced a confusion that was very hard to resolve. The best entertainment, Browne discovered, was his own thoughts. And then, as a kind of puzzle, there was the radio.

Browne had managed to locate the missionary station again. The reader, who sounded like an English-speaking African, announced that a dramatization from Genesis would be broadcast at 2000 Greenwich Mean Time. Browne decided to celebrate. In order to keep his thoughts clear, he had been fasting, living mainly on unheated, unmixed consomme. To accompany the broadcast, he undertook to prepare a homely feast—frankfurters Southern-style from his Fannie Farmer Cookbook, with canned tomatoes, chopped onion, thyme, and oregano.

Browne's feat proved a disappointment. He had spent the afternoon trying to clear his generator's fuel injectors; when he turned to in the galley, his hands were still fouled with diesel fuel. It was extraordinary the way the stuff managed to contaminate the ingredients of his proposed meal. Finally he gave up on it and opened a can of corned beef instead. He ate the corned beef with saltines and settled down to listen to the night's drama.

The missionaries' radio play was about Isaac and his family. Jacob was played by a young Canadian. Isaac sounded like an elderly Southern white man. Esau was played, somewhat humorously, by an African. Rebekah was played by a young woman with a sweet clear northwestern voice who reminded Browne of a woman from Oregon he had once known. It was apparent that there was some doubling up. Isaac was also Laban. Rebekah was both Rachel and Leah.

A narrator, who might have been the English lady Browne had been listening to before, reminded the audience of how Isaac had been spared sacrifice and of his adventures among the Philistines in the land of Gerar. She pointed out that even in today's world, travelers must be careful to protect their loved ones.

"How many of our listeners," she asked, "have been sojourners, have been among those of some other nation? How many have feared for their safety? Do we know," she inquired, "how we shall behave when our loved ones are threatened?"

Browne wrapped the remaining corned beef in foil, turned on his Kemper heater, and wrapped himself in a dry navy blanket on his bunk as the dramatization began.

"Oh, that red pottage," said Esau, "that red pottage smells so good to me. I am faint with hunger."

"Would you like some?" Jacob asked. He sounded honest enough, a wholesome North American. "Then sell me your birthright."

Esau seemed to consider the offer in a stage whisper.

"I am afraid I'm going to die. What good is some old birthright to me?"

Browne thought he heard voices rising all over Africa. No! Esau!

"Then Jacob gave Esau bread and pottage of lentils," recited the English lady, "and he did eat and drink and rose up and went his way." She paused. "Thus," she proclaimed severely, "Esau despised his birthright."

The scene shifted to the tent of old Isaac. Rebekah instructed her son to kill the goats and she would make them into a dish the old man liked. Then young Jacob would bring it to him, and Isaac would bless him before he died. The girl of whom Rebekah reminded Browne had been the daughter of the captain of the USS *Pollux* out of Bremerton.

"But, *Mother*," said Jacob in a slightly epicene tone, "brother Esau is hairy! My skin is smooth. Father might feel my arm. Then he'd say I was a deceiver. He'd give me a curse instead of a blessing."

Rebekah's reply was sweet as country water. She sounded more resigned than conniving, like someone doing what she had to do.

"Upon me be the curse, my son. Only obey my voice and go fetch them."

So, of course, Jacob did. Any boy would.

There was one line that caught Browne's particular attention because he had often heard his father use it. "The smell of my son is as the smell of a field the Lord has blessed."

Later, when Esau found he had been displaced from his father's blessing as well as his birthright, his anguish was unsettling. The actor's voice trembled terribly. Who knew

Browne thought, over there in Africa, what his life was like, what things he'd seen?

"Have you only one blessing, Father? Please bless me, Dad. Bless me also." But he was out of luck.

"And Esau lifted up his voice," declared the stern English lady, "and wept."

Browne listened to all of it, huddled in the blanket. He was unaware of the tears that coursed down his cheeks. Isaac let poor Esau know that he was basically on his own. Then Jacob went to work for Laban and Laban deceived him, substituted Leah for Rachel, extorted his labor. Then he returned and simple-hearted Esau welcomed him and miracles ensued.

When the dramatization was over, the lady came back on.

"When Esau came in from the field," she asked the public, "was he really starving to death? I hardly think so. Wasn't he only being greedy after a day in the field? Listeners will remember how he despised his birthright. Wasn't he a thoughtless young man?"

The English lady allowed that many listeners would feel sorry for Esau because of the way things turned out for him. She admitted it was only natural to do so.

"But what are we to think of Jacob's behavior?" she asked. She paused again for general reflection. "Didn't he act wrongly? What do listeners think?"

Jacob's behavior was absolutely unjustified, the lady maintained. It was wrong of him to impersonate Esau. She made no comment regarding Rebekah.

"What are we to think of this story?" the lady asked. "What message does it hold for us?"

"Good question," Browne said from his rack.

"Its message," the lady replied, "is that of God's almighty will. Never forget that God is strong. What is God's is likewise strong. The will of God binds the world and everyone in it. There is no setting it aside. There is no pleading against it."

Browne stirred in the bunk, his teeth set in rage.

"When we say that our God is a fortress," the lady declared, "we proclaim his strength. Would a weak God be worshipful? Would a weak God be worthy of love?"

In spite of the tender emotions he was experiencing—the self-pity, the loneliness, the disappointment—Browne found himself compelled to admit that a weak God would not be worthy of love. As for the English lady, she had no doubts whatsoever.

"Certainly not!" she declared vigorously. "The weakness of a little child is moving," the lady said. "We have all seen sick unhappy children. There are millions of them today. We pity them. We help them. This does not mean that we are worshipers of weakness. Almighty God is our all-eternal father, the Lord of hosts and stronger than the strong. Almighty God makes provision for the weak in his mercy," the lady went on, "as provision was made for Esau. But his weakness and heedlessness were not blessed. They were forgiven but not forgotten. There was no covenant with Esau.

"Doesn't all of nature proclaim the great strength of God? Can we not see the strong plants forcing their way through the earth? Can we not see our strong cattle thriving and providing for us? Don't we rejoice in the strength of our young men? Whom would listeners prefer for a son? Esau or Jacob?"

Browne considered his daughter the only child close to his heart. She was without guile. There were many things he wanted to explain to her.

"I think they should prefer Jacob," the lady declared. "Just as Rebekah did. In preferring Jacob, Rebekah anticipated God's will. She was its instrument."

Browne pondered the admission into which he had just heard the Christians trick themselves. They were talking to Africa, engaging in primary process. You had to come a long way, he thought, to the margins of the world, to get the message straight. Of course, the woman was absolutely right.

"When God had made his covenant with Jacob, Jacob was raised up into Israel," the lady concluded. "It is easy for God to raise man to His purposes, when that is His Almighty will."

During the white night, the glitter of distant ice beguiled his mind's eye and denied him sleep. Around one he started up the engine to charge his batteries and found one of the starboard fuel tanks contaminated with algae. His other tanks, it turned out, were fine, but the injectors were glutted now with an animal-vegetable-mineral jelly that took him hours to clear away. Eventually, he was able to hook up and charge.

Wiping the scum off his hands, Browne considered God's will, how hard it was. Toward morning, he climbed into his bunk. For a long time he lay awake. His mind was racing and it struck him suddenly that there might be some form of false thought, notions that had their origin outside the brain and even outside ordinary reality. He went to sleep trying to work it out.

Sleeping at last, he dreamed. In the dream, he was swimming with difficulty, his chin raised awkwardly for breath. In reality, Browne was a strong and skilled swimmer. There was turmoil in the water behind him, and he was paddling away from it. There was a gray sky and angry voice. Browne knew that his father was behind him, drunk and enraged. It was some kind of swimming lesson. He woke up breathless and terrified.

Something had happened in life to suggest the dream, Browne thought. Then he was aware of the noise. It was a rending, the kind of sound that could be made by tearing open a taped package but ten times magnified. It was not the ordinary noise of bulkheads creaking, although he heard that as well. In the galley, hanging pans rang together. He climbed out of his bunk. *Nona* was rolling in heavy seas. The wind had come with a vengeance.

Browne hurried up the companionway and opened the hatch to see the gray sky of his dreams looming above a scattered ocean.

Listening to the wind, Browne recalled that, with luck, noise was the worst part of certain experiences. Lashed within his bubble, he struggled with the helm. For hours it had been blowing more than sixty miles an hour. His own intermittent headway was off the scale; sometimes it exceeded fourteen knots. Surfing down the crests brought on a double vertigo. Each slide promised to bottom out in nothingness itself, each stalling of the rudder brought him the sickening impotence of an unresponding helm. After each trough his bow dug deeper into the froth, the vessel shuddering as though scalded as she tried to rise. He felt as though he were riding the edge of a green wall that closed off possibility, thinly balanced, accelerating and about to fall. Spinning out, every minute.

The wind sounded as though things had stopped putting up with him. When their patience was expended, Browne considered, things had the forbearance of an insect and the same random energy. At first he had shouted back at it all, ready to sing along. At first it had sounded familiar—the good old thrashing main, school of liberty, cradle of the race. After a while, when it had compelled his closer attention, he heard the stone annihilation, the locust's shriek magnified from the abyss.

"Christ that my love was in my arms," he said.

The gale whistled in his slackening shrouds like incoming fire. He laughed in despair. He could imagine the long-legged crabs of Fiddler's Green rosining up their bows for him. He felt warm, sweet, and powerless, a morsel, a portion. Above all, alone. Also the wind, for all its fury, was not the only sound he heard. There was a worse sound below that made him prefer it.

The sound from below was nasty indeed. He could not remember when he had begun hearing it. Just below the doldrums, probably, in the rising of the southeast trades. There was something human in its nastiness, a squeal, a squawk. It sounded like the gutter, like an obscene threat, a New York objection. Plastic. Listening, he clenched his teeth.

Its whine suggested loud vulgar language and cheap macho menace. Bad workmanship and sharp practice. Phoniness and cunning. Fucking plastic, he thought, enraged. It sounded like a liar burning in hell. Plastic unmaking itself.

That was what it was. And, of course, he should have known. He had been seeing the crazes and having trouble with the locker doors. Like a little tin soldier in a paper boat, he thought, biting his lip, headed for the drain. He was riding a decomposing piece of plastic through an Antarctic storm.

"You bastards!" he shouted, trying to outdo the wind. "What have you done to me? You fucking filthy swine!"

It was hard to force himself down into the cabin where the whine was loudest. It reminded him of the kind of dirty laughter it was sometimes expedient not to hear. You are not called *Nona*, bitch, he told the boat. Fake bitch. You have no name. But she was not even a bitch. Just plastic.

He sat down at the navigation table and started going through the chart drawers in search of the boat's design drawings. He had not seen them for months. The first document he laid hands on was the rough copy of a brochure he had written himself. He stood up and, holding fast to the overhead rail, got to read his own prose.

"Altan 36! Master-crafted! A seasoned winner in the newest design! All the elements of the precision-designed racer—attainable! Affordable!"

They were his own words. And, of course, he had approved the boat. More than that—in imagination he had invented a perfect boat for it to be. It had been salesmanship by ontology, purveying a perfect boat for the perfect ocean in an ideal world. The very thing for a cruise to the perfect island, the one that had to exist because it could be imagined. He had been his own first, best customer.

With every gust the fiberglass screamed. The urgency in the sound was genuine, and he understood that, under sail, she could not stand up to weather any longer. He went on deck and, laboring furiously with the cockpit open to black sky and rain, dropped and lashed the main and genoa and raised a storm jib. He brought the boat to a close leach, all but hove to, a humble penitent posture.

Below again, he had to strip the boards of the cabin sole with a crowbar to reach the mast-step. The devilish, spider-webbed craze patterns across its surface were worse than anything he had imagined. The makers of the boat had simply piled on extra fiberglass. With each tightening of the stays, Browne realized, he had been driving the mast-step down and bending the hull.

Clinging to the overhead rail, he began to smash the bulkhead cabinets with his crowbar. They were his own work, poor quality, of cheap material. When he had stove in the lockers that adjoined the main bulkhead, he saw that there too the glass was crazing. So it was no wonder, he realized, that his shrouds were slack, since the chain plate was secured there. All the secondary bonds were giving way. Again and again, Browne brought his crowbar down on the shiny, cosmetic cabin-fittings of his worthless boat. With the sails down, the boat was pitching relentlessly. Browne lay across the cabin sole, his legs braced against the bulkhead, trying to buttress the mast-step with the ruins of the floorboards. He jammed the fragments of his cabinets against the angle between the hull and the main bulkhead. Every few minutes he had to turn away from work to retch over a bucket.

The suffering plastic ground on. It was like a last, terrible laugh. There is justice here, Browne thought. He had been trying to be someone else. He had never really wanted any of it.

The tie rods he found under the liner were not stainless steel rods but appeared to have been rigged out of galvanized wire. It made him laugh to see the way they had stretched because it was like a practical joke. Like a cartoon in which some furry creature's flying machine deconstructed itself element by element until the poor thing was left about to fall, humorously embarrassed and terrified, naked and unsupported over emptiness. Flightless furry me, Browne thought.

Drenched with sick sweat, he hammered the slats into place. Gradually he realized that the noise in the cabin had diminished. With the sails down, the pressure eased, the boat was relieved of its misery. He went on deck and felt ashamed to face the gale.

Eventually, he decided that he could not risk lying a-hull. When the wind shifted to southeast, he put out a drogue, winched it securely, and started northeasterly with the wind on his quarter. The drogue kept his speed down, but he had to stay at the helm to keep the course.

Hours later the wind eased, and he raised a storm jib again and went below to rest. Sleep eluded him in spite of his fatigue. Sickness came and went. Petty hallucinations assailed him. He found himself absurdly concerned with appearances. Everyone must have seen the poor set of the main. Anyone could have found him out, exposed his lack of knowledge and experience. It had all been pretending, he thought, as far back as memory. He was at the root of it. He was what raised the stink at the heart of things. There would always be something to conceal.

The sleep that finally came was shallow and thirst-ridden. In dreams, he was trying to overcome his father's loony drunken scorn with quiet logic. It was necessary to be patient because his father was highly intelligent and knew no limits and was capable of saying anything.

But reasonableness had been the strategy. There was always a chance you could surprise him and strike a spark of approbation. You had to stage an ambush to wring a good word.

Half waking, Browne felt the peculiar anxiety with which he had always awaited his father's laughter. If I'm not careful, he thought, thrashing in the bunk, he'll have me laughing too.

Browne thought he heard that little bubbling up of humor in the throat that preceded one of the old boy's amusing sallies. His heart fluttered, in fear of embarrassment. Then he heard the voice itself, dry and theatrical, heartless.

"Everybody loves you when you're someone else, son."

That was a good one, Browne thought.

Miguelito

Douglas Unger

e moved back to the confinement of San Miguel after our night of tango and our three-day weekend at the Plaza Hotel. We felt low and depressed. The reality struck home that we had spent in a few days more than the spare money we had left. Worse, we were avoiding each other, as though guiltily, waking up each morning just to get through the day. Betty Ann stuck close to Mama and helped with domestic chores. I was in the small cottage most of the time, reviewing tapes, taking notes, waiting for what more I might learn at the trials. The weather changed. Temperatures dropped to freezing. Most days were misty, with a low covering of dark clouds. Looking out through the high iron fences of the estate, broke and irritable, we felt as limited and enclosed as if under house arrest.

The Sunday barbecue was held as usual at San Miguel. Even in the cold, the family set up tables under the trees. The Beneventos and their guests ate their meats and salads and drank their wine bundled up in sweaters, jackets, scarves, and hats. Jorge Gallo and his two young daughters were there. His girls cried easily. Any kind of brattiness was tolerated by their father, who was drinking too much, letting them run around, screaming, out of control. Jorge was in one of his more abusive, dark moods. He started ranting about yanqui exploitation of the world, forcing every country it could into "obscene consumerism." He directed his remarks straight at me, across the table. I gritted my teeth and pretended to ignore him. Only once did I ask a question—if he hated the United States so much, why was he trying to get a work visa and go there to live?

After the meal, Mama and Betty Ann did winter chores in the gardens, mulching the flower beds. Papa and Martin retired to one of the bedrooms in the main house to review some legal papers for the trials, then sleep a siesta, while Alicia tried to quiet the children enough for a nap. Jorge staggered off to the guest cottage, appropriated my bed, and passed out cold.

That left Amalita and me still at the table, getting reacquainted. Amalita was a spinster, a close friend of the family. We called her Tia Amalia, like an aunt. I had vague memories from my year as an exchange student that this woman had been at family gatherings, holiday tables, even at graduation from secondary school with Martin Segundo. She was shy, had turned gray at a young age, and was so quiet and in the background most of the time that it was as if she wished no one would notice her.

It wasn't long before we were driven out of our chairs by a cutting breeze. We walked around the grounds briskly, clapping our gloved hands together to stay warm. We found ourselves walking in circles near the corner of the garden that

Mama had reserved for brown failed experiments with tropical plants. There was a particularly unfortunate banana tree there, its long boats of leaves yellowed by frost, hanging like limp shredded rags.

Amalita talked about her life. She described her mainly solitary existence without sorrow or regret, her small apartment, her nights spent reading and knitting, her days at her good job as a laboratory technician for a large medical practice in the city. She reminded me that she had been in the room or at important events during the year I had been an exchange student, and all through the years when my brothers were growing up. "Nobody realizes in this family that I was actually very close to the boys," she said. "That was especially so with Alejo and Miguel at the end. Except for Martin Segundo, I was the last one to see either of them alive."

"When was that?" I asked.

"I don't like to talk about it," she said. "It's been the main topic around here far too long, in my opinion. Those were terrible, terrible years. But that's over now, God willing. There are thirty million Argentines who have to go on living. The best thing is to put those years behind us, to get them over with once and for all so this country can function again. Isn't that what people are supposed to do when they wake up from a nightmare?"

She pulled a pack of cigarettes out of her jacket pocket. They were the cheapest brand available, a kind that smelled like burning sawdust. I took out a good American brand and offered her one. We fumbled, clumsily, with gloves and matches and cigarettes.

"I don't agree with the family on this subject, as you can see," Amalita continued. She smoked in short puffs, without inhaling, like someone unaccustomed to smoking. "I have a very different view of what happened to the boys. They were running with a very bad crowd. Colonel Dipaoli, you remember him? He had a son who went to school with you and the boys. The colonel visited Martin at his law office. He warned him, 'Watch out for your sons. They're running in very dangerous things.' But what did Martin do? Oh, maybe he tried to persuade them to stay out of politics, but he clearly didn't do enough. None of us did. We should have knocked them over their hard heads and shipped them out of the country before they woke up. It was hell in Buenos Aires by then. Bombs were going off everywhere, and there was shooting in the streets. Do you know what happened to Miguelito? The story of how he was expelled from school?"

"No," I said. "The family doesn't talk much about him. I keep thinking it's because Papa is going to testify about him, but I don't know. . . ."

"Come on, Diego, seriously. They avoid talking about Miguelito because of what he did. Getting expelled from school was just the beginning. Miguel ran with a gang of the militancy among his classmates. They packed pistols, showed off their guns in the hallways. They were wild, and nobody studied. Miguelito was suspended for being caught painting slogans, 'Down with the dictatorship,' on the walls of the school in broad daylight. The family had lost all control of him by then. Martin was desperate. He talked the administration into giving Miguel one more chance. Then he was with the group of boys who rebelled during a chemistry exam. Like it was all a joke, they drew out their guns and shot up the lab tables, the blackboards, the windows.

"That's about the time Alejo and Martin Segundo moved out of the house, for good reasons. They weren't concerned only for themselves, but for their parents. By that time, Miguelito was in thick with the worst of the militant gangs. They planted bombs. They shot people. Even though I'm like an aunt to this family, at a certain point, it was too much. I grew afraid to have anything to do with him. I shouldn't be talking about this. My God, I'm getting upset now."

We were strolling back from the brown corner of the garden and found ourselves near the tables. There was a large bottle of wine left there. I found two glasses, picked the wine up by its basket handle, and poured them full. Amalia shook her head once, no, then reached out and took a glass.

"Those boys were the closest I ever knew to having children of my own," she said.

We sat down and drank together in silence. I was unsure if that was all she was going to say, and I didn't feel it was the right moment to press her for anything more. There was a far-off look in her eyes as she stared out across the cold landscape into the trees.

"One of my cousins, on my mother's side, had a job in the Public Works Administration Building," she said after a while. "The building was bombed. My mother's family is from Cordoba, and they didn't have much money. I was the closest relative to this cousin in the capital. He was new to the city, happy about his state job, and he would come over to dinner once a week. After the bombing, naturally, I was the one they called to identify his body. Then before his body was shipped home, there was a mass memorial service, and I stood in for my mother's family. Coffins were set up on stands, with flags draped over them. I'm not the kind of person to be at that kind of service. I mean, what's the point? What was the military trying to say?

"Still, I stood by my cousin's coffin, facing crowds of people and the press. Comandante General Videla was there with all the other important generals and admirals. Videla gave a speech that declared war on the urban gorillas. Thousands of people cheered him on. Then the general marched down the line of coffins and shook hands with the families of the dead. He got to me. I was face to face with him. He seemed very polite, a very sincere and caring man to me then. He reached for my hand and I felt his mustache when he kissed my cheek. It was then that I said to him, 'Find out who did this. Find out who killed my cousin and punish them.' He answered, 'Don't worry, senora. I'll see they are punished.' God forgive me. But nobody knew how far he would go. Nobody knew."

Amalia stopped talking. She reached up and rearranged some messy ends of white hair sticking out from under her stocking cap. She looked at me strangely, as if she needed reassurance about what she had said.

"I don't believe that nobody knew," I said. "I've been finding out since I got here that plenty of people must have known what would happen."

"In this country, nobody ever knows what's going to happen," she said "Think about the 1950s, when the generals threw out Peron. They were far less bloody than the elected government had been. Think about that and tell me who knew."

"Alejo knew," I said. "Miguelito probably knew."

"Miguelito didn't even know how to make his own coffee," Amalia said sharply. Her tall body stiffened. Two thin, blue-veined hands came up out of her lap suddenly and pressed against her cheeks. She looked away from me, her mouth tightly closed, trying to avoid an argument.

"I appreciate your telling me what happened," I said.

"I'm telling you because someone has to tell you. I'm only sorry it has to be me," she said. "Everyone else in this family is living in a delirium. Here. Give me another cigarette, please."

As I was removing my gloves, taking out my pack and matches, and lighting one for her, she said, "Actually, I hate smoking. I do it because I grew up thinking smoking might make me more attractive to men. That's the way it was then, just look at the movies from that era. Men and women smoked first and then they kissed. Now look at how the world has changed."

She drew in one of her short, mouthy puffs, not really smoking so much as nervously playing with her cigarette. We sat for a long moment in silence.

"The best I can tell you is how the boys were, the last time I saw them," she continued. "A few days before Alejo disappeared, his mother got a message to him that he could meet me at a theater, so I could pass him some money, and some clothes and things. She couldn't do that herself for fear the death squads were watching the house. I got there and saw Alejo standing at the edge of the crowd in line to buy tickets. This was at the San Martin Theater, inside, in the lobby. Alejo didn't see me coming. I walked up next to him and touched his shoulder. I'll never forget the way he jumped. He turned and gave me such a frightened look. It's clear to me now. He must have known how close they were to catching him. Oh, he recovered, it took just a minute. You know Alejo, how he had such good spirits.

"I had bought us both tickets to the play that night, thinking how much he always liked to go to plays and movies. He was surprised that I had done that, and he thanked me, then said he couldn't. He had to be somewhere. We hugged and kissed in the lobby. I passed him a small tote bag with the money and things his mother had given me. He melted away into a line of people who were leaving the theater. I went in to see the play alone. But I didn't stay. That look he gave me when I touched him was as if I had poked him with the point of a knife. I told his mother about it. She and Martin were busy trying to make arrangements to get Alejo into exile. They were too late. Except for Martin Segundo, that was the last time anyone in the family saw him. Excuse me," she said.

Amalia began fumbling around in the pockets of her drab camp jacket for a handkerchief. Her mouth was trembling, her eyes watering. I thought she had started to cry. I fished around in my own pockets for tissues but couldn't find any. I picked a linen napkin off the table and held it out for her.

"It's all right," she said. She pulled a dainty lady's handkerchief from her pocket and waved it once at me in irritation. "I'm all right," she said again, sharply. "Call it allergies. It happens every time I come out to San Miguel. There's something out here that makes my nose start running. I turn into a mess."

She blew her nose and dried her eyes, turning away from me so I wouldn't see.

When she looked at me again, she had a hard expression on her face. Something in the set, unmoving wrinkles around her eyes and mouth, and her eyes that seemed now a darker shade of brown, made me think of Spanish widows who dressed in black for the funeral mass, resolved never to wear colors again for the rest of their lives.

"The case of Miguelito is different," Amalia said. "After he helped to shoot up the school, he went underground. He told his mother and father not to worry if they didn't hear from him. If anything bad happened to him, he didn't want them to know. This was shortly after Alejo disappeared. Miguel was a self-centered, uncaring boy, really, to say such a thing. Martin tried to stop him. He had everything in place to get the two sons he had left across the river and out of the country. The times Miguel did get in touch—oh, maybe once a month he would turn up out here on a weekend—the arguments the two had about saving him were terrible. Miguel grabbed some food and money and just took off for the train station. This went on for almost a year. . . .

"One night, Miguelito turned up at my apartment. It was late, almost midnight. He was soaking wet from a rain, and he was dragging his right leg. Of course, I let him in. He was wounded. I tried to put him on the couch, but he refused to lie down anywhere but on the kitchen door so he wouldn't get blood on anything. I tried to get his pants off but ended up cutting them off. He had several very deep wounds in his thigh, bleeding badly, and black at the edges like burns. I asked him what had happened. He said, 'I was just fooling around with some friends.' He laughed through his pain. He was doing everything to pretend it didn't hurt him. And why had he come to me? He knew I worked for a medical practice and had things in the house to give first aid.

"He tried to keep me from using the telephone, but I did. My friend Dr. Giezeman came over, the same doctor who had been with the Benevento family all the boys' lives. We put Miguel up on my dining room table, which I had prepared. Dr. Giezeman gave him local anesthetics. Then he worked for more than an hour taking pieces of shrapnel out of Miguelito's leg. When he finished, the boy looked about done for. He was so thin, and he hadn't shaved. His clothes were filthy. He smelled like he had been living in the subway.

"Dr. Giezeman bandaged him. Then he told Miguel that this was the last time he was going to treat him for anything. He wasn't going to waste his time sewing up anyone fool enough to play with hand grenades. I tried to reach Martin on the telephone but remembered the family had left to go out to San Miguel, partly in case Miguel might turn up out there again. In those days, they had the phone here disconnected for security reasons. Miguelito sat up on the table. He let himself down, and was already trying to walk on his wounded leg. Dr. Giezeman threw up his hands and told him he was impossible, he was going to rip through his stitches and start bleeding again. Miguel insisted that he had to go, walking or not. Dr. Giezeman gave some pain pills to him. Miguel didn't take them. He dropped the pills in his dirty T-shirt pocket. Then Dr. Giezeman went home.

"I tried to get Miguelito to spend the night at least, so he could get some rest and food. What was his hurry? When I saw he meant to leave anyway, I really got mad. 'Why can't you stop?' I shouted. 'What can you possibly gain now by gambling with your life?'

"Miguel just stood there, testing his leg. After my shouting at him, he was looking at me with this infuriating smirk. Then he asked me for his clothes. The doctor had made him take off most of his filthy clothes before he worked on the wounds. Miguel was in his underwear and a T-shirt. I found the rotten bundle of his clothes, opened the balcony window, and tossed them down six stories. I shouted that if he was planning to leave my apartment before his parents talked to him, he was going to have to do it naked. He laughed at that, and at me. Oh, how he laughed and laughed. It was a bitter, painful, terrible sound. 'Don't you know your father could have you on a boat to Uruguay by tomorrow?' I shouted. Miguel turned serious then. 'My parents can't do anything for me, and neither can you, because I'm not going. That's final,' he said. 'What kind of a hold do they have on you?' I asked. 'Are you afraid of someone? Or are you doing this for something so foolish as a feeling of loyalty?'

"He looked at me then with this terrible thing in his eyes. The pain in his leg was there, but that wasn't it. I still dream about that look sometimes and wake up with a shout. It was hatred, pure hatred, hatred of everything. I felt then all that he must have suffered, God knows, the way he had been living. 'I don't care anymore,' he said. 'I've made my decision. I'm going to keep fighting. Please, Amalita, go get some food I can take with me.'

"What could he possibly have been thinking? He would have thrown a coat over his underwear and walked out that way if I had let him. Don't ask me to explain, but there were some men's clothes in the apartment. They were too big for him, but he could still manage in them, and anything was better than the ones I had tossed out. I helped him into the clothes. I gave him one of my sweaters, which fit him. I started to fill the pockets of his coat with food. He stopped me. He took this big black pistol out of one of the pockets. He checked the pistol, cocked it, I think, then shoved it under his belt. It makes me shiver to think of it. Here he was hardly a man yet. That gun looked so big in his hands. It was like watching him as a boy, playing cops and robbers. You knew Miguel then. You knew how he always got into trouble. Maybe he would have been just as wild anywhere else in this world. In your country, he would probably have been in trouble with drugs. There he was, with that gun he carried. I could see he knew how to use it, and the most terrible thing was that he was proud of himself with it, just by the sure way he handled it I could see what he thought of himself. . . .

"But what was he fighting against? Over the years since it happened, I keep telling myself that whatever he ended up doing, no matter how many crimes, he must have started out feeling he was doing it for something good. Don't you see? All his life, he was the youngest, not as good at things as his brothers. He had trouble in school. He was always getting into trouble at home. He must have started off in the militancy thinking that now, yes, he was going to show everyone. He was going to be a guerrilla, a soldier, the best fighter of them all. And I think about what he had come to by that night. I think about that look he kept giving me, the one so filled with hatred. Only someone who has seen it knows what I mean. There's no other way to say it. It was the cold hard look of a killer. He had killed people. And he was going to leave my apartment that night so he could keep on killing.

"So, there it is. Am I saying he deserved to die? Maybe even the way he did? No.

I'm just telling you what I saw. I loved Miguelito. Maybe he was the one who needed my love the most and I hadn't given enough to him, or the right kind, when he was growing up, and then it was too late. That night, I emptied out all the money in my purse for him. I found my big black umbrella that he could use as a cane. I hugged and kissed him in the doorway. I sent him off into the night, praying to God to keep him safe. No one in this family ever saw him alive again.

"The next day, I took a train out here. I told his mother and father what had happened. Martin Segundo was with them. We were all upset, out of our minds with worry. Then the three of us ganged up on Martin Segundo and begged him to go into exile. He kept saying, 'Why me? Why would they be after me?' He had quit all his involvements since Alejo had disappeared, and enough time had gone by that he was starting to feel safe again. Can you believe it? He still didn't want to go. . . ."

"'Go!' We told him. 'Go! Go now! Go!' And that day, it worked. He finally said he would go. His mother and father had him packed up and ready in about thirty minutes. You know the story. He was sent across the river to Uruguay that evening, in a tourist boat, under a false name. Later, arrangements were made for him in Rio, and then he was able to get to France and he was safe.

"You said before that you don't believe that nobody knew. I'm telling you that we didn't know, or at least not what it meant, that young people were being tortured and disappeared. It was just too unimaginable for us that here, in Argentina, there were concentration camps. The day Martin Segundo went into exile, we even believed there was a good chance Alejo was still alive, maybe in some kind of secret prison. Or it might be that he had been hurt so badly he didn't know who he was. He was being taken care of in some hospital until this nightmare was over and we could find him. We talked about the wildest ideas, still looking for some hope.

"And just you consider the way Martin was thinking. He should have known better than any of us. Still, he had the idea that the death squads would leave him alone. Does that sound to you like someone who knew what was going on? I'm telling you. Nobody knew. Or nobody really knew. I'm just grateful for the rest of my life to Martin that he made his decision. We can all thank God that at least one of them had enough good sense to save himself and escape."

newborn thrown in trash and dies

John Edgar Wideman

They say you see your whole life pass in review the instant before you die. How would *they* know. If you die after the instant replay, you aren't around to tell anybody anything. So much for they and what they say. So much for the wish to be a movie star for once in your life because I think that's what people are hoping, what people are pretending when they say you see your life that way at the end. Death doesn't turn your life into a five-star production. The end is the end. And what you know at the end goes down the tube with you. I can speak to you now only because I haven't reached bottom yet. I'm on my way, faster than I want to be traveling and my journey won't take long, but I'm just beginning the countdown to zero. Zero's where I started also so I know a little bit about zero. Know what they say isn't necessarily so. In fact the opposite's true. You begin and right in the eye of that instant storm your life plays itself out for you in advance. That's the theater of your fate, there's where you're granted a preview, the coming attractions of everything that must happen to you. Your life rolled into a ball so dense, so superheavy it would drag the universe down to hell if this tiny, tiny lump of whatever didn't dissipate as quickly as it formed. Quicker. The weight of it is what you recall some infinitesimal fraction of when you stumble and crawl through your worst days on earth.

Knowledge of what's coming gone as quickly as it flashes forth. Quicker. Faster. Gone before it gets here, so to speak. Any other way and nobody would stick around to play out the cards they're dealt. No future in it. You begin forgetting before the zero's entirely wiped off the clock face, before the next digit materializes. What they say is assbackwards, a saying by the way, assbackwards itself. Whether or not you're treated to a summary at the end, you get the whole thing handed to you, neatly packaged as you begin. Then you forget it. Or try to forget. Live your life as if it hasn't happened before, as if the tape has not been pre-punched full of holes, the die cast.

I remember because I won't receive much of a life. A measure of justice in the world, after all. I receive a compensatory bonus. Since the time between my wake-up call and curfew is so cruelly brief, the speeded-up preview of what will come to pass, my life, my portion, my destiny, my career, slowed down just enough to let me peek. Not slow enough for me to steal much, but I know some of what it contains, its finality, the groaning, fatal weight of it around my neck.

Call it a trade-off. A standoff. Intensity for duration. I won't get much and this devastating flash isn't much either, but I get it. Zingo.

But the future remains mysterious. Even if we all put our heads together and became one gigantic brain, a brain lots smarter than the sum of each of our smarts, an intelligence as great as the one that guides ants, whales or birds, because they're smarter, they figure things out not one by one, each individual locked in the cell of its head, its mortality, but collectively, doing what the group needs to do to survive, relate to the planet. If we were smarter even than birds and bees, we'd still have only a clue about what's inside the first flash of being. I know it happened and that I receive help from it. Scattered help. Sometimes I catch on. Sometimes I don't. But stuff from it's being pumped out always. I know things I have no business knowing. Things I haven't been around long enough to learn myself. For instance, many languages. A vast palette of feelings. The names of unseen things. Nostalgia for a darkness I've never experienced, a darkness another sense I can't account for assures me I will enter again. Large matters. Small ones. Naked as I am I'm dressed so to speak for my trip. Down these ten swift flights to oblivion.

Floor Ten. Nothing under the sun, they say, is new. This time they're right. They never stop talking so percentages guarantee they'll be correct sometimes. Especially since they speak out of both sides of their mouths at once: *Birds of a feather flock together. Opposites attract.* Like the billion billion monkeys at typewriters who sooner or later will bang out this story I think is uniquely mine. Somebody else, a Russian, I believe, with a long, strange-sounding name, has already written about his life speeding past as he topples slow-motion from a window high up in a tall apartment building. But it was in another country. And alas, the Russian's dead.

Floor Nine. In this building they shoot craps. One of many forms of gambling proliferating here. Very little new wealth enters this cluster of buildings that are like high-rise covered wagons circled against the urban night, so what's here is cycled and recycled by games of chance, by murder and other violent forms of exchange. Kids do it. Adults. Birds and bees. The law here is the same one ruling the jungle, they say. They say this is a jungle of the urban asphalt concrete variety. Since I've never been to Africa or the Amazon I can't agree or disagree. But you know what I think about what they say.

Seven come eleven. Snake eyes. Boxcars. Fever in the funkhouse searching for a five. Talk to me, baby. Talk. Talk. Please. Please. Please.

They cry and sing and curse and pray all night long over these games. On one knee they chant magic formulas to summon luck. They forget luck is rigged. Some of the men carry a game called Three Card Monte downtown. They cheat tourists who are stupid enough to trust in luck. Showmen with quick hands shuffling cards to a blur, fast feet carrying them away from busy intersections when cops come to break up their scam or hit on them for a cut. Flimflam artists, con men who daily use luck as bait and hook, down on their knees in a circle of other men who also should know better, trying to sweet-talk luck into their beds. Luck is the card you wish for, the card somebody else holds. You learn luck by its absence. Luck is what separates you from what you want. Luck is always turning its back and you lose.

Like other potions and powders they sell and consume here luck creates dependency. In their rooms people sit and wait for a hit. A yearning unto death for more, more, more till the little life they've been allotted dies in a basket on the doorstep where they abandoned it.

The Floor of Facts. Seventeen stories in this building. The address is 2950 West 23rd Street. My mother is nineteen years old. The trash chute down which I was dropped is forty-five feet from the door of the apartment my mother was visiting. I was born and will die Monday, August 12, 1991. The small door in the yellow cinder block wall is maroon. I won't know till the last second why my mother pushes it open. In 1990 nine discarded babies were discovered in New York City's garbage. As of August this year seven have been found. 911 is the number to call if you find a baby in the trash. Ernesto Mendez, forty-four, a Housing Authority caretaker, will notice my head, shoulders and curly hair in a black plastic bag he slashes open near the square entrance of the trash compactor on the ground floor of this brown-brick public housing project called the Gerald J. Carey Gardens. Gardens are green places where seeds are planted, tended, nurtured. The headline above my story reads "Newborn Is Thrown in Trash and Dies." The headline will remind some readers of a similar story with a happy ending that appeared in March. A baby rescued and surviving after she was dropped down a trash chute by her twelve-year old mother. The reporter, a Mr. George James who recorded many of the above facts, introduced my unhappy story in the Metro Section of the *New York Times* on Wednesday, August 14, with this paragraph: "A young Brooklyn woman gave birth on Monday afternoon in a stairwell in a Coney Island housing project and then dropped the infant down a trash chute into a compactor ten stories below, the police said yesterday." And that's about it. What's fit to print. My tale in a nutshell followed by a relation of facts obtained by interview and reading official documents. Trouble is I could not be reached for comment. No one's fault. Certainly no negligence on the reporter's part. He gave me sufficient notoriety. Many readers must have shaken their heads in dismay or sighed or blurted Jesus Christ, did you see this, handing the Metro Section across the breakfast table or passing it to somebody at work. As grateful as I am to have my story made public you should be able to understand why I feel cheated, why the newspaper account is not enough, why I want my voice to be part of the record. The awful silence is not truly broken until we speak for ourselves. One chance to speak was snatched away. Then I didn't cry out as I plunged through the darkness. I didn't know any better. Too busy thinking to myself, *This is how it is, this is how it is, how it is . . .* accustoming myself to what it seemed life brings, what life is. Spinning, tumbling, a breathless rush, terror, exhilaration and wonder, wondering is this it, am I doing it right. I didn't know any better. The floors, the other lives packed into this building were going on their merry way as I flew past them in the darkness of my tunnel. No one waved. No one warned me. Said hello or good-bye. And of course I was too busy flailing, trying to catch my breath, trying to stop shivering in the sudden, icy air, welcoming almost the thick, pungent draft rushing up at me as if another pair of thighs were opening below to replace the ones from which I'd been ripped.

In the quiet dark of my passage I did not cry out. Now I will not be still.

A Floor of Questions. Why.

A Floor of Opinions. I believe the floor of fact should have been the ground floor, the foundation, the solid start, the place where all else is firmly rooted. I believe there should be room on the floor of fact for what I believe, for this opinion and others I could not venture before arriving here. I believe some facts are unnecessary and that unnecessary borders on untrue. I believe facts sometimes speak for themselves but never speak for us. They are never anyone's voice and voices are what we must learn to listen to if we wish ever to be heard. I believe my mother did not hate me. I believe somewhere I have a father, who if he is reading this and listening carefully will recognize me as his daughter and be ashamed, heartbroken. I must believe these things. What else do I have. Who has made my acquaintance or noticed or cared or forgotten me. How could anyone be aware of what hurtles by faster than light, blackly, in a dark space beyond the walls of the rooms they live in, beyond the doors they lock, shades they draw when they have rooms and the rooms have windows and the windows have shades and the people believe they possess something worth concealing.

In my opinion my death will serve no purpose. The streetlamps will pop on. Someone will be run over by an expensive car in a narrow street and the driver will hear a bump but consider it of no consequence. Junkies will leak out the side doors of this gigantic mound, nodding, buzzing, greeting their kind with hippy-dip vocalizations full of despair and irony and stylized to embrace the very best that's being sung, played and said around them. A young woman will open a dresser drawer and wonder whose baby that is sleeping peaceful on a bed of dishtowels, T-shirts, a man's ribbed sweat socks. She will feel something slither through the mud of her belly and splash into the sluggish river that meanders through her. She hasn't eaten for days, so that isn't it. Was it a deadly disease. Or worse, some new life she must account for. She opens and shuts the baby's drawer, pushes and pulls, opens and shuts.

I believe all floors are not equally interesting. Less reason to notice some than others. Equality would become boring, predictable. Though we may slight some and rattle on about others, that does not change the fact that each floor exists and the life on it is real, whether we pause to notice or not. As I gather speed and weight during my plunge, each floor adds its share. When I hit bottom I will bear witness to the truth of each one.

Floor of Wishes. I will miss Christmas. They say no one likes being born on Christmas. You lose your birthday, they say. A celebration already on December 25 and nice things happen to everyone on that day anyway, you give and receive presents, people greet you smiling and wish you peace and goodwill. The world is decorated. Colored bulbs draped twinkling in windows and trees, doorways hung with wild berries beneath which you may kiss a handsome stranger. Music everywhere. Even wars truced for twenty-four hours and troops served home-cooked meals, almost. Instead of at least two special days a year, if your birthday falls on Christmas, you lose one. Since my portion's less than a day, less than those insects called ephemera receive, born one morning dead the next, and I can't squeeze a complete life cycle as they do into the time allotted, I wish today were Christmas. Once would be enough. If it's as special as they say. And in some matters we yearn to trust them. Need to trust something, someone, so we listen, wish what they say is true. The holiday of Christmas seems to be the best time to be on earth, to be a child and awaken with your eyes full of dreams and expectations and believe for a while at least that all good things are possible—peace, goodwill, love, merriment, the raven-maned rocking horse you want to ride forever. No conflict of interest for me. I wouldn't lose a birthday to Christmas. Rather than this smoggy heat I wish I could see snow. The city, this building snug under a blanket of fresh snow. No footprints of men running, men on their knees, men bleeding. No women forced out into halls and streets, away from their children. I wish this city, this tower were stranded in a gentle snowstorm and Christmas happens day after day and the bright fires in every hearth never go out, and the carols ring true chorus after chorus, and the gifts given and received precipitate endless joys. The world trapped in Christmas for a day dancing on forever. I wish I could transform the ten flights of my falling into those twelve days in the Christmas song. *On the first day of Christmas my true love said to me . . . angels, a partridge in a pear tree, ten maids a milking, five gold rings, two turtledoves.* I wish those would be the sights greeting me instead of darkness, the icy winter heart of this August afternoon I have been pitched without a kiss through a maroon door.

Floor of Power. El Presidente inhabits this floor. Some say he owns the whole building. He believes he owns it, collects rent, treats the building and its occupants with contempt. He is a bold-faced man. Cheeks slotted nose to chin like a puppet's. Chicken lips. This floor is entirely white. A floury, cracked white some say used to gleam. El Presidente is white also. Except for the pink dome of his forehead. Once, long ago, his flesh was pink head to toe. Then he painted himself white to match the white floor of power. Paint ran out just after the brush stroke that permanently sealed his eyes. Since El Presidente is cheap and mean he refused to order more paint. Since El Presidente is vain and arrogant he pretended to look at his unfinished self in the mirror and proclaimed he liked what he saw, the coat of cakey white, the raw, pink dome pulsing like a bruise.

El Presidente often performs on TV. We can watch him jog, golf, fish, travel, lie, preen, mutilate the language. But these activities are not his job; his job is keeping things in the building as they are, squatting on the floor of power like a broken generator or broken furnace or broken heart, occupying the space where one that works should be.

Floor of Regrets. One thing bothers me a lot. I regret not knowing what is on the floors above the one where I began my fall. I hope it's better up there. Real gardens perhaps or even a kind of heaven for the occupants lucky enough to live above the floors I've seen. Would one of you please mount the stairs, climb slowly up from floor ten, examine carefully, one soft, warm night, the topmost floors and sing me a lullaby of what I missed.

Floor of Love. I'm supposed to be sleeping. I could be sleeping. Early morning and my eyes don't want to open and legs don't want to push me out of bed yet. Two rooms away I can hear Mom in the kitchen. She's fixing breakfast. Daddy first, then I will slump into the kitchen Mom has made bright and smelling good already this

332

morning. Her perkiness, the sizzling bacon, water boiling, wheat bread popping up like jack-in-the-box from the shiny toaster, the Rice Krispies crackling, fried eggs hissing, the FM's sophisticated patter and mincing string trios would wake the dead. And it does. Me and Daddy slide into our places. Hi, Mom. Good morning, Dearheart. The day begins. Smells wonderful. I awaken now to his hand under the covers with me, rubbing the baby fat of my tummy where he's shoved my nightgown up past my panties. He says I shouldn't wear them. Says it ain't healthy to sleep in your drawers. Says no wonder you get those rashes. He rubs and pinches. Little nips. Then the flat of his big hand under the elastic waistband wedges my underwear down. I raise my hips a little bit to help. No reason not to. The whole thing be over with sooner. Don't do no good to try and stop him or slow him down. He said my Mama knows. He said go on fool and tell her she'll smack you for talking nasty. He was right. She beat me in the kitchen. Then took me in to their room and he stripped me butt-naked and beat me again while she watched. So I kinda hump up, wiggle, and my underwear's down below my knees, his hand's on its way back up to where I don't even understand how to grow hairs yet.

The Floor That Stands for All the Other Floors Missed or Still to Come. My stepbrother Tommy was playing in the schoolyard and they shot him dead. Bang. Bang. Gang banging and poor Tommy caught a cap in his chest. People been in and out the apartment all day. Sorry. Sorry. Everybody's so sorry. Some brought cakes, pies, macaroni casseroles, lunch meat, liquor. Two Ebony Cobras laid a joint on Tommy's older brother who hadn't risen from the kitchen chair he's straddling, head down, nodding, till his boys bop through the door. They know who hit Tommy. They know tomorrow what they must do. Today one of those everybody-in-the-family-and-friends-in-darkclothes-funeral days, the mothers, sisters, aunts, grandmothers weepy, the men motherfucking everybody from god on down. You can't see me among the mourners. My time is different from this time. You can't understand my time. Or name it. Or share it. Tommy is beginning to remember me. To join me where I am falling unseen through your veins and arteries down down to where the heart stops, the square opening through which trash passes to the compactor.

The Liar

Tobias Wolff

y mother read everything except books. Advertisements on buses, entire menus as we ate, billboards; if it had no cover it interested her. So when she found a letter in my drawer that was not addressed to her she read it. "What difference does it make if James has nothing to hide?"—that was her thought. She stuffed the letter in the drawer when she finished it and walked from room to room in the big empty house, talking to herself. She took the letter out and read it again to get the facts straight. Then, without putting on her coat or locking the door, she went down the steps and headed for the church at the end of the street. No matter how angry and confused she might be, she always went to four o'clock Mass and now it was four o'clock.

It was a fine day, blue and cold and still, but Mother walked as though into a strong wind, bent forward at the waist with her feet hurrying behind in short, busy steps. My brother and sisters and I considered this walk of hers funny and we smirked at one another when she crossed in front of us to stir the fire, or water a plant. We didn't let her catch us at it. It would have puzzled her to think that there might be anything amusing about her. Her one concession to the fact of humor was an insincere, startling laugh. Strangers often stared at her.

While Mother waited for the priest, who was late, she prayed. She prayed in a familiar, orderly, firm way: first for her late husband, my father, then for her parents—also dead. She said a quick prayer for my father's parents (just touching base; she had disliked them) and finally for her children in order of their ages, ending with me. Mother did not consider originality a virtue and until my name came up her prayers were exactly the same as on any other day.

But when she came to me she spoke up boldly. "I thought he wasn't going to do it anymore. Murphy said he was cured. What am I supposed to do now?" There was reproach in her tone. Mother put great hope in her notion that I was cured. She regarded my cure as an answer to her prayers and by way of thanksgiving sent a lot of money to the Thomasite Indian Mission, money she had been saving for a trip to Rome. She felt cheated and she let her feelings be known. When the priest came in, Mother slid back on the seat and followed the Mass with concentration. After communion she began to worry again and went straight home without stopping to talk to Frances, the woman who always cornered Mother after Mass to tell about the awful things done to her by Communists, devil worshipers, and Rosicrucians. Frances watched her go with narrowed eyes.

Once in the house, Mother took the letter from my drawer and brought it into the kitchen. She held it over the stove with her fingernails, looking away so that she would not be drawn into it again, and set it on fire. When it began to burn her fingers, she dropped it in the sink and watched it blacken and flutter and close upon itself like a fist. Then she washed it down the drain and called Dr. Murphy.

The letter was to my friend Ralphy in Arizona. He used to live across the street from us but he had moved. Most of the letter was about a tour we, the junior class, had taken of Alcatraz. That was all right. What got Mother was the last paragraph where I said that she had been coughing up blood and the doctors weren't sure what was wrong with her, but that we were hoping for the best.

This wasn't true. Mother took pride in her physical condition, considered herself a horse: "I'm a regular horse," she would reply when people asked about her health. For several years now I had been saying unpleasant things that weren't true and this habit of mine irked Mother greatly, enough to persuade her to send me to Dr. Murphy, in whose office I was sitting when she burned the letter. Dr. Murphy was our family physician and had no training in psychoanalysis but he took an interest in "things of the mind," as he put it. He had treated me for appendicitis and tonsillitis and Mother thought that he could put the truth into me as easily as he took things out of me, a hope Dr. Murphy did not share. He was basically interested in getting me to understand what I did, and lately he had been moving toward the conclusion that I understood what I did as well as I ever would.

Dr. Murphy listened to Mother's account of the letter, and what she had done with it. He was curious about the wording I had used and became irritated when Mother told him she had burned it. "The point is," she said, "he was supposed to be cured and he's not."

"Margaret, I never said he was cured."

"You certainly did. Why else would I have sent over a thousand dollars to the Thomasite Mission?"

"I said that he was responsible. That means that James knows what he's doing, not that he's going to stop doing it."

"I'm sure you said he was cured."

"Never. To say that someone is cured you have to know what health is. With this kind of thing that's impossible. What do you mean by curing James, anyway?"

"You know."

"Tell me anyway."

"Getting him back to reality, what else?"

"Whose reality? Mine or yours?"

"Murphy, what are you talking about? James isn't crazy, he's a liar."

"Well, you have a point there."

"What am I going to do with him?"

"I don't think there's much you can do. Be patient."

"I've been patient."

"If I were you, Margaret, I wouldn't make too much of this. James doesn't steal, does he?"

"Of course not."

"Or beat people up or talk back."

"No."

"Then you have a lot to be thankful for."

"I don't think I can take any more of it. That business about leukemia last summer. And now this."

"Eventually he'll outgrow it, I think."

"Murphy, he's sixteen years old. What if he doesn't outgrow it? What if he just gets better at it?"

Finally Mother saw that she wasn't going to get any satisfaction from Dr. Murphy, who kept reminding her of her blessings. She said something cutting to him and he said something pompous back and she hung up. Dr. Murphy stared at the receiver. "Hello," he said, then replaced it on the cradle. He ran his hand over his head, a habit remaining from a time when he had hair. To show that he was a good sport he often joked about his baldness, but I had the feeling that he regretted it deeply. Looking at me across the desk, he must have wished that he hadn't taken me on. Treating a friend's child was like investing a friend's money.

"I don't have to tell you who that was."

I nodded.

Dr. Murphy pushed his chair back and swiveled it around so he could look out the window behind him, which took up most of the wall. There were still a few sailboats out on the Bay, but they were all making for shore. A woolly gray fog had covered the bridge and was moving in fast. The water seemed calm from this far up, but when I looked closely I could see white flecks everywhere, so it must have been pretty choppy.

"I'm surprised at you," he said. "Leaving something like that lying around for her to find. If you really have to do these things you could at least be kind and do them discreetly. It's not easy for your mother, what with your father dead and all the others somewhere else."

"I know. I didn't mean for her to find it."

"Well." He tapped his pencil against his teeth. He was not convinced professionally, but personally he may have been. "I think you ought to go home now and straighten things out."

"I guess I'd better."

"Tell your mother I might stop by, either tonight or tomorrow. And James—don't underestimate her."

While my father was alive we usually went to Yosemite for three or four days during the summer. My mother would drive and Father would point out places of interest, meadows where boom towns once stood, hanging trees, rivers that were said to flow upstream at certain times. Or he read to us; he had that grown-ups' idea that children love Dickens and Sir Walter Scott. The four of us sat in the backseat with our faces composed, attentive, while our hands and feet pushed, pinched, stomped, goosed, prodded, dug, and kicked.

One night a bear came into our camp just after dinner. Mother had made a tuna casserole and it must have smelled to him like something worth dying for. He came into the camp while we were sitting around the fire and stood swaying back and forth.

My brother Michael saw him first and elbowed me, then my sisters saw him and screamed. Mother and Father had their backs to him but Mother must have guessed what it was because she immediately said, "Don't scream like that. You might frighten him and there's no telling what he'll do. We'll just sing and he'll go away."

We sang "Row Row Row Your Boat" but the bear stayed. He circled us several times, rearing up now and then on his hind legs to stick his nose into the air. By the light of the fire I could see his doglike face and watch the muscles roll under his loose skin like rocks in a sack. We sang harder as he circled us, coming closer and closer. "All right," Mother said, "enough's enough." She stood abruptly. The bear stopped moving and watched her. "Beat it," Mother said. The bear sat down and looked from side to side. "Beat it," she said again, and leaned over and picked up a rock.

"Margaret, don't," my father said.

She threw the rock hard and hit the bear in the stomach. Even in the dim light I could see the dust rising from his fur. He grunted and stood to his full height. "See that?" Mother shouted: "He's filthy. filthy!" One of my sisters giggled. Mother picked up another rock. "Please, Margaret," my father said. Just then the bear turned and shambled away. Mother pitched the rock after him. For the rest of the night he loitered around the camp until he found the tree where we had hung our food. He ate it all. The next day we drove back to the city. We could have bought more supplies in the valley, but Father wanted to go and would not give in to any argument. On the way home he tried to jolly everyone up by making jokes, but Michael and my sisters ignored him and looked stonily out the windows.

Things were never easy between my mother and me, but I didn't underestimate her. She underestimated me. When I was little she suspected me of delicacy, because I didn't like being thrown into the air, and because when I saw her and the others working themselves up for a roughhouse I found somewhere else to be. When they did drag me in I got hurt, a knee in the lip, a bent finger, a bloody nose, and this too Mother seemed to hold against me, as if I arranged my hurts to get out of playing.

Even things I did well got on her nerves. We all loved puns except Mother, who didn't get them, and next to my father I was the best in the family. My specialty was the Swifty—"'You can bring the prisoner down,' said Tom condescendingly." Father encouraged me to perform at dinner, which must have been a trial for outsiders. Mother wasn't sure what was going on, but she didn't like it.

She suspected me in other ways. I couldn't go to the movies without her examining my pockets to make sure I had enough money to pay for the ticket. When I went away to camp she tore my pack apart in front of all the boys who were waiting in the bus outside the house. I would rather have gone without my sleeping bag and a few changes of underwear, which I had forgotten, than be made such a fool of. Her distrust was the thing that made me forgetful.

And she thought I was cold-hearted because of what happened the day my father died and later at his funeral. I didn't cry at my father's funeral, and showed signs of boredom during the eulogy, fiddling around with the hymnals. Mother put my hands into my lap and I left them there without moving them as though they were things I was holding for someone else. The effect was ironical and she resented it. We had a sort of reconciliation a few days later after I closed my eyes at school and refused to open them. When several teachers and then the principal failed to persuade me to look at them, or at some reward they claimed to be holding, I was handed over to the school nurse, who tried to pry the lids open and scratched one of them badly. My eye swelled up and I went rigid. The principal panicked and called Mother, who fetched me home. I wouldn't talk to her, or open my eyes, or bend, and they had to lay me on the backseat and when we reached the house Mother had to lift me up the steps one at a time. Then she put me on the couch and played the piano to me all afternoon. Finally I opened my eyes. We hugged each other and I wept. Mother did not really believe my tears, but she was willing to accept them because I had staged them for her benefit.

My lying separated us, too, and the fact that my promises not to lie anymore seemed to mean nothing to me. Often my lies came back to her in embarrassing ways, people stopping her in the street and saying how sorry they were to hear that _____. No one in the neighborhood enjoyed embarrassing Mother, and these situations stopped occurring once everybody got wise to me. There was no saving her from strangers, though. The summer after Father died I visited my uncle in Redding and when I got back I found to my surprise that Mother had come to meet my bus. I tried to slip away from the gentleman who had sat next to me but I couldn't shake him. When he saw Mother embrace me he came up and presented her with a card and told her to get in touch with him if things got any worse. She gave him his card back and told him to mind his own business. Later, on the way home, she made me repeat what I had said to the man. She shook her head. "It's not fair to people," she said, "telling them things like that. It confuses them." It seemed to me that Mother had confused the man, not I, but I didn't say so. I agreed with her that I shouldn't say such things and promised not to do it again, a promise I broke three hours later in conversation with a woman in the park.

It wasn't only the lies that disturbed Mother; it was their morbidity. This was the real issue between us, as it had been between her and my father. Mother did volunteer work at Children's Hospital and St. Anthony's Dining Hall, collected things for the St. Vincent de Paul Society. She was a lighter of candles. My brother and sisters took after her in this way. My father was a curser of the dark. And he loved to curse the dark. He was never more alive than when he was indignant about something. For this reason the most important act of the day for him was the reading of the evening paper.

Ours was a terrible paper, indifferent to the city that bought it, indifferent to medical discoveries—except for new kinds of gases that made your hands fall off when you sneezed—and indifferent to politics and art. Its business was outrage, horror, gruesome coincidence. When my father sat down in the living room with the paper Mother stayed in the kitchen and kept the children busy, all except me, because I was quiet and could be trusted to amuse myself I amused myself by watching my father.

He sat with his knees spread, leaning forward, his eyes only inches from the

338

print. As he read he nodded to himself. Sometimes he swore and threw the paper down and paced the room, then picked it up and began again. Over a period of time he developed the habit of reading aloud to me. He always started with the society section, which he called the parasite page. This column began to take on the character of a comic strip or a serial, with the same people showing up from one day to the next, blinking in chiffon, awkwardly holding their drinks for the sake of Peninsula orphans, grinning under sunglasses on the deck of a ski hut in the Sierras. The skiers really got his goat, probably because he couldn't understand them. The activity itself was inconceivable to him. When my sisters went to Lake Tahoe one winter weekend with some friends and came back excited about the beauty of the place, Father calmed them right down. "Snow," he said, "is overrated."

Then the news, or what passed in the paper for news: bodies unearthed in Scotland, former Nazis winning elections, rare animals slaughtered, misers expiring naked in freezing houses upon mattresses stuffed with thousands, millions; marrying priests, divorcing actresses, high-rolling oilmen building fantastic mausoleums in honor of a favorite horse, cannibalism. Through all this my father waded with a fixed and weary smile.

Mother encouraged him to take up causes, to join groups, but he would not. He was uncomfortable with people outside the family. He and my mother rarely went out, and rarely had people in, except on feast days and national holidays. Their guests were always the same, Dr. Murphy and his wife and several others whom they had known since childhood. Most of these people never saw each other outside our house and they didn't have much fun together. Father discharged his obligations as host by teasing everyone about stupid things they had said or done in the past and forcing them to laugh at themselves.

Though Father did not drink, he insisted on mixing cocktails for the guests. He would not serve straight drinks like rum-and-Coke or even Scotch-on-the-rocks, only drinks of his own devising. He gave them lawyerly names like "The Advocate," "The Hanging Judge," "The Ambulance Chaser," "The Mouthpiece," and described their concoction in detail. He told long, complicated stories in a near-whisper, making everyone lean in his direction, and repeated important lines; he also repeated the important lines in the stories my mother told, and corrected her when she got something wrong. When the guests came to the ends of their own stories, he would point out the morals.

Dr. Murphy had several theories about Father, which he used to test on me in the course of our meetings. Dr. Murphy had by this time given up his glasses for contact lenses, and lost weight in the course of fasts which he undertook regularly. Even with his baldness he looked years younger than when he had come to the parties at our house. Certainly he did not look like my father's contemporary, which he was.

One of Dr. Murphy's theories was that Father had exhibited a classic trait of people who had been gifted children by taking an undemanding position in an uninteresting firm. "He was afraid of finding his limits," Dr. Murphy told me: "As long as he kept stamping papers and making out wills he could go on believing that he didn't *have* limits." Dr. Murphy's fascination with Father made me uneasy, and I felt traitorous listening to him. While he lived, my father would never have submitted himself for analysis; it seemed a betrayal to put him on the couch now that he was dead.

I did enjoy Dr. Murphy's recollections of Father as a child. He told me about something that happened when they were in the Boy Scouts. Their troop had been on a long hike and Father had fallen behind. Dr. Murphy and the others decided to ambush him as he came down the trail. They hid in the woods on each side and waited. But when Father walked into the trap none of them moved or made a sound and he strolled on without even knowing they were there. "He had the sweetest look on his face," Dr. Murphy said, "listening to the birds, smelling the flowers, just like Ferdinand the Bull." He also told me that my father's drinks tasted like medicine.

While I rode my bicycle home from Dr. Murphy's office, Mother fretted. She felt terribly alone but she didn't call anyone because she also felt like a failure. My lying had that effect on her. She took it personally. At such times she did not think of my sisters, one happily married, the other doing brilliantly at Fordham. She did not think of my brother Michael, who had given up college to work with runaway children in Los Angeles. She thought of me. She thought that she had made a mess of her family.

Actually she managed the family well. While my father was dying upstairs, she pulled us together. She made lists of chores and gave each of us a fair allowance. Bedtimes were adjusted and she stuck by them. She set regular hours for homework. Each child was made responsible for the next eldest, and I was given a dog. She told us frequently, predictably, that she loved us. At dinner we were each expected to contribute something, and after dinner she played the piano and tried to teach us to sing in harmony, which I could not do. Mother, who was an admirer of the Trapp family, considered this a character defect.

Our life together was more orderly, healthy, while Father was dying than it had been before. He had set us rules to follow, not much different really than the ones Mother gave us after he got sick, but he had administered them in a fickle way. Though we were supposed to get an allowance we always had to ask him for it and then he would give us too much because he enjoyed seeming magnanimous. Sometimes he punished us for no reason, because he was in a bad mood. He was apt to decide, as one of my sisters was going out to a dance, that she had better stay home and do something to improve herself. Or he would sweep us all up on a Wednesday night and take us ice-skating.

He changed after he learned about the cancer, and became more calm as the disease spread. He relaxed his teasing way with us, and from time to time it was possible to have a conversation with him which was not about the last thing that had made him angry. He stopped reading the paper and spent time at the window.

He and I became close. He taught me to play poker and sometimes helped me with my homework. But it wasn't his illness that drew us together. The reserve between us had begun to break down after the incident with the bear, during the drive home. Michael and my sisters were furious with him for making us leave early and wouldn't talk to him or look at him. He joked: though it had been a grisly experience we should grin and—bear it—and so on. His joking seemed perverse to the others, but not to me. I had seen how terrified he was when the bear came into the camp. He had held himself so still that he had begun to tremble. When Mother started pitching rocks, I thought he was going to bolt, really. I understood—I had been frightened too. The others took it as a lark after they got used to having the bear around, but for Father and me it got worse through the night. I was glad to be out of there, grateful to father for getting me out. I saw that his jokes were how he held himself together. So I reached out to him with a joke: "'There's a bear outside,' said Tom intently." The others turned cold looks on me. They thought I was sucking up. But Father smiled.

When I thought of other boys being close to their fathers I thought of them hunting together, tossing a ball back and forth, making birdhouses in the basement, and having long talks about girls, war, careers. Maybe the reason it took us so long to get close was that I had this idea. It kept getting in the way of what we really had, which was a shared fear.

Toward the end Father slept most of the time and I watched him. From below, sometimes, faintly, I heard Mother playing the piano. Occasionally he nodded off in his chair while I was reading to him; his bathrobe would fall open then, and I would see the long new scar on his stomach, red as blood against his white skin. His ribs all showed and his legs were like cables.

I once read in a biography of a great man that he "died well." I assume the writer meant that he kept his pain to himself, did not set off false alarms, and did not too much inconvenience those who were to stay behind. My father died well. His irritability gave way to something else, something like serenity. In the last days he became tender. It was as though he had been rehearsing the scene, that the anger of his life had been a kind of stage fright. He managed his audience—us—with an old trouper's sense of when to clown and when to stand on his dignity. We were all moved, and admired his courage, as he intended we should. He died downstairs in a shaft of late afternoon sunlight on New Year's Day, while I was reading to him. I was alone in the house and didn't know what to do. His body did not frighten me but immediately and sharply I missed my father. It seemed wrong to leave him sitting up and I tried to carry him upstairs to the bedroom but it was too hard, alone. So I called up my friend Ralphy across the street. When he came over and saw what I wanted him for he started crying but I made him help me anyway. A couple of hours later Mother got home and when I told her that Father was dead she ran upstairs, calling his name. A few minutes later she came back down. "Thank God," she said, "at least he died in bed." This seemed important to her and I didn't tell her otherwise. But that night Ralphy's parents called. They were, they said, shocked at what I had done and so was Mother when she heard the story, shocked and furious. Why? Because I had not told her the truth? Or because she had learned the truth, and could not go on believing that Father had died in bed? I really don't know.

"Mother," I said, coming into the living room, "I'm sorry about the letter. I really am."

She was arranging wood in the fireplace and did not look at me or speak for a moment. Finally she finished and straightened up and brushed her hands. She stepped back and looked at the fire she had laid. "That's all right," she said. "Not bad for a consumptive."

"Mother, I'm sorry."

"Sorry? Sorry you wrote it or sorry I found it?"

"I wasn't going to mail it. It was a sort of joke."

"Ha ha." She took up the whisk broom and swept bits of bark into the fireplace, then closed the drapes and settled on the couch. "Sit down," she said. She crossed her legs. "Listen, do I give you advice all the time?"

"Yes."

"I do?"

I nodded.

"Well, that doesn't make any difference. I'm supposed to. I'm your mother. I'm going to give you some more advice, for your own good. You don't have to make all these things up, James. They'll happen anyway." She picked at the hem of her skirt. "Do you understand what I'm saying?"

"I think so."

"You're cheating yourself, that's what I'm trying to tell you. When you get to be my age, you won't know anything at all about life. All you'll know is what you've made up."

I thought about that. It seemed logical.

She went on. "I think maybe you need to get out of yourself more. Think more about other people."

The doorbell rang.

"Go see who it is," Mother said. "We'll talk about this later."

It was Dr. Murphy. He and Mother made their apologies and she insisted that he stay for dinner. I went to the kitchen to fetch ice for their drinks, and when I returned they were talking about me. I sat on the sofa and listened. Dr. Murphy was telling Mother not to worry. "James is a good boy," he said. "I've been thinking about my oldest, Terry. He's not really dishonest, you know, but he's not really honest either. I can't seem to reach him. At least James isn't furtive."

"No," Mother said, "he's never been furtive."

Dr. Murphy clasped his hands between his knees and stared at them. "Well, that's Terry. Furtive."

Before we sat down to dinner Mother said grace; Dr. Murphy bowed his head and closed his eyes and crossed himself at the end, though he had lost his faith in college. When he told me that, during one of our meetings, in just those words, I had the picture of a raincoat hanging by itself outside a dining hall. He drank a good deal of wine and persistently turned the conversation to the subject of his relationship with Terry. He admitted that he had come to dislike the boy. Then he mentioned several patients of his by name, some of them known to Mother and me, and said that he disliked them too. He used the word "dislike" with relish, like someone on a diet permitting himself a single potato chip. "I don't know what I've done wrong," he said abruptly, and with reference to no particular thing. "Then again maybe I haven't done anything wrong. I don't know what to think anymore. Nobody does."

"I know what to think," Mother said.

"So does the solipsist. How can you prove to a solipsist that he's not creating the rest of us?"

This was one of Dr. Murphy's favorite riddles, and almost any pretext was sufficient for him to trot it out. He was a child with a card trick.

"Send him to bed without dinner," Mother said. "Let him create that."

Dr. Murphy suddenly turned to me. "Why do you do it?" he asked. It was a pure question, it had no object beyond the satisfaction of his curiosity. Mother looked at me and there was the same curiosity in her face.

"I don't know," I said, and that was the truth.

Dr. Murphy nodded, not because he had anticipated my answer but because he accepted it. "Is it fun?"

"No, it's not fun. I can't explain."

"Why is it all so sad?" Mother asked. "Why all the diseases?"

"Maybe," Dr. Murphy said, "sad things are more interesting."

"Not to me," Mother said.

"Not to me, either," I said. "It just comes out that way."

After dinner Dr. Murphy asked Mother to play the piano. He particularly wanted to sing "Come Home Abbie, the Light's on the Stair."

"That old thing," Mother said. She stood and folded her napkin deliberately and we followed her into the living room. Dr. Murphy stood behind her as she warmed up. Then they sang "Come Home Abbie, the Light's on the Stair," and I watched him stare down at Mother intently, as if he were trying to remember something. Her own eyes were closed. After that they sang "O Magnum Mysterium." They sang it in parts and I regretted that I had no voice, it sounded so good.

"Come on, James," Dr. Murphy said as Mother played the last chords. "These old tunes not good enough for you?"

"He just can't sing," Mother said.

When Dr. Murphy left, Mother lit the fire and made more coffee. She slouched down in the big chair, sticking her legs straight out and moving her feet back and forth. "That was fun," she said.

"Did you and Father ever do things like that?"

"A few times, when we were first going out. I don't think he really enjoyed it. He was like you."

I wondered if Mother and Father had had a good marriage. He admired her and liked to look at her; every night at dinner he had us move the candlesticks slightly to right and left of center so he could see her down the length of the table. And every evening when she set the table she put them in the center again. She didn't seem to miss him very much. But I wouldn't really have known if she did, and anyway I didn't miss him all that much myself, not the way I had. Most of the time I thought about other things.

"James?"

I waited.

"I've been thinking that you might like to go down and stay with Michael for a couple of weeks or so."

"What about school?"

"I'll talk to Father McSorley. He won't mind. Maybe this problem will take care of itself if you start thinking about other people."

"I do."

"I mean helping them, like Michael does. You don't have to go if you don't want to."

"It's fine with me. Really. I'd like to see Michael."

"I'm not trying to get rid of you."

"I know."

Mother stretched, then tucked her feet under her. She sipped noisily at her coffee. "What did that word mean that Murphy used? You know the one?"

"Paranoid? That's where somebody thinks everyone is out to get him. Like that woman who always grabs you after Mass—Frances."

"Not paranoid. Everyone knows what that means. Solsomething."

"Oh. Solipsist. A solipsist is someone who thinks he creates everything around him."

Mother nodded and blew on her coffee, then put it down without drinking from it. "I'd rather be paranoid. Do you really think Frances is?"

"Of course. No question about it."

"I mean really *sick?*"

"That's what paranoid is, is being sick. What do you think, Mother?"

"What are you so angry about?"

"I'm not angry." I lowered my voice. "I'm not angry. But you don't believe those stories of hers, do you?"

"Well, no, not exactly. I don't think she knows what she's saying, she just wants someone to listen. She probably lives all by herself in some little room. So she's paranoid. Think of that. And I had no idea. James, we should pray for her. Will you remember to do that?"

I nodded. I thought of Mother singing "O Magnum Mysterium," saying grace, praying with easy confidence, and it came to me that her imagination was superior to mine. She could imagine things as coming together, not falling apart. She looked at me and I shrank; I knew exactly what she was going to say. "Son," she said, "do you know how much I love you?"

The next afternoon I took the bus to Los Angeles. I looked forward to the trip, to the monotony of the road and the empty fields by the roadside. Mother walked with me down the long concourse. The station was crowded and oppressive. "Are you sure this is the right bus?" she asked at the loading platform.

"Yes."

"It looks so old."

"Mother—"

"All right." She pulled me against her and kissed me, then held me an extra second to show that her embrace was sincere, not just like everyone else's, never having realized that everyone else does the same thing. I boarded the bus and we waved at each other until it became embarrassing. Then Mother began checking through her handbag for something. When she had finished, I stood and adjusted the luggage over my seat. I sat and we smiled at each other, waved when the driver gunned the engine, shrugged when he got up suddenly to count the passengers, waved again when he resumed his seat. As the bus pulled out, my mother and I were looking at each other with plain relief.

I had boarded the wrong bus. This one was bound for Los Angeles but not by the express route. We stopped in San Mateo, Palo Alto, San Jose, Castroville. When we left Castroville it began to rain, hard; my window would not close all the way, and a thin stream of water ran down the wall onto my seat. To keep dry I had to stay away from the wall and lean forward. The rain fell harder. The engine of the bus sounded as though it were coming apart.

In Salinas the man sleeping beside me jumped up but before I had a chance to change seats his place was taken by an enormous woman in a print dress, carrying a shopping bag. She took possession of her seat and spilled over onto half of mine, backing me up to the wall. "That's a storm," she said loudly, then turned and looked at me. "Hungry?" Without waiting for an answer she dipped into her bag and pulled out a piece of chicken and thrust it at me. "Hey, by God," she hooted, "look at him go to town on that drumstick!" A few people turned and smiled. I smiled back around the bone and kept at it. I finished that piece and she handed me another, and then another. Then she started handing out chicken to the people in the seats near us.

Outside of San Luis Obispo the noise from the engine grew suddenly louder and just as suddenly there was no noise at all. The driver pulled off to the side of the road and got out, then got on again dripping wet. A few moments later he announced that the bus had broken down and they were sending another bus to pick us up. Someone asked how long that might take and the driver said he had no idea. "Keep your pants on!" shouted the woman next to me. "Anybody in a hurry to get to L.A. ought to have his head examined."

The wind was blowing hard around the bus, driving sheets of rain against the windows on both sides. The bus swayed gently. Outside, the light was brown and thick. The woman next to me pumped all the people around us for their itineraries and said whether or not she had ever been where they were from or where they were going. "How about you?" She slapped my knee. "Parents own a chicken ranch? I hope so!" She laughed. I told her I was from San Francisco. "San Francisco, that's where my husband was stationed." She asked me what I did there and I told her I worked with refugees from Tibet.

"Is that right? What do you do with a bunch of Tibetans?"

"Seems like there's plenty of other places they could've gone," said a man in front of us. "Coming across the border like that. We don't go there."

"What do you do with a bunch of Tibetans?" the woman repeated.

"Try to find them jobs, locate housing, listen to their problems."

"You understand that kind of talk?"

"Yes."

"Speak it?"

"Pretty well. I was born and raised in Tibet. My parents were missionaries over there."

Everyone waited.

"They were killed when the Communists took over."

The big woman patted my arm.

"It's all right," I said.

345

"Why don't you say some of that Tibetan?"

"What would you like to hear?"

"Say 'The cow jumped over the moon.'" She watched me, smiling, and when I finished she looked at the others and shook her head. "That was pretty. Like music. Say some more."

"What?"

"Anything."

They bent toward me. The windows suddenly went blind with rain. The driver had fallen asleep and was snoring gently to the swaying of the bus. Outside the muddy light flickered to pale yellow, and far off there was thunder. The woman next to me leaned back and closed her eyes and then so did all the others as I sang to them in what was surely an ancient and holy tongue.